i.C. No. 48 - 1021
ordered 11-12-57

W9-AGU-916

John Hancock

JOHN HANCOCK, THE PATRIOT, IN 1765. FROM A PORTRAIT BY JOHN
SINGLETON COPLEY. BY COURTESY OF THE MUSEUM OF FINE ARTS,
BOSTON.

John Hancock

Patriot in Purple

BY HERBERT S. ALLAN

NEW YORK:

THE BEECHHURST PRESS

1953

Wingate College Library

COPYRIGHT, MCMXLVIII, BY HERBERT S. ALLAN

All rights reserved—no part of this
book may be reproduced in any form
without permission in writing from
the publisher, except by a reviewer
who wishes to quote brief passages in
connection with a review written for
inclusion in magazine or newspaper.

Second Printing

PRINTED IN THE UNITED STATES OF AMERICA

pur.

11-12-57

TO MY WIFE

MADELEINE

8008

Preface

$\mathscr{O}$NE OF THE strangest paradoxes in history is that a vast majority of Americans know the name John Hancock but only a small minority know the man who bore it.

Because of the showy form in which it is inscribed on the Declaration of Independence "John Hancock" has been incorporated into the English language as a synonym for autograph. This top signature with its large, bold, symmetrical script is the most expressive of the fifty-six appended to the Declaration; yet the fascinating personage for whom it stands is least understood or appreciated of all the important founding fathers. Few names of noted patriots have been so perpetuated; but the memory of no other's personality and achievements has been so thoroughly obliterated.

Named after Hancock are an aircraft carrier celebrated for her contribution to the defeat of the Japanese during the Second World War; a nationally known life insurance company and numerous firms of sectional repute; counties, towns, and streets throughout the eastern part of the United States. Still, it is doubtful that more than one person in a thousand—even among the educated—is aware of this man's significant role in the birth of a nation. He is remembered as the first to sign the Declaration and is quoted—somewhat derisively—as having declared melodramatically after adding the final flourish: "There! John Bull can read my name without spectacles."

Hancock is the most neglected and maligned of famous figures in the annals of America. For more than a hundred years after his death on October 8, 1793, his own state of Massachusetts ignored him completely while rearing monuments and statues to many lesser men. In 1894, when the legislature of the commonwealth, of which he had been the original governor under its independent constitution, got around to making an appropriation for a memorial to be erected over his grave in the Old Granary Burying Ground at Boston, the resolution was introduced by a Negro representative—fitly, for the former chief magistrate had stanchly befriended his race. Not until September 10, 1896, was the simple granite shaft unveiled by Mary Elizabeth Wood, greatgrandniece of the patriot.

Prior to that time neither his beloved state nor his beloved widow, Dorothy Quincy Hancock Scott, did anything to mark his last resting place beyond inserting, in the near-by wall of the cemetery, a sandstone slab bearing the inscription: "No. 16, Tomb of Hancock." This crumbling marker, stuck at a crazy angle in the ground covering his remains, may be seen there today.

Historians have been equally neglectful. Even now, a century and a half after his decease, books for popular consumption that treat of him at length total no more than ten. Only one— Lorenzo Sears' *John Hancock, the Picturesque Patriot*, which appeared in 1912—may justly claim to be a biography; and its author does not pretend to be comprehensive or definitive. The other works concentrate on certain phases of Hancock's life. They are Abram E. Brown's *John Hancock: His Book*, composed chiefly of transcriptions from the letterbooks, or copy files, kept by John and his uncle, Thomas Hancock; W. T. Baxter's *House of Hancock*, a study of the two Hancocks' business careers; James S. Loring's *Hundred Boston Orators*; William Sullivan's *Familiar Letters on Public Characters*; Ellen C. D. Woodbury's *Dorothy Quincy, Wife of John Hancock*; Stephen Higginson's *Ten Chapters in the Life of John Hancock*; John R. Musick's *John Hancock: A Character Sketch*; Kenneth B. Umbreit's *Founding Fathers*, and Mabel M. Carlton's *John Hancock, Great American Patriot*.

Yet plenty of source material is available to any one who takes the trouble to investigate. It is scattered among innumerable unpublished manuscripts; contemporary letters, diaries, journals, commentaries; newspapers and magazines of the Revolutionary period; historical society publications, general histories, and biographies of the other founders.

Only two serious attempts have been made previously to gather enough data for a well rounded study. According to a mysterious statement by a Professor Warren of Dover, New Jersey, quoted in the Boston *Transcript* of February 11, 1884: "A gentleman was engaged not long since by descendants of Hancock to gather material to write a history of Hancock's life. Material was collected and read, when the members of the family immediately offered the writer $1,000 to hand over the work and not make further investigation. The writer took the money, and the book was never published."

The library of the American Antiquarian Society of Worcester contains a voluminous collection of notes and disconnected manuscripts compiled by Henry A. Phillips of neighboring Millbury, Massachusetts, preparatory to a formal biography. But Phillips died in 1926 without having undertaken it.

Most writers apparently have been baffled by Hancock's personality. In 1817 John Adams—once a caustic critic of his fellow founder—implied as much in an inscrutable and presumptuous prophecy to William Tudor, the historian:

"I am not writing the life of Mr. Hancock; his biography would fill as many volumes as Marshall's *Washington* and be quite as instructive and entertaining. . . . His life will, however, not ever be written. But if statutes, obelisks, pyramids, or divine honors were ever merited . . . John Hancock deserved these from the town of Boston and the United States."

In "Portrait of an Empty Barrel," a *Harper's Magazine* article which takes its title from John Adams' alleged characterization of Hancock, James Truslow Adams wrote in 1930:

"We can only patch and guess toward a conception of an enigmatic character. Was it really as poor and shallow and puffy as it appears from the evidence today? Or was there more to it than we can see? Was there any justification for the changed estimate of John Adams in his not very reliable old age when, altering the opinions of his prime and intellectual vigor, he expressed a higher one of Hancock's ability than was his wont? Will the biography of him that Adams said would never be written yet come into being?"

Like John Adams, many of Hancock's contemporary detractors—most of whom were political enemies swayed by prejudice during a period of partisanship as bitter as any in the annals of this country—contradicted themselves in their comments upon him. Whatever chance he may have had to obtain a consistent and just verdict at the bar of history, when enough time had elapsed to scan the evidence in true perspective, was all but killed in 1865 by William V. Wells' *Life and Public Services of Samuel Adams.*

Wells, who was a great-grandson of the protagonist, glorified Adams at the expense of Hancock, his pre-Revolutionary protégé. And almost all subsequent commentators have used this work as a primary source of information about the patriot in purple.

It must be admitted that there is a modicum of truth in the derogation of Hancock. He had a full measure of the faults and foibles common to humanity. He compared unfavorably with some other founding fathers in intellectual power and originality of thought. He was vain, arrogant, egotistic, hypersensitive, petulant, exhibitionistic, capricious, vacillating, intemperate, susceptible to flattery, improvident, and was somewhat of a demagogue and much of a faker.

Yet the antitheses of all these traits crop up frequently as one studies his most complex character. He was the Hamlet of the great American historical drama.

This book is designed primarily to fill a long-existent gap in the biographical scrolls of the United States; secondarily, to meet the challenge connoted in the words of John Adams and James Truslow Adams. It is neither a eulogy nor an apologia. It is an attempt to portray Hancock not only as he appeared to his contemporaries but also as he looks in retrospect after the passage of many years.

On the other hand, it is not intended to be a history of the period during which Hancock lived, although certain aspects of life in America throughout the seventeenth and eighteenth centuries are reinterpreted. No more historical narrative will be found in these pages than is necessary to clarify the relationship of the principal character to the events with which he was associated, their influence upon him, and his upon them.

The author has consulted original sources whenever and wherever accessible. Among the repositories that he has visited in Boston and vicinity are the Athenaeum, New England Historic Genealogical Society, Massachusetts Historical Society, Bostonian Society, Society for the Preservation of New England Antiquities, Museum of Fine Arts, Old South Meetinghouse, Massachusetts Statehouse, John Hancock Mutual Life Insurance Company, Old Granary Burying Ground, Widener and Baker libraries of Harvard University, Hancock-Clark House and Buckman Tavern at Lexington, and the Quincy homes at Quincy. He also has worked at the American Antiquarian Society in Worcester; at the Historical Society of Rhode Island and the John Carter Brown Library of Brown University in Providence; at the Historical Society of Pennsylvania, American Philosophical Society, and Independence Hall group of buildings in Philadelphia; at the Yale University Library in New Haven; at the Fairfield Historical Society in Fairfield, Connecticut; at the New York Historical Society, Pierpont Morgan Library, and Frick

Art Library in New York; and at public libraries in most of the foregoing places.

By voluminous correspondence with authorities at institutions such as the Library of Congress and with private individuals, the biographer has gained access to papers and facts unused heretofore. In the interest of readability he has modernized spelling and punctuation in quoting from old manuscripts but has not changed the meaning in any case.

Although there are no direct heirs, the writer has gleaned much additional information through personal contact and communication with numerous collateral descendants. He is deeply indebted to Arthur R. Wendell of Rahway, New Jersey, great-great-grandnephew of Elizabeth Wendell Quincy, Dorothy Quincy Hancock's mother, for many hours spent in clearing up moot points of genealogy and in trying to unearth letters written by Mrs. Hancock. The utter disappearance of these epistles, a number of which Hancock acknowledged, is a mystery. Thanks are due also to Edmund Quincy, Boston artist, who likewise can trace his ancestry back to the beginning of the Quincy line in America; to Mrs. Samuel B. Doggett of Wiscasset, Maine, and to Miss Dorothy M. Vaughan of Portsmouth, New Hampshire.

For assistance in the preparation of this volume the author wishes to express his appreciation particularly to his college classmate, Leonard Woods Labaree, Farnam Professor of History and chairman of the history department at Yale University. An outstanding authority on the American colonial period, Dr. Labaree has given unstintedly of his time and knowledge to perfect the work.

Others whose courtesy and cooperation have been of invaluable help are: Norman Cousins, editor of the Saturday Review of Literature, who urged the writer to undertake the biography and encouraged him during the five years consumed in completing it; Clifton A. Follansbee of the John Hancock Mutual Life Insurance Company, who placed the firm's unique collection of Hancockiana at his disposal and aided him in countless ways; the late Dr. Allyn B. Forbes, director of the Massachusetts Historical Society, Stephen T. Riley, librarian, and his assistant, Miss Dorothy Fox; Dr. Arthur H. Cole, librarian of the Baker Library; Mrs. Franklin E. Scotty, librarian of the New England Historic Genealogical Society; M. A. De Wolfe Howe, historian and head of the Boston Athenaeum; Miss Harriet Swift of the reference division, Boston Public Library; James L. Bruce, clerk of the Bostonian Society; Dr. Clifford K. Shipton, librarian of the American Antiquarian Society; Mrs. John A. Forsythe, Jr., assistant curator of the Fairfield Historical Society; Capt.

H. A. Baldridge, director of The Museum, United States Naval Academy; Miss Beatrice Pinkney Jones of Washington, D. C.; Mrs. Katharine McCook Knox of Washington, D. C.; Miss Virginia Seery of the Frick Art Library; Sylvester L. Vigilante, chief of the American history department, New York Public Library; his associate, F. Ivor D. Avellino; and their former co-worker, Miss Dorothy P. Miller.

Contents

Illustrations

John Hancock

Prologue

T HE REVEREND JOHN HANCOCK, "Bishop of Lexington," Massachusetts, throughout the first half of the eighteenth century, was as forbearing toward the foibles of his flock as a man of God should be. But something was going on in his parish that had aroused his righteous wrath; so he decided to put a stop to it.

Two of Parson Hancock's parishioners had long been wrangling over the bounds of their contiguous properties. This is no cause for wonder in view of the vague verbiage used to define Lexington land at that period, even in the official records. The town, which had broken away from Cambridge in 1713, had scarcely improved upon the method employed in the parent settlement seventy-eight years before, when it had been known as Newtown. According to an inventory of householders taken in 1635, Nathaniel Hancock, grandfather of the Bishop and first of the New England Hancocks to emigrate to America, owned a house "with back side about half a rod, William Town southwest, Hester Musse southeast, the common pond northeast, Water Street northwest." [1] The real estate now in dispute was described with similar precision.

Still, this was no reason, in the eyes of their pastor, for men in the Christian colony of Massachusetts Bay to carry on a silly quarrel every time they met. So the Reverend Mr. Hancock suggested that Joseph and Reuben (fictitious names invented by the Reverend Theodore Parker in retailing the story handed down by ancestors who had lived in the same parish) should accompany him to the boundary line in question and bring along their deeds. Since a suggestion from the Bishop was tantamount to a command, they complied without hesitation. After listening to the rival claims and inspecting the legal papers on which they were based he ordered:

"Take your axes and cut some stakes."

I

When they meekly obeyed he directed:

"Drive this stake down here. . . . Now drive that stake down there."

The stakes having been driven, the benevolent dictator brought the issue to a close:

"Now, Reuben and Joseph, your line runs there; and there let it run forever! . . . And let us have no more quarreling about this matter." [2]

There was none.

Fifty or seventy-five years after this little scene in the Lexington meadows a grandson and namesake of the Reverend John Hancock played the vastly more important role of mediator in a drama watched by the whole world. At the Massachusetts convention for ratification of the Federal Constitution—an assemblage that went far toward determining the fate of the dis-United States—the latter-day John Hancock helped to save the Union from disintegration into thirteen separate dominions as quarrelsome as Joseph and Reuben had been. As chairman he introduced into the bitterly factionalized meeting a series of amendments that served as enabling acts for nation-wide adoption of the great set of governmental principles under which this country lives and prospers today.

Another traditional anecdote recounted by Parker illustrates how a predominant trait in the Bishop of Lexington reappeared, on a magnified scale, in the "King of America," as he was called sardonically by Tories in the British Parliament.

Toward the close of his fifty-four-year pastorate the Reverend Mr. Hancock received a visit from his two deacons. They thought that he was taking his unofficial title of Bishop too literally, and they resented having their picayune authority flouted by this clerical tyrant. So they proposed asking the parish to appoint them ruling elders to assist him and, by way of dissembling their motive, based their plan on the professed desire to lighten the burden that he carried on his aging shoulders.

"Well, I should like it," Hancock replied diplomatically, "but what do you think is the business of ruling elders?"

On their pleading ignorance (which was unfeigned, for such functionaries were rare in American colonial meetinghouses) he explained:

"I should like to have one of them come up to my house before meeting on Sunday and get my horse out of the barn and then saddle him and bring him up to the door and hold the stirrup while I get on. The other may wait at the church door and hold him while I get off. Then, after the meeting, he may bring him up to the steps. This is all of my work I ever can consent to let the ruling elders do for me." [3]

The job of elder was not filled before the Bishop's death at the venerable and—in his case—vigorous age of eighty-one.

John Hancock, the patriot in purple, inheriting this flair for smart politics from John Hancock, the individualist in black, used it to excellent advantage. In 1780 he thwarted the efforts of Sam Adams' party to keep him out of the governorship of Massachusetts, a post unequaled in prestige anywhere in the young nation at the time. By the same means he got himself reelected annually, except for two years, until his death in 1793. Popularity, which the grandfather enjoyed in a small circle, the grandson attained in the grandest manner ever known in this country.

A third Lexington legend recorded by Parker points up still more the remarkable bond of heritage between the Reverend Mr. Hancock and his illustrious grandson.

On his appointed rounds the Bishop visited a well-to-do farm family about noon one day, probably with a not entirely pastoral purpose. It was haying time, and only the lady of the house and the children were at home. After the usual amenities had been exchanged the good wife set before her good shepherd a meal of the plain but succulent victuals for which New England women have been noted from that day to this —cider, brown bread, and a whole "rat" cheese.

"Where shall I cut this cheese, Mrs. Smith?" queried the visitor.

"Cut it where you have a mind to, Mr. Hancock," answered the hostess.

"Then I think I will cut it at home," was the prompt rejoinder.[4]

Disarmed by the candid cleric, Mrs. Smith told one of her offspring to put the cheese into his saddlebag and served some more in slices. So the Reverend John had his cheese and ate it, too.

The politically irreverent John Hancock who allegedly asserted, while inscribing his famous bold signature first on the Declaration of Independence, "There! John Bull can read my name without spectacles," had his cake and ate it, too. He gained renown as a great democrat while living as a great aristocrat.

Another characteristic common to the original John Hancock and his grandson was imperious worldliness. Although the one gave wing to the human spirit for the good of his parish and the other did so for the good of his *patria,* neither ever let his feet leave the ground.

In a sermon preached at the ordination of his eldest son, the second Reverend John, the Bishop declared:

"Those who are called by office to preach the word of God have power of rule, also. . . . And therefore are the keys of the kingdom to be committed unto them. Not only the key of doctrine but of discipline. The keys are an emblem of power. . . . I might have added—their power to ask and receive wages for this their service. . . . And the laws of Christ have given them this power to take wages for their work and to take it not as alms or charity but as justice; and I know no more reason they have to thank them [the parishioners] for giving it than there is for you to thank them [the pastors] for receiving it. For they are maintained out of God's right and revenues and not out of yours, for the tithes of all are the Lord's; and it is easy enough to prove that such as withhold God's dues from him are guilty not of petty larceny but of sacrilege itself." [5]

How the congregation took this unspiritual special pleading in behalf of Parson Hancock's profession, with its implied application to his son, is not recorded. They probably smiled indulgently and forgave the man who practiced—if he did not always preach—the precept of selflessness.

Just so did the mass of the people forgive the Hancock of the future for requesting of George Washington an escort of horse for his journey from Philadelphia to Boston while on leave from the Presidency of the Continental Congress in 1777. It meant nothing to the Congressional leader, as far as his personal pride was concerned, that Washington was in the midst of his most heartbreaking campaign; that he had suffered defeat at Brandywine Creek and Germantown, Pennsylvania, within the preceding five weeks, or that, as he wrote to John, "the severe duty the horse have been obliged to perform for a long time past has rendered many of them unfit for service" and "we are under a necessity of keeping several considerable patrols of them constantly along the enemy's lines." The President received not only an escort, consisting of "Cornet Buckmer and twelve dragoons," but an apology from the commander in chief for its "being so small"! [6]

Most of the Revolutionary statesmen, realizing with Tom Paine that theirs were "the times that try men's souls," would have been content with a guard of ordinary militia, even though part of the route ran through hostile territory—but not John Hancock. He insisted on traveling in his accustomed style, not because he was afraid (he stuck his neck figuratively into a British noose more than once) but simply because he regarded it as a right, like the wages about which his grandfather had preached. The later Hancock's social equals denounced him caustically, but the masses overlooked his egotism because they realized that he was risking for their sake one of the greatest fortunes amassed in colonial times and was spending an estimated total of $100,000 of his private funds to make them free.

This line of thought leads directly to a sermon delivered by the first John Hancock before Governor Jonathan Belcher and the General Court of Massachusetts in Boston.[7] It contains a passage that proved to be amazingly pertinent to his own flesh and blood. The Bishop thus raised a touchy issue:

"And what good may men of great fortunes . . . do with their estates? . . . They should be spoken to about it, that they may lay such pious and useful foundations for which future generations may call them blessed. . . . If they have . . . great possessions they must be told it is God that gave them or their ancestors power to get wealth. . . . You may see some persons, when their riches are increased or when the government has promoted them, assume an air of pride and defiance."[8]

It required courage to utter this exhortation, indirect though it was, before such an august audience, who were not used to being told what to do with their money or to being criticized for their arrogance—even by a highly respected minister. And courage was an important part of the third John Hancock's spiritual endowment from his grandsire.

This excerpt is oracular in a twofold sense. God did give a collateral ancestor of the Reverend John's grandson "power to get wealth." The Bishop's second son, Thomas, became one of the greatest merchants ever produced by a land famed for them; and he bequeathed to his brother's boy the modern equivalent of $1,000,000, representing the profit from his world-wide mercantile operations. Furthermore, the heir did turn out to be proud and defiant in consequence.

The uncle exerted upon the extremely impressionable nephew, whom he adopted at the age of seven, the influence of environment which complements that of inheritance in molding men. He and his childless wife Lydia took the lad into their magnificent mansion on Beacon Hill in Boston, showered upon him all the advantages within their ample means, and refined the raw stuff of character which his grandparent had passed on to him, until he became a unique man of destiny.

∽ 1 ∽

ROOTS OF A MAN AND A NATION

*M*UCH WATER had flowed over the beaches of New England during the decade since the landing of the Pilgrims in 1620 at Plymouth. But few first-hand accounts of this epic emigration or of those which followed it had percolated to the rural regions of old England. So it was natural that the folks back home in the country districts should be eager to obtain the "inside story" of the great movement which enthralled the world of the seventeenth century.

One of these curious persons was the "Right Honorable, my very good Lady, the Lady Bridget, Countess of Lincoln"—as her husband's former steward, now the Honorable Thomas Dudley, deputy governor of the Massachusetts Bay Colony, addressed her on March 12, 1631.[1] Although the countess must have received sketchy reports of the historic colonization in a roundabout way, she wanted the facts straight from a man who was in a position to give them to her authentically. Her desire probably was stimulated not only by thirst for knowledge of the grand adventure but by hunger for revelations that would raise the eyebrows of the parochial lords and ladies who gathered around her tea table. Such news would be the sensation of the social season in the county of Lincoln on the east coast of England, too distant from London to hear word-of-mouth narratives from returned colonists.

Lady Bridget had been importuning Dudley in letters "which are not common nor cheap," as her ex-retainer obsequiously acknowledged them, to bring her up to date on what was taking place across the Atlantic. But the deputy governor apparently had been too busy to comply since arriving at Salem with the third group of Massachusetts Bay pioneers during the summer of 1630. Even now he required more than two weeks to tell the tale, for the recital he started on the 12th did not come to an end until the 28th. The inordinate time consumed was due partly to the difficult and distracting circumstances under which he wrote from his residence in Boston, the seat of provincial government. He had to do it "rudely, having yet no table nor other room to write in than by the fireside upon my knee in this sharp winter; to which my family must have leave to resort, though they break good manners and make me many times forget what I would say and say what I would not." [2]

Dudley, however, managed to present a clear, concise picture of all the principal settlements made or attempted during the last eleven years in New England and to treat the founding of his own plantation in more detail. He told how John Endicott, first governor of Massachusetts Bay, and a small party had preceded the main body of colonizers in 1628; how in 1629 "we sent divers ships over, with about 300 people and some cows, goats, and horses, many of which," he added in the revealing manner of a pioneer accustomed to a low percentage of survival, "arrived safely," and how he himself had followed in another argosy of seventeen vessels.

The deputy governor then related that his particular contingent, sailing in four ships, had landed during June and July at Salem, "where we found the colony in a sad and unexpected condition, above eighty of them being dead the winter before and many of those alive weak and sick; all the corn and bread amongst them . . . hardly sufficient to feed them a fortnight." With remarkable resignation he continued:

"But, bearing these things as we might, we began to consult of the place of our sitting down; for Salem . . . pleased us not. . . . We found a place three leagues up Charles River and thereupon unshipped our goods into other vessels and . . . brought them in July to Charlestown; but, there receiving advertisements . . . from London and Amsterdam of some French preparations against us . . . we were forced . . . to plant dispersedly."

In enumerating and locating the various plantations thus launched—Charlestown, Medford, Watertown, Roxbury, Saugus, Dorchester, and Boston—Dudley dismissed what was to be "The Hub of the Universe" so perfunctorily as to make the souls of yet unborn Beacon Hill Brahmins turn over on their fleecy clouds. He stated merely that some settled on the south side of the Charles, "which place we named Boston." [3] Then he resumed:

"And of the people who came over with us, from the time of their setting sail from England in April 1630 until December following, there died by estimation about 200 at the least. . . . So, after divers meetings, . . . on the 28th of December we grew to this resolution: to bind all the Assistants . . . to build houses at a place a mile east from Water-town near Charles River the next spring and to winter there the next year; . . . that so, by our examples, . . . all who were able might be drawn thither and such as shall come to us hereafter . . . be compelled so to do; and so, if God would, a fortified town might there grow up." [4]

Governor John Winthrop, who had superseded Endicott; Simon Bradstreet, one of the assistants, and Dudley carried out their part of the bargain in 1631 by erecting "country homes" within a palisade surrounding the town, which was called Newtown until its name should be changed to Cambridge five years later. But Winthrop soon tore his down and removed it to Boston, thereby precipitating a bitter quarrel with the deputy governor; and the rest of the leaders apparently reneged on the agreement. Yet the power of Dudley's and Bradstreet's examples was sufficient to encourage other enterprising spirits to move into the fortified area. At least enough had done so by July 26 for it to be included in an order issued on that date by the Court of Assistants providing for the military training of all able-bodied men.[5]

The impetus of emulation, however, was short-lived. No sizable body of colonists settled in Newtown until the occasion arose for "such as shall come to us hereafter" to "be compelled so to do" by a court decree of August 14, 1632.[6] Under this directive the Reverend Thomas Hooker's "Braintree company"—so named after the village at which they had just arrived a year in advance of their pastor—moved to the fortified town. By December 24 they had "built the first house for public worship at Newtown . . . with a bell upon it," although the community was not to have an ordained minister until the following October.[7]

Writing in 1633, a Massachusetts Bay historian asserted: "This is one of the neatest and best-compacted towns in New England, having many fair structures, with many handsome-contrived streets. The inhabitants—most of them—are very rich and well stored with cattle of all sorts, having many hundred acres . . . paled in with one general fence, which is about a mile and a half long." [8] Even when the evident exaggeration concerning the physical features is liberally discounted this description stamps Newtown as an up-and-coming place by comparison with most of its sister settlements.

· 2 ·

Significantly Nathaniel Hancock, great-great-grandfather of the titular character of this book, picked out a locality with such an auspicious origin to settle in with his wife Joanna and probably John, their first-

born, some time before January 5, 1634.[9] On that day he was granted
two acres "behind pine swamp" with the understanding that "whoso-
ever hath any lot granted by the town and shall not improve the same,
then it is to return to the town." [10]

Nathaniel did improve his patch of planting-ground by joining in sowing the seeds of a nation which his distinguished descendant was to help
bring to fruition one hundred and fifty years later.

Little more can be told about the circumstances surrounding the emigration of the man who founded the Hancock line in New England
than that he came out of the nowhere into the here. Even his birth date
is conjectural. He is known to have belonged to an old English family
and is believed to have been connected with the branch that had its
roots in the vicinity of London. According to the heraldic interpretation,
the first syllable of his surname was derived from the Teutonic-Hebraic
appellation Hans, a nickname for John, and the second from the Anglo-
Saxon word "cock." So the literal translation is "John of the Cock"—the
form in which it appears on the Hundred Rolls of the Domesday Book.

Nathaniel, however, probably knew little and cared less about his
family tree. Like most of the bold Britons who fared forth to build a new
world in the seventeenth century, he was chiefly concerned about the
trees on which men who spoke their minds in England might be strung
up. He seems to have been a member of the farmer class, for he expanded
his American holdings rapidly and possessed more than fourteen acres at
his death.

There is no record as to the exact time when Hancock first set foot
in Newtown. The two-acre grant contains the earliest mention of his
name. He may have come over in the after-party of the Braintree company led by Thomas Hooker. This divine had reached Boston on September 4, 1633, from Holland, whither he had fled to escape imprisonment for heretical preaching. He had taken pastoral charge of his old
flock in the fortified town on October 11. But Samuel Stone, his assistant,
is the only person identified as having accompanied him.

In any event, by February 8, 1635, Nathaniel had a house in the
"west end." [11] This was the building which presented its back side to William Town and Hester Musse, as noted in the graphic inventory previously referred to.

But no Newtownite was allowed to pick up lots indiscriminately or to
use them as he pleased. The settlement was laid out in accordance with
a crude version of modern municipal zoning methods. Houses could be
erected only within the town proper or the west end. Cultivation was

restricted to the territory within the impaled "neck," or upland. Hancock's original grant behind pine swamp was situated in this area. Grazing land for cows, goats, and swine was not assigned to individuals during the first century of Newtown's existence but was utilized communally under the designation of "commons." [12]

· 3 ·

Almost all of Nathaniel's activities and those of his fellow settlers revolved around the meetinghouse. In Puritan New England this was the object closest to the hearts of most men, with the possible exception of their families. And the attachment was not merely spiritual. It was a temporal, pragmatic, workaday relationship which impinged upon the lives of the colonists at every turn.

The Massachusetts Bay Colony had been established no longer than a year when its leaders set up Congregationalism as the official state religion and concentrated political authority in the hands of its devotees. A General Court resolution of 1631 decreed that "for time to come no man shall be admitted to the freedom of this body politic [that is, made a voter] but such as are members of some of the churches within the limits of the same." [13] Although the purpose of this measure was to foster harmony that would strengthen the plantation through the union of secular and clerical government, the system eventually bred as much discord as did the politicoreligious British hierarchy from which the Puritans had fled. The persecution crusades against Roger Williams, Anne Hutchinson, and others who dissented from the dissenters are well known cases in point.

Identification of church and colony extended all the way down the line to the smallest village. Every town was constituted a parish at its inception. Even the business of the two organizations was conducted jointly. The meetinghouse, where the town officials assembled on weekdays and in company with ordinary folk on Sundays, derived its name from this dual use.

The "freedom of this body politic" conferred full civil rights upon those qualified; but, as a rule, it was bestowed only on condition that the community support a minister and provide an opportunity for public worship. Lack of clergymen, rather than unwillingness to meet this requirement, probably accounted for the delay of a year and a half before the building of the church "with a bell upon it" in Newtown.

Although discouraged from talking out of turn by this absolute cleri-

calism, Hancock and his fellow citizens received a stimulus to the imagination in 1637. Nicholas Danforth was authorized by the General Court
to "sell wine and strong water" in what now was Cambridge.[14] Three
years later Thomas Chesholme was to be licensed to "draw wine" there.[15]
But the provincial authorities chose very carefully the persons whom they
entrusted with the privilege of dispensing the blessings of Bacchus. Danforth was a member of the House of Representatives and a townsman,
predecessor of the selectman.[16] Chesholme was a deacon and subsequently steward of Harvard College. His business (a home enterprise)
was further sanctified by being conducted next door to the meetinghouse
on Dunster Street. This circumstance made it especially convenient for
Nathaniel, who lived on the same thoroughfare.

There was scarcely any diversion for Hancock and his neighbors except
tippling and attending the semiscriptural lectures, instituted about this
time on weekday mornings in Boston and a few other towns. A half-
holiday was declared to enable Bostonians to hear the Thursday discourse
by the Reverend John Cotton. To moderns it would seem that this
must have been a busman's holiday for the theology-surfeited Puritans.
But residents of places like Cambridge, where there were no such disser-
tations, contrived to make a lark out of the sugar-coated soul-saving
medium. They—presumably including Nathaniel—would play hookey
from the deadly routine of colonizing chores ostensibly to drink in Cotton's uplifting words but actually to absorb the less ennobling atmosphere
of the metropolitan pleasure spots. Pretended lecture-going soon developed into a religious racket among the more worldly-minded. This dodge
finally became so prevalent that the authorities contemplated banning the
so-called entertainment; but they refrained lest such action should be interpreted as discouragement of piety.

· 4 ·

Soon after Hancock's arrival Cambridge took the play away from the
pseudointellectualism of its big sister settlement through the founding of
a bona fide seat of learning—Harvard. On October 28, 1636, the General
Court appropriated £400 as the nucleus of a fund for building a school
or college; and on November 15 of the following year it granted permission for construction to begin.[17] In 1638, according to an anonymous historian of the period, "it pleased God to stir up the heart of one Mr. Harvard . . . to give the one-half of his estate (it being in all about £1700)
towards the erecting of a college, and all his library." [18] Meanwhile the

town had contributed nearly three acres to the good cause. In 1640 the oldest, most revered institution of advanced education in the United States started to make history.

But a grammar school erected concurrently on a lot adjacent to the Harvard grounds to prepare students for the college probably was of more immediate interest to Nathaniel; for he had a young, fast-growing family by 1639.[19] His second son Nathaniel was born in that year, and John must have been about seven. There were also two—possibly four—girls; but formal schooling was not for the weaker sex in those days.

This seminary figured in the lives of two future generations of Hancocks. Within its roughhewn walls Nathaniel II obtained the rudiments of knowledge that helped to train him for prominent citizenship. His son John supplemented a skill in expounding Congregational doctrine by acquiring there the experience that enabled him to impart secular lore to his parishioners.

If Nathaniel I had any intellectual curiosity he must have been excited by the establishment of another institution in Cambridge almost simultaneously with these scholastic projects. That was the installation in 1638 of a public printing press in the home of the Reverend Henry Dunster, president of Harvard. The General Court went on record as recognizing Stephen Day to be "the first that set upon printing" in the American colonies.[20]

And so the pioneer Hancock lived out the remainder of his short span wresting a livelihood from the reluctant soil to provide for his perennially increasing dependents. He seems to have worked as hard at creating life as at producing crops, for the little ones kept coming along as regularly as the seasons until 1646, when the tally reached eight.

Cambridge, as well as its worthy son, had won a secure place in the colonial world by the middle of the seventeenth century. It no longer had to be fortified, for it had come to terms with the Indians. At a sitting of the General Court in 1639 "Mr. Gibons was desired to agree with the Indians for the lands within the bounds of Watertowne, Cambridge, and Boston."[21] The Redskins were ruled by a "squaw sachem," who was by no means politically primitive. For closing the deal she had demanded and obtained a bonus, which had been provided for in a court decree that "Cambridge is to give Squa-Sachem a coat every winter while she liveth."[22]

In 1652, about a decade after this prototype of the modern American career woman began to collect her commission, the first Nathaniel, approximately at the age of forty, went to his reward. He deserved a rich

Wingate College Library

one, for he had helped to implant in New England the sturdy stock that was to attain its full flowering four generations later.

· 5 ·

Nathaniel Hancock II, only son of the emigrant to reach manhood, took unto himself a wife, Mary Prentice, at the age of twenty-four in 1663. Presumably he brought his bride to his mother's home, for there is no record of his setting up a separate establishment until three years afterward. By that time living space in the old family homestead must have been somewhat cramped. The young couple already had passed on the Hancocks' favorite name to little Nathaniel and were about to have a daughter. So it is not surprising to read in the selectmen's minutes that "liberty is granted for felling timber on the common . . . to Nathaniel Hancock for ground sills and clapboards." [23]

Probably in anticipation of becoming a householder he had taken title to a ten-acre lot across the street from the pioneer rooftree and had obtained in "cow common" the use of another acre—the nucleus of more than a hundred grazing plots that he eventually owned.[24] But he does not seem to have been in any hurry to complete his house. Perhaps he was too busy cultivating his land and sticking to his last as a shoemaker to work at it steadily. In any event, the annals do not show definitely that he had a habitable dwelling of his own until 1670.[25]

The second Nathaniel soon began to exhibit the flair for politics which in his great-grandson became genius. At the election of municipal officers in 1673 he was chosen town constable, most important of the four law enforcement agents in the township of Cambridge.[26] Two years later he was shouldered with a thankless task as one of a committee "to have inspection into families, that there be no by-drinking nor any misdemeanor whereby sin is committed and persons [kept] from their houses unseasonably." [27] In 1677 it became his still more odious and odorous duty, with the assistance of another citizen, "to look after the swine for the town." [28] And he improved his spare time by serving as official drummer of the community. The municipality was not very appreciative of his work in this connection; for in 1685 he had to sue to obtain compensation amounting to only eight pounds "for drumming and the maintenance of drums for sundry years past." [29]

Nathaniel probably needed all the odd jobs he could pick up to support his rapidly-increasing family. Another Nathaniel (named after the first-born, who had died) was the eldest son, aged nineteen; but John, at

REVEREND JOHN HANCOCK, GRANDFATHER OF THE PATRIOT. FROM
A PORTRAIT BY JOHN SMIBERT IN THE HANCOCK-CLARK HOUSE AT
LEXINGTON, MASS.

THOMAS HANCOCK, UNCLE OF THE PATRIOT. FROM A PORTRAIT BY
COPLEY IN THE FOGG MUSEUM OF ART AT HARVARD UNIVERSITY.

seventeen, already was showing the greatest promise of all the thirteen children in 1687, when Mrs. Hancock gave birth to the last of her brood —a daughter who died young.[30] Infant mortality was heightened by Mother Mary's procreative pace—a new arrival every eighteen months —under conditions that were hardly conducive to the raising of babies.

Responsibilities continued to shower upon Nathaniel, Sr. In 1694 he attained the zenith of his political career—the office of tithingman.[31] There is more truth than raillery in this characterization of the Cambridge portfolio. The function of tapping misbehaving parishioners on the head with the knobby end of a long staff and tickling sleepy ones with the fox tail attached to the other extremity carried considerable prestige. It was dignified by the General Court to the extent of being invested under oath.

This post and several others conferred upon the popular politician kept him prominent in the settlement until after the turn of the century. But as his progeny grew up and became capable of fending for themselves he seems to have settled down into a more leisurely life, made possible presumably by moderate affluence. In 1707 he purchased a house from four members of a family named Green who had left town. His wife had died, and in 1699 he had wedded Widow Sarah Green. His probable reason for buying the home, in which she had an interest, was to move there with her and leave his original residence to one or more of his married offspring.

Nathaniel II, now Deacon Hancock, died on April 2, 1719, in his eightieth year. Although he had been able to look back with satisfaction, in the twilight of his life, to many solid achievements, he must have realized that his most significant contribution to the world was John, aged forty-eight at his father's death and already widely known as the Bishop of Lexington.

· 6 ·

Old Nathaniel seems to have recognized that his second surviving son had exceptional qualities even in early youth, for the lad enjoyed the advantages of a college education usually bestowed first upon the eldest boy. But John did not receive this nourishment for the mind out of a silver spoon. He had to earn part of his tuition, at least, by tutoring while an undergraduate at Harvard, where he became both a Bachelor and a Master of Arts—the latter in 1688. So he was well prepared when, in 1691, the Cambridge selectmen "called Sir Hancock to keep school for the town to teach both grammar and English, with writing and ciphering," as successor to Master Elijah Corlett, who had built up a far-flung reputation in half a century of service.[32] The title of "Sir" was conferred upon all holders of a B.A. (which could be acquired in three years) who remained in residence for another year to obtain an M.A. But elevation to the academic "nobility" carried no pecuniary preferment: the young "knight" had to wait until 1693 for his remuneration—and the town proprietors were forced to sell some common land to raise it.[33]

In the meantime John had improved his spare hours by training himself for the ministry practically as well as theoretically. He had preached as a substitute at Groton and Medford. In 1697 he paved the way still further for the pursuit of his ultimate calling by moving from Cambridge to "The Farms," a suburb, and by placing one foot in the ecclesiastical door through which the Farmers' former pastor, the Reverend Benjamin Estabrook, had just passed into eternity. The young lay preacher spent more than a year in proving to his new congregation, as was the custom, that he was worthy to become a consecrated apostle of Christ. After serving on this trial basis for a consideration of eighteen shillings per week he not only qualified for the pastorship but enjoyed the honor of delivering his own ordination sermon on November 2, 1698.

The Reverend Mr. Hancock had made an agreement with the parish whereby he was to receive an annual salary of £40, supplemented by the usual settlement gift, or bonus, amounting to £40 more. This was regarded as generous compensation for a novice dominie of twenty-seven.[34] It enabled him, at least, to buy a fifty-acre tract of land in Cambridge Farms and to start construction of what has become one of the most historic houses in America. This was a single-story structure measuring twenty-four feet by twenty-one, into which were squeezed a kitchen, a study, and two tiny bedrooms tucked up under a gambrel roof. Here John and his wife, Elizabeth Clark, whom he had married in 1700, reared five children.

When the Hancocks set up housekeeping the population of the Farms could not have exceeded forty families totaling approximately three hundred persons; and not more than half a dozen dwellings besides their own could have clustered around the village green. A great majority of the inhabitants lived on widely scattered farms, to which the only means of access were wagon trails winding through the woods. To the north and west stretched the pine swamp behind which Nathaniel I had staked out his first piece of American real estate.

The meetinghouse where Nathaniel's grandson embarked upon his career stood at the southern end of the common within short walking distance of his home. Near by were the stocks—possibly so situated as to make delinquents more conscious of their guilt. The Reverend John's congregation comprised only thirty-three souls when he was ordained. But the parish had done an excellent promotional job by inducing the Council of Massachusetts Bay and representatives from five churches outside Cambridge Farms to attend the ceremonies.

The youthful clergyman soon justified his parishioners' faith in him. By 1713, when the Farms was incorporated as the independent town of Lexington, his magnetism had attracted to the new house of worship, built that year on the site of the old, the first families of Cambridge proper as well as the Farmers.

· 7 ·

Parson Hancock's popularity was based partly on his ability to satisfy the craving for flagellation of conscience. He was a "painful preacher," and, although he did not indulge in dogmatic damnation of sinners to the extent of his celebrated contemporaries Increase and Cotton Mather, he was enough of a Puritan to compel wrongdoers to stand up in meeting and confess their transgressions. His learning was comprehensive rather than narrowly theological, and he imparted it to his people with a witty tongue. Every Sunday throughout the year he delivered from manuscript two sermons an hour long; but they were not nearly so dry as the average.

This unusual minister drew his subject matter largely from his commonplace book—a huge compendium of 500 pages packed with notes on general science, medicine, botany, zoology, history, biography, philosophy, and wise sayings of great men. With such catholic intellectual interests he could not be a fundamentalist in religion. As a matter of fact, he was skeptical—almost heretical—toward holy writ. "How was it possible," he asked himself in his jottings, "if the flood was universal, for water enough to have fallen in forty days to have covered the tops of the highest mountains?"

He also was ahead of his time in questioning the accepted standards of social relationships, such as intermarriage among persons of differing faiths. "Is it lawful for an educated Protestant woman to marry a Roman Catholic if he agrees not to disturb her religion?" he queried in his written meditations—and answered, with surprising tolerance and a characteristic dig at the Papists: "It would not be sinful for her to marry a pagan, no more to marry a Catholic, especially where better is not to be had." [35]

The Reverend John employed the same analytical and judicious reasoning in guiding his parish through its most perilous period—that of the Great Awakening. This was an evangelistic movement launched, strangely enough, by an ordained minister of the conservative Church of England—George Whitefield. The colonial branch of the Congregational Church had been stagnating, probably in reaction from its pioneering, rebellious beginnings. Jonathan Edwards had been injecting considerable new vigor into it from his Northampton pulpit since 1734. But Whitefield was the man who stirred the sluggish pool of theological thought into a seething caldron. He thundered against the outward observance of religious ritual as dissimulation for lack of inward and spiritual grace. But he saved souls at the expense of unity in the body politic of the church—an unwise and dangerous proceeding in an embryonic nation where ecclesiastic and civic life were so interdependent.

Boston, where Whitefield started his revival tour of New England in earnest, was sufficiently sophisticated to take his disturbing diatribes in stride. Governor Belcher's enthusiastic sponsorship of his cause helped to prevent a breach between his adherents and his opponents there. Almost twenty thousand people listened to his farewell exhortation on the Common without becoming unduly agitated. But his preaching had a different effect in the smaller towns. The Concord congregation was split wide open by disputation over his doctrine; a serious schism was created at Medford, and cleavages of varying degrees were caused in most of the other Massachusetts parishes.

But the Lexington pastor's flock continued to pasture peacefully on the comforting food for thought which he provided. He did not reject the underlying principles of the new movement. His mind was as receptive as any minister's to ideas that would illuminate the darkness of men's souls. But he knew that the light shed by Whitefield was too dazzling for these simple folk. So he shaded it in such a way as to make them see the eternal verities clearly instead of becoming blinded by transitory fanaticism.

· 8 ·

The Bishop was not blind, either, to the materialistic side of life. He saw to it that he and his family got their modest ministerial share of this world's goods. At a parish meeting in 1702 he had wangled a salary increase of £20 per year, plus permission to cut timber on the common land for the repair of his farm buildings and fences. In 1725 he had talked the town authorities into giving him a £20 gratuity, probably on the ground that the currency had depreciated by 50 per cent.[36]

But it was in the sermon (cited partially heretofore) at the 1726 ordination of his son John that Parson Hancock put on the pressure most unashamedly for appreciation in the form of cold cash.[37] One can visualize from the portrait of him by John Smibert, leading colonial painter of the early eighteenth century, how impressively he must have claimed for the clergy the power that goes with "the keys of the kingdom." The black, buttonlike eyes must have flashed as they peered down the long nose at the congregation; the locks of the fluffy wig that framed a fleshy face must have shaken violently, and the prominent jaw must have wilted the starched Puritan collar as the massive head, crowning a burly body, wagged admonishingly.

In the same homily the outspoken cleric interpolated what looks like a broad hint that he wished the church would legalize his unofficial title: "He that desires the office of a bishop desires a good work." With paternal pride the Bishop then addressed his son. He told him that "you are where God would have you to be; . . . you have not begged the office nor invaded it nor shuffled yourself into it . . . but have tarried till a wide . . . door is opened unto you." [38]

The consecration and settlement of his third boy, Ebenezer (John, Jr., had been born in 1702, and Thomas in 1703), as assistant to his father in 1734 was another memorable and gratifying episode in the Bishop's career.[39] The pleasure he derived from seeing a second child—and perhaps the most brilliant of all—follow in his footsteps was changed to sorrow six years later, however, by the youth's death at the age of thirty.

The Reverend John senior, of course, was chosen to grace the pulpit at the consecration. Again he could not resist the temptation to brag and gloat a bit about "me and mine" as he pointed out that Ebenezer's "invitation to a settlement elsewhere was [extended] with such repeated earnestness that it pushed on his settlement here faster than some desired. But you did see apparently that you must take him now or never." He also boasted of his own well-being—justifiably so—and of his economical administration of the parish as he recalled that "my God has blessed me with health to that degree that, for the space of six and thirty years, I have been but a little confined; and, if continued at any time, I have supplied the pulpit without any care or cost unto you."

Being a politician at heart, he was careful to pay his parishioners a compliment—a sincere one: "You are an industrious and consequently a thriving people. There's no drinking clubs or companions that have their appointed places and times to meet and drink and game and spend their precious time, as I know of."

After reviewing briefly the history of his pastorate, reminding his hearers that about three hundred communicants had been added to the rolls and a thousand persons had been baptized, he admitted he was not quite the man he once had been. The tenor of his confession—"I feel the outward man decay"—was to be strangely echoed by his grandson more than half a century afterward.[40]

But the Bishop underestimated the toughness of his constitution, for he seems to have worked harder than ever during the two concluding decades of his life. He responded to constant demands to act as chairman of ecclesiastical councils, as organizer of parishes, and as leader in all kinds of religious projects in neighboring communities in addition to his own.

The "outward man" did not decay. He collapsed and died suddenly on December 6, 1752, three months before his eighty-second birthday. According to the Reverend Nathanael Appleton, who eulogized him on the Sunday following the funeral, the Bishop went "to bed as well as usual the night after the 5th . . . and, awakening some time after midnight with a great pain in his stomach, died in a few minutes." [41]

The town granted the widow £200 to pay for the obsequies and five hundred bricks to line the grave. When a bill of £219 for the services and burial, including the cost of rings for the bearers (worn in violation of the law), was presented to the selectmen they readily honored it.[42]

So the citizens of Lexington did not stint on the outlay essential to the proper speeding of their beloved pastor's soul into the next world any more than he had husbanded his strength in saving theirs. They were fully aware of the truth in the Reverend Mr. Appleton's tribute to him:

"He had an uncommon vivacity of spirit that made him diligent, active, and cheerful. . . . Few ministers have been so much concerned in the various affairs of their people . . . ; for you yourselves were so sensible of his wisdom and goodness . . . that . . . you seldom or never engaged in any important or difficult affair without consulting him upon it. And Oh! what a happy talent had he to prevent quarrels and differences among you . . . ! That facetious temper and turn of wit which was natural to him and which, although some people of a different make might think at some times abounded, . . . he made a very good use of . . . in general. . . . But few ministers have been so much employed in ecclesiastical councils as he was, for . . . he has been even as a bishop among us. . . . I understand that he himself, a few days before his death, observed that he had given the solemn charge to twenty-one ministers, which I believe no minister in this country besides has been able to say. . . . Yet he did not outlive his usefulness, for he retained his spirits and the powers of his mind with uncommon vivacity and vigor even to the last." [43]

· 9 ·

During his comparatively short occupancy of the pulpit the second Reverend John Hancock must have been a source of much happiness to the first. Although apparently lacking his father's intellectual powers and commanding personality, he was a worthy offspring of an extraordinary character.

There is no positive indication in the records as to how John II spent his time between graduating from Harvard and qualifying for the cloth. He seems to have followed his eminent parent's example by filling in for absent clergymen until he was given pastoral charge of the North Precinct of Braintree (the present Quincy) on November 2, 1726—just twenty-eight years, to the day, after John I was ordained at Lexington. He had received his call, at an annual emolument of £110, four months previously and was granted £200 more on settlement—almost quadruple the sum paid to his sire at the start.[44] But these figures represented highly inflated values.

The Bishop probably handled the financial part of the agreement. A shrewd request in his son's letter of acceptance sounds as if it was inspired by the canny cleric. "I would just take leave," it reads, "to recommend to your consideration the article of wood, which I understand is, or is likely to be, pretty dear and scarce in this place." This implied condition put the parish under a moral obligation, which it fulfilled in 1733 by compensating its pastor to the extent of £20 for the cost of fuel.

Thoughts of the hearth flame must have been in the mind of the young Reverend Mr. Hancock even oftener than hell fire during those early years of his ministry; for up to 1732, when a new meetinghouse (a Quincy landmark to this day) was built, the bleak, stone edifice erected in 1666 had continued to serve. The old church had become so dilapidated by the winter of 1730 that "cartloads of snow" had drifted into it.[45]

But warm blood had been coursing through the veins of numerous parishioners in the meantime. Typical of several entries in the minister's memorandum book is the following:

"January 21, 1728—Joseph P—— and Lydia, his wife, made a confession

before the church, which was well accepted, for the sin of fornication
with each other before marriage."

Although only seven persons, in addition to this overhasty couple—all
except one of whom were women—spoke up in meeting to the effect that
they had been sinfully ardent during the eighteen years while Pastor
Hancock shepherded his flock, the annals do not include erring non-
members.[46] Since this group embraced illiterates and most servants, the
unholy worship of Venus probably was more prevalent in North Braintree than the clerical evidence reveals. And yet, according to a careful
docket maintained by Colonel John Quincy, Suffolk County justice of
the peace, scarcely more than two hundred cases of sexual immorality
came before him between 1716 and 1761.[47] So—relatively speaking—the
inhabitants of the Reverend John's parish, which was part of that county,
were far more circumspect than the general run of eighteenth century
New Englanders, whose reputation for chastity was distinctly malodorous.

After its flurry of scandal the community settled down to a comparatively virtuous life. The erstwhile wayward members, on the whole, emulated their pastor, who entered into holy matrimony with Widow Mary
Hawke Thaxter in 1733 before starting to raise a family. They produced
a daughter Mary in a good Christian manner two years later. With continued rare restraint for that prolific period the Hancocks let an equal interval elapse before giving a son to the world—but he was well worth
waiting for.

John Hancock, prospective patriot in purple, arrived on January 23,
1737 (New Style), at the parsonage which stood on the site of what now
is the Adams Academy in Quincy.[48] The Reverend John, who had
baptized another of the future founding fathers—John Adams—in 1735,
dedicated his own boy to Christianity four days after birth, although
he recorded the ceremony in accordance with the Old Style calculation
of time. The entry in the annals of the First Church reads simply: "John
Hancock, my son, Jan. 16, 1737."[49]

There is not much more to relate concerning the North Braintree clergyman—a modest man of laudable intentions but mediocre attainments.
Glimpses of his character are provided by two contemporaries.

John Adams, who was nine years old when the Reverend John died,
and who was a playmate of young John, affords an indirect insight into
the nature of the father while writing of the son: "He inherited from his
father, though one of the most amiable and beloved of men, a certain
sensibility, a keenness of feeling, or—in more familiar language—a peevishness of temper that sometimes disgusted and afflicted his friends."[50]

In a funeral oration on the last Parson Hancock the Reverend Ebenezer Gay stressed his middle-of-the-road philosophy, to which all three John Hancocks subscribed. Referring particularly to the Great Awakening, he said:

"As a wise and skilful pilot he steered you a right and safe course in the late troubled sea of ecclesiastical affairs, guarding you against dangerous rocks on the one hand and on the other; so that you have escaped the errors and enthusiasms which some, and the infidelity and indifferency in matters of religion which others, have fallen into. . . . The churches in this neighborhood and land have cause to lament the death of one who affectionately cared for their state."

On May 7, 1744, after "pining sickness and pain," the helmsman of God had been relieved of the tiller and had followed Brother Ebenezer to an impatient grave at the age of forty-two.[51] He had left his widow with three children: Mary, aged nine; John, seven; and Ebenezer, a three-year-old, who was to be a lifelong burden to his brother.

So passed the man whose primary mission was to bridge the generation between one who had gained regional fame and one whose renown was to become universal.

II

BOY INTO HARVARD MAN

ALTHOUGH JOHN HANCOCK was born into a family of law-abiding and fundamentally conservative citizens for at least four generations, the place of his birth had a rebellious history more consonant with the spirit which eventually converted him into one of the most recalcitrant Revolutionary leaders. The town, known as North Braintree when he first opened his eyes upon it, had been settled as Mount Wollaston on a hillock still so designated and kept green in the minds of New Englanders by Nathaniel Hawthorne's essay, "The Maypole of Merry-Mount."

Concerning the man who gave his name to the site around which Quincy has grown up there is little in the records, which refer to him only as Captain Wollaston. He sailed into Boston Bay in the spring of 1625 at the head of a small party of adventurers, including thirty or forty indentured servants, and established a trading post. But one Massachusetts winter was enough for him, and he shipped off to Virginia with a group of the bondmen, leaving the rest of the colonists in charge of an associate. When, a few months later, he sent word to his lieutenant to follow him with more of the articled vassals, the remaining settlers contemplated abandoning the plantation.

They did not reckon, however, on the persuasive persistence of another Wollaston henchman—Thomas Morton "of Clifford's Inn, Gent.," as he presumptuously styled himself.[1] This "gentleman" had been a shyster lawyer of London and had been accused by the prejudiced Deputy Governor Dudley—whose narrow Puritanical principles he had flouted —of being implicated in several dastardly deeds, including murder. But he was quite a man, for all that.

Morton had visited New England first in the summer of 1622, had helped to found a settlement at Wessagusset a few miles from the site of Mount Wollaston, and had returned to England in the fall. An ardent

24

nature lover and sportsman as well as a shrewd Indian trader, he had seen in this new country a glorious future of pleasure combined with business. He seized the opportunity presented by Wollaston and probably picked out the place where the captain's company located.

When the colonists were on the point of following their leader to Virginia, according to Governor William Bradford of the Plymouth Plantation, Thomas "got some strong drink and other junkets and made them a feast." As soon as they were in an amenable mood he talked them into remaining with dire warnings that they would be sold into slavery, like their fellow bondmen, if they should go south.

Morton made life pleasant, even if not permanently profitable, for the Mount Wollastonites and launched a picturesque, though abortive, rebellion against the dour Puritanical philosophy. As related by Bradford: "They fell to great licentiousness and led a dissolute life," "maintained . . . a school of Athisme," "set up a Maypole, drinking and dancing about it many days together," and changed the name of their place to "Merie-Mount." [2]

The Plymouth authorities denounced—and averted horrified eyes from —this cesspool of iniquity reeking on their borders but did nothing about it for a year. Perhaps they thought that their vengeful God would visit retribution upon it in due course. But when, by the spring of 1628, Morton started to sell rum and firearms to the Indians on such a large scale as to menace the safety of all the colonists they dispatched Miles Standish with a party of eight men to arrest him. The prisoner was sent to England, but returned to his beloved Merry-Mount eighteen months afterwards, only to find that it had been rechristened Mount Dagon, that Governor Endicott of Massachusetts Bay had had his beautiful eighty-foot Maypole chopped down, and that his drinking companions had been dispersed.

But this did not discourage Morton from continuing to tweak the Puritans' blue noses through the medium of various escapades. In 1630 his personal belongings were confiscated, his house burned, and he was shipped back once more to where he had come from. Even a term in jail, however, did not cure him of running wild in the American wilderness. He yielded to it again in 1643 and turned up at Plymouth like the proverbial penny. He was banished from the colony almost immediately and took refuge in Maine. But the strange lure of Merry-Mount soon brought him back for the fifth time. Although apprehended and fined by the Massachusetts government, he enjoyed one short, last laugh at the expense of his oppressors, who persecuted him, he wrote, because he "endeavoured to advance the dignity of the Church of England." [3] They released him after a year's imprisonment to die a free man in 1647 because they were tired of supporting him!

The revolt against social despotism thus carried to inward victory even in outward defeat by Thomas Morton of Clifford's Inn, Gent., was to be paralleled by a completely successful revolution against political dictatorship more than a century later. And it would be done with the invaluable assistance of a genuine gentleman who had spent his early childhood in the exhilarating atmosphere of Mount Wollaston—John Hancock.

· 2 ·

Morton's flamboyant frolics had passed into the realm of half-forgotten legend by the time that Hancock was born in 1737 within easy walking distance of Merry-Mount. The gaiety which one of the few first-rate playboys of the Puritan period had injected fleetingly into its somber life had vanished; and the North Precinct of Braintree, which had developed around the scene of his protest against stuffiness, was a stolid, circumspect community, much like all the rest of the smaller towns in the province of Massachusetts Bay. Its population, which had been about 500 in 1708, when the township of Braintree was divided into north and south precincts, had increased by only two or three hundred at the arrival of the future patriot in purple.

Even a century after the early settlements had been made New England rural life still was hard and primitive. In the very best homes (not to mention the poor parsonage where Hancock lived until the age of seven) the long, bleak winters were almost unbearable—or so they would have seemed to modern Americans. The only heat available was supplied by open-hearth fires, which toasted the faces of those who huddled around them while drafts chilled their spines. On Sunday January 15, 1716, Judge Samuel Sewell had written in his diary: "An extraordinary cold storm of wind and snow. . . . Bread was frozen at the Lord's Table. . . . At 6 o'clock my ink freezes so that I can hardly write by a good fire in my wife's chamber." [4] And the climate had not moderated, nor had the heating system been improved, when Hancock was being rocked in his cradle twenty-one years later.

Household furnishings were not calculated to offset the discomfort caused by the weather. There were few beds, and the mattresses were usually made of lumpy wool or cornhusks. The chairs (as people of today with friends who go in for colonial antiques do not have to be told) were no cozier. Clothing was homespun and was worn until threadbare. Puritan hats are known to have passed down from father to son through three generations.

There was little solace or novelty for the inner man, either, in North Braintree. Indian cornmeal was the staple food. Flour was a delicacy enjoyed only by the well-to-do. Fresh meat was a rare luxury. Even the wealthy had to salt down a pig or a side of beef in the fall in order to make it last through the shut-in winter.

This practice accounts in part for the insatiable thirst of the early New Englanders. They did not have to quench it, of course, with incredible quantities of rum; but, in the absence of other good cheer, they hardly can be blamed for doing so—or for tapering off with hard cider and beer. The Braintree brewery was built in 1640, the year in which the original town was incorporated.

Probably it was in their native North Precinct that John Adams acquired the lifelong habit of tossing off a huge tankard of cider before breakfast, and that Hancock got in the way of keeping a gallon jug of hot rum punch on the sideboard in his Beacon Hill mansion at all hours of the day and night. It is true, to be sure, that both left home as young boys—but the children of that era were brought up not to be sissies.

Existence was dull, by present standards, in this birthplace of two American Presidents—John Adams and his son, John Quincy Adams. But while the first Adams and Hancock (who was to be a presidential precursor) were playing obliviously on its spacious common the inhabitants had the saving grace of many and various occupations.[5] In addition to agriculture every essential trade was represented there. Except for special requirements, the people had little occasion to go to Boston. To meet everyday needs which the general store could not supply there were blacksmith, bootmaker, mason, carpenter, fishmonger, and peddler of miscellaneous merchandise—the last two of whom also purveyed news of the outside world as they tramped through the town signaling their approach by tooting a horn.[6]

Hancock may have been too young to be deeply impressed either by the hardships or by the meager conveniences of life in North Braintree. But he must have carried into later years certain memories such as suffering through his father's sermons and, perhaps, sticking pins into his pal Adams without getting caught by the tithingman; studying with his playmate, as the future President wrote in old age, "at the same school together as soon as we were out of petticoats"; visiting his grandfather, the

Bishop of Lexington, during the last illness of that venerable prelate; and, above all, shivering into his clothes at dawn on frigid days in the parsonage.[7]

After leading the simple life of a typical country boy little John must have thought that he, too, was being transported to heaven on the death of his father in 1744, when rich Uncle Thomas carried him off to the fairy palace on Beacon Hill. And his childish fancy, as subsequent events were to prove, did not lead him very far astray, at that.

· 3 ·

Thomas Hancock was firmly established as a merchant prince when he took his nephew and adopted son to Boston, but had been too busy making money to order from London the resplendent chariot which later stamped him definitely as one of the economic royalists of his day. So young John probably embarked upon his great adventure in the old family coach.

But it is more than likely that the child of fortune was dressed up to the minute for the occasion—somewhat in the manner of Tommy Coffin, who eventually became commissary general of the British army in America. Tommy was five, two years the junior of Johnny Hancock, when put on canvas by John Singleton Copley, who had superseded Smibert as the preeminent portrait painter in the colonies. According to an old catalogue of Copley's works:

"He is dressed in a low-necked sacque of green satin over a dress of white satin, richly embroidered with lace and with ruffles at the wrists. In his plump and pretty right hand he holds two cherries, while on his left are two white turtle-doves. The plumes of his hat are seen behind the left hand." [8]

To describe the youthful Hancock by analogy to this prettified picture may not seem consistent with the impression of a perfectly normal boy already conveyed to the reader; but the likeness is in keeping with the sartorial superlativeness favored by the uncle and emulated by the nephew throughout their lives. Furthermore, Thomas, a childless man who was infinitely proud of his good-looking foster son, would have gone the limit to attract the attention of Bostonians to his newest acquisition as he drove the lad to his home.

And what a home it must have appeared to wide-eyed Johnny as he stood at the foot of the dozen stone steps leading up to the front door under a balustraded balcony! Even though he probably had visited there many times, the idea of living in the show place of the big town must have struck him dumb with awe.

The Hancock residence was a two-story structure of granite from the Braintree quarries, with quoins of Connecticut freestone from Chatham and a tiled gambrel roof, the summit of which was spanned by a wooden railing that connected a pair of slender brick chimneys. It had a frontage of about fifty-three feet and a depth of approximately sixty-three. It was lighted by fifty-four windows, including three dormers overlooking the famed Common across Beacon Street. A vast entrance hall divided the mansion in the center and extended through to the rear, where it gave upon a group of the loveliest gardens in Boston, laid out on the hillside against which the house nestled.

The great parlor, or drawing room, opened off at the right. It was furnished luxuriously in mahogany and draped with damask curtains. Several clusters of tall brass candlesticks looked like burnished gold as they reflected the flames in the fireplace—one of many which supplied whatever heat there was in all the apartments.

Across the reception hall was the family sitting room. Behind it, in a wing, were the dining room and the kitchen. Opposite was a combination library and office. The rich and costly furnishings of the whole main floor were in keeping with those of the "company" parlor. Rising along the left wall of the foyer was a grand staircase with hand carved balusters; and on the landing where the stairs curved up through a spacious well to the second floor were an arched window and a settee, where portly Thomas probably would stop on hot days to catch his breath and to admire his meticulously landscaped grounds.

Directly above the great parlor was the historic guest bedchamber, decorated and fitted in yellow damask. Hugh, Earl Percy, it is believed, slept in its canopied four-poster during the British occupation of Boston; and from one of its windows Sir William Howe, according to legend, descried with dismay, on the morning of March 5, 1776, the intrenchments thrown up by Washington on Dorchester Heights during the preceding night—a sight that determined him upon evacuation twelve days later.

Opposite this capacious compartment was the room originally occupied by Uncle Thomas and Aunt Lydia; subsequently by Governor John and his Lady, Dorothy Quincy Hancock. Its appointments were done in a warm crimson. The remainder of the second floor was taken up by two more bedrooms, for which the hospitable Hancocks of future years, like the first occupants, found good use.

The entire piece of property, which also embraced a barn and a coach house, covered almost two acres and stretched back over the section of Beacon Hill on which a wing of the Statehouse now stands. It was valued at £5,000—a princely sum even for the demesne of a merchant prince in those days.

· 4 ·

The plan for the mansion upon which Johnny Hancock gazed so rapturously on the day when it became his permanent address had been born in his uncle's brain four years before the boy's birth. It had been fathered through an association of ideas by Daniel Henchman, leading Boston bookseller and stationer, whose daughter Thomas had married after going into partnership with him. In 1733, on Queen Street (now Court), Henchman had built a house that bespoke his prosperity and thereby had put the notion of doing likewise into the head of his rapidly rising son-in-law.

Two years later the shrewd young merchant picked up, at a bargain, an ideally situated tract of land on Beacon Hill that had been used for pasturage ever since the town's settlement a century before.[9] In December, 1736, with the pride and detailed interest he took in all his concerns, he opened a long correspondence regarding every aspect of the magnificent estate he had in mind. To the London horticulturist James Glin he wrote, referring to Francis Wilks, his agent in the British capital:

"I have sent my friend Mr. Wilks a memo to procure for me two or three dozen yew trees, some hollys and jessamine vines; and, if you have any particular curious things . . . [that] will beautify a flower garden, send a sample. . . . Pray send me a catalogue of what fruit you have that are dwarf trees and espaliers. . . . My gardens all lie on the south side of a hill, with the most beautiful ascent to the top; and it's allowed on all hands the Kingdom of England don't afford so fine a prospect as I have. . . . Neither do I intend to spare any cost or pains in making my gardens beautiful or profitable."

Either Glin tried to palm off on Hancock inferior flora, or the long ocean voyage was too much for them. In any event, the Englishman felt the prick of his customer's trenchant pen during the following June. Thomas informed him that all the trees he had shipped, except the yews, had arrived half dead; that the holly vines had expired altogether; that none of the flower seeds had sprouted, and that he expected the loss to be made good.[10] The British dealer presumably acquiesced, for the landscaping of the Beacon Hill domain eventually became the talk of the town.

Hancock even commissioned sea captains to keep on the lookout for exotic vegetation that could be transplanted to his estate. In August he sent word to one bound for Bilbao, Spain, to bring him a few mulberry, peach, nectron, and apricot trees—and "any small thing to beautify my garden." [11]

By this time the landed gentleman had hired a London architect to draw plans for the mansion and had engaged Joshua Blanchard, noted American builder whose initials are carved in the cornerstone of the Old South Meetinghouse, to construct it. The structure was virtually completed during 1737.

Meanwhile Thomas had begged of Wilks "your particular care about my window glass, that it be the best and every square cut exactly to the size." [12] Early in 1738 he asked John Rowe, a Boston merchant traveling in Europe, to pick up for him some English wallpaper with a pattern of peacocks, macaws, squirrels, fruits, and flowers. He emphasized that it should be "extraordinary neat and the figures and colors beautiful." [13]

In December—presumably after he and his ménage had been installed in the home of his dreams—the epicurean parvenu set about acquiring the piece of furniture with which he evidently hoped to stun Boston society. He desired Wilks to procure for him a chiming clock of the latest design, made of black walnut in a veneered tree case with "dark, lively branches" and "three handsome carved figures, gilt with burnished gold," to stand ten feet high and to cost fifteen or twenty guineas. But Thomas did not fancy his agent's conception of handsome figures; for in July, 1739, he dispatched instructions to exchange them for "Fame, Peace, and Plenty, to be ten inches long." [14]

A few months later Hancock made his boldest attempt to scale the social ladder by asking Jarvis Maplesden, another of his London agents, to "look into the Herald's Office and take out my arms"; and specified: "Let it be a well-cut crest and arms in silver and fixed to ivory for the use of a counting-room." [15] Whether this request was complied with is not known; but the economic royalist had no right to the coat-of-arms he referred to, anyway, for his family's connection with the Hancocks who had created it was decidedly nebulous.

· 5 ·

Uncle Thomas—quite likely at the insistence of doting Aunt Lydia—kept Johnny out of school for a year after he went to live with them. Most boys of that period, when there were no kindergartens, started their schooling as early as the age of six; but young Hancock, always pampered by his foster parents, was tutored at home until he was well over eight.

This may have been due partly to his health, which never was robust and gradually deteriorated into chronic illness that terminated his life at fifty-six. His new father and mother may have realized, also, that too much responsibility was placed upon little children, causing them to age so rapidly that few men lived out the biblical span of threescore and ten.[16]

At all events, it was not until July, 1745, that Johnny entered the Public Latin School, which now is the oldest educational institution in the United States. But from then on he had to work much harder than pupils of today, for by 1750 he had matriculated at Harvard after completing a more advanced curriculum in five years than modern lads do in eight.

The entrance requirements for elementary school were deceptively easy. They consisted merely of reading a few passages from the Bible. But during his first year young Hancock had to master, among other assignments, Cheever's *Accidence, Nomenclatura Brevis,* and Corderius' *Colloquies* (in Latin). The major subjects in the second year were Aesop's *Fables,* Eutropius, and Lilly's Grammar. By the end of his fourth year he had to be able to write Latin and to read fluently Caesar, Cicero, and Virgil. At graduation he was expected to be proficient in Xenophon, Homer, and the New Testament (in Greek). The long grind was alleviated by vacations of a week each at Thanksgiving and Christmas and three weeks in August.

Almost as much stress was laid upon penmanship as upon Greek and Roman culture at Public Latin School. The last hour of the school day, extending from seven o'clock in the morning to five in the afternoon, was devoted to the perfection of handwriting and the mending of quills. In Hancock's case this early training was to produce some of the finest, although belated, results in colonial chirography. Up to 1770 his autograph was scraggly, but within six years it acquired the copper-plate precision and beauty for which his signature on the Declaration of Independence is famous.

Under schoolmaster John Lovell, a martinet of the first order, the young student from Beacon Hill and most of the other prospective leaders of the Revolution in New England were thoroughly and painfully prepared. As a boy, the artist Smibert was one of Lovell's pupils. He created the teacher's likeness which hangs in Harvard Memorial

Hall today by working on it "while the terrific impressions of the pedagogue were yet vibrating on his nerves."

Although a Tory, the pedagogue did not let his political predilections
curb the freedom of thought in which he believed passionately, and
which made him a great master. But when it became evident that the
colonists were going to back up their free thinking with force he would
not go along with them. As soon as he sighted Lord Percy's brigade, bound
for Lexington and Concord on April 19, 1775, at the head of the street
on which the school was situated he dismissed his class with the cryptic
announcement: "*Deponite libros.* War's begun and school's done." [17]
When the British evacuated Boston on March 17 of the following year
he sailed with them.

· 6 ·

The term "Commencement Day" connoted the beginning of undergraduate, as well as graduate, life in mid-eighteenth century academic
circles. It was the day in the middle of July on which Master John Hancock, at the dignified age of thirteen, became a Harvard sub-freshman.

Entrance examinations were held at the college shortly before the commencement exercises, and successful candidates were admitted at approximately the same time as the seniors were going out into the world.
The tests were oral, except for the writing of an essay in Latin. In the
presence of the president and the tutors the students were required "*ex
tempore* to read, construe, and parse Tully, Virgil, or such like common
classical Latin authors; and . . . ordinary Greek, as in the New Testament; Isocrates, or such like, and decline the paradigms of Greek nouns
and verbs." [18]

After matriculation the entering class was free to go home and await
the start of the fall term in the middle of August. Those who lived at a
considerable distance from Cambridge probably did not remain for commencement; but it is likely that young Hancock, who resided only six
miles away, was present at the big doings to enjoy his new, proud status
of "Harvard man." Uncle Thomas and Aunt Lydia must have attended
regularly this most important Massachusetts social function of the year.

Since there was no bridge over the Charles, they would have traveled
from Boston by way of Brookline, Roxbury, and the "Neck" unless they
risked a ducking on the unseaworthy ferry. The land route is more probable, for Lydia's weight alone might well have sunk the frail river craft.

It is almost certain, too, that they used the handsome new chariot which Thomas had ordered from London two years before, and which had arrived within a month or two. He had sent to Christopher Kilby, another of his British factors, minute specifications for the carriage. This vehicle symbolized the success of a self-made man and was a source of preening pride to its owner.

The detailed instructions for its construction were justified by Mrs. Hancock's bulk. "You know," her husband wrote in September, 1748, after referring to former correspondence about the conveyance, "Mrs. Hancock is none of the shortest and smallest of folks, though I'd prefer as light a one as possible to her size." He repeated, and amplified by implication, the directions given to Maplesden back in 1739: "My and her arms (the Henchman) are to be met with at the Heraldry Office." But there is no more evidence of such a meeting than of success in the previously requested search. Hancock probably invented an escutcheon to be painted on his carriage, as his nephew was to do. Apparently sensing that Kilby, an expatriated Bostonian who "knew him when," would suspect him of putting on airs, he added: "I hope you won't think it savors too much of vanity in all this, as it's for [the] benefit of Mrs. Hancock's health." [19]

This letter does not seem to have brought action. In a follow-up addressed to Kilby & Barnard (Christopher's firm) in February, 1749, the merchant exhorted: "Let it be a new, neat, and very good one. As it will last for life, let everything be of the best and fashionable. . . . I keep three, and sometimes four, horses. . . . Please to send me the following: . . . A neat, roomy, genteel chariot . . . with a pack carriage; the doors to have double slides for glass and canvas sashes; the lining of a good light cloth or scarlet, which[ever] is most fashionable; one neat seat, cloth with a handsome fringe; one ditto, plain, for common use and bad weather; one pair harness . . . of the best leather and strong; one pair of spare worsted reins; two or three whips; four dozen small harness bells fixed on wires to put on in the winter."

Thomas still was waiting for his chariot in November, as is indicated by another letter directed to the London concern. He was annoyed at the delay because "Mrs. Hancock is often ill, and we live so far from town and church that an open chaise is very inconvenient for her." Besides, he had meanwhile become envious of a friend in Boston's upper crust and wanted "also a chaise on long shafts . . . such a one as Sir Harry Frankland* bought. . . . Inclosed is the account of particulars and cost; which is cheaper than I can have one made here, and [one of domestic

* Collector of the port.

manufacture] won't be half so good. I would have a step on each side fixed for a woman to get in and out and some neat, light, leather seat fixed for a boy to sit before to drive." [20]

The seat undoubtedly was intended for Master John, who was twelve at this writing. In view of the slow action on the chariot, however, the chaise probably did not reach the uncle in time for the nephew to hold one of the reins and crack the whip on the momentous journey to Cambridge.

In December the elder Hancock again put pressure on Kilby concerning the first vehicle. He reiterated that it must "be easy to get in and out and hang low, with good, broad steps; for Mrs. Hancock, [by reason of] a fall, is a little weak in her knees." Thomas had decided not only to emulate but to outdo the highest society in the matter of splendor on wheels. He sniffed at "two or three chariots sent here for Mr. Pitts; Bowdoin, and Flucker* [as being] the worst I ever saw. . . . I would not accept of either if given me." He also had made up his mind to add a touch of swank to his equipage but, characteristically, had an eye to the practical side of this acquisition as well: "If you could send me a good coachman, sober and honest and one that understands a kitchen garden, to keep from being idle, . . . I should be very glad of one . . . not younger than twenty-six or twenty-eight nor older than thirty to thirty-six."

The vehicular episode was brought to a partially happy conclusion— one that surprisingly satisfied the exacting merchant to some extent—in the spring of 1750. Hancock wrote once more to Kilby in May: "The chariot is come safe. A little rubbed, not being well packed. It's only too rich and good. But, as it pleases Mrs. H. and all my friends, I care not for other folk. . . . The chaise I don't think the Gentlemen Earlington & Co. have done me justice. It's no way equal to Sir Harry's." [21]

· 7 ·

Commencement Day provided the largest safety valve for the release of pent-up emotions in repressed Massachusetts. It was the lone opportunity for the people to give vent to their animal spirits in a province where the only other festivities were such formal, ritualistic affairs as the Thursday lecture, ministerial ordinations, general muster of militia, and execu-

---

* James Bowdoin, who was to be governor of the state; Thomas Flucker, the treasurer of the province.

tions accompanied by the inevitable sermon. The annual college celebration was almost completely uninhibited. Shops were closed in Boston and vicinity on the great day, and the holiday atmosphere prevailed for a week afterwards. During this period Cambridge common was dotted with booths containing food, liquor, and games of chance. The festival was the unbridled precursor of the New England county fair.

During the year before Hancock arrived on the campus the students had painted the town a real Harvard crimson. As a result the fathers of three undergraduates had offered the authorities £1,000 on condition that they would exclude the general public from the exercises. This proposition was acceptable to the Harvard corporation, but was turned down by the superior board of overseers for fear of popular resentment.

The younger generation had its way throughout Master John's residence in the halls of learning. Every annual exodus of seniors was an occasion of joy unrestrained. But in April, 1755, there was a reaction. Even the overseers became convinced that things had gone too far. They veered around to the corporation's point of view in recommending that entertainment of all kinds be prohibited not only on Commencement Day but during the entire academic year. By 1760 the pendulum had swung so far that the Reverend Edward Holyoke, president of the institution, was instructed to "put an end to the practice of addressing the female sex." [22]

Sartorial splendor, as well as jollification, was at its height when the boy from Beacon Hill first attended the graduation ceremonies as a matriculated student. In 1750 he witnessed what must have seemed to him an awe-inspiring procession moving from Harvard Hall to Holden Chapel.[23] President Holyoke, at its head, was followed by Governor William Shirley, his guard of honor, and the whole student body in order of classes. When the parade reached the chapel there were seated on a platform surrounding the pulpit all the academic, civil, and military dignitaries gorgeously attired in ermine, velvet, and silk habiliments or red-and-gold uniforms.

The undergraduates, too, were dressed in the latest fancy fashions and radiant colors. This offended the Puritanical college authorities' sense of propriety and led to a ukase passed just in time to cramp the style that already had become so dear to Hancock. Shortly before his own commencement in 1754 the ruling powers must almost have broken his heart by decreeing that "on no occasion any of the scholars shall wear any gold or silver lace or silver brocade in the college or town of Cambridge; and on Commencement Day every candidate for his degree who shall appear dressed contrary to such regulation may not expect to receive his degree." [24]

But as a spectator in 1750 John would not have been Thomas's adopted son if he had not been garbed, like the merchant prince and other leaders of society, in a coat of peach bloom or lavender; an embroidered satin waistcoat; velvet smallclothes, and rainbow-patterned or similarly bizarre stockings, with silver knee and shoe buckles. Aunt Lydia, too, would have felt dowdy without one of the modish towering coiffures which compelled milady to keep her head projecting from a window of her low carriage, or one of the hoop skirts which ballooned so that only two could be accommodated in a coach.

John and his foster parents presumably had front-row seats in Holden Chapel when President Holyoke arose from a triangular dais of turned wood behind the pulpit, with its canopylike sounding-board, to deliver the invocation. They were entitled to this place of honor by virtue of Uncle Thomas's high social standing. On one occasion the merchant was invited to dine with the exclusive Harvard pooh-bahs, although they doubtless were actuated as much by the desire to curry favor with this wealthy and influential citizen as by respect for his gentility.

After squirming through the Reverend Mr. Holyoke's ensuing salutatory oration and several learned discourses in Latin, Master John saw the gowned and mortarboarded graduates receive the sheepskin to which he aspired. For once in his life he probably experienced genuine humility.

When the ceremonies were over the academicians and students repaired to the commons or to their chambers for refreshments while the other functionaries and spectators went home or, in the case of the celebrating masses, prepared to spend the night in tents pitched on the common. By sunset the exhilaration induced in Cambridge's dons and denizens alike by the inspiring events of the day had reached flood tide. But the current of feeling, on the whole, was of a spirituous, rather than a spiritual, nature.

· 8 ·

John Hancock's aristocratic outlook was intensified during his freshman year at Harvard. When the "frosh" reported for the first semester in August the college steward "placed" them temporarily in accordance with their families' standing in society; and in the following spring the faculty assigned them to permanent rungs on the social ladder. This meant that their names were posted, in order of rank, on a wall of the "buttery hatch"—a refreshment room, or bar, where the students congregated in their leisure hours. Since there was, of course, no way of determining beyond dispute the relative blueness of the young men's blood, this practice led to much back-scratching and backbiting. But, once the sheep were separated from the goats, they retained their respective positions throughout their undergraduate careers unless degraded for misconduct. Even in that event, they could regain their original station before Commencement Day by expressing contrition for their sins.

A high rating brought more tangible privileges than that of snubbing inferiors. It carried the right to occupy the more desirable chambers, to march in the van of academic processions, to sit in the forward rows at chapel, to grace the head table in commons, and to enjoy first choice of food.

Hancock was conceded to be one of the elect, even though his foster family had no more than the claim of the *nouveau riche* to social distinction. Uncle Thomas' blood may have looked blue in the dazzling light emitted by his horde of pounds sterling.

But the special treatment accorded the "little marster" did not apply to the curriculum. He and all the rest of the student body had to get up in time for six-o'clock chapel, with Scripture reading in Hebrew or Greek, a spiritual discourse by the president or a tutor, and a prayer. At half past six he was obliged to report for his first recitation, which lasted an hour. Then he was permitted to snatch a bite of breakfast in chambers or the buttery hatch, where biscuits, coffee, chocolate, milk, and beer were dispensed.

The remainder of the morning was given to class work, interspersed with between-meals snacks called "bevers." At noon the entire group of undergraduates assembled in commons for the main repast of the day. Served by student waiters, it consisted of a pound of meat and vegetables, washed down by swigs from two huge pewter mugs of cider circulated like loving cups at each table. Sanitary precautions were further ignored in the kitchen, where the drinking vessels were scoured but once a week and the plates no oftener than every two or three months. What could the boys expect, however, for weekly board of only seven shillings?

After a recreation period lasting until two o'clock the students were shut up in their rooms for study until suppertime. The evening meal, which provided a choice of bread and milk or meat pie and a half-pint of beer, was supposed to sustain the young men through another long battle of the books in their chambers; but frequently it merely laid the foundation for an all-night bout with the bottle—a sport seemingly well mastered by Hancock.

John's intellectual fare in freshman year comprised Cicero, Virgil, Greek versions of the Bible and the Calvinist catechism; rhetoric, and Ramus' *Definitions*. As a sophomore he struggled with Burgerdiscius' *Logic*, Heerboord's *Melemata*, and Wallebius' *Divinity*, in addition to reading the classics every day. His junior program embraced physics, metaphysics, ethics, and religion. The modern order of educational progression was reversed, for his senior curriculum included such comparatively simple subjects as elementary arithmetic, geometry, geography, and astronomy. These courses were offered to "Bachelors" who intended to go into business as alternatives to the regular fourth-year requirements for those planning to enter the professions.[25]

As a freshman John was compelled to bow to the even more implacable decrees of college tradition enforced by the sophomores. He was prohibited from wearing a hat in the Yard "except it rains, snows, or hails, or he be on horseback or hath both hands full," and he had to bare his head in the presence of seniors.[26] He was warned against raising his voice in the corridors or playing ball on the campus. He was forbidden to "mingo" against the walls of buildings or to use the fellowship students' "cuz|ohn"—colonial slang for answering the calls of nature, and the place provided for it.

"Frosh" Hancock was forced to respond to the slightest whim of an upper-class man. The principal errands he was called upon to run were taking wigs to be curled or clothes to be pressed, delivering orders of food and drink from taverns, and acting as messenger boy for academic superiors who wished to communicate with one another.

In one respect, however, collegians of that time—even freshmen—enjoyed as much freedom as those of today. They had six weeks' vacation in summer and five in winter. In addition they were permitted to go home for four days in every month if they lived within ten miles of Cambridge and for periods of twenty-one days twice annually if they had farther to travel. It was typical of Hancock's lifelong luck that the midwinter holiday, starting on the first Wednesday in January and designed to give the poorer students a chance to eke out their tuition by teaching school, should have been instituted during the year before he entered Harvard.

· 9 ·

A modern commentator says that John was "simply a respectable, good-mannered lad, obedient to his superiors, and a faithful scholar in school." [27] But this paragonlike characterization does not quite jibe with the facts. Two-fisted tippling was at its peak during his affiliation with the college, and he was no exception to the rule of riotous living.

Probably at no other period in the history of the Cambridge institution has so much liquor been consumed per capita as during the second half of the eighteenth century. Although the Gargantuan guzzlers of the 1920's throughout the United States absorbed synthetic gin by the bathtubful, it is doubtful if their capacity equaled that of their Harvard prototypes in the latter 1700's. To be sure, the beverages imbibed during the earlier era were not so lethal as those of the later; but the quantity lapped up on the colonial campus would have made speak-easy habitués appear temperate by comparison.

The capacious tankards, mugs, and beakers preserved in Robinson Hall testify to the vast volume of spirits that went down when the students "bottomed up" in Hancock's day. Rum was the favorite potion. It usually was taken straight but often formed the base of a punch. Those who preferred to be titillated more gradually indulged in Madeira, flip, or negus. Flip was a staggering mixture of ale, beer, cider, "etc." (according to Webster), sweetened, spiced, and heated with a glowing iron in the manner of the current hot toddy. Negus was a seemingly innocuous concoction consisting of wine, water, sugar, nutmeg, and lemon juice; but it had remarkable creeping qualities.

One of the traditional means by which the Harvardians expressed their exhilaration when under the influence of such drinks was to invite Titus, a Negro slave and town character, to the party, ply him with refreshment, and induce him to perform. Whether he ever entertained Hancock is not known; but it is recorded that Master John and Samuel Quincy, a cousin of Dorothy Quincy, were severely disciplined "for being most remarkably active in making drunk" another colored man "to such a degree as greatly endangered his life." [28]

Although this incident suggests that John was not always a "faithful scholar," he seems to have been faithful to his ties of kinship. In the earliest letter extant from his pen he displayed devotion to his sister Mary and evinced interest in her coming nuptials. On May 1, 1754, he wrote to her:

"There was, nay, now is a report that you are going to be married very soon. I should be glad to know to whom. I hope you will give me an invitation. . . . I enjoy at present perfect health and should be very glad to see you. Accept my kind love to you. . . . Dear Sister, your ever loving brother till death shall separate us." [29]

When Widow Hancock had married for the third time Mary had

taken the name of her stepfather, the Reverend Daniel Perkins. She was now to wed without changing it, in accordance with a common colonial custom of intrafamily matrimony. Her intended husband was Richard Perkins, son of Daniel.

John received his Master of Arts degree at the age of seventeen on the July 17 following the date of his brotherly note. And so he went out into the world with the college graduate's characteristic determination to conquer it. His world was small in an immediate sense but vast in prospect. He had not far to go to start making his way—no farther than his uncle's countinghouse, where he was to spend the next six years learning the ropes in a business of tremendous ramifications and complexity. From this experience would emerge a man with a fantastic future.

$\mathcal{O}$ III $\mathcal{O}$

MERCHANT PRINCE AND PRINCELING

$\mathcal{T}$HERE HAD BEEN no such comparatively soft berth awaiting Thomas Hancock in Boston's hard-bitten commercial community in 1717 as the one his nephew rolled into thirty-seven years later. Besides, John owned a Harvard sheepskin with which to brush aside many of the obstacles that might have stood in his way; whereas his uncle possessed only such normally slow-working equipment as industry, ambition, imagination, and an ingratiating personality when he set about making a place for himself in a business society already characterized by a grim, self-seeking chase after the almighty pound sterling that was to lead right up to the muzzles of British guns.

Furthermore, Thomas was no more than fourteen years old when he fared forth from home with the blessings of the Reverend John Hancock. The boy may have envied his elder brother John, then a junior at Cambridge; but he probably accepted philosophically the usual fate of a second son in families of moderate means at the time. In fact, the enthusiasm with which he went into trade and the eminent success he made of it would indicate that he considered his lot an opportunity rather than a handicap.

Even the prospect of a seven-year apprenticeship, which must have discouraged many a less earnest youth, did not dampen Thomas's ardor for getting on in the world. He must have chafed occasionally, however, under the rigid restrictions imposed upon his private life by the indenture with which his father bound him over to Samuel Gerrish, a bookbinder whose shop was near the Old Brick Meetinghouse in Cornhill (now Washington) Street, and his wife Sarah. It stipulated that he must serve his "master and mistress well and faithfully" and "their secrets keep." Also: "Matrimony he shall not contract. Taverns and ale-houses he shall not frequent. At cards, dice, or any other unlawful games he

42

shall not play." In return the Gerrishes were to teach him bookbinding and provide him with "meat, drink, washing, and lodging." [1]

There is some doubtful evidence, in the form of a document signed at Plymouth, England, by a person named Hancock, that Thomas went abroad at the conclusion of his apprenticeship on July 1, 1724. How he could have raised the money for the journey, however, is hard to conceive. In any event, it would have been a hurried one at a period when transatlantic crossings required six weeks or more; for he was running a bookshop of his own in Ann, or Drawbridge, Street (known as North today) by the end of the year.

From the very start of his first venture Hancock displayed the extraordinary aptitude for trading that eventually made him one of the greatest merchants of his day—or any other. With a capital of less than £100, probably furnished by the Bishop of Lexington, he earned within two years a profit that enabled him to hire a bookbinder and to devote all his energy to expanding the enterprise. By 1727 he was laying the foundation for the House of Hancock in an establishment that was to become famous during the next four decades as the "Bible and Three Crowns." [2] He had not moved but simply had dressed up his original store with this catchy name for purposes of advertising, which he employed to an extent far in advance of his time.

Thenceforth he used as his address, indiscriminately, "Ann Street near the Drawbridge" and "Drawbridge Street near the Town Dock." This section was the principal market place of Boston's 14,000 inhabitants.

By 1728 his business had grown so large that he contracted with another dealer to dispose of 3,000 volumes for him on a commission basis and obtained big consignments of costly literary wares from two British agents. Even at this early date he exhibited the flair for gambling, partly with his own but mostly with other people's money, which led him into the fancy finance typical of eighteenth century commerce. A few months after entering into negotiations with him one of his English representatives refused to deliver any more goods until payment should be guaranteed by a third party.

It was during this same fateful year that Thomas formed the previously mentioned partnership with Henchman, whose daughter Lydia became Mrs. Hancock in 1730. As John's adoring aunt and foster mother she was to exert upon him an influence second in importance only to that of his uncle.

This combined commercial and social union was the most profitable of the many associations cannily cultivated by Thomas at the beginning of his career. Out of it came the funds with which he expanded his interests into fields entirely foreign to books and far more lucrative.

The bewildering rapidity with which he branched out during the next ten years was due partly to his enterprise but almost as much to chance. The literary market had become glutted through the decision of Thomas Cox, a London exporter, to compete for colonial business on the spot by sending a representative to Boston with a tremendous stock. Hancock, always quick to sense which way the trade winds were blowing, relegated books to his back shelves and started to push a wide assortment of other commodities through both domestic and foreign channels. He eventually imported cloth, tea, paper, and cutlery from England; exported codfish, lumber, whalebone, and whale oil to Britain—to mention but a few of the products he dealt in. He gradually broadened the scope of his merchandising to include Novia Scotia, the West Indies, Holland, and Spain.

But these operations were not nearly so simple as they may seem. And many of them would not meet with the approval of the Rotary Club today.

· 2 ·

Before delving into Hancock's amazing manipulations it is well to consider briefly the mechanics of bargaining in the middle of the eighteenth century, and the ingenious devices employed at the time to circumvent the virtually prohibitive obstacles to trading.

Cash was so scarce in New England as to be nonexistent for all practical purposes. This was due to the paucity of products for the British market, to the insistence of the English mercantile class on keeping the balance of trade preponderantly in their favor, and to the Britons' equally shortsighted policy of restricting colonial trade almost exclusively to the mother country.

So Boston merchants had to approach customers with a modified barter proposition. If Thomas, for instance, discovered that his butcher was interested in a best seller he might deliver a book to the good man on credit. Then when Lydia desired a loin of pork she would collect the debt in kind. Her husband would refine this process in transactions with farmers. He would accept a whole hog in payment for a Bible and would export it in settlement of a claim from an overseas creditor for manufactures that he had imported.

Frequently the three-sided deal would be entirely maritime. Hancock would consign to Newfoundland a cargo of foodstuffs unacceptable in

England; his agent there would ship to London a load of fish equal in value, and his British representative would send the equivalent in manufactures to Boston. Or this triangular transfer might take the form of an exchange of credits: the merchant and his customer would call in a third party who had accounts with both, and induce him to act the part played by the modern banker on a bill-of-exchange basis.

But the system sometimes broke down—and Thomas along with it. He must have tossed through many a night before he made his name as a tycoon and financier, for his foreign creditors often would not accept a slab of meat or a mess of fish in place of hard coin. He simply had to scrape up pounds sterling now and then.

This necessity proved to be the mother of discovery. Hancock learned that there was a strong demand in England for the products of whaling off the Grand Banks—particularly for the oil. He set about filling the need in partnership with William Tyler, a well-to-do Bostonian, and did this successfully until 1736, when he abandoned it in favor of a more profitable quest—the rewards of smuggling.

Through the first of many such illicit ventures Thomas revealed the devious working of his scheming mind. The Navigation Acts decreed that certain goods exported from the colonies to European nations must be routed through British ports, and that most products of those countries and their possessions imported into the colonies must be shipped by way of Britain, so that customs could be collected. But the regulations did not prohibit direct exportation to the dependencies. The wily Boston merchant slipped through this loophole. Taking partners on a temporary basis to minimize the per capita risk, he sent a vessel with a legal cargo to Surinam (Dutch Guiana); but he instructed the captain to bring back a load of contraband wares from South America.

Hancock took elaborate precautions to avoid running afoul of the law on the homeward trip. He wrote to the shipmaster: "Closely observe, when you come on our coasts, not to speak with any vessels *nor let any of your men write up to their wives* when you arrive at our lighthouse." [3]

The many-sided man of affairs probably owned a "piece" of this ship as of numerous others. Shipping was another phase of the expansionist policy he had adopted six years before. With various associates he had built up a private merchant marine, more from expediency than from volition. It was essential, for several reasons, that they should be part owners of the bottoms which carried their merchandise. They could not depend on transportation of their wares by outsiders to places off the few regular trade routes. They had to exercise control over the time consumed by a voyage in order to derive the maximum benefit from dizzily fluctuating oil prices. And if they were to evade import duties they needed authority to enjoin secrecy upon the masters of the smuggling vessels. Besides, they could turn many an extra profit by selling their shares in these ships along with the cargoes at the port of destination.

Within the span of a decade after going into business for himself Thomas fashioned the House of Hancock into one of the most imposing edifices in colonial mercantile circles—chiefly by means of hard and straight, though not always ethical, thinking. The more naïve contemporaries of the thirty-year-old Boston merchant were utterly mystified by his achievement. Thomas Hutchinson epitomizes their reaction thus: "He had raised a great estate with such rapidity that it was commonly believed among the vulgar that he had purchased a valuable diamond for a small sum and sold it at its full price."[4] But Hutchinson and others in the know were aware that one primary source of his already huge fortune, unlike the precious stone, would not be improved in appearance by the light of day.

· 3 ·

Yet no particular stigma attached to smuggling at that period—far less, in fact, than was borne in the Volstead era by bootlegging, which was condoned and abetted in private while being hypocritically condemned in public by the "best people." Evasion of customs had not attained the status of the holy commercial crusade which John Hancock was to lead as a plumed knight in the armor of patriotism, with the wholehearted approval and support of the populace. But most of the New England merchants who had the necessary resources and gumption indulged in it without forfeiting the respect of the community. Men of affairs could easily soothe their collective conscience, at a time of low mercantile morality, with the subsequently idealized contention that they were carrying the torch for freedom in protest against unfairly restrictive British trade regulations.

So Thomas could hold his head as high as anybody else when he strolled of an afternoon along the covered walk surrounding the Town House (known later and to this day as the Old Statehouse), gossiping with other merchants about conditions, exchanging market tips, and making deals. It was customary, according to a contemporary chronicler, for the businessmen to "shut up their warehouses at 1 o'clock and go on 'change and return about 4 o'clock."[5]

DOROTHY QUINCY HANCOCK, WIFE OF THE PATRIOT, ABOUT 1772.
FROM A PORTRAIT BY COPLEY. BY COURTESY OF MRS. ATHERTON
LORING, JR., OF BANGOR, ME., AND THE MUSEUM
OF FINE ARTS, BOSTON.

JOHN HANCOCK AND HIS WIFE, DOROTHY QUINCY. FROM A PORTRAIT
BY EDWARD SAVAGE. BY COURTESY OF THE CORCORAN GALLERY OF
ART, WASHINGTON, D.C.

Even Hutchinson admitted that the merchant prince enjoyed the esteem of his fellow citizens. Writing in later years with the rectitude of a Crown officer, although Boston-born, he stated that the secret of Hancock's mushrooming success lay in "his importing from St. Eustatia * great quantities of tea in molasses hogsheads, which sold at a very great advance," and that "by importing, at the same time, a few chests from England he freed the rest from suspicion and always had the reputation of a fair trader." [6]

Tea, however, was a negligible part of Thomas's stock when his smuggling was at its height, and Hutchinson probably exaggerated its importance as an illicit source of his fortune. At all events, he did not have to resort to subterfuge in disposing of his wares. Displayed in great profusion and variety, they must have made his shop resemble an old-fashioned general store. Dress goods constituted two-thirds of his merchandise, including such items as coarse cloth, ribbons, buckles, and fans. Hardware—comprising brass compasses, fire steels, hourglasses, larding pins, and swords—made up about a tenth; so did provisions, among which rum had the quickest turnover. An equal proportion was composed of leather, lime, salt, and such staple products. Smaller percentages of the total were formed by tea, coal, ships' stores, stationery, and books—so far had the proprietor departed by 1740 from the line that had given him a foothold in Boston.

Although the bulk of his clientele, both wholesale and retail, was local, he had customers in all parts of Massachusetts and Connecticut and even on Long Island. His trade relations with the other American commercial centers New York, Philadelphia, and Charleston—were exceedingly few. The markets in these growing, but as yet undeveloped, colonial seaports were poor as compared with London and the West Indies.

The accounting and correspondence systems that kept the House of Hancock in order would make a modern efficiency expert feel like biting chunks out of the ledgers. The base of operations for both was the "compting-room," where John Hancock was to sweat out his unofficial apprenticeship. A staff of clerks handled the books and mail by a quill process rendered more laborious, in its foreign phase, by constant but necessary duplication. The first step in writing a letter to an overseas agent was for Thomas to dash off a rough draft on a piece of scratch paper. A scribe would make a clean copy of this for posting; but, before sealing it, he would transcribe the contents in a letterbook—precursor of the present-day carbon file.

* St. Eustatius in the Dutch West Indies.

During the quarter-century starting in 1739, in which England was at war with Spain and France almost continuously, a transatlantic communication was just about as likely to land on the floor of the ocean as to reach the other side. So four or five extra copies were dispatched by as many different ships in the hope that at least one would get through. And, as an additional precaution, especially pertinent paragraphs were lifted from facsimiles of previous messages and incorporated in those of the moment. The clerical force at the Bible and Three Crowns must have suffered chronically from writer's cramp.

· 4 ·

While fortune's wheel was spinning giddily to Hancock's advantage during the 1730 decade the general business cycle was swinging downward in America. Toward the close it struck bottom, and the miracle merchant suddenly found his trade plunged into the doldrums. In 1739 he wrote to the wife of his London agent, Maplesden, who supplied him with fabrics and related articles, that the market had declined precipitously.[7] The Newfoundland oil harvest had begun to decrease two years earlier, and now this "commodity pay" could not be had in profitable quantities in exchange for rum. To aggravate the situation, the British government chose the next season to tighten enforcement of the Molasses Act prohibiting colonial trade with the West Indies. This caused Thomas's sweet smuggling racket to turn sour.

By this time, too, inflation had become rampant in Massachusetts. Deacon Samuel Adams, father of the patriot, induced a thousand hard-pressed Bostonians to join him in organizing a "Land Bank" to help the desperate debtor class. But it gave additional impetus to the inflationary spiral by printing notes with insufficient security behind them. As an offset to this ruinous venture the comparatively conservative merchants of the town, including Hancock, created a more soundly financed "Silver Bank." But a few months later Parliament outlawed both projects.

Although better fortified against the slump than the majority of the people, the Beacon Hill entrepreneur was in a precarious position because of extravagance, typified by the vast amount of money he had poured into his mansion within the preceding few years. His British agents were reluctant to continue replenishing the silver stream through long-term credits.

At this critical juncture luck and opportunism, mainstays in the lives of both the uncle and the nephew, came to Thomas's rescue. News of war between England and Spain, of which the opening phase was known as the War of Jenkins' Ear, reached the colonies in the spring of 1740. But the mercantile marvel had long since learned of its imminence through his globe-circling grapevine of information and was prepared to profit—and to profiteer—by it.

So accurate was Hancock's tip as to when hostilities would start that he was able to make plans far in advance. In October, 1739, considerably before the fighting began on this side of the Atlantic, he ordered 100 barrels of gunpowder from Wilks and shrewdly pointed out to his London representative, as an inducement to make the consignment, that the ships carrying the remittances would be protected by British convoys.[8]

Thomas girded his loins for the fray—as a not-so-innocent bystander—in numerous other ways. He liquidated his assets by sharply curtailing investments in foreign products so that he would be in position to provision the military campaigns—mainly American-waged—which Britain was mapping against Spanish possessions in the New World. He knew that payment would be made in precious pounds sterling, and must have rubbed his hands in glee at the prospect. He schemed to get the most out of the rise in prices that was certain to result from an uncontrolled wartime economy. He began adding new links to his chain of overseas agents and replacing old ones for the purpose of taking fullest advantage of transatlantic trade opportunities—including the greatly improved chance of slipping by customs barriers—when Mother England became too preoccupied to bother much about the disobedience of her colonial offspring.

Hancock never took a wiser step than when he reorganized and expanded his system of foreign factors. Reliable and well connected agents were indispensable to maritime trading in his day, when buyer and seller were so remote from each other and communication was so slow. Wilks and Mrs. Maplesden had served adequately as London representatives, but the lady had died recently; anyway, changing conditions called for more enterprising and influential contacts in the British capital. So when Christopher Kilby sailed for England in 1739 as a special emissary of the Province of Massachusetts, Thomas arranged to have him handle important deals there. This was a timely move, for Wilks also passed on three years later.

· 5 ·

Kilby was a man of the world. He had embarked upon a promising business career in Boston but had found the town too confining. Leaving his wife and two children, he had sought a wider outlet abroad for his versatile talents. He had returned to his family after two years without a fortune but with a copious fund of experience. He had resumed merchandising and had engaged in politics on the side as a representative in the General Court. But Mrs. Kilby had died soon afterward, and he had eagerly accepted the London post offered him by the colony.

This was the ideal man to look after Hancock's interests in Britain. As a merchant and a politician he was able to further Thomas's ambitions in a sphere where experience in both fields was essential. And he became still more valuable in 1742 on succeeding Wilks as official agent of the province. Most important of his earlier favors was to swing to his associate several British government contracts for rehabilitating the shattered forts in Newfoundland and at Annapolis, Nova Scotia, supplying them with arms and ammunition, and providing food for the English garrison which took over Louisbourg after its capture by an expedition from New England in 1745. This was the second year of King George's War, which came to be known globally as the War of the Austrian Succession.

Kilby's influence with the Board of Ordnance was particularly important in clinching the Newfoundland and Annapolis deals, which proved to be immensely beneficial to Hancock's private trade. The military engineer, John Bastide, who represented the board in Nova Scotia, became one of the merchant's stanchest advocates in that part of the world and continued to be, long after Thomas temporarily got rid of Charles Apthorp, a Boston competitor with whom he was forced to share his martial business.

Thus did Kilby help to solidify and extend the empire of the House of Hancock. Adrian and Thomas Hope, powerful Amsterdam bankers, performed a similar service in Europe; and Martin Godet of St. Eustatius, in the West Indies. Hancock was flying high on the wings of war.

· 6 ·

Meanwhile, as he was starting to lay the groundwork for these grandiose politicocommercial enterprises, the merchant prince was rendered still more military-minded by the plumping of preparations for the war with Spain right down in his front yard. By a twofold appeal to loyalty and self-interest Britain induced Massachusetts and other colonies to take a lion's share in the attack upon the Spanish islands in the Caribbean. Boston alone raised 1,000 men and drilled them on the Common. In August, 1740, Thomas reported to Kilby, "We have the pleasure of seeing 'em disciplined every day from 5 in the morning to 8 and from 5 afternoon till night before our house," and added, with rueful recognition that even a nice, profitable war is not an unmixed blessing, "We have not the less company for it but a quicker draft for wine and beer." [9] But Hancock could well afford to slake the thirst of a regiment when he was being paid in sterling, at kiting prices, to provide a sizable section of the whole colonial expeditionary force with beef and pork.

As King George's War swung into full stride in 1745 Thomas tried to infiltrate the lush Louisbourg contractual territory and to force Apthorp out of it by cultivating the friendship of Bastide and every other government official who could be of any assistance. He gave dinners for numerous provincial functionaries, including Governor Shirley himself. He put pressure on Kilby and Jonathan Barnard (Kilby's successor as British factor for the House of Hancock) to use their influence with the Board of Ordnance. He expressed a willingness to grease palms, too, by instructing Barnard, "if a few guineas be necessary to expend in the affair, let it be done." [10] Finally, after eighteen months of intricate machinations, during which he himself was frequently in danger of being shoved aside by the now resurgent Apthorp, the Machiavelli of Beacon Hill procured a contract for half of the Louisbourg business, in partnership with his rival, for the duration.

Hancock also took extensive fliers in New England real estate. He invested in numerous pieces of profitable Boston business property, including Clark's Wharf, which he renamed after himself; in farm land throughout Massachusetts and Connecticut, and vast timber tracts in the wilderness of what now is Maine. These last were speculative purchases which failed to appreciate materially in value even in the lifetime of John Hancock, who inherited most of them. Those listed with their sizes in the appraisal of the nephew's estate totaled more than 50,000 acres.

In his spare time, which must have been at a premium during the greater part of his hectic career, Thomas served as executor of wills and administrator of estates; managed the affairs of Bostonians living abroad; looked after relatives of absent family heads—in short, transacted any business that anybody wished to entrust to him. He did it for a price in most cases but often acted out of the goodness of his heart. His genuine kindliness, and a self-righteousness hard to reconcile with the skulduggery which characterized his trade practices, are revealed in two of his letters. In the first, informing a certain George Brice, resident in England, of a brother's death, he wrote:

"Great pains are taken by some designing persons to get his affairs into their hands. . . . He offered to make me any satisfaction for my trouble and kindness to him, even to half his estate. . . . But far be it from me to take advantage of mankind in any affair. . . . I have given him a place in my tomb." [11]

The other missive, addressed to Kilby, points out that the benefactor of humanity (on occasion) "wholly maintained old Mr. Bulkley and wife for many years, except what of your goodness you advanced to her when at Boston . . . and if there is no help for me from you out of that estate at Epsom I must wait for my reward in the other world." [12]

· 7 ·

It was not long between wars in the eighteenth century—but too long for Hancock. He complained to Kilby at the close of King George's fracas in 1748 that "peace hath put a stop to all our trade." And that was only the beginning of his tribulations. Prices tobogganed during the next few years, and the old cry of scarce money was heard again in the land. By 1752 Thomas had £10,000 worth of goods cramming his shelves and no prospect of moving them. Besides, he could not collect debts to tide himself over the lean period. "I have 200,000 due me . . . and can't raise 1000 to save my life," he wailed to his London agent. [13]

Despite this sad state of affairs the resourceful head of the House of Hancock had managed to keep the edifice shored up, largely by resorting to his always present help in time of trouble—smuggling by way of the West Indies and Amsterdam, a route that was safe once more from war-legalized piracy. Hancock still did business in 1749 on a scale sufficient to warrant dispatching to his London tailor the following order: "One yard superfine Saxon green cloth; . . . seven and a half yards gold lace. . . . Let it be the best, double strong, handsome, or the most fashionable lace to be had in England." [14]

Thomas decided to be the cock of the walk in military trade and finance as well as in dress. He saw a chance to twist the British Lion's tail and to make him like it.

At the end of the war Britain had handed Louisbourg back to the French under a treaty dictated by expediency rather than the honor and glory for which the gullible colonists who had won it thought that they had been fighting. So the government had concluded that it would be wise to build a naval base in Nova Scotia called Halifax to offset France's refortification of her recovered stronghold.

Edward Cornwallis, uncle of the general in the Revolution, was appointed governor. He applied to Hancock and Apthorp for construction materials but deemed their terms exorbitant—as they were. He shopped around and bought from other merchants on a cash basis with borrowed money, but within a year had committed himself far in excess of the funds appropriated by Parliament. So he finally had to go back, cap in hand, to the partners and beg a loan of £3,000. They accommodated him but declared that henceforth they would neither finance nor supply him unless they received a complete monopoly of the business. Supplementary government grants relieved Cornwallis of further knuckling under to the Boston Shylocks. He then excoriated their high-handed actions in a letter to the Lords of Trade:

"Some gentlemen of Boston who have long served the government, because they have not the supplying of everything, have done all the mischief they could. Their substance . . . enables them to distress and domineer. Without them, they say, we can't do and so must comply with what terms they think proper to impose. These are Messrs. Apthorp and Hancock, the two richest merchants in Boston—made so by the public money and now wanton in their insolent demands." [15]

Repercussions from high places soon made the would-be monopolists realize that lording it over His Majesty George II did not pay, and they regretted their rashness. But the traditional Hancock luck extricated them from this embarrassing predicament and gained the substance of their demands. Cornwallis resigned in 1752; and his successor, Peregrine Hopson, was so compliant as to shake virtually all the Nova Scotia trade plums into their laps.

These juicy pickings lasted only until Hopson went out of office at the close of the year, but the perspicacious merchants succeeded in accumulating enough to keep themselves well nourished until another —and much more delightful—war came along in 1756. Thomas enjoyed the French and Indian War almost to the day of his death eight years later, but in the meantime he began to ponder the ephemeral nature of all human felicity and to insure the continuance of the House of Hancock after he was gone. Primarily for this purpose he welcomed Nephew John within its portals.

Although the population of Boston was only about 20,000 in 1754, when seventeen-year-old John Hancock left Harvard, he must have found the transition sharp. Young Hancock, to be sure, was no stranger to urban life, for he had seen it from the aloof but excellent vantage point of his uncle's Beacon Hill mansion. But, except for the impressions received on occasional visits to Thomas's shop during vacations, the hurly-burly in the heart of the commercial district must have been a new and thrilling experience to him.

The creak of cranes, the thud of barrels, and the shouts of dock workers at near-by Long Wharf—projecting half a mile into the harbor —as the more than 500 ships that cleared the port of Boston annually were loaded and unloaded must have dinned into John's ears as he tried to concentrate on his writing in ledgers and letterbooks.

During lulls in this raucous racket he must have been disturbed by the high-pitched voices of housewives haggling with tradesmen in the market on the ground floor of the original Faneuil Hall virtually across the street. Quite possibly, too, his attention was arrested, as he sat near an open window in the Hancock "compting-room" in summer, by the thunderous protests registered against England's Navigation Acts in town meeting upstairs in the same public building. Even the imprecations of the merchants upon these restrictive measures uttered on 'change beneath the Town House around the corner may have formed a part of the clamor that initiated the green clerk into the disconcerting mysteries of life among men of affairs in the capital of Massachusetts.

In short, noise was the dominant characteristic of what later generations of Americans have come to think of as a peaceful, almost somnolent community. It is doubtful if the roar of traffic and the blasts of taxicab horns in New York today could match the Babel that was Boston in the mid-eighteenth century.

Even in the residential section the air was rent almost incessantly by the cackle of patent medicine peddlers, fishmongers, chimney sweeps, and town criers. The *clop-clop* of horses' hoofs on cobblestones, the clatter of cart wheels, and the ringing of bells could be heard everywhere and always, except in the dead of night. Gongs were struck to summon fire fighters and to signalize the repeal of obnoxious London-made laws; chimes were played to call citizens to meeting, whether religious or political; handbells were tinkled by the innumerable street venders to attract attention, and schoolmasters rang to round up their pupils.[16]

· 9 ·

As John Hancock, probably seated beside Uncle Thomas in one of the family carriages, headed homeward after his day's work the route at first followed King (State) Street, the busiest thoroughfare in the metropolis, and crossed what now is Washington. This narrow way, changing its designation every few blocks, successively to Marlborough, Newbury, and finally Orange, meandered toward the closely guarded town gates, where it deteriorated into a dirt road that wound past the gallows and the pasturage of the communal bull.

After the Hancocks turned left into Treamount (Tremont) and right to ascend the steep slope of Beacon the sights that met their eyes differed as much as the sounds that smote their ears from the corresponding features of modern Boston. The Hill was as high as the Statehouse which crowns its summit today and towered over two other hills that no longer exist. These heights have been razed, and Beacon itself has been shaved down, to fill in Roxbury Harbor, Back Bay, and Mill Cove —mud flats which, together with the Charles River and Boston Harbor, formed an aquatic periphery around a roughly circular peninsula two miles in diameter, connected at the southwest with the mainland by the Neck, a strip only two hundred yards wide. Castle Island, which now may be approached on solid ground, was well out to sea in those days.

The view of a predominantly rural landscape, semi-urbanized by approximately sixteen hundred homes, a disproportionate number of high-steepled churches, and a scattering of other public buildings, which John and Thomas enjoyed of an evening as they rolled slowly up the long ascent to the mansion, would sometimes—especially as the boy grew older—have been a bit blurred. They would have stopped at one of the numerous taverns near their place of business. Their favorite, for swank as well as convenience, probably was the Royal Exchange hard by the Town House. When in the mood to make the rounds after a particularly trying day, they might have dropped in also at the Crown Coffee House; at Colonel Joseph Ingersoll's Bunch of Grapes, later headquarters of the Whigs; at Luke Vardy's, in front of which the "Boston Massacre" was to occur; at the British Coffee House, where a performance of *The Orphans* so scandalized the town that it would legislate against stage plays in 1758; or at the Blue Anchor, principal resort of magistrates and clergy. In an unusually venturesome mood the Hancocks could have wound up at the Sun and Half Moon or the Golden Ball, waterfront dives patronized by seamen; or at the Ship Tavern on Clark's Wharf (to see, incidentally, whether their future tenants were prospering); or at the Green Dragon, where Sam Adams subsequently held the caucuses by which he bossed local politics and where, it is said, he stoked his fiery "Mohawks" with liquid fuel in preparation for the Tea Party.

Aunt Lydia could not count on her menfolk coming home for dinner. The male sex ate out to a greater extent even than in the modern era of widespread restaurant dining. Banquets, liberally augmented by Madeira and rum punch, were given for every conceivable purpose—and often for no purpose at all except guzzling. In the middle 1750's and afterward the merchant prince could truthfully send word to his wife that he was "unavoidably detained," for he was duty-bound to attend numerous official feasts in his capacity as a member of the governor's Council; and it is safe to assume that he made a practice of taking the heir apparent along to introduce him to the "right people."

Most of these functions were staged at the Province House, the chief executive's majestic mansion. Surrounded by lush lawns and terraced gardens that sloped up to the Old South, this edifice was the supreme architectural expression of eighteenth century Boston's social life.

It is small wonder that dinner parties were popular among Bostonians of the period. In the first place, there were few other forms of entertainment; secondly, food was excellent, abundant, and cheap. Writing of his travels through New England in the 1740's, the Englishman Joseph Bennett recorded that beef, mutton, and lamb were as plentiful and succulent in Boston as in London; that, although pickled pork was used as a substitute for bacon, poultry was "as fine as can be desired," and that "as good a turkey may be bought for about two shillings sterling as we can buy at London for six or seven, and as large and fine a goose for tenpence as would cost three shillings and sixpence or four shillings in London. . . . They sell a fine fresh cod that will weigh a dozen pound or more . . . for about twopence sterling. Salmon [weighing fifteen pounds] they have, too, in great plenty, which is as fine as any I ever eat of anywhere in my life, for about a shilling apiece." [17]

· 10 ·

In colonial days young men were precocious with respect to wine, women, and song. But it is doubtful that John Hancock's strict foster parents would have allowed him to do the town on his own, even as he approached the age of twenty-four and the end of his informal apprenticeship. Unless accompanied by Uncle Thomas, he must have had to confine his recreation to the simple and innocent pleasures provided by a Boston just emerging from Puritan repression. These included walking, riding, hunting, fishing, boating, picnicking, skating, sledding, lecture going, dancing—in private homes and at assemblies in a hired hall. Of this newfangled caper of the younger generation, Bennett had written only fifteen years before: "They have set up an assembly to which some of the ladies resort. But they are looked upon to be none of the nicest in regard to their reputation."

Judged by his subsequent hedonistic propensities, John might reasonably be presumed to have risked the wrath of Aunt Lydia to sneak out to such affairs; but at this period he seems to have been too dutiful a nephew for that. It is more likely that he contented himself with the typical diversions of his class, as thus described by the Englishman:

"When the ladies ride out to take the air it is generally in a chaise or chair, and then [pulled by] but a single horse; and they have a Negro servant to drive them. The gentlemen ride out here as in England, some in chairs and others on horseback, with their Negroes to attend them. . . . For their domestic amusements every afternoon . . . the gentlemen and ladies walk in the Mall [Common] and from thence adjourn to one another's houses to spend the evening—those that are not disposed to attend the evening lecture, which they may do . . . six nights in seven. . . . And the ladies here visit, drink tea, and . . . neglect the affairs of their families with as good a grace as the finest ladies in England." [18]

It is probable that Aunt Lydia, if not Uncle Thomas, usually tagged along even when young Hancock engaged in such proper pastimes, and that she thwarted the possibility of his making eyes at the Beacon Hill damsels. He may have derived an occasional thrill from itinerant showmen like William Clagget, who had staged at a house in King Street during the fall of 1747 the "wonderful phenomena of electrical attraction, repulsion, and flamific force; particularly the new method of electerising several persons at the same time, so that fire shall dart from all parts of their bodies." [19]

But John must often have longed to be on the loose like Captain Francis Goelet, a London-bound New York merchant whose ship was forced by a storm to put into the port of Boston for repairs in 1750. In his journal Goelet recorded dining at a certain Mr. Sheppard's in "a company of about forty gentlemen . . . in a very elegant manner upon turtle, etc.; drank . . . toasts and sang a number of songs and were exceeding merry until 3 o'clock in the morning. From whence went upon the rake. . . . Surprised a company [of] country young men and women with a violin at a tavern, dancing and making merry. Upon our entering the house the young women fled; we took possession of the room, having the fiddler and the young man with us, with the keg of sugared rum. We were very merry. From thence went to Mr. Jacob Wendell's,* where we were obliged to drink punch and wine, and about 5 in the morning made our exit and to bed." [20]

· 11 ·

Although the inhibitions clamped upon John Hancock by his upbringing and his conscientious attitude toward his job must have restrained him from such dark-to-dawn revelry, he probably cut as dashing a figure as any young man about town in the high society where Goelet had whiled away an enforced visit. Even in his middle twenties the scion of the House of Hancock quite likely was beginning to answer Bennett's description of the gentry as dressing in the gay fashion of "courtiers in England on a coronation or [royal] birthday." [21]

Several years were to pass before John attained affluence through his uncle's death, but it stands to reason that he would have been decked out by clothes-conscious Thomas even at this period in a manner befitting the nephew of a merchant prince. Toward the end of the 1750's the Hancocks must have looked much as they are represented in Copley portraits painted somewhat later.

In a picture for which he evidently posed at home Thomas is depicted as a thick-set gentleman of medium height with features and build resembling those of his father, the Bishop of Lexington, although not so massive. He is attired in a red velvet cap; a blue damask dressing gown lined with a lighter shade of the same color; a white satin, embroidered waistcoat; black satin breeches; white silk stockings, and red morocco slippers. In another study he is shown in street clothes, with a powdered neck-length wig caught up in a queue under a three-cornered hat; a gold-laced coat of blue broadcloth with long lace ruffles at the wrists; shoes adorned with silver buckles, and the sword he had ordered from London in 1756 in accordance with the following specifications: "I want a very handsome sword for myself. Let it be a fashionable one, whether a neat silver-washed or one most in taste that gentlemen wear." [22]

* Granduncle of Dorothy Quincy—a babe of three at the time.

John is delineated as a tall, willowy, graceful figure. The aristocrat with the instincts of a democrat—a combination that was to command the respect of the gentry and the adoration of the commonalty during his political career—is portrayed in his high forehead, penetrating but tolerant eyes, finely molded nose, firmly set mouth, and determined chin. There is no evidence of the pettiness, hypersensitiveness, opportunism, vacillation, or vainglory that were to be the despair even of his best friends at the peak of his public life. The womanish hands and tapering fingers suggest the esthete rather than the statesman but explain the artistic perfection of the celebrated signature.

The younger Hancock's taste in dress was as correct as his uncle's, but far less conservative. He fancied equally expensive, London-tailored suitings but added a dash of lavender to his jackets and a touch of lilac to his pants—the foundation of a wardrobe which eventually became so extensive that one of his trunks was found, after his death, to contain ninety-two items of apparel. He was a much more lacy person than Thomas. There were frills not only on his cuffs but on his shirt front. He was every inch a dandy from his bob wig down to his fancy-buckled shoes, which set off to good advantage the "well turned calf" that heroines in old-time historical novels admired in their swains.

Even in early manhood John was well on the way to becoming the fashion leader of Boston and of all New England. He finally achieved this distinction by introducing a scarlet coat which created such a stir that Dr. Nathan Jacques, noted pedestrian of West Newbury, hiked the thirty miles to the metropolis to obtain a piece of cloth from which to have a similar garment made.

But the merchant princeling did not let his sartorial side line interfere with his principal vocation. After working for his uncle a year he was widely recognized as a model of industry as well as fashion. He apparently took to heart the verses displayed in Thomas's office. They counseled:

> The sloth, the canker of good men and parts,
> Of health, of wealth, of honor, and of arts;
> Such as court Fame must not their senses please;
> Her chariot lags when drawn by sloth and ease.[23]

John Adams, reminiscing toward the close of his life, thus characterized the House of Hancock and its admirable addition:

"And what a school this was! Four large ships constantly plying between Boston and London and other business in proportion. This was in 1755. He [John] became an example to all the young men of the town. Wholly devoted to business, he was as regular and punctual at his store as the sun in his course." [24]

Adams might have added that, so far as Boston's populace was concerned, the sun was to rise and set in accordance with the comings and goings of John Hancock.

~ IV ~

MASTER JOHNNY TURNS ESQUIRE

*H*AVING BRACED the House of Hancock against the vicissitudes of the future, as he thought, by installing his promising foster son and intended heir on the ground floor, Thomas Hancock turned his attention to making it secure for the present. Characteristically, however, he not only prepared it to weather the approaching French and Indian War by disposing of his shipping interests and reducing his European trade to a minimum, but rehabilitated those parts of his business structure which would enable him to capitalize to the limit on what promised to be the best of all possible wars.

By this time Hancock and his distasteful but indispensable partner, Apthorp, were so generally recognized as *the* military provisioners of the British government in America that they no longer had to dicker for contracts. Long before the formal fighting broke out in 1756 Charles Lawrence, who had succeeded Hopson as governor of Nova Scotia, sought out Thomas and offered him the monopoly which Cornwallis had so bitterly opposed. The ubiquitous Kilby, who had been appointed agent for Lawrence's province as well as for Massachusetts, probably had something to do with the windfall.

This boon, however, was not an outright gift. Hancock was to finance, though at a low interest rate, a projected sneak attack upon Fort Beauséjour, which commanded the isthmus between Nova Scotia and Canada, by an expedition including 2,000 New England volunteers. Since the merchant prince did not have the necessary funds, he was compelled to call in Apthorp once more on a partnership basis. In return for a huge outlay of cash and the extension of unlimited credit they were to have all the business stemming from the impending hostilities.

With his nostrils distended by the provocative odor from 600 half-

61

barrels of pistol powder, which he had foresightedly ordered from London, Thomas now turned into a full-fledged, fire-eating merchant of death. All through the spring of 1755 he raced around Boston beating the drum for the "cause," lining up transports, canvassing every local dealer for martial accouterments, sending to Philadelphia for wheat, and throwing himself into the fringe of the fray. He even tried to arouse the English masses from their apathy toward this war. In a letter to Kilby dated August 4, probably designed for publication and prefaced with the news of General Edward Braddock's notorious defeat on July 9 near Fort Duquesne, he exhorted, "For God's sake . . . let us root the French blood out of America," and concluded, evidently referring to Braddock's fatal refusal of Washington's advice to order the tradition-bound Redcoats to take cover when ambushed by Indians: "Give us ships, money, artillery (no regulars), and let us fight them in their own way." [1]

War hysteria had so gripped the once pacific Boston merchant that he played an important part in driving the storied Acadians into exile. Military necessity may have justified the British government in taking this action—but not in the means employed. After the Beauséjour stronghold had been reduced Governor Lawrence, suspecting that the 6,000 French-speaking natives of western Nova Scotia were disloyal to their new sovereign, ruthlessly uprooted them and dispersed them among the southern American colonies. At his behest Hancock (calling the refugees "vermin") and Apthorp rounded up the ships in which to carry out this needlessly cruel purge, with indecent eagerness. [2]

However, Thomas apparently repented on coming into contact with a party of the exiles who were seized at Boston, presumably on their way back home. The merchant, who was given the job of feeding them during their two-week incarceration, was so touched by their plight that he pleaded with Governor Shirley's Council to "compassionate their unhappy circumstances" and permit them to remain as free settlers. [3] His recommendation was adopted.

Perhaps Thomas's change of heart toward the Acadians was due as much to pangs of conscience as to considerations of common humanity. He must have realized that the success of his business, which reached its highest peak during the first two years of the French and Indian conflict, rested largely on wars and rumors of wars—a thought not comfortable to go to sleep with.

But there was little occasion for Hancock to be introspective during his waking hours. He had become so important in his own eyes, as well as in those of the British government and its colonies, that he probably had an astigmatic view of his shortcomings. He now was almost as great a power in politics as in commerce. He had been a Boston selectman—with prestige entirely disproportionate to the intrinsic worth of the office —since about 1740; and he recently had been honored with the impressive title, "His Majesty's Agent for Transports." This gave him authority to pay enlistment bounties to seamen; to provision vessels of the royal fleet; to hire freighters for the service of the Crown and appraise their tonnage; to issue sailing orders, and to discharge crews on their return from a voyage.

But Thomas must have derived greatest satisfaction from pulling one of the strings that set in motion the appointment of a new commander in chief of the British army in America on the death of Braddock. Two months after the general had fallen the "king maker" of Beacon Hill wrote to no less a personage than the Earl of Halifax, president of the Board of Trade: "I beg leave to say that it will be a favor to the colonies and spirit them much to the service if General Shirley* may have the command of all His Majesty's forces in North America." [4]

Within a matter of weeks the post was conferred upon Shirley. Hancock's judgment, however, apparently was not as strong as his influence. His man led an expedition bound for Niagara, but it bogged down at Oswego. After returning to Boston under suspicion of treason (the charges were based on prejudiced testimony) he was relieved of his command in June, 1756, and was recalled to England in September.

Opportunistic Thomas even managed to anticipate the turn of the official tide against the soldier-governor's fortunes and did a hasty flip-flop that headed him in the direction of the Whitehall current. In April he confided to Kilby regarding Shirley: "I am of the opinion great fault may be found with his conduct as general." [5]

Both Hancocks were experts at swimming with the stream; but the uncle never developed his talent beyond the point of high skill, whereas the nephew ultimately raised his to the level of an art.

· 2 ·

If Thomas was superstitious he may have thought, in the fall of 1755, that the God in whose name he had advocated extermination of the entire French population in North America was punishing him and his bloodthirsty compatriots for their unholy and fundamentally selfish

* Who was still governor of Massachusetts.

crusade. On the morning of November 18 Boston was rocked to its foundations by "the most surprising earthquake that ever was known here since the settlement of this country. It's done vast damage in town but, by God's mercy, not one person hurt. Had it continued many moments longer, it's thought the town would have been buried in its ruins. Thank God I had no hurt done to my house nor anything in it, though we expected nothing but that the house would sink or fall to pieces in a moment." [6]

Hancock's account of this paroxysm of nature is corroborated and amplified by John Tudor, a deacon of the New Parish Church, who noted in his diary that it "came on like the noise of several coaches rattling. There was two shocks so terrible that 'twas thought . . . that most of the houses in town would . . . [be] shook down. . . . The principal damage was near the Town Dock." [7] But presumably it did not extend to the Bible and Three Crowns.

Aside from this scary but relatively harmless upheaval, the Hancocks had little to worry about during the next four years. Although they were as busy as a farmer making a good deal more than hay while the sun shone for them through the clouds of war, they found time for filial amenities.

Two undated letters written by John, probably late in 1759 or early in 1760, illustrate this point. In the first, directed apparently from the home of the Reverend Daniel Perkins at Bridgewater to his foster mother, he spread his literary wings in phrasing that reflects the more stodgy of his classical studies. "My stepfather," he inversely addressed Aunt Lydia, "I accompany this afternoon to Lexington in a chaise. If you have any commands there, shall be happy in the execution of them. My grand-mama will be happy to receive a word or two from you, as will your nephew in committing to memory what shall proceed from an amiable and beloved aunt; and, as the original will not be present, the proxy must answer as a feeble representative." [8]

The "grandmama" mentioned was Mrs. Elizabeth Hancock, widow of the Bishop of Lexington. In 1755 Parson Jonas Clark, who had succeeded him as pastor of the parish and had married his granddaughter, Lucy Bowes, had moved his growing family into the parsonage to live with the old lady. There was comparatively ample room then, for Thomas had built a two-story addition about the time when he erected his mansion. John often visited this house, which was to be the scene of his most exciting adventure—eluding capture by the British on the eve of the Revolution.

To Clark, his cousin by marriage, he wrote in the second of the undated missives while his grandmother awaited death:

"My uncle . . . is very sorry to hear his mother is so ill and desires, if she grows worse or wants anything, you would send Jack down (who is gone up) to let him know it. The bearer will deliver two oranges and six lemons. Perhaps my grandmother may eat an orange." [9]

This gift was a rare treat at that period in New England, when citrus fruits were auctioned off at what was known as "sale by candle" (the dwindling of the flame corresponded to the "Going, going, gone" of the modern auctioneer).

In February, 1760, the feeble spark of life in the matriarch of the Hancock clan was finally extinguished. She had been in her grave only a month when one of the worst fires in the history of pre-Revolutionary Boston swept over the town. Raging from the 20th to the 22nd of March, it razed 174 dwellings and 175 warehouses. The General Court appropriated £3,000 for the relief of 220 families. But the buildings owned by the outstanding man of property in the metropolis were not damaged severely enough to warrant mention in his correspondence.

Whatever loss he may have sustained, Thomas still was financially able to provide for the future of his two nephews. In a letter to Ebenezer during May Mrs. Perkins alluded to the immediate prospects of both. After expressing anticipation of a visit from her younger son before his graduation from Harvard, where he was being maintained by his generous uncle, she cautioned him, "I hope you won't come without your uncle and aunt are freely willing," and added that "doubtless they will consent to it if your brother comes, whom we all expect to see before he goes for London." [10]

Thomas had decided that John was sufficiently well grounded in the workings of the home office after six years of hard, conscientious plugging, and that it was time for him to familiarize himself with overseas operations; to make the acquaintance of the foreign agents, most of whom he knew only by name; to meet the leaders of British trade and finance who could help him when he should become head of the business; and, in general, to acquire the urbanity resulting from association with Old World culture. To this end he was to sail for London in June —an opportunity enjoyed by few Americans until the nineteenth century was well advanced.

Ebenezer Hancock, whom his mother advised in the letter already quoted to "deliberate well" upon a vocation and make a "good choice now of that calling you may be qualified for," was about to have the problem solved for him by his uncle. In July the younger nephew was to go to work in the warehouse. But the new employee was to be no adornment to the House of Hancock.

· 3 ·

Thomas paved the way for John in London by writing on May 21 to his old friend Kilby's firm:

"I have given my nephew, Mr. John Hancock, who has been with me many years in business, an opportunity of going to London to see my friends and settle my accounts . . . and he has taken his passage . . . on board the ship *Benjamin and Samuel*. Will sail in about ten days. . . . By him I shall write you again; and I am to desire you be so kind as to provide him with good lodgings, where you think will be most convenient for him, with reputable people. He goes with Governor Pownall. . . . Should he be taken on his passage and carried to France or elsewhere, I have given him leave to draw upon you for what money he may want."

Two days later the Boston merchant penned the note that his nephew was to carry with him. In it he told, for the first time in writing, what he thought of his intended heir. He called him "a sober, modest young gentlemen" whose "industry, abilities for business, and good behavior has recommended him to me in such manner that on his return to New England I propose to take him a partner with me." [11]

Thomas mentioned June 2 as the date of John's departure (although he was to refer to it later as the 3rd) in a letter to Governor Thomas Pownall's brother John. It reveals the understandable misgivings with which people in that day of sailing ships contemplated their loved ones braving an ocean voyage, rendered more hazardous still by war.[12] This was the first real test of physical courage for a man who was to give repeated evidence of it during the ensuing quarter-century.

On July 5, when his nephew still was on the high seas, Thomas wrote: "Your aunt has been much concerned for you, and I have been put to it to keep up her spirits. . . . Take care of yourself and observe the advice to a son [Polonius' to Laertes?]. . . . Let me know who receives you with respect. . . . Write me how the world goes on the other side of the water. . . . Be frugal of expenses, do honor to your country, and furnish your mind with all wise improvements." And he added, with a characteristically incongruous transition from idealism to materialism, in a postscript: "Keep the pickpockets from my watch." [13]

After escaping the perils both of Neptune and Mars, apparently without incident, John and the retiring governor landed in England on July 12. That they were enjoying the ministrations of Pownall's slave Derry is indicated by Thomas in a communication relaying a query from his personal servant, Cato, to the other Negro concerning his opinion of London.[14]

Four months later the scion of the House of Hancock attended the funeral of King George II, who died on October 25 and was succeeded by his grandson, George III. John apparently observed the obsequies from the close vantage point reserved ordinarily for royalty, high government officials, and leaders of society. But he naturally did not comprehend their significance with respect to the future of his own country and was bored by their dampening effect upon the gay life of the British capital. In a letter to his stepfather, written four days after the death, he touched lightly—almost casually—upon the historic events:

"I am very busy in getting myself mourning upon the occasion . . . of the death of His Late Majesty King George the 2d, to which every person of any note here conforms. Everything here now is very dull. All plays are stopped, and no diversions are going forward; [so] that I am at a loss how to dispose of myself. On Sunday last the Prince of Wales was proclaimed King through the city with great pomp and joy. His coronation . . . will not be till April, [so] that I can't yet determine whether I shall stay to see it; but rather think I shall, as it is the grandest thing I shall ever meet with." [15]

· 4 ·

Writing to Ebenezer in December, John betrayed the nostalgia he often expressed while abroad. After a typical big-brother lecture about attending to business and remembering that "the diligent hand maketh rich" he inquired about the family domestics: "How is Molly and how does Cato behave? Is Agnies a-brooding? Is Prince as gouty as ever and Hannibal as peevish as formerly?"

In the same epistle he spoke of having been ill but of being on the mend under the care of "a young woman who is remarkably tender and kind to me" at the home of Jonathan Barnard.[16] Whether the Hancocks' wandering boy reciprocated this tenderness in a non-Platonic manner is not known. But there is later evidence, weakened materially by its prejudicial source and the time of its presentation, that he banished the dullness of London with the solace of hired girls in the house of a host named Lane. Years afterwards, when John had made himself one of the outstanding targets of Tory vilification by signing the Declaration of Independence in a provocatively large hand, a London scandal sheet stated:

"In the younger part of his life his supposed want of spirit and ambition brought on him much raillery, particularly respecting his amours with the female domestics of Mr. L., a merchant in London to whom, on his visiting England, he was recommended. . . . On this subject of Mr. Hancock's gallantry it is even said he was an accomplished Lothario. Thanks to the laws against female seduction in New England, however, he could not abuse the credulity of the fair in that country as he might in old England; Miss Q., his present wife, taking advantage of those laws to hold him fast in the bonds of lawful wedlock." [17]

This retroactive smear campaign had begun in 1772 and may have been carried on from start to finish by one and the same writer. The man who fired the opening blast has been identified as the Scotch bookseller, John Mein, who earlier plying his trade in Boston had aroused the wrath of antigovernment leaders by attacking them in a book. He fled to London in 1769 and eventually was thrown into jail there, through Hancock's efforts, for nonpayment of debts. The Tory scribbler sought revenge by penning and publishing the following slander:

"When . . . [Hancock] was in London about twelve years ago he was the laughing-stock and contempt of all his acquaintances. . . . He kept sneaking and lurking about the kitchen of his uncle's correspondent, drank tea every day with the housemaid, and on Sunday escorted her to White Conduit House* . . . but his old schoolfellows and intimates know that, though nature had bestowed upon him a human figure, she had denied him the powers of manhood. The girl was therefore in perfect safety." [18]

There may have been some truth in the accusation of skulduggery in the scullery, but there certainly was none in that concerning sexual impotence; for John eventually produced two children. The main object in citing this libelous statement is to show how much license political pamphleteers possessed in eighteenth century England and how far they would go to defame the character of an enemy.

Perhaps this alleged dalliance had something to do with putting young Hancock on the defensive against a suspicion of extravagance harbored by Uncle Thomas. Writing to his provider in January, 1761, the Beau Brummell entered this revelatory and ingenuous plea of not guilty:

"I observe, in your letter, you mention a circumstance in regard to my

* A social and cricket club on the outskirts of the city.

dress. I hope it did not arise from your hearing I was too extravagant that way, which I think they can't tax me with. At same time I am not remarkable for the plainness of my dress. Upon proper occasions I dress as genteel as any one and can't say I am without lace. I endeavor, in all my conduct, not to exceed your expectations in regard to my expenses; but, to appear in character, I am obliged to be pretty expensive. I find money, some way or other, goes very fast but I think I can reflect it has been spent with satisfaction and to my own honor."

In his two concluding paragraphs John promised to send "the mitts for my aunt and the shoes for you, with a cane if I can meet one suitable," and added, with indirect admiration for His Majesty George III that seems strikingly ironic in the light of later events, "The King is very popular and much beloved." [10]

· 5 ·

It was inevitable that George should be popular at this period. Even if he had not had the advantage over his two German-born predecessors of being reared in England, he ascended the throne when the nation was at the all-time height of its power and prosperity and could not help being loved by the people. Within the last four years the British had laid the foundations of empire with the victories over the French of Robert Clive at Plassey in India and James Wolfe on the Plains of Abraham near Quebec. And by 1763, the end of the Seven Years' War, Great Britain was to become supreme on both sides of the world in triumphal alliance with Frederick the Great of Prussia against the coalition of France, Austria, Russia, Sweden, and Saxony.

The chief maker of the British triumph was the first William Pitt, Secretary of State, who had gained ascendency over the Crown in the time of George II and was immensely popular among military and mercantile empire builders and among the masses, whose heavy tax burden he had drastically reduced. But the new King displayed despotic tendencies in the very beginning of his reign, at the instigation of his Saxon princess mother, Augusta; and, jealous of his minister's popularity, he soon managed to bring about Pitt's separation from office.

Young Hancock, being neither an imperialist nor a member of the British masses, was not particularly interested in these epochal affairs. In fact, he was downright disillusioned and homesick, as is indicated by this letter, penned in March to the Reverend Mr. Perkins:

"I am almost satiated with London and . . . shall, with satisfaction, bid adieu to this grand place, with all its pleasurable enjoyments and tempting scenes, for the more substantial pleasures . . . in the enjoyment of my friends in America . . . whom I prefer to the showy and . . . superficial, flattering sincerity of many here, who are very ready to be thought industrious to serve you but no farther than they think to be interested by you."

Even so early in her history America inspired in her sons an affection that caused them to yearn for home after a brief absence. It was the first flowering of a peculiarly provincial love expressed, by a people who eventually became the world's champion globe trotters, in the well known words, "Such-and-such is wonderful to visit, but I wouldn't live there if they gave me the place." To his stepfather the Boston traveler phrased it thus: "A man of fortune might live here as happy as possible; but for me . . . the greatest estate in England would be but a poor temptation . . . to spend my days here."

John also reacted like the typical American male of today toward the female idea of sartorial beauty. With a neat dig at his sister Mary's vanity he asked the Reverend Daniel to tell her: "I shall bring her a Capuchin or a more fashionable thing, and of consequence more ugly; though what's fashionable must be thought pretty and may cut a figure in a meeting-house." [20]

This bit of sarcasm at the expense of poor "sis" came with something less than good grace from one who was planning to cut quite a figure himself, in a get-up not without lace (one may safely assume), at the Court of St. James's. He fully intended to be on hand for the coronation, even though it had been put off until September 22 so that King George, who was to marry Charlotte of Mecklenburg on the 8th of that month, would have a consort to share it with him.

But Uncle Thomas upset his nephew's calculations. "Mrs. Hancock and I have been willing you should stay for the coronation . . . and I have given you leave," he wrote in March. "But on our maturely . . . considering it yet to be postponed and bring it to be late in the fall before you can reach New England, and the many dangers that will attend a fall voyage, we . . . desire your return . . . may be as soon as possible." [21]

A reputed opportunity (not, however, substantiated by the Hancock papers) to be presented at court, of which John is supposed to have taken advantage, may have been an even stronger inducement than the crowning of His Majesty for the merchant princeling to defer his departure. It probably would have been well-nigh irresistible to a young man with his predisposition toward empty, though pride-tickling, honors. There is a similarly unverified account of his being given a snuffbox with the royal likeness by the sovereign who was to attempt to have him hanged fifteen years later.

· 6 ·

In any event, the once restrained youth who at last had broken out of the elder Hancock's harness stalled until July, when he informed his uncle that "unexpected detentions have arisen, both with respect to want of goods and convoy." [22] He added that he expected to set out for Portsmouth within a few days and to be under way to America within a week. He evidently left for the English port on the 14th, for that is the date of a letter of hand given him by Barnard. But he either had to wait about a month for passage or ran into trouble while crossing the Atlantic aboard the *Boscawen,* convoyed by the man-of-war *Alcide;* for he did not reach Boston until October 3. His arrival is recorded by Thomas in an acknowledgment of Jonathan's communication, which apparently was written at the request of the bearer in anticipation of avuncular displeasure over bills that were to follow.[23]

"If his expenses while here has been more than you may have expected," reads the shock-absorbing message, "I am sure you'll excuse it; for I can assure you no young gentleman I know of, from any part of America, has laid it out with more propriety and frugality, always keeping up such a character as was agreeable to the connections you were pleased to grant him. He is a very worthy, well-disposed young gentleman and despises the thing that is mean and low; and I doubt not he will be a comfort both to you and Mrs. Hancock." [24]

John had good reason to fear that his exacting uncle and aunt, who could be stern as well as affectionate, would upbraid him for his expenditures. He could not have forgotten the chilling formality of this note from Thomas, written a year earlier with a quill dipped in venom:

"Dear Sir . . . Two Lisbon vessels have just arrived, but no letters from you. Your aunt begins to think hard of you for not writing. . . . I am, Dear Sir, Your humble servant." [25]

The dutiful nephew had answered, in a letter already quoted in part, with an abject apology and an explanation that he had dispatched letters by thirteen ships.[26] The presumption is that the vessels had been sunk, intercepted by French privateers, or driven off their course. Trying to please such inconsiderately demanding foster parents may have been a psychological cause of his unusually strong desire in later years to be all things to all men.

John himself, probably in consequence of the mental strain thus put upon him, could be hypersensitive over a fancied wrong. He had picked a quarrel with Trecothick & Co., the most powerful bankers in England, because they refused to advance £1,100 more than was authorized by his uncle. On hearing of this the Boston merchant inconsistently had become enraged at the "insult" and had transferred his account to Kilby & Barnard. Thus did the prospective patriot in purple betray another weakness that was to make enemies for him when issues affecting the welfare of his country were at stake.

But, on the whole, John had done an excellent job for his benefactor in foreign parts—one which Thomas appreciated when he reflected calmly upon the results of the inexperienced youth's trip. He amply rewarded the lad two years later by naming him residuary legatee of his huge estate. The young ambassador of good will had cemented his uncle's far-flung, loosely organized commercial empire into a compact, solid unit. He had put the credit of the House of Hancock on a sound foundation by settling its accounts—generally to the advantage of the proprietor. He had gathered inside information about the Board of Ordnance which proved invaluable in the handling of the important war contracts. Above all, he had established personal contacts not only in London but in other parts of the British Isles, in Germany, and in Holland. These were of incalculable benefit to the Hancock interests at a time when transatlantic trade was at best catch-as-catch-can.

So, loaded down with souvenirs from the capital of the world, including a cap and a French horn for Cato, John probably received a warm welcome from lonely Uncle Thomas and Aunt Lydia on his return. A delightful surprise was awaiting him, too; for he now found himself, at twenty-four, an uncle in his own right. While he was on the high seas a son, Daniel, had been born to Sister Mary and Richard Perkins.

· 7 ·

On his homecoming the heir of the House of Hancock found it as sturdy as when he had left—but its head considerably less so. The long continued tension of the struggle to keep the mammoth mercantile establishment preeminent in a highly competitive, war-torn world; day-after-day bouts with the Madeira flagon, and frequent attacks upon overladen banquet boards had taken their toll of Thomas's health. His joints were puffed up by gout, and his nervous system was breaking down.

In his letter of July, 1760, he had indicated a desire to get away from it all. "I design to leave the town and go into the country or to London," he had confided.[27] A month after his nephew's arrival in Boston, during a temporary slump in business, he wrote to an English firm: "Trade is on such a footing here I am of opinion it will be better for me to sell all and go to England and spend my days in quiet; and Mrs. Hancock is quite willing."[28] And by the following January his spirits were still lower. He moaned through the mail to Bastide that "we are all just creeping about pretty poorly."[29]

Even if he had not been viewing his economic situation through the distorting lens of self-pity, Thomas would have had a strong inducement to retire. His father-in-law, Daniel Henchman, had died in April, 1761, and had provided that he and Lydia should inherit the bulk of his fortune—which compared favorably with Hancock's own—after the decease of Mrs. Henchman.

Part of Thomas's heritage, incidentally, was a pirated edition of the Bible, the first in English to be published on the American continent. Henchman, a highly respectable and respected citizen, apparently had no more scruples than his son-in-law about violating a British statute. He had a legitimate copy of the Holy Book, which could be printed legally only in England by holders of royal patents. Importing paper and type from London, he had a reprint made surreptitiously and marketed it at his usual handsome profit. One of the volumes eventually passed on to John.[30]

In spite of his huge accumulation of earned and reversional wealth, the merchant prince, like so many men who live to make money instead of making money to live, could not bring himself to abdicate—especially when there was a chance to add more sterling to his pile. That opportunity came to him now in an offer from Matthew Woodford, an Englishman who had had charge of victualing the Nova Scotia and Newfoundland forts for thirty years, of a subcontract which promised to net an annual income of £3,000.

Thomas was too astute to accept this proposition on the proffered terms. Payment was to be made on a basis of the number of men fed— an indeterminate and unstable figure because of the continual shifting of personnel.

The shrewd Bostonian, however, did agree with the British contractor to supply the forts under a commission arrangement that left Woodford shouldering the risk. During the four years intervening before his death Hancock often regretted having undertaken this job at all; for it turned out to be "the most intricate, perplexed affair I ever had to do with and has taken me up more time than all my other business." [31] It involved such exasperating tasks as making out long itemized accounts and ration lists, disentangling transportation snarls caused by bad winter weather, and fighting a government embargo on New England shipping. In general it was a mess emitting a very strong odor, and made Thomas an inadvertent party to a deal which offended even his none too squeamish sensibilities.

By the autumn of 1762 Woodford was sustaining big losses from spoilage caused by delays in shipment. So, in order to recoup, he sent back to Boston a batch of Nova Scotia provisions condemned by the inspectors. With Hancock's connivance he had the best of the vermin-infested food repacked and returned to the northern province for distribution among the British common soldiers and the French prisoners. In extenuation of Thomas it should be pointed out that he abetted this practice to extricate his English colleague from financial difficulties. But he betrayed a guilty conscience in a letter to Woodford the following summer. It explained how he had arranged to cover up by dispatching "a quantity of higher-prized bread for the officers . . . to help it off and make 'em easy." [32]

· 8 ·

It must be assumed that John was privy to these shady goings-on in the House of Hancock; for, if the facts of eighteenth century business life had gone over his head while it was buried among the ledgers, they must have struck him squarely in the face during the past seven months; for Thomas had carried out his announced intention of raising his nephew to a partnership status. He informed his London agents under date of January 1, 1763, that he had taken such action on that day and instructed them to charge his latest order of goods to "Thomas Hancock & Company." [33] It is quite possible that a long siege of illness had hastened his decision to invest his prospective successor with official authority to run the business, for in March he disclosed: "Having been confined these three months with the gout . . . don't expect to be able to attend to very little business again, if any." [34]

But the hardy veteran of many militant mercantile campaigns, at the age of sixty, managed to get back on his swollen feet to wage, with the help of his full-fledged lieutenant, the most dramatic one of all before going down for the last time.

Shortly after his gout attack Thomas set out to corner the market in whale oil, which he had neglected for more than two decades because the industry had been virtually ruined by the series of wars. Now he organized a syndicate, with the Nantucket firm of Folger & Gardner doing the buying; his own house, the shipping; Barnard & Co., the selling.

Especially for this trade the three parties to the combine agreed to build one of the tiny merchant vessels so numerous in the transatlantic service of that day, called packets, which ranged from 120 to 180 tons, and averaged in length between sixty and eighty feet. This one—a 160-tonner —was to be christened the *Boston Packet* and, according to the elder Hancock's prideful description, would be "a prime-going ship, handsome and to carry well, plain but neat." [35]

In this connection Thomas mentioned a man who was to become intimately involved in John's life. On a recommendation brought from England by his nephew the merchant sought for master of the new craft Captain James Scott. But Scott was abroad during the construction of the *Boston Packet* and did not return in time to take command of her when she was launched in September.

Because of John Folger's failure to acquire enough oil to make up a full cargo and his tardiness in having it transported to Boston, the ship's departure was delayed for two months. This proved fatal to the venture, for another exporter (probably William Rotch, with whom John Hancock was to engage in bitter rivalry) got the jump on the would-be monopolists. He loaded a vessel and dispatched her at top speed direct from Nantucket to London, where she arrived considerably ahead of the packet.

Thomas bewailed the misfortune in writing to Barnard & Co.: "The schooner from Nantucket sailing to your place with oil was very unlucky, more especially as it fetched so great a price, as it may be a means of . . . keeping up the price . . . here." Intimating that the oily triumvirate were stooping to slick practices in restraint of trade, he continued: "Captain Folger did all he could to prevent her sailing, but they were determined upon it." [36]

Thus did old warrior Hancock lose the first battle of his final campaign. But he took defeat only as a spur to redoubled effort and immediately began laying plans for a new drive in 1764. Perhaps to boost morale he ordered some splendid headgear for his aide from his London factors:

"Our J. H. asks the favor that Mr. Harrison will please get made and sent him one neat bag wig and one neat bob wig, fashionable and of a light color." [37]

The Hancock syndicate now decided to siphon out of Rotch's reach and that of every other competitor all the oil they could lay their hands on. But the archenemy did not take this challenge lying down. Outbid in local and neighboring markets, he scoured the country. The result was that prices ballooned and stores shrank precipitately while the *Boston Packet* and its rival sailer, the *Hale Galley*—docked in close proximity—were being filled up in a theatric atmosphere preparatory to racing for London.

Toward the end of June the combine determined to supplement their incomplete cargo with tar, staves, and other products and to cut their vessel loose while Rotch's schooner still was tied up at her wharf. No sooner had they done so than the proverbial Hancock luck enabled Thomas to pick up a whole shipload of oil from a previously undiscovered source. So it was feverishly stowed aboard the *Lydia,* a stout new brigantine appropriately named after Mrs. Hancock and commanded by Captain Scott. Both the packet and the brig left the *Hale Galley* far behind and discharged their contents at London in August for sale at a substantial net profit. The *Lydia* consignment entailed a small loss, but that did not detract from the glorious personal victory scored by the House of Hancock over its formidable foe.

Death, however, robbed the triumphant general in this war of what would have been his sweetest satisfaction. Thomas, whose blood pressure must have soared during these hectic days, died of apoplexy on August 1, 1764.

· 9 ·

Hancock passed on, at the age of sixty-one, in what was then regarded as ripe maturity—and rightly so, for the perils of disease were great.

Smallpox, which broke out periodically, was the most dreaded of the potentially fatal ills that beset mankind in the eighteenth century. An epidemic had been raging in Boston since the previous December. The General Court, recognizing just after the turn of the year that the crude and unsanitary inoculation then administered was often more inimical than the disease to the general welfare, had prohibited the practice until thirty families should be infected. By March the pestilence had assumed such proportions that a third of the community fled into the country, and the selectmen granted the inhabitants permission to submit to the so-called immunity treatment.[38]

Governor Francis Bernard and the General Court were among those who had taken flight. They had adjourned to Cambridge in January and had carried on the public business at the college—the Council in old Harvard and the House in Hollis Hall, which had just been erected. They had been in session there only a couple of weeks, during which the students were on vacation, when fire gutted the councillors' quarters and destroyed many of John Hancock's valuable belongings. How he happened to be living there is not known; but he, too, probably was a refugee from the plague.

An eyewitness, daughter of President Holyoke, described the conflagration to her husband in London. She wrote that on Tuesday night January 24, "about 12 o'clock, in the severest snowstorm I ever remember, I heard the cry of fire. One moment brought me to the window, when I saw the old Harvard College on fire; and it was with the greatest difficulty they saved the other buildings. . . . The whole library . . . demolished. . . . Mr. Hancock, who lodged out on account of the storm, lost everything except the clothes he had on. . . . The Governor and a great number of the Court assisted in extinguishing the fire. . . . I'll tell you the proceeding of our worthy Court the next day. The first vote that passed was for rebuilding the college at the expense of the Province immediately, and 2000 [pounds] . . . voted to begin with; and a sum to Mr. Hancock to repair his loss, which, with what of money, plate, etc., they have found in the ruins, I hope will make his loss light." [39]

Why the province should have reimbursed a private citizen for loss by fire is not explained by the writer, but there is a logical answer to the question. Thomas now was a member of the Council; and John, as a prominent young man of affairs, may have been engaged in government business in his own right. Chafing under the trade restrictions imposed by England, he was to become deeply involved in politics within a year. So he may have set up headquarters in Cambridge, together with the official functionaries, and may thus have established a moral claim upon the Court in the event of damage sustained in the performance of his duties. As to his salvaged money and plate, he naturally would have taken along a large supply of funds and silverware—particularly drinking utensils—to "appear in character."

· 10 ·

By July the Hancocks must have been reunited in Boston; for Thomas was sinking fast, and the family would have been rallying around his sickbed. In a letter written apparently during the early part of that month John requested Barnard & Harrison to send an eiderdown quilt for his uncle by the *Boston Packet* on her return voyage. "Pray be very particular in the choice of a good one," he cautioned, "as it is for our T. H.'s own use in the gout."

The same communication implies that doughty old Thomas was determined to die as he had lived—with plenty of good wine at his elbow: "If the brigantine [*Lydia*] goes to New Castle, pray order us from thence ten gross of the best quart champaign bottles for own use." [40]

But the patient did not last long enough to taste the sparkling water. He must have gone into a serious decline shortly after his sixty-first birthday, for a piece of business correspondence copied in one of the letterbooks on that day, July 13, is followed by four blank pages and is the last to be composed until after his death. The merchant prince, however, died with his buckled boots on. The Boston *Gazette* of Monday August 6 thus relates the circumstances of his passing:

"Wednesday last, about noon, the Honorable Thomas Hancock, Esq., one of His Majesty's Council for this Province, was seized with an apoplexy just as he was entering the Council chamber and expired about three o'clock P.M. at his seat [the mansion], to which he was carried soon after he was taken with the fit. He . . . was one of the most noted merchants in New England. His remains are to be interred this afternoon at half-past four o'clock."

Thomas had been an expert on funerals (one might almost say a connoisseur, so much pleasure did he take in well conducted rites) by virtue of having handled so many in behalf of absentee family heads. In the letter to George Brice, already quoted,[41] concerning the death of that gentleman's brother he had reported with pride: "His funeral was decent, honorable, in good order, and conformable to the established Church of England, and attended by many gentlemen of the first rank here."

So Hancock's rotund shade must have glowed with satisfaction at his own obsequies. His spurious escutcheon was hung on the balcony over the entrance to the mansion. The house was made as funereal as possible, by closing the shutters, covering mirrors and every other bright object with sheets; in short, by forcing upon the mourners' attention the solemnity and sepulchral nature of the occasion. As an indication that the Hancocks still were a law unto themselves, as on the day of the Bishop's funeral twelve years before, mourning rings were worn illegally. At the head of the long, imposing cortege marched the leading dignitaries of the town. And—as the man in whose honor the ceremony was held would have wished most to know—it was genteel.

It will be noted that Thomas, merchant to the last, rendered a final accounting to his Maker on the first of the month. A mortal audit shows, against the large debit of business immorality, a sizable balance in his favor, based on his great contribution to the commercial development of America.

V

THE POLITICAL BUG BITES

A YEAR INTERVENED between his uncle's death and the conversion of John Hancock into an active patriot under the banner of rebellion being raised unobtrusively by Sam Adams. But he was clothed, by the will of Thomas Hancock, in the purple that was to make him unique among the political leaders of the Revolution. As residuary legatee of the merchant prince's fabulous estate and beneficiary of the reversionary rights to his aunt's heritage he fell heir to an estimated sum of £80,000—the equivalent of at least $1,000,000 in modern purchasing power—at a time when millionaires were almost unheard of in the American colonies.[1]

John, named co-executor with Lydia, presented Thomas' last testament for probate on August 10, 1764, before Lieutenant Governor Hutchinson, who was doubling as a judge. Hutchinson, more friendly at this period than after his accession to the governorship, admitted the document on the same day.

The first of many bequests provided for the widow. Mrs. Hancock was to receive £10,000 in cash or securities, whichever she preferred; the Beacon Hill mansion and grounds; the silver plate and household furniture; the horses and carriages,[2] and the Negro slaves. Cato was to be set free on attaining the age of thirty and was to be given about six pounds if his conduct in the interim should prove satisfactory to his mistress. Harvard College was to get the income from a trust fund of £1,000 for the support of a professor of oriental languages specializing in Hebrew and avowing the "Protestant Reformed religion." An equal amount was bequeathed to the Society for Propagating Christian Knowledge Among the Indians in North America. The town of Boston was to have £600 to help defray the cost of building a badly needed insane asylum.

Thomas remembered his father's Lexington meetinghouse with a gift of £20 for the purchase of two silver communion cups and left a similar donation to his own Brattle Street Church; but he attached to both provisions the characteristically qualifying clause, "in case I do not give 'em in my lifetime." His relatives, friends, and servants came in for a total of approximately £5,000 and more than 19,000 acres, mostly on the Kennebec River. Ebenezer's share was slightly more than £666 and 3,200 acres.

This nephew, who had the more reason to be economical, soon frittered away his cash inheritance through bad judgment, laziness, and improvidence; but the other worked as hard and diligently (although with his uncle's reckless disregard of general business conditions) as if he had been disinherited. In a letter after John Hancock's death to William Tudor, biographer of James Otis, John Adams asserted:

"No alteration appeared in Mr. Hancock, either from his travels in England or from his accession to the fortune of his uncle. The same steady, regular, punctual, industrious, indefatigable man of business; and, to complete the character with the ladies, always genteelly dressed, according to the fashions of those days. . . . What shall I say of his fortune, his ships? His commerce was a great one. Your honored father told me . . . that not less than a thousand families were, every day in the year, dependent on Mr. Hancock for their daily bread. Consider his real estate in Boston, in the country, in Connecticut, and the rest of New England. Had Mr. Hancock fallen asleep to this day, he would now awake one of the richest men. Had he persevered in business as a private merchant, he might have erected a House of Medicis." [3]

But John's first year as sole proprietor of the House of Hancock was far from emulation of Rip Van Winkle. In fact, he must have had difficulty catching forty winks a night while carrying on the manifold activities of the incredibly complex enterprise his uncle had built up. Immediately upon assuming control he had to break in a new assistant, William Palfrey. Ebenezer, probably with delusions of grandeur brought on by his inheritance, had left the firm and gone into the hardware trade in partnership with a man named Blanchard—and, of course, the backing of big-hearted Brother John.

In the midst of these adjustments the international mercantile structure slipped out of joint. The severe slump that had set in at the end of the Seven Years' War was becoming acute; and Parliament, in an effort to pay for the long, exhausting struggle that had almost emptied the exchequer, slapped heavy import duties on wine and silk. The customs officers plugged up the smuggling leaks to such an extent that the number of ships plying between New England and the West Indies was reduced by 80 per cent.

· 2 ·

But John Hancock forged blithely ahead with plans for expanding the business, on the one hand, and getting the better of his uncle's old enemy Rotch, on the other. In two letters dated August 17 to Barnard & Harrison he notified them of his intention to carry on, told of having made arrangements during a trip to Nantucket for as much whale oil as he wanted, "which, of course, takes from the other channel and is very chagrining to Mr. R——h; but he knows my mind," and offered them a chance to join a big combine to market it in England.[4] They took him up on it a month later.

Like the former head of the House of Hancock, he thereupon gave his Nantucket suppliers an unprecedented order for £17,000 worth of oil and bone. Six vessels, including his own *Boston Packet* and *Lydia*, were required for transporting these products to London. When they arrived two of the cargoes proved to be of poor quality and sold at unprofitably low prices. Lacking the shrewd skepticism of his uncle, John had relied on the honesty of the American dealers and had neglected to have the shipments inspected en route through Boston.

But the Nantucket agents were not the only ones with whom he became annoyed. Barnard & Harrison were sending him defective merchandise, failing to comply with his orders, affronting him by shipping Rotch's goods in the *Boston Packet,* and insinuating that he was misrepresenting the cost of his exports—so high were the figures he reported in his invoices. He threatened to sever connections with his factors on both sides of the Atlantic but was himself too vulnerable to push the point. He was so slipshod in financial matters that he felt constrained to patch up the differences. Thus his first year as head of Hancock & Co. revealed an energetic but by no means astute businessman. His shortcomings, however, were due in part to the tremendously complicated problems and overwhelming responsibilities he had to face without benefit of his uncle.

One of the compensating developments was the speeding up of transatlantic crossings. On October 20, 1764, one shipmaster set a new record of twenty-six days for the London-Boston passage, which previously had consumed periods varying from five to eight weeks. By 1769 another navigator had covered the run from Glasgow in the breath-taking time of twenty-two days. Hancock then had an interest in a fleet of about twenty vessels, exclusive of whalers; and he probably could boast, when the Revolution interrupted his mercantile ventures, that several of them had equaled or bettered this pace.

But the brighter future for trade did not lessen the darkness of John's present situation. His trouble-studded initial year as an entrepreneur ended in deep gloom, partly of his own making. Softness both of head and of heart added materially to his difficulties. He had begun, however, to learn by experience and had decided to quit being a gull in business. In December he served notice upon his London representatives: "I am now determined not to . . . carry on the whole of other people's business with my money. I have long enough done that. . . . I have paid every farthing cash for the whole cargo of *Boston Packet* and had it all to provide, as much as if J. F. [John Folger] had no connection with her. . . . I can't no way advance my own money and give others the advantage of it." [5]

Of all the irritations the young merchant had to contend with during this trying twelvemonth none was more vexing than the smallpox, which had not yet run its course. The *Lydia*, which had recently put into Boston harbor with an infected Negro aboard, was quarantined. This delayed her next outward trip, with resultant loss of potential profits. The disease was virulent enough in the town to cause Hancock to wind up his business correspondence for 1764 on the doleful note: "The dullness of trade the year past, owing to the smallpox, has left me a stock of goods for some time." [6]

So John concluded the opening phase of his stewardship in the House of Hancock with his affairs, both foreign and domestic, in a stagnant state; although with sufficient faith in the future to order a dozen pairs of "very neat" custom-made shoes from London and to advertise in a newspaper on Christmas Day that there were on sale at his "Store No. 4 at the east end of Faneuil Hall Market a general assortment of English and India goods; also choice Newcastle coals and Irish butter, cheap for cash." [7] That he still had plenty of fight left, too, is shown by the threat in the advertisement:

"Said Hancock desires those persons who are still indebted to the estate of the late Hon. Thomas Hancock, Esq., deceased, to be speedy in paying their respective balances to prevent trouble."

· 3 ·

In New England business circles the year 1765 began even less auspiciously than its predecessor had ended. Several prominent Boston merchants went bankrupt—the most disquieting eventuality in the career of the foremost to date. In a January letter John Hancock betrayed to his London factors profound alarm over the situation.

"The great uneasiness . . . here, owing to the failure of some persons of note," he confided, "has put us all into great anxiety, as trade has met with a most prodigious shock and the greatest losses to some people . . . ever known in this part of the world. . . . Times are very bad and precarious here; and take my word, my good friends, the times will be worse here." [8]

He was even frightened into attempting to effect a truce and a monopoly with Rotch for the purpose of keeping down the purchase price of oil. He did so at the urging of Barnard but was very skeptical of the plan's feasibility because there were so many buyers who would pay almost anything to get the precious stuff. He reported to Jonathan in April that his biggest rival appeared "disposed to be upon amicable terms . . . and tells me he will strictly abide by the instructions" from a fourth firm in the projected syndicate. "How far, time can only discover. You are not so well acquainted with that gent as I am." [9]

Hancock's doubts were justified. "That gent" went right ahead buying up oil stocks at any price he could bargain for. But John was in no position to throw stones, for he had started to do likewise immediately after their agreement. He also began to acquire shares in four whalers, had a third merchant vessel built for his sole use, and took a one-third interest in another ship that was to be constructed for a three-cornered partnership excluding Rotch. Thus he created a hedge against failure of negotiations for peace with his foe. This double double-cross undermined the proposed combine, and by summer the old policy of every man for himself was in full swing once more.

In the meantime events of much greater significance in the life of Hancock and America were getting under way in England. The Stamp Act, designed to extend a long established system of imposts to the colonies, had been introduced in Parliament by George Grenville. It provided that all commercial and legal documents should be written on stamped paper. This would inflict a heavy financial burden upon colonial merchants, who used reams of such foolscap to record their complicated transactions. The measure was passed with little or no debate; but, much to the surprise of the unimaginative politicians in London, it caused an avalanche of protest on the other side of the Atlantic and eventually became the basis of the Liberty party's slogan, "No taxation without representation."

As far back as June, 1764, Thomas Hancock & Co. had complained to Barnard & Harrison about an impending increase in taxes. Now the new head of the House of Hancock grumbled more emphatically and began subconsciously to develop into an American patriot.

"I hear the Stamp Act is like to take place," he wrote in the next April. "It is very cruel. We were before much burthened. We shall not be able much longer to support trade, and in the end Great Britain must feel the effects of it. I wonder the merchants and friends of America don't make a stir for us." In the middle of May, after the act had become law, he penned to his English confidants a phrase that reveals his dawning sympathy with the political campaign opened by Sam Adams during the same month: "I am heartily sorry for the great burthen laid upon us. We are not able to bear all things but must submit to higher powers." [10]

The "higher powers" were the farsighted English statesmen led by Edmund Burke who defended the American claim concerning taxation, and to whom Adams was appealing in the set of instructions drafted for presentation to the General Court, denying the right of the British government to tax the colonies without their consent. This document was read in the Assembly, which voted in June to send a letter of similar import to its London agent, Jasper Mauduit, directing him to fight for the colonists' stand.

· 4 ·

The political bee had been buzzing around Hancock's ears for at least three years. Since October, 1762, he had been a member of the Masonic Lodge of St. Andrews. This and St. John's Lodge included such influential citizens as Otis, Sam Adams, Dr. Joseph Warren, and Colonel Josiah Quincy. At joint meetings the brotherhood of man was, of course, frequently discussed. This subject led naturally to conversations about the underdog—a category in which the colonials were beginning to picture themselves as more and more trade restrictions were clamped upon them by their autocratic mother country. Out of these talks came some of the earliest rebellious ideas; although most of the men who took part in them, including Hancock, had then no conscious thought of disloyalty to the Crown.

At about the same time John joined the newly formed Long Room

Club along with Paul Revere, Thomas Dawes, Dr. Benjamin Church, the Reverend Samuel Cooper, Otis, Warren, and others who were to be leaders in the Revolution. It met above the Edes & Gill print shop, where the inflammatory, widely read Boston *Gazette* was published. This club, it is believed, was the first of many to foment revolt.

A third organization with which the embryonic patriot became affiliated at this period or slightly later was the Merchants Club. Among the members were Thomas Cushing, his future henchman; Harrison Gray, treasurer of the province; and the ubiquitous Otis. They gathered monthly at the British Coffee House, the Bunch of Grapes, or the Vernon's Head Tavern to discourse upon business conditions, to draw up grievances against the Board of Trade, and to vent indignation over their treatment by Britain in general.

After being exposed to all these influences John was in a receptive frame of mind when offered an opportunity to run for selectman. He was voted in with six other candidates on March 11 and thus was launched officially upon his political career.

Now that he was a "statesman," Hancock apparently decided he should look the part by putting on a bit of swank. He ordered a Negro named Frank from London to be his personal servant, just as he would have requisitioned a batch of Irish butter. The man's death in 1771 is recorded on a moss-covered slab in Boston's Old Granary Burying Ground near John's own tomb—an enlightening commentary on the master's genuine affection for the lowly, despite the many charges of demagoguery leveled at him by historians; for markers seldom were placed on domestics' graves in those days.

The squire of Beacon Hill may have regretted the extravagance of buying and supporting a flunky, for in July he was experiencing the pinch of the economic depression. "I must beg," he apologized to Barnard & Harrison, "that you will excuse me at this juncture that I have drawn on you. . . . Out of all my debts . . . I can collect no money and am reduced to this method . . . to raise cash." [11]

Later in the month John, perhaps, felt the need of alcoholic solace. At any rate, he requested "two pipes of the very best Madeira for my own table" from his agents on the island and further specified: "I don't stand at any price. Let it be good. I like a rich wine." [12] This letter strikingly illustrates his slavish imitation of Thomas even after his uncle had been dead almost a year. He must have turned to the letter-books for a copy of a similar application dispatched by the old gentleman in 1757, for the phraseology of the two passages is identical.

Whether or not he replenished his wine cellar at this time for a particular purpose, the merchant-politician soon had compelling cause to do so. Within a month indignation against the Stamp Act flared into the first serious display of violence against England.

· 5 ·

As soon as the list of stamp distributors, headed by Andrew Oliver, Lieutenant Governor Hutchinson's brother-in-law, was made public on August 8 the Boston *Gazette* came out with a rabble-rousing article. On the 14th a mob, believed to have been inspired by crafty Sam Adams, assembled under a large elm at the corner of what are now Washington and Essex streets which came to be known as the Liberty Tree. This meeting was directed by the famous Sons of Liberty, who were to develop into the most radical organization in America. It stemmed from the committees of correspondence promoted by Adams throughout the colonies to keep the revolutionary spirit alive.

These malcontents hung Oliver in effigy from a limb of the symbolic tree and then dispersed until evening, when they cut down the stuffed figure and carried it on a bier through the Town House, where Governor Bernard and his Council were in session on the second floor. Shouting, "Liberty, property, and no stamps!" as they passed beneath the seat of government, they proceeded to King Street and destroyed the framework of what was to be the stamp agent's headquarters. From there they pushed on to Oliver's beautiful estate, from which he had been persuaded by friends to flee with his family. On the following night the rioters, now acting independently of the Sons of Liberty, but with their secret approval, again moved against Oliver's mansion, to which he had returned, and were dissuaded from demolishing it only by his promise to resign. He was a fourth-generation resident of Massachusetts and a more or less innocent victim, for he had vigorously opposed passage of the Stamp Act and had reluctantly accepted the appointment to enforce it.

Still determined to visit their artificially stimulated wrath upon the King's representatives, the insurgents next turned their attention to Hutchinson, who was falsely reported to have favored the revenue measure. They made his palatial home the target of two attacks, the second of which, on August 26, wrecked the interior just after the lieutenant governor and his family had escaped.[13]

All this unbridled license was very disturbing to Hancock. He, like

the rest of the "respectable" Boston businessmen, was politically con-
servative and feared mob action against constituted authority far more
than he hated what he considered the unfair exercise of that authority.
A long process of education by Sam Adams was required to convince
John that the end justified the means of opposition to the Crown.
Although one of the stanchest supporters of orderly protest against the
Stamp Act, he was shocked by the plundering of Hutchinson's property.
He thus opened his heart to Barnard & Harrison on the subject:

"The injury that has been done the lieutenant-governor . . . is what
I abhor and detest as much as any man breathing and would go great
lengths in repairing his loss. But an opposition to the Stamp Act is highly
commendable." [14]

The now somewhat muddled merchant probably was among the large
group of citizens who gathered in Faneuil Hall on the morning after
the outrage and denounced it. But he and the other town fathers disclaimed responsibility, while the provincial government abstained from
effective action in the absence of Bernard and Hutchinson, who had
fled to Castle William in fear for their lives.

· 6 ·

Having shrugged off his civic obligation to prosecute disturbers of the
peace, John turned to his private concerns once more and resumed
his personal agitation against the object of the disturbance. In a letter
of September 30 to his London representatives, after arrival of the first
shipment of stamped sheets, he referred to them as "the most disagreeable
commodity . . . that were ever imported into this country." The Stamp
Act "will entirely stagnate trade here, for it is universally determined
. . . never to submit to it. . . . For God's sake use your interest to relieve
us." And he concluded ominously, "I dread the event."

Two weeks later, as the enforcement deadline of November 1 approached, he worked himself into a profane dither over the significant
seals. "I now tell you," he declared prophetically, ". . . that the people
of this country will never suffer themselves to be made slaves of by a
submission to that d——d act. . . . A thousand guineas—nay, a much
larger sum—would be no temptation to me to . . . apply for a stamp. . . .
Under this additional burthen . . . I cannot carry . . . on to any profit."
And in a postscript he put himself on record to this effect:

"This letter I propose to remain in my letterbook as a standing monu-
ment to posterity, and my children in particular, that I by no means

consented . . . to this cruel act and that my best representations were not wanting in the matter." [15]

Within another week John reached the climax of his correspondence campaign against the Stamp Act. This communication is an excellent epitome of the colonists' official attitude toward the statute. Directed to Barnard & Harrison, it shows that his personal opposition, as well as that of the people as a whole, was based on constitutional principle.

"I believe," he wrote, "that not a man in England, in proportion to estate, pays the tax that I do. What would a merchant in London think of paying £400 sterling annually, which my late uncle paid to this province and county? . . . And I now pay yearly . . . £300 sterling, besides all duties, imposts, ministers, and many other additional taxes. . . . I will not be a slave. I have a right to the liberties and privileges of the English Constitution and I, as an Englishman, will enjoy them." [16]

These three letters—especially the last—mark an important turning point in Hancock's career. They prove that in theory, at least, he believed Britain's liberty-curbing legislation should be resisted, even though he was not prepared at this time to put his ideas into practice by overt means. He undoubtedly was actuated partly by the ulterior motive of protecting his widely ramified business interests, which, of course, were seriously affected by such a heavy drain of taxation. But so were the concerns of the other big Massachusetts merchants. And yet, although none of them had as much at stake as he, few adhered so loyally to the several nonimportation agreements. Of all those who counted in the commercial life of the province he displayed the greatest courage of conviction, although he weakened on one occasion under extenuating circumstances. So tremendous was his influence that, if he had lost heart, the rest probably would have done likewise; and the progress of the Revolutionary movement might have been arrested for a long period, despite Sam Adams's untiring efforts to keep it going by exerting his power over the lowest, financially impotent strata of society. It is a logical conclusion, therefore, that John's opposition to the Stamp Act and the other anticolonial tax measures was founded fundamentally on the concept that no self-respecting Englishman could submit to oppression—physical, political, or economic.

· 7 ·

That Hancock was becoming more politically inclined in fact as well as in theory is indicated by several developments during the summer and fall of 1765. First he was appointed to a committee for the instruction of Boston's representatives in the General Court as to the line they were to follow in debates on the big issues of the day, with particular reference, of course, to the Stamp Act. Then he was nominated for a vacancy in the Court—his highest governmental aspiration so far—but ran a bad last, with only forty votes, in a special election held on September 27. Slightly more than a month later he took his longest and most significant stride to date into the field of politics—one that marked the real beginning of Sam Adams's influence, which continued off and on until the end of the Revolution.

The occasion was Pope's Day, the New England version of Guy Fawkes Day, which had been celebrated in Britain on every 5th of November for one hundred sixty years. In the smaller towns the ceremony was as innocuous as the New Orleans Mardi Gras. On a huge float was placed an illuminated paper lantern large enough to contain five or six persons. Behind it was ensconced an image of the Pope surrounded by imitation monks, friars, and other clergy of the Roman Catholic Church. At the rear of the platform stood a representation of the Devil, with horns, tail, and pitchfork. Sometimes dancers, fiddlers, and likenesses of unpopular politicians were added to the ensemble. The figures were manipulated with strings by little boys walking beneath the wagon. Under the direction of a captain and two lieutenants it was drawn through the streets by young men while a great crowd of obstreperous youths followed, beating drums and blowing whistles.

In Boston two pope's carriages were employed because of the internecine rivalry between the North and South End gangs. The vehicles advanced toward each other from the respective extremities of the metropolis. Their hundreds of escorts were mostly of the hoodlum type and itched for a good fight, which inevitably ensued when the processions met. As time went on these battles became more and more violent. Many of the participants were maimed by paving stones, bricks, and cudgels of all sorts used as weapons by the opposing forces in their efforts to capture the enemy's effigies.

For twenty-four hours, starting at sundown, the town was at the mercy of this riffraff. The General Court tried to curb these excesses by legislation; but neither the government of the province nor that of the town had any enforcement agency except a poorly trained militia, the sheriff, and a dozen constables. Unsupported by public opinion, they were entirely inadequate to interfere with such a deeply rooted custom. So it continued to thrive until 1765 in what was a lawless community at best.

Ever since the festival of the previous year, when the fighting had been particularly savage and had caused the death of a child, Sam Adams had been mulling over the idea of harnessing these tough characters to his political chariot. If they could intimidate the provincial and town authorities (he reasoned) they might in time, when welded into a single unit, be made the nucleus of a power that could effectually defy the King himself. Much of the early success of the Revolutionary movement was due to his ability to stir up trouble at psychological moments through his control of this reckless element.

Adams worked through the loutish leader of the mob that had assaulted Hutchinson's residence, Ebenezer Mackintosh, whom he probably had been instrumental in getting released from imprisonment for the offense. As captain of the victorious side in the popery war of 1764 this rawboned, ignorant, ludicrously conceited bully was a hero to both factions. Through his prestige, played upon like a violinist by the great master of the rhythm of rebellion, the two gangs were induced to make peace and to join forces. In the meantime Adams, already sensing what a boon to the patriot cause would be the support of a wealthy, upright citizen like Hancock, had cultivated his friendship and had capitalized on his bitterness against the British government.

So on November 5, 1765, the North and South Enders paraded together in military formation, keeping in well drilled step and maneuvering with soldierly precision. At their head was Mackintosh, marching arm in arm with Colonel William Brattle of the local militia, who was glad, of course, to cooperate in this scheme designed ostensibly to restore law and order. Brattle heaped flattery upon the "captain," who was decked out in a uniform of sunset-red and sky-blue topped by a gold-laced hat as he twirled a cane and shouted commands through a speaking trumpet.

Although they had buried the hatchet as between themselves, the mobsters did not overlook the opportunity to dig it up and bury it again in the sensitive flesh of Governor Bernard and his Council. They dragged a float bearing, as usual, the pope and the devil together with several other figures dangling from gibbets beneath an inscription reading, "The Devil take him who takes his commission"—obviously a warning to Oliver not to go back on his promise to resign. The procession halted long enough below the windows of the Council chamber, where the General Court was in session, for the Crown officials to catch the significance of the display and then proceeded to the Green Dragon. There the demonstrators sat down to a harmony feast also attended by Adams, Hancock as master of ceremonies, and numerous other members of the budding Whig party.[17]

According to William H. Sumner's reminiscences of a talk with Dorothy Quincy in her old age,[18] John forked out the equivalent of $1,000 to pay for this affair and gave the first important exhibition of the eloquence that was to be such a tremendous factor in the creation of a new nation. He impressed upon his awed audience, which had profound respect for the native aristocracy, that unity was essential to the success of resistance to England's ruinous taxation policy. Probably in the hyperbolic vein to which orators of the day were addicted he inflamed his hearers with hatred for the "tyrannical" mother country.

This speech made Hancock solid with Adams and the rest of the Whigs but naturally did not endear him to the American Tories, one of whom wrote in an indictment of sixty-one "dangerous" colonial leaders prepared for publication in a British newspaper that he was a "milch cow to the Faction." [19]

· 8 ·

Although he now owed Barnard & Harrison the disturbingly large sum of more than £19,000, Hancock made a costly contribution to Harvard. Toward the end of October, in the midst of his first essay into Anglo-American politics and his financial worries, he ordered from London for spring delivery 1,098 books at the cost of about £516 to help repair the loss of 6,000 in the fire of the preceding year and start a new library.

Contrary to an assertion of James Truslow Adams,[20] John was not obligated by a legal bequest on the part of his uncle to give these volumes. At most he was morally bound only by a private commitment of £500 which the deceased merchant is alleged to have imparted to him. Furthermore, although he attempted to drive a good bargain like any businessman, there is no indication in his letter on the subject that he insisted on cheap works, as Adams contends. On the contrary, they were to be "the best editions and well bound . . . if to be had at any price." [21]

But Hancock must have been more concerned at this time about the appearance of his account books as the Stamp Act threatened momentarily to increase the red entries in his ledgers. Fortunately for him, the virulent agitation against this measure had so deeply impressed the King's officers in Massachusetts that they refrained from putting it in force on the effective date of November 1. By the middle of the month several vessels, led by John's *Boston Packet,* had been allowed to sail without stamped clearances. The customs officials had given the ship-masters certificates stating that stamps were unavailable. This probably was true, but it was palpably an excuse for evading an unpleasant responsibility.

Sam Adams and his Whigs, however, were not satisfied with this negative nullification of the Parliamentary decree. Hearing that Oliver was reconsidering his agreement to resign as chief distributor, they decided to forestall any backsliding. On the morning of December 17 the town was placarded with notices summoning the Sons of Liberty to assemble beneath the Liberty Tree at noon to witness the official's resignation under oath. Oliver pleaded for the courtesy of being permitted to perform the humiliating act in the comparative seclusion of the Town House. Mackintosh, now called "Governor" by the cunning higher-ups in the patriot councils, pretended to comply in spirit by letting him put his renunciation in writing before a gathering of magistrates and merchants in a private dwelling but adhered to the original plans for his ultimate abasement.

This occurred on the symbolic spot specified in the broadsides. Before about 2,000 people, with Mackintosh glowering at his side, Oliver swore never to attempt to enforce the Stamp Act. The oath was administered by Richard Dana, one of the most active Sons, from whose near-by home the Council and selectmen observed the proceedings. It is not known whether Hancock was among the witnesses; but he, as one of the town fathers, presumably would be on hand for such a momentous occasion. This unjustifiably degrading spectacle, in which the radical wing of the Liberty party took great delight and the more conservative branch spinelessly acquiesced, wound up with a speech by the victim, who said quite truthfully that he detested the Stamp Act. Thereupon he was cheered derisively and dismissed.

This, however, was not the end of the opposition to the abhorrent tax law. The rabble's desire to flout authority had been satiated temporarily, but the merchant class could not rest easy as long as the act remained on the statute books. So while Adams and his henchmen were using strong-arm tactics the more dignified, though not more docile, part of the community was resorting to a boycott. In a letter to his London agents a few days after the Oliver incident Hancock issued the following indirect ultimatum to the government:

"In case the Stamp Act is not repealed my orders are that you will not . . . ship me one article. I have wrote . . . this in consideration of the united resolves of not only the principal merchants . . . of this town but of those of the other trading towns of this province, and which I am determined to abide by." [22]

Although neither the harsh political undertones of the colonial resistance movement nor the self-pitying note in John's correspondence struck a responsive chord in the breasts of Barnard & Harrison or the other British representatives of the House of Hancock, the nonimportation agreement did. All of them immediately bestirred themselves to have the obstacle to this lucrative source of business removed. Barnard worked incessantly for repeal through his connections in the House of Commons; Devonshire & Reeve, the Bristol factors, carried on a propaganda campaign to the same purpose, and Barlow Trecothick, in his strategic position as chairman of the English merchants' committee, applied more direct pressure.

· 9 ·

Even though Hancock had no definite assurance at the turn of the year that these efforts would be productive, he showed the enterprising, almost foolhardy spirit of his uncle by adopting a broad expansionist policy. Palfrey, who had become his right-hand man, with the understanding that he was to be permitted to work for himself on the side, had built up a prosperous trade of his own and had left the House of Hancock early in 1765. Now, because of the prohibitive import duties imposed upon the products in which he dealt, he gladly accepted his former employer's offer to let him manage a new retail shop under a profit-sharing arrangement. This association continued until 1776, when Palfrey first became aide-de-camp to Washington and later paymaster general of the army. In 1780 Congress appointed him consul general to France; but he was lost at sea on the way to his post. His former boss obviously made a wise choice in renewing relations with him.

Hancock's speculation in whale oil and bone during 1766 was not as successful as his gamble on the stuff of human nature. He doubled his original fleet of four whalers; bought the Nantucket catch on an unheard-of scale as a partner in the old combine embracing his British and American agents, drove Rotch out of the market—in short, did everything in a large way except turn a profit. After increasing his indebtedness to Barnard & Harrison to the staggering total of £25,000 he wound up the year deeper in the hole than ever before as the result of a sudden decline in prices while his cargoes were on the high seas.

John's second failure in the whaling field undoubtedly was due to his increasing preoccupation with politics. Back in January he had written, "My situation ever since my uncle's death has been a scene of hurry," and now he was "reduced to the evening to finish my letters." [23]

The aristocratic and now whole-souled politician from the silk-stocking district of Beacon Hill was engaged in another campaign for election as one of Boston's four representatives in the General Court. This time, on May 6, he coasted into office along with Sam Adams, Cushing, and Otis on a high wave of 437 votes.

Although the triumph, at the age of twenty-nine, reflected John Hancock's popularity, it was due chiefly to his good standing with the Whig machine, which was well broken in even at this early date. He had forced himself upon the attention of the people as front man in the reconciliation of the popery gangs; had attained prominence in business circles through spectacular commercial deals, and had won a certain amount of admiration as a conscientious selectman. But if he had not been endorsed by the bosses he still would have been an also-ran.

It is a common misconception that the Boston town meeting of pre Revolutionary days expressed the will of the people directly. Actually it was no more democratic than a party convention today and was less representative than a modern election, for only 3.5 per cent of the population exercised the right of suffrage. For at least a decade before the battle of Lexington hand-picked candidates were steam-rollered into office. The caucus, which had its earliest and highest development in America, was already in 1766 the predominant instrument of political action. John Adams recognized this three years before when he wrote in his diary:

"This day learned that the Caucus Club meets at certain times in the garret of Tom Dawes. . . . There they smoke tobacco till you cannot see. . . . There they drink flip, I suppose, and there they choose . . . selectmen, assessors, collectors, wardens, firewards, and representatives . . . before they are chosen in the town. . . . Adams, Cooper,* and . . . others are members." [24]

Even though Hancock's election meant little to the man in the street it was fraught with the deepest significance to the men in the garret. To John Adams posterity is indebted for the following first-hand account of its import and effect upon the new incumbent:

"At the time of this prosperity I was one day walking in the Mall and accidentally met Samuel Adams. In taking a few turns together we came in full view of Mr. Hancock's house. Mr. Adams, pointing to the

* Samuel Adams, William Cooper.

stone building, said, 'This town has done a wise thing today.' 'What?' 'They have made that young man's fortune their own.'

"His prophecy was literally fulfilled, for no man's property was ever more entirely devoted to the public. The town had that day chosen Mr. Hancock into the legislature of the province. The quivering anxiety of the public under the fearful looking-for of the vengeance of the King, Ministry, and Parliament compelled him to constant attendance in the House. His mind was soon engrossed by public cares, alarms, and terrors; his business was left to subalterns; his private affairs neglected and continued to be so to the end of his life. If his fortune had not been large he must have died as poor as Mr. S. Adams or Mr. Gerry." [25]

· 10 ·

Meanwhile repercussions of the Stamp Act's effect in America had reached England. The cumulative protests from a congress at which nine colonies had been represented during 1765 in New York, together with individual remonstrances from Hancock and other merchants, reinforced by the nonimportation agreements, had finally brought on a debate in Parliament. Lord Mansfield had answered the colonists' "No taxation without representation" argument by pointing out that only 1,000,000 of the 9,000,000 adult British males were entitled to vote in elections for seats in the House of Commons, but that all were taxed, anyway. Pitt, however, had rebutted successfully with the contention that this line of reasoning did not apply to America because conditions were different there. So "that d——d act" was repealed on March 17, 1766.

First news of the revocation reached New England May 16. The luck of the Hancocks put John in position to announce it, for his new brig, *Harrison*—named after the junior partner in the English firm whose good will meant much to the merchant-politician—was the carrier.

The selectmen designated May 19 as a day of celebration. So happy were the good burghers that they could not even wait for dawn. At one o'clock in the morning the church bells started to ring, and soon virtually every bell in town was pealing. Blaring of bands, thumping of drums, and discharging of guns increased the din, and at daylight the Liberty Tree, public buildings, and private homes were festooned with flags. Debtor prisons were emptied by the Sons of Liberty, who paid what the inmates owed.

In the evening the greatest illumination yet seen in New England, including a pyramid of 280 lamps four stories high and a pyrotechnical exhibit under the direction of the Sons, was staged on the Common. Hancock, now rapidly learning the tricks, matched the fireworks spectacle with one on the lawn in front of his mansion. He also had pipes of Madeira placed there for the delectation of the populace while he held open house for the gentry in his brightly lighted show place.

John Rowe, the merchant, kept a diary in which he describes the event and a banquet for twenty-nine gentlemen at the Bunch of Grapes, where fifteen toasts were drunk. His strange comment, "Mr. Hancock behaved very well on this occasion and treated every person with cheerfulness," [26] suggests that the moodiness which eventually alienated so many of the young politician's associates may already have become manifest under pressure.

Governor Bernard, who had been among the Crown officers to urge the rescinding of the Stamp Act, celebrated "Repeal Day" with his Council by drinking His Majesty's health at Province House in the afternoon and then mingled with the commoners in the Mall.

Hancock probably joined the chief magistrate in paying homage to King George and undoubtedly raised his glass in testimony to his loyalty at the dinner described by Rowe. It cannot be emphasized too strongly that at this time he still was unprepared intellectually, if he was disposed emotionally, to embrace the secret belief of Sam Adams that rebellion should be the ultimate aim of the colonies. The current of conservatism in the complex nature of Adams' protégé ran too deep to be dammed up by minor obstacles to contentment interposed by Mother England. And his innate fealty to the Crown asserted itself repeatedly, to the disgust of Adams, for several years to come. He thus expressed it in a letter acknowledging receipt of the repeal announcement:

"Our rejoicing has been conducted in a very decent, reputable manner; and I hope now peace and harmony will prevail. My best influence and endeavors to that purpose shall be used. I doubt not but the colonies will make all the grateful returns in their power." [27]

· 11 ·

The rejoicing with knife and fork in pre-Revolutionary Boston was an art closely allied to that of politics. John Hancock practiced both jointly and assiduously, although he was so busy during the summer of 1766 that he must temporarily have lost his trencher touch.

"I have been, and still am, so excessively hurried," he wrote to his London agents, "that I scarcely have time to sleep. What with attending

Court in the House of Assembly, my own store, and ships in and out . . .
I have enough to do; but you and I love hurry, which will be my lot
while I live." [28]

Yet the Beacon Hill gourmet must have found time to account for a
fair share of the tavern consumption of food. Midafternoon was the
fashionable hour for dinner, and nine o'clock for supper. The components of the main meal—enough for three average four-course repasts
today—were substantial English dishes. No hors-d'œuvres or soups are
mentioned in the diary kept by Rowe, an inveterate banqueter. Diners
evidently concentrated on viands into which they could sink their teeth.
The choicest were venison, turtle, and salmon. Green peas are the only
vegetable noted. The favorite dessert was fruit—cherries and strawberries,
usually served in tarts, and plums in cake.[29]

Prodigious quantities of wine, of course, were swilled at every feast
and were the inspiration of almost endless toasts. Rowe records [30] the
doings at a dinner given for a shipmaster by the leading merchants,
including Hancock, on December 2 at the British Coffee House—where
the most pretentious affairs were held. Healths were drunk, in order
(and probably on a descending scale of intelligibility), to the King, the
Queen, and the royal family; to Parliament, the Ministry, various earls,
dukes, and military figures; to the Chancellor of the Exchequer, the
Lords of Trade, the Lords of the Admiralty, the army and the navy; to
exshtention of trade and commersh; to y'nited and insheparable int'res'
of Great Britain and her c-c-colonies; to proshperity of Nor' Amurrica,
and to a goo' voyash for goo' ship *Jamaica*.

It may or may not have been due to pure coincidence that John picked
the following day, when headaches must have been prevalent, to tell
Harrison & Barnard that their "treatment really vexes me, and I see so
much of the world that I am almost tempted to say I will not concern
myself in trade any longer. . . . I am almost tired." [31]

As the new year dawned Fortune displayed toward her favorite the
fickleness for which she is notorious. What appears to have been the
most disastrous fire in Boston's colonial period broke out in the bakehouse
of one of his tenants during the night of February 3-4, 1767, and razed
more than twenty buildings, including several of Hancock's. But the
town's leading landlord made a political virtue of misfortune—and
showed his natural kindness—by supplementing with hundreds of
guineas the General Court's appropriation of £400 for the relief of the
fifty families rendered homeless. By this and other means, such as
distributing huge stacks of wood among the poor during the severe New

England winters, he built up a reputation of sympathy for the underprivileged which was to stand him in excellent stead throughout his life.

John likewise won the everlasting loyalty of the influential clergy and impressed his name upon the minds of parishioners in his own and surrounding towns by costly gifts to meetinghouses. In April he ordered from abroad a three-hundred-pound bell for a church in Jamaica Plain, where he had a summer residence.[32] This was the first of many donations —of cash, pulpits, communion tables, seats for needy widows, window glass, and Bibles—which flowed from him at intervals over a span of fifteen years.

The seeds of support for his steadily mounting political ambition began to bear rich fruit in May. At the annual election of delegates to the provincial legislature his growing popularity was reflected in his poll of 618 votes—44 more than that of Boss Sam Adams himself, who was returned to office, too, along with Otis and Cushing. This indication of higher regard probably put into the head of the protégé the ideas of superiority he ultimately turned to account at his patron's expense.

· 12 ·

In September, 1767, the burgeoning revolutionary patriot must have purpled while replying to a proposal from Harrison & Barnard that they send an inspector across the Atlantic to pass on his oil shipments for the sake of eliminating the numerous substandard cargoes. "What you mean, Gentlemen," this bristling note reads, "I am at a loss to know. When I am in want of a guardian our laws will appoint one. . . . I will never submit to have a man sent over to inspect my business to make me the ridicule of the merchants." [33]

Relations with the leading and long established foreign factors of the House of Hancock had become more and more strained. Now came the crack-up. In the middle of October John assailed them bitterly for declining to ship some goods to Palfrey on credit. He interpreted this as a reflection on his own integrity; told them he was seeking a connection with Haley & Hopkins, another London firm, and added loftily: "I look on myself a man of capital and am not to be put on a footing with every twopenny shopkeeper that addresses you. . . . You have affected me in the tenderest point." [34] On the same day he suited the action to the word by soliciting an arrangement with George Haley, at whose house he had stayed while in England.[35]

With typical presumption, justified in his eyes by self-esteem, Hancock dispatched consignments and requests for merchandise to his potentially new representative without waiting for acceptance of his proposition. Fortunately Haley acquiesced. The bargain was sealed with several exchanges of gifts—wood ducks, fish, pickled peppers, and a picture of Boston from John; peacocks, beer, and a dressing table (probably for Aunt Lydia) from George. Thus was sealed a beautiful friendship that was to last for two decades.

Early in November, with equally characteristic irresolution, the merchant of many moods made overtures of reconciliation to his dismissed agents but gave them to understand that he was determined henceforth to deal on a cash basis, to keep only one vessel in operation, and to act independently in his shipping ventures.[36] He failed to carry out any of these intentions and resumed full-scale relations with the Harrison house at the end of two years.

Meanwhile there had been developing a situation which gave John good reason for acquiring new agents in England and for clinging to old ones. The respite from oppressive taxation afforded the colonists through repeal of the Stamp Act had come to a close during the summer of 1767 with the passage of the Townshend Acts, which levied import duties on tea, paper, and glass. This was an implementation of the legislative principle enunciated in the Declaratory Act, which reasserted the right of King and Parliament to make any laws they saw fit for the colonies. It had been ignored by most Americans in their joy over release from the stamp regulations. So Hancock and his fellow merchants once more had need of all the cooperation obtainable from the politically potent businessmen of London in combating this new assault upon the liberties they had arrogated to themselves.

Ninety-eight Boston traders initiated the opposition at a meeting held on March 1, 1768, by agreeing to take up again the cudgel that had proved so effective previously—nonimportation. The entrepreneur of Beacon Hill was one of them and was placed on a committee of nine to report at the next session on the best means of carrying out the compact.

As if he were not sufficiently harassed by mercantile troubles, John was called upon three weeks later to help get Sam Adams out of a serious financial predicament and thereby pay the first debt of his own career as a politician. Sam had been sued by the town treasurer in June of the preceding year for £1,463, tax arrears for which he was personally responsible as collector. Execution of the judgment given against him was to begin in March, but he had failed to raise the money and was petitioning for a stay of six months. On the 22nd a committee, including Hancock, was appointed to seek the reprieve from Treasurer Gray, who granted it.

Partly out of sincere sympathy for the underdog, partly in deference to political expediency, and partly through sheer business inefficiency, Adams had made only a half-hearted attempt to collect the taxes. Even now he felt little compulsion to change his course of action—or inaction. He did garner a few small payments from unimportant delinquents but borrowed enough from his beholden protégé to cover the bulk of the people's indebtedness. When the period of grace was up the boss and his henchman wielded so much power in the government of Massachusetts that nobody dared to prosecute the suit further. And in 1772 a committee named to inquire into the matter reported that £50 still was outstanding, but that there was no chance of collecting.

Hancock's patriotism was rapidly assuming a deeper tinge through his association with the reddest of the Revolutionists.

✍ VI ✍

A NEW WHIG IS DYED

*U*P TO THE SPRING of 1768 Hancock's opposition to the British government was of two distinct kinds—commercial and political—running along roughly parallel lines. They occasionally converged as he was drawn by the magnet of his desire for freedom of action, first concretely expressed through the nonimportation agreement, toward the rebellious ideology of Sam Adams. That was when he tentatively espoused the cause of the Whigs by standing for election to the General Court on their ticket. But he probably did not consciously associate trade with politics, as an abstract, objective concept. It is almost certain that he thought of the Liberty party's slogan, "No taxation without representation," only in terms of its application to the practical business of buying and selling. Now the two conduits of his resistance to the Crown were to cross, and the contact was to touch off the initial spark of the Revolutionary conflagration. Henceforth his motives for defying King and Parliament were to be indistinguishable.

Hancock and the other Boston merchants received a pointed indication in the fall of 1767 that England did not intend to be talked and bluffed out of enforcing the Townshend Acts. She sent six customs commissioners, with a large staff of clerks, to join the two who had proved so inadequate to carry out the royal will.

The new officials soon learned, however, from the most outspoken of the town's businessmen that he, at least, could not be overawed by numbers. In a letter to the Lords of the Treasury during the following March, His Majesty's representatives reported that he "is one of the leaders of the disaffected," and that "early in the winter he declared in the General Assembly that he would not suffer any of our officers to go even on board any of his London ships." [1]

John Hancock had a chance to make good this threat on April 8, the day after the *Lydia* arrived with a cargo from London. He was too late to prevent Owen Richards and Robert Jackson, tidesmen hired by the commissioners, from setting foot on deck; but he carried out his defiance.

Acting on the suspicion of their employers that there were tea, paper, and other dutiable articles in the hold of the brig, Richards and Jackson boarded her. A few hours afterward her owner appeared and, on being informed of their mission by the inspectors, ordered her master, Captain Scott, not to allow them to go below. So they went away.

But Richards returned during the next night and found his way into the steerage. At about eleven o'clock Hancock, who must have had numerous informers among the tenants of his wharf, led aboard eight or ten strong-arm men, with a Negro slave—probably Cato—holding a lantern. He demanded Richards' credentials, which proved to be technically unofficial because they bore no date. Thereupon the renegade patriot made his first show of force against Mother England. Under his orders the mate and the boatswain thrust the intruder up on deck, where he received permission to search every part of the vessel except the hold. But the tidesman, now thoroughly scared, declined.

By this time a large crowd, presumably attracted by the sound of the scuffle and the angry voices of Hancock's muscle men, had gathered on the dock. Writing shortly afterward to an agent of the province in England, Lieutenant Governor Hutchinson recounted: "Mr. H. was escorted up the wharf, he having the approbation of the spectators. He was obliged to entreat them not to [demonstrate?] through the town."[2]

Professor W. T. Baxter states: *

"It is, perhaps, unsound to say of such a deep-rooted and wide-spread movement as the American Revolution that it began with any one incident; yet, since the hustling of Owen Richards from the *Lydia* was the first act of physical opposition to Crown officers by respectable citizens, John's admirers have some grounds for claiming that he started the Revolution."[3]

The basis of this contention would seem to be as valid as that of any other theorizing about historical cause and effect in connection with the War for Independence. Although, as Baxter points out, the argument is open to dispute, it is as sound as the generally accepted reasoning that the so-called "battles" of Lexington and Concord brought on the great struggle. Even in those instances a full-scale war could have been averted if either side had been willing to give in after what amounted

* See *The House of Hancock* (Harvard University Press, Cambridge, 1945). Reprinted by permission.

to an unorganized and largely unpremeditated uprising on the part of a few hundred disobedient, but by no means fundamentally disloyal, colonists.

In the *Lydia* case Britain was to yield; but Hancock had forged a strong link in a chain of events that would lead straight up to the Declaration of Independence. James Otis had aroused the indignation of the people with his impassioned utterances against the Writs of Assistance;[4] Sam Adams was to crystallize their sentiment in favor of forcible methods through his committees of correspondence, and Patrick Henry would stir them with "Give me liberty or give me death." But it was Hancock's strange fate that, lacking the intellectual stature of these men, he should be responsible for one of the first acts of violence against His Majesty George III.

· 2 ·

By ordering the manhandling of a British government representative— even the humble hireling of a small subdivision—John Hancock had, of course, committed a very serious offense if there was proof that he had acted without just cause. But the fantastic Hancock luck came to his rescue once more.

The commissioners immediately inquired of Attorney General Jonathan Sewell (husband of Dorothy Quincy's sister Esther) whether the owner of the *Lydia* was liable to prosecution. On investigation of the law the worthy barrister discovered that it was extensively perforated with loopholes. It authorized customs men (and, by inference, their employees) to go on board a ship for the twofold purpose of searching her and observing whether her cargo was being put ashore. But the statute did not specify whether "on board" meant on deck or in the hold. Furthermore, Richards had asserted that he did not wish to search the vessel.

Sewell pussyfooted on the question and advised against legal action on the ground that it "might in the end be rather prejudicial than advantageous to the interests of the Crown." The royal solicitor probably was influenced by the hostile temper of the people and possibly, also, by Hancock's close friendship with the Quincys in the early North Braintree days. At all events, he let John off with a gentle wrist-slapping to the effect that "though Mr. Hancock may not have conducted himself so prudently or courteously as might be wished; yet, from what appears, it is probable that his intention was to keep within the bounds of the law." [5]

Thus did the stupid officials of the great British Empire, American- as well as English-born, continue to pursue alternately their equally ineffective policies of exploitation and appeasement until, like the fabled ass that starved to death while trying to decide between two bales of hay, they eventually lost their most valuable colonial possessions. The namby-pamby attitude of the Massachusetts jurist emboldened Hancock to declare in public, according to the commissioners, that "if we . . . are not recalled he will get rid of us before Christmas." [6]

However, before he was officially informed that the attorney general winked at his violation, "this infatuated man" flouted the authority of the revenue agents even more boldly. On the night of May 9 Thomas Kirk and another tidesman boarded the *Liberty*, which had just arrived from Madeira with a consignment of wine, to check on the suspiciously small entry of twenty-five casks made by her master, James Marshall, as the total number subject to tax. Marshall got wind of the visit and went to investigate, with a gang of waterfront toughs, at about nine o'clock. He found Kirk alone (his assistant having gone home to sleep off a drunk) and asked his permission to remove the spirituous contents of the hold. On receiving a firm refusal the skipper and his cohorts pushed the tidesman down into the cabin and nailed up the companionway. From then until midnight, the prisoner testified later, he heard the creak of hoisting gear steadily at work. When the job was finished Marshall released him with a warning that if he did not keep his mouth shut he would lose his property and possibly his life. So the frightened hireling told his superiors that no wine had been taken out of the sloop, and that the quantity reported was correct.

During the ensuing month the *Liberty* was unloaded and reloaded preparatory to her next voyage. Meanwhile the *Romney*, a fifty-gun frigate, had nosed into Boston Harbor to strengthen the tax collectors' hands. In the interim, also, Marshall had died.

On June 10 Kirk, relieved of the fear of reprisal, confessed the true story of the Madeira smuggling to the commissioners. Thereupon they made up their minds to seize Hancock's ship without delay. In the evening of the same day Benjamin Hallowell, comptroller of customs, and his brother Joseph, chief collector, marched down to the wharf and had the broad arrow (indicating government property) painted on her side. By their order John Corner, commander of the *Romney*, then put a de-

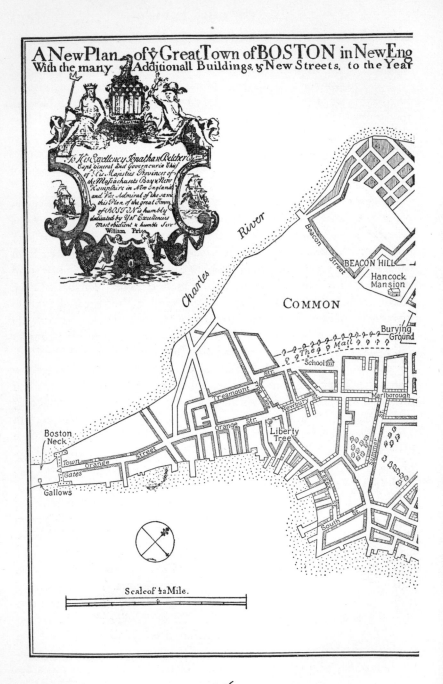

A New Plan of y Great Town of BOSTON in New Eng
With the many Additionall Buildings, & New Streets, to the Year

To His Excellency Jonathan Belcher Esq
Capt General and Governour in Chief
of His Majesties Provinces of
the Massachusets Bay & New
Hampshire in New England
and Vice Admiral of the same
this Plan of the great Town
of BOSTN is humbly
dedicated by Yor Excellencies
Most obedient & humble Serr
William Price

Charles River

Beacon Street

BEACON HILL

Hancock Mansion

COMMON

Burying Ground

The Mall

School

Str

Treamount

Newbury

Marlborough

Orange Str

Liberty Tree

Boston Neck

Town

Orange

Street

Gates

Gallows

Summer

Sea

South

Scale of ½ a Mile.

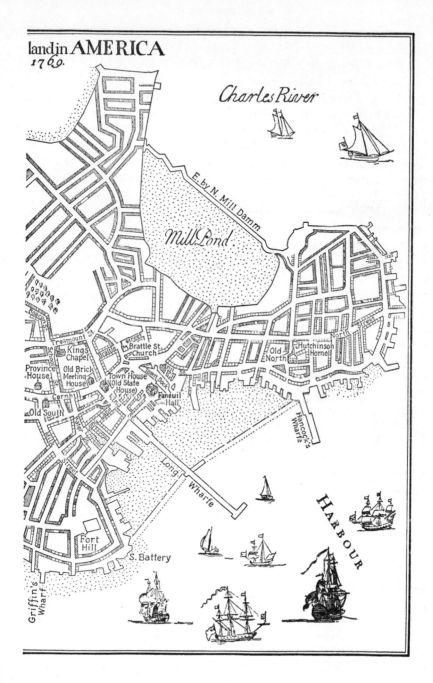

land in **AMERICA**
1769.

Charles River

E. by N. Mill Damm

Mill Pond

Treamount

Kings
Chapel

Brattle St.
Church

Old
E North

Hutchinson
Home

Province
House

Old Brick
Meeting
House

Town House
(Old State
House)

Cornhill

Faneuil
Hall

Old South

Hancock's
Wharfe

Long Wharfe

HARBOUR

Fort
Hill

S. Battery

Griffin's
Wharfe

tachment of marines aboard the sloop and moored her under the man-of-war's guns.

This infuriated the colonial sailors in the vicinity, especially because the seizure was to be performed by Corner, an ornery, ruthless old salt typical of officers in the royal navy at that period. He already had incensed the maritime population of Boston by resorting to a long established British practice which was to become a contributory cause of the War of 1812—impressment of American seamen. He also added insult to injury by declaring: "The town is a blackguard town and ruled by mobs; . . . and, by the eternal God, I will make their hearts ache before I leave." [7]

So, while Corner's crew were cutting the *Liberty* loose, a wrathful crowd gathered on the dock and pelted them with stones. The captain ordered his men to fire upon the mob; but they refrained and proceeded to tow the vessel, with barges, out to the *Romney*.

By this time the rabble, always spoiling for trouble, had joined the seafarers and was helping them chase the Hallowells. Hurling rocks, bricks, and mud, they followed the terrified commissioners all the way to their homes and smashed their windows. Three days later the whole customs personnel took refuge aboard the *Romney* and finally in the Castle. In the meantime another group of hoodlums had lifted the chief collector's boat out of the water, had carried it to the Common and had set fire to it—but not, according to Sam Adams, on Hancock's doorstep as was eventually reported to England.

Adams, in a letter to the London agent of the Massachusetts House of Representatives, an ardent champion of the Whigs, belittled the whole affair with injured innocence. He also tried to exonerate Hancock and the majority of the citizens from implication in it—even asserting that Hancock was a restraining influence. The butter-melting missive reads:

"We cannot help taking notice here of a notorious instance of the inveterate temper of our enemies, in a representation made in a certain letter, of this riotous assembly's having burnt a beautiful barge belonging to the Collector of the Customs *before Mr. Hancock's door*. As this worthy gentleman sustains a public character and is one of the principal inhabitants in the province, it is apparent that the malice of the writer . . . was not confined to a single gentleman but extended to the public. The truth is, the barge was burnt on a common surrounded with gentlemen's seats; and the scene could not be said to be before Mr. Hancock's door any more than before the doors of divers other gentlemen in the neighborhood. The mean insinuation that it was done under the in-

fluence of Mr. Hancock is so far from the least shadow of truth that it is
notorious here that the tumult was finally dispersed principally by his
exertions, animated by his known regard to peace and good order." [8]

Sam now was taking full advantage of the opportunity to clothe his
disreputable conception of idealism in the purple robes of his patrician
protégé.

· 3 ·

Undaunted by the Damoclean danger of the two major prosecutions for
smuggling that were hanging over his head, John Hancock was concerned only about the prospects of getting the *Liberty* back into his merchant fleet. After dickering for two days with Collector Hallowell he
agreed that, if the sloop should be restored to his custody, he would
turn her over to the British government in case the admiralty court
should declare her forfeit. But Adams and Otis, John's legal adviser, apparently decided to press home the juridical victory achieved in connection with the *Lydia* and induced their political pawn to adopt an
uncompromising attitude respecting his other ship. After a long council
of war lasting until midnight of June 12 at his mansion the obliging
front man of the Whigs sent word to the commissioners that all negotiations were off.

The King's advocate in London, to whom the matter was then referred, had him arrested in November on the charge of importing 100
pipes of wine valued at £3,000 without paying the tax, and asked a penalty of £9,000, plus possession of the *Liberty* and other fines amounting
in all to the stupendous sum of £100,000. John, released in £3,000 bail,
retained John Adams as his counsel. But, for lack of conclusive evidence
(Kirk's being weakened by the hearsay manner in which it was collected), Attorney General Sewell gave up after a three months' trial in
1769 and terminated the main part of the action with the statement:
"Our Sovereign Lord the King will prosecute no further hereon." [9]

So, thanks to his phenomenal luck, Hancock once more escaped the
feeble clutches of the English law. But the good ship *Liberty* remained
in the more tenacious grip of His Majesty's navy and figured, according
to the belief of most historians, in another celebrated case three years
later. The consensus is that she was masquerading as the *Gaspee* when
the burning of that British revenue cutter by Providence patriots on
June 9, 1772, almost precipitated the Revolution prematurely.

Hancock now enjoyed the paradoxical position of having gained immeasurably by the loss of the *Liberty*. His popularity heretofore had

been based chiefly on kind-heartedness. Henceforth it was to have the additional prop of stout-heartedness. The masses were profoundly impressed by his willingness to risk his vast fortune for the sake of a principle. Even the poorest and lowliest, who were but little affected by the import duties on wine and other luxuries, felt that he was standing up for their self-respect as free men. They admired his courage and what they interpreted as his public-spiritedness, without analyzing his motives.

Such an analysis would have been futile, anyway; for students of John Hancock's character have been attempting it, without conclusive results, for nearly two centuries. It is doubtful that he himself knew, or even stopped to consider, what impelled him, in this first of many instances, to challenge the power of the great British Empire when submission or compromise must have seemed to be the more expedient course at the time. The taxation of which he complained was, to be sure, "burthensome" as compared with corresponding levies in England, although they also were high enough to cause evasion on a large scale. But the colonial imposts were by no means prohibitive to a merchant of Hancock's resources. He could have continued indefinitely to make a good living by minding his own business while Sam Adams and the rest of the Whigs were ranting about liberty; for the Lords of the Treasury, greedy, and shortsighted though they were, never would have allowed taxes to become confiscatory.

So there must have been a strain of idealism—or its bastard brother, pride—in his make-up, as is indicated in his letters of protest against the Stamp Act and other inequitable taxation. True, the expression of this feeling through the illegitimate medium of smuggling was far from being idealistic. But the loftiest ideals often are adulterated with the basest materialism. Who can say, in John's case any more than in his uncle's, whether he smuggled and defied the King's prosecutor primarily for profit or for principle?

In any event, he now was an American patriot by conviction as well as by persuasion. It was inevitable that, from this time forward, he would go along with the radical element in the Revolutionary movement. He would be guilty of temporary backsliding, but whenever the situation should call for a showdown he would be found holding the red cards.

· 4 ·

The Whig caucus struck while the iron in Hancock's soul was hot. In May the bosses had seen to it that the big four—Sam Adams, Otis, Cushing, and John—were reelected to the General Court. Now they engineered the calling of a special town meeting for June 14 at Faneuil Hall to protest against the threatening presence of the *Romney* in Boston Harbor. So large was the turnout that the conclave had to be adjourned to the Old South. A committee, including Hancock, was appointed to petition Governor Bernard on the same day for removal of the frigate. "Menaces have been thrown out, fit only for barbarians," reads the richly embroidered recital of grievances; they "threaten us with famine and desolation . . . and the town is . . . in a situation nearly such as if war was formally declared against it." [10]

It was decided to dress up the presentation of this appeal to His Excellency, like its language, in impressive fashion—quite likely at the suggestion of the style-conscious gentleman from Beacon Hill. The committee met at his mansion and drove out to Bernard's country home in Roxbury in eleven of Boston's twenty-two privately owned carriages, with John beside Otis in the leading vehicle. This probably was the "neat, roomy, genteel chariot," drawn by four high-stepping horses and driven by the imported coachman, that Thomas had ordered from London.

The diplomatic governor greeted his visitors cordially, treated them to wine, smoothed them down, and made most of them like the manner of his refusal, on the ground that he lacked authority, to grant their plea— "especially that part of them," according to his written account, "which had not been used to an interview with me." [11] Hancock would not have been overawed by such royal condescension, but he and the other leaders of the delegation must have realized the validity of their host's excuse; for such well informed Whigs would have been aware that Captain Corner was taking his orders directly from the commissioners.

While His Excellency was handling the Bostonians with kid gloves His Majesty, as represented by the revenue agents, decided to use the mailed fist. Shortly after the *Liberty* incident it had been reported that General Thomas Gage, commander in chief of the British forces in America from 1763 until after the outbreak of the Revolution, had received a request at his New York headquarters from the customs officers to send troops to the Massachusetts capital. At about the same time Bernard prorogued the General Court and forbade the holding of town meetings. In a letter vaguely dated June, Hancock thus described the citizens' reaction to these disturbing developments:

"We have now two regiments, part of a third, and a train of artillery in this town. . . . The report of the troops coming here alarmed the people much . . . but . . . the people are quiet and peaceable, and not the least disturbance has taken place. It is a great grief to this people that they are deprived of the benefits of a General Assembly." [12]

In July, Boston's leading merchant and others held a conference at the behest of the town and protested against the armed intervention, but to no avail. It was then that Sam Adams, says William V. Wells, his great-grandson and biographer, came "to the conclusion that American independence was a political and natural necessity" and admitted to a friend "that from this moment he struggled unremittingly for the accomplishment of that object." [13]

Since early spring Hancock had been fighting the war of nerves against Britain on two fronts—the one essentially political, the other mercantile. The nonimportation agreement of 1767 had broken down because no town except Boston had stuck to it. Thereafter John had resumed his old policy of ordering English goods on a lavish scale, and by the end of the current year he was to bring in more than £8,000 worth. But on August 1 a new, all-inclusive pact was signed, to apply to every article manufactured in England for export and to go into effect on January 1, 1769.

This boycott proved to be a disguised blessing to the man whom, one might suppose, it should have injured most. Although the value of his imports dropped to £2,000, Hancock was compelled by circumstances, against his poorer judgment, to redress the balance of trade in his favor through large exports of whale oil. He also took the opportunity to pay off his burdensome foreign debts. His domestic sales increased tremendously as customers rushed to his store to hoard against the impending shortage. A time was to come—in 1770—when his shelves would be virtually empty and the home market would be stagnant. But by then he would care little, for his main business would have become America's business.

· 5 ·

Rebuffed politically by the royal government, Hancock and Boston had started—in the spring of 1768—to retaliate socially. He had bought a concert hall and deeded it over to the town with the stipulation that no British revenue, army, or navy officer should be admitted. The civic fathers had accepted this lead in ostracism. They had voted, if the commissioners should be in the gubernatorial party, to exclude the governor and his staff from the annual May election day dinner, to which it was customary to invite all important provincial functionaries. Hutchinson reported, "An affront of the same nature was, at the motion of Mr. Hancock, . . . offered by a company of cadets." [14] This was the famous Independent Corps of which John would be put in command after the lieutenant governor became chief executive in 1772, when the Beacon Hill politico was powerful enough to require appeasing.

But Hancock was in no mood to be mollified now. During September, at a town meeting in Faneuil Hall, "where four hundred muskets lay upon the floor," he gladly accepted appointment to a committee formed to ask Bernard why troops had been dispatched to Boston and why more were expected; also to request him to reconvene the General Court.[15] Learning on the following day that the governor, a good politician, had nothing to say, the Liberty party decided to hold a convention of representatives from all sections of Massachusetts—in other words, to organize an assembly of their own that could act in place of the non-functioning, duly constituted one.

The first session on September 22 was attended by delegates from sixty towns. Thirty-six more and eight districts—virtually all the settlements in the province—had a voice in the proceedings before the six-day meeting ended. Boston's regularly qualified quartet of Hancock, Adams, Otis, and Cushing were on hand.

The only action taken was to draw up another fruitless petition for relief from taxation and from military coercion. It made a special point of denying any intention to usurp the legislative rights of the House. But this was a uniquely significant assemblage, nevertheless; for it was the initial attempt to organize the whole provincial population and to express their unified will in disregard of the royal prerogative to convene or dissolve the General Court.

It worried Bernard so much that he tried to split the Whigs. Realizing that the loss of Hancock's support would be an almost mortal blow to the "Faction" at this germinative period, he offered to slip him into a vacant seat in the Council. To the aristocrat of Beacon Hill the offer must have been very tempting, for he would have enjoyed mingling with the blue-bloods of His Majesty's government; but he spurned it.

As if to show the Crown's contempt for such gatherings as the September convention, a squadron of warships brought the long dreaded additional troops from Halifax on the day it closed. To the accompaniment of drums and fifes, with flags rippling belligerently in the breeze, two regiments of foot soldiers debarked on Long Wharf and marched to the Common, where they staged a clocklike drill designed to impress the gaping populace. The 1,000 men were equipped with sixteen rounds of ammunition and attired in full battle regalia. Their commander, Colonel William Dalrymple, bivouacked the Twenty-ninth Regiment in the great green quadrangle frowned upon by Hancock's formidable mansion and demanded quarters for the Fourteenth. But neither the Council nor the selectmen were sufficiently impressed by the demonstration. Only the compassion of the citizens for the Redcoats, shivering in the chill evening, induced the Sons of Liberty to admit them to Faneuil Hall.

When the Fifty-ninth Infantry and a battery of artillery joined the garrison a few days later the inhabitants repented of their humane attitude and became bitterly resentful—especially toward the governor for ordering the Town House thrown open for billeting. Hancock made their indignation articulate by getting up in meeting and denouncing the use of public buildings for such a purpose.

By this time the British government might well have taken cognizance of the colonists' increasing hostility, not only in Boston but throughout America. But the King's officers on the spot were no more aware than the King in his palace that armed rebellion was brewing. Hutchinson was above the average colonial official in intelligence and sensitiveness to currents of popular feeling; but even he indicated his conviction in a letter to London that there was no danger of revolution. He wrote:

"I cannot think that, in any colony, people of any consideration have ever been so mad as to think of revolt. Many of the common people have been in a frenzy and talked of dying in defense of their liberties and have spoke and printed what is highly criminal; and too many of rank above the vulgar, and some *in public posts,* have countenanced and encouraged them until they increased so much in their numbers and in their opinion of their importance as to submit to government no further than they thought proper." [16]

While this communication was in transit Sam Adams probably was in transports.

· 6 ·

Hutchinson must still have been thinking of the trouble caused by those "of rank above the vulgar" in positions of public trust when Hancock was elected speaker of the House, *pro tem,* on April 18, 1769. The lieutenant governor, in Bernard's temporary absence from the province, exercised a dubious right of veto. Dr. Joseph Warren, a Whig just as stanch as John but not so conspicuous, was then selected in his stead with the approval of Hutchinson.

But neither he nor any other power in the government could prevent

Boston from returning Hancock and his three running mates to office at the May election for representatives. As if in answer to the royal appointee's opposition to its idol, the town gave 500 of the 508 votes cast to each of the four perennial candidates. This combination was now almost impregnably intrenched in the favor of the caucus-controlled electorate.

The veterans took their seats on May 31, when Bernard called the General Court into session for the first time in a year—because he was compelled to do so by the Massachusetts charter, but also because he was dependent upon the Assembly for his salary and had not been paid since proroguing it.

The first business to come before the court was the removal of the troops from Boston. When Governor Bernard again disclaimed authority to do anything about it the legislative body refused to take action on any other measure—not even the appropriation of funds for billeting—until he should find the means to get rid of the hated soldiery. After waiting two weeks for the legislators to change their minds he acted in a way which formed a bone of contention until the Revolution: he adjourned the sitting to Cambridge.

Where the Assembly should meet had been a moot question throughout the eighteenth century. It now became a significant one because it involved the fundamental theory of the King's prerogative—that is, the assumed right to impose his will upon the colonists through the royal governors. In other words, one of the constitutional issues underlying the Revolutionary movement was at stake.

In the instance under discussion the reason for Bernard's decision to shift the General Court to the halls of Harvard College was to get it away from the inflammatory atmosphere of the provincial capital. But even councilors and representatives who were not in sympathy with the resistance to military pressure opposed the governor's decree on principle. Concerning this controversy Professor Leonard Woods Labaree, an authority on colonial government, writes: *

"The position taken by the general court in this contest marks the high point of colonial opposition to the prerogative. . . . The threat of revolution was important, but at least equally significant was a further point which Samuel Adams implied in his argument. Hitherto no one had ventured to deny the right of the king to instruct his governor within the limits of the constitution or to question the governor's duty to obey

* See *Royal Government in America* (Yale University Press, New Haven, 1930). Reprinted by permission.

such instructions. But Adams dared to enter upon this forbidden ground. Instructions which were injurious to the people were not binding, he said. . . . Therefore the governor must not be permitted to obey them. From this position the conclusion seems inescapable . . . that the assembly . . . must be the interpreters of such documents. . . . To have permitted such a privilege to the assembly would have meant that the British government had abandoned its fundamental claim to authority in America. . . . No more sweeping challenge than this was made to the system of royal government in the provinces before the actual expulsion of the governors upon the outbreak of the Revolution. And so, though the meeting-place of the assembly was not in itself a vital point in the colonial system, it gave rise to controversies which went to the heart of the provincial constitution." [17]

By the time of his adjournment order Bernard had wearied of squabbling with the incorrigible Massachusetts provincials over what seemed to him entirely unreasonable and dangerously radical demands. So he announced his intention of going to England on a short leave of absence and dumping the whole disgusting mess into the lap of the King. This, of course, was just what the nagging Whigs had been trying to bring about. On hearing of the governor's plans the General Court petitioned the Crown to make his sojourn at home permanent and at last caught the royal ear, for the governor never returned to America.

Carrying the sentiment of all Boston town with them, the Sons of Liberty sped Bernard on his way on August 1 with wild demonstrations of joy, ringing bells, waving flags, burning bonfires, and firing cannon— from Hancock's Wharf.

· 7 ·

The Sons flaunted their increasing power in the faces of the Crown officers two weeks later by turning out, 350 strong, for the annual ceremonies marking their birthday. After toasts had been drunk under the Liberty Tree in the morning 139 carriages were required to transport the celebrators to Robinson's Tavern in Dorchester. Hancock again headed the procession—a mile and a half long—with Otis bringing up the rear. Since Boston's private owners could not provide even one-sixth of the vehicles in line, the gospel of freedom from British "tyranny" must have been spreading extensively among the surrounding towns. And the seriousness of its apostles is implicit in John Adams' comment that not a single person was intoxicated.

In November, Hancock showed his earnest support of the doctrine of passive resistance by criticizing his London factors for a shipment of goods in disregard of the nonimportation agreement. He also announced that he was shipping back in his vessels, freight-free, not only his own consignment but those destined for other merchants, and that he even had offered to supply crates for the return of wares already unpacked by his competitors.[18]

Meanwhile he had been taking a more active part in promoting the "cause," too. In October he had visited New York and Philadelphia in the interest of intercolony union. He had called upon John Dickinson in the Quaker town to thank and to praise him for his resounding denunciation of the Townshend Acts in the "Farmer's Letters."

And so the old year waned as the Whigs kept their political fences in repair and as the Tories, represented by the King's officers, clung to the hope that the barriers to colonial cooperation would break down. But no sooner had 1770 dawned than Hutchinson upset the equilibrium once more by trying to suppress the merchants' meetings of protest against the revenue laws. In January he wrote to one of the mercantile leaders a sharp note insisting, in His Majesty's name, that these conferences be discontinued. Replying in behalf of his fellow businessmen, Hancock penned a letter which the acting governor deemed incriminating enough to preserve against a possible future trial for treason.

The rash young man from Beacon Hill may have realized that he had exceeded even the broad latitude of expression permitted the colonists by their rulers. In any event, he declined to serve on a committee formed at the urging of Sam Adams and William Molineux, a rabid Factionist, to lead a mass demonstration against Hutchinson because his sons, Thomas, Jr., and Elisha, had imported English products. Even when Otis and William Phillips reconsidered after having declined appointment, John Hancock continued to lie low. A crowd of two thousand stormed up to the acting governor's house and demanded that the goods be turned over to them. But Hutchinson faced them with a solemn warning that their ultimatum was illegal and induced them to disperse.

This first sign of backsliding in his invaluable protégé and the citizenry in general was a setback for Adams, but he could afford to smile wryly and to bide his time.

· 8 ·

Sam had not long to wait. On Monday March 5, the fateful Boston "Massacre" occurred.

Feeling between the British troops and the inhabitants had been running high. Heckling of the irritating Redcoats, or "lobsters," by the chip-on-shoulder water-front gang had led to several brawls with soldiers of the Twenty-ninth Regiment on the previous Friday.

On the night of the 5th, while the town snuggled restively under a blanket of snow, Captain John Goldfinch of the Fourteenth Regiment emerged from his company's barracks on Brattle Street, around the corner from the Town House, to check up on the main guard in King Street. As he entered that thoroughfare a tough little urchin employed by a barber to whom Goldfinch owed money pointed at him and broadcast the fact in loud, obscene language. The officer ignored him; but a sentry named Hugh Montgomery, stationed outside the near-by customhouse, stepped up and slapped the boy's face hard enough to knock him down. Immediately a crowd gathered, screaming that the lad was being murdered.

In the meantime about two hundred sinister-looking characters had been listening to a harangue by a tall gentleman in a red cloak and a white wig at the entrance of Faneuil Hall. This probably was Molineux. At the end of the speech they rushed to the scene. Almost simultaneously a third group in the neighborhood of the barracks joined the throng at the corner of King and the section of Long Lane known as Congress Street today.

It was now shortly before nine o'clock. Suddenly the bell in the Old South steeple started ringing furiously. Under the impression that there was a fire people poured out of their homes carrying buckets and swelled the large number surrounding Montgomery. The sentry was becoming panicky.

"If you come near me," he shouted, "I'll blow your brains out!"

"Fire and be damned!" retorted some one in the menacing multitude.

Montgomery rammed a charge into his musket. At this juncture Crispus Attucks, a massive mulatto, pushed forward. He was brandishing a club and leading a band of American sailors. Shaking the cudgel at the "lobster," he threatened to "have off one of his claws."

Thereupon the sentry yelled, "Turn out the main guard!" [19] At once, from the other side of the street, seven men came double-timing under Captain John Preston of the Twenty-ninth, officer of the day. Ordering his squad to load, he placed himself in front of them as a precaution against nervous triggers.

Captain Goldfinch and several of the cooler heads in the crowd tried to break up the altercation, but Attucks felled Montgomery with his weapon as the milling mob advanced toward the other Redcoats. During the ensuing scuffle between the mulatto and the sentry the throng pressed still closer to the corporal's guard.

In a few moments the command "Fire!" was heard. Subsequent testimony proved that Preston did not give it, but none of the witnesses would reveal who did.

Montgomery was the first to obey. He killed Attucks with two balls aimed point-blank at his chest. Three more civilians quickly dropped dead beside Crispus; another was mortally wounded; and six others were shot, but not fatally.

That was the Boston "Massacre."

Preston now got his charges under control and warded off a second volley. At the sound of the firing virtually all the British troops in Boston had run pellmell, with fixed bayonets, to the spot. Acting Governor Hutchinson rushed to the Town House and addressed the populace from the balcony. He denounced the King's men and the townsmen with equal severity. Both parties to the ominous incident, becoming afraid of the possible consequences, listened meekly to authority and then dispersed—the soldiers to their barracks and the citizens to their homes.

But the dire deed had been done. The witches' brew, agitated so patiently by Sam Adams, had boiled over at last.

· 9 ·

Whether Adams had a part in this ebullition of long strained feelings is unknown, but the circumstantial evidence points to the affirmative. John Adams, his second cousin but not a kindred soul, wrote insinuatingly of the events leading up to the tragedy:

"Endeavors had been systematically pursued for several months by certain busy characters to excite quarrels, rencounters, and combats . . . in the night between the inhabitants of the lower class and the soldiers and . . . to enkindle a mortal hatred between them. I suspected that this was the explosion which had been intentionally wrought up by designing men who knew what they were aiming at better than the instruments employed." [20]

Sam Adams unquestionably was one of the "designing men"—if not in this case, then in most similar instances—and had notified all the towns in the vicinity of Boston that, on the night of March 5, there might occur an incident which would require the assistance of liberty-loving citizens. He now tried to capitalize on what had happened. He called the British troops butchers and painted the bloodletting in lurid colors. But he overplayed the part of avenger. Months before the trial of the soldiers involved in the shooting, who were arrested on charges of murder but were acquitted in November chiefly as a result of John Adams' conscientious and honorable conduct of their defense, the affair boomeranged upon Sam. The Massacre helped the Whig cause materially but reacted just as considerably upon the party's most radical member. He was suspected of having deliberately encouraged bloodshed to effectuate his ruthless concept of patriotism.[21]

The testimony does not connect Hancock with this episode. He probably would have condemned in private whatever accessory role his patron may have played in it; for his humane nature would have revolted at the thought of sacrificing five lives, even on the altar of freedom, at this time.

But the humanitarian quickly reiterated in public his approval of the agitation which had eventuated in the bloody developments. On the day after the Massacre he agreed to head a committee chosen to demand that Hutchinson withdraw the troops. Adams also was a member; but the Faction apparently decided that, in view of the impression obtaining especially in government circles that his hands were stained, it would be advisable to have the ultimatum conveyed by clean ones. According to Hancock's reminiscences concerning these negotiations, the acting governor, when approached at his home, countered with a compromise proposal that only the Twenty-ninth Regiment should be pulled out. On being told then that ten thousand armed men were ready to enforce the people's mandate he tremblingly requested—and obtained—a few hours' grace in which to consider it. He finally consented to transfer all the forces to the Castle.[22]

Although Adams had done most of the talking, his protégé gained most of the prestige attached to this signal diplomatic triumph by reporting it to the town meeting, which waited at Old South until dark to hear the verdict. His announcement before nearly four thousand citizens "was received with a shout and clap of hands which made the meeting-house ring." [23]

But Hutchinson stalled at least six days; for on the 12th another committee, including Hancock, was authorized to ask Colonel Dalrymple for an explicit commitment as to when his superior's promise was to be performed. This brought almost immediate action.

The acting governor, however, was determined not to yield an inch more than he had to. Pursuant to Bernard's policy, he convened the General Court at Cambridge on March 15. Its Whig majority protested once more, but to no avail. This pattern of convoking and proroguing the

Assembly—on the Harvard campus during Hutchinson's tenure as chief magistrate and at Salem during that of Gage, his successor—was repeated with monotonous regularity and with equally inconclusive results until it faded into the fiery background of the Revolution.

· 10 ·

Ironically, on the very day of the Massacre Lord North, British Prime Minister and leader of the "King's Friends" party, had moved to rescind all provisions of the Townshend Acts except the duty on tea. That was to be retained to symbolize the right of Parliament to tax the colonists without their consent. The motion had passed.

Again one of Hancock's ships—the *Haley*, in command of his now favorite master, Captain Scott—brought the glad news to Boston on April 24. The good will redounding to her owner helped him to lead the ticket in the May election of representatives. But James Bowdoin, who was to become his only successful rival for the governorship of the Massachusetts Commonwealth, beat out Otis.

Two days later Hancock revealed that power and popularity were going to his head. Because an Otis supporter had had the temerity to assert that he was somewhat less than perfect he threatened to resign. He was dissuaded by that hardened campaigner Sam Adams, in a letter of the 11th:

"Your resolution yesterday to resign your seat gave me very great uneasiness. . . . You say you have been spoken ill of. What then? Can you think that, while you are a good man, . . . *all* will speak well of you? If you knew the person who has defamed you, nothing is more likely than that you would justly value yourself upon *that* man's censure as being the highest applause. Those who were fond of continuing Mr. Otis on the seat were . . . among your warmest friends. Will you, then, add to their disappointment by a resignation merely because one contemptible person, who perhaps was hired for the purpose, has *blessed* you with his *reviling*? Need I add more than to entreat it as a favor that you would alter your design?" [24]

Adams was to have more of such petulance from his temperamental henchman and was himself to be the target of a large share of it. And Sam was not always to be successful in pacifying him with common-sense arguments.

The combined pressure of business and politics, and the incidental travel, probably had something to do with Hancock's irascibility at this time. In June Palfrey, who now handled most of his mercantile transactions, wrote to London: "The removal of the General Court to Cambridge obliges Mr. Hancock to be often there. He has directed me . . . to acquaint you that he has chartered the ship *Pratt* for a voyage to South Carolina." [25]

Soon the rapidly burgeoning first citizen of Boston had two more responsibilities heaped upon him. In August he was chosen moderator of the town meeting, and in September, chairman of a society to promote arts, agriculture, manufactures, and commerce throughout the province.

Another worry on Hancock's mind was the blunting of the Whigs' sharpest weapon for cutting down taxation. He and Adams admitted early in the winter that nonimportation was being rendered ineffectual by a few merchants who were welshing on the agreement. In December, John wrote to Haley: "In the matter of non-importation I . . . have been most fully, freely, and cruelly used." [26]

Meanwhile the firm of Blanchard & Hancock had gone into bankruptcy; and Elizabeth Lowell, wife of its junior partner, Ebenezer, had become pregnant. His brother, of course, had had to bail him out of his financial difficulties. Finally, in January, 1771, John felt that his hapless relative could emerge into the light of day without falling into the clutches of the sheriff and so apprised him in a stone-throwing letter from the glass House of Hancock:

"Your affairs are now brought to such a close that you are at liberty to come abroad and keep abroad. You will deliver me all the notes, etc. Those at Providence and in the country it will be best you ride after and collect as soon as possible. . . . And one word more: as you are now coming out afresh into life, my serious advice to you is that you would calmly reflect on your former imprudencies and resolve to quit yourself like a man. . . . Great . . . is my burthen and loss in these matters of yours. I shall never throw it in your teeth but always conduct towards you as a brother; but the consideration of that near connection must, by no means, prevent your looking out for yourself. You must expect to undergo some hardships, and it will be for the best. But always remember that by diligence and industry and good conduct a man will rub through this world with comfort; but, above all, . . . be steadfast and unmoveable, always abounding in the work of the Lord; and then you may be assured that your labors shall not be in vain for time and eternity." [27]

Not long after giving this fraternal advice John ordered a consignment of goods from London "for my brother, whom I am determined to establish in business again in hopes he may better succeed, and over whom

I shall be careful to keep a watchful eye." [28] Thus did the leading altruist
of eighteenth century New England almost invariably act with greater
credit to his heart than to his head.

· 11 ·

Hancock could not have had much time to "keep a watchful eye" on
Ebenezer, for he soon was importing on his erstwhile grandiose scale
and was more deeply involved in politics than ever.

In March, Hutchinson was appointed governor in accordance with
royal instructions which stipulated that his salary should be paid by the
Crown, thus releasing the legislature's strongest hold upon him. But
this did not relieve the steadily mounting pressure being exerted for
approval of Hancock as a councilor. He had been chosen for this post
shortly after being reelected to the General Court in May with his former
trio of colleagues, Adams, Cushing, and Otis.

During April the new chief executive had written to England that
John Hancock was one of the few political figures of consequence in
Massachusetts who still bucked him. [29] Now he decided it would be smart
to make a deal with the party of this disturbingly influential citizen,
and three weeks after the election he reported to John Pownall—ironically, in view of the addressee's fraternal connection with Thomas Hancock's old friend:

"I wished to avoid negatives and offered privately before the choice,
if they would bring in the secretary,* to take Hancock [as councilor]
with him; but they could not be prevailed upon, and I thought it would
be giving them too much to take him without." [30]

The governor's eyes were opened still wider, within a few days, to
the potency of the opposition personified by the Beacon Hill aristocrat,
and he imagined that he descried a rift between the patriot in purple
and the drab proletarian, for on June 5 he confided to another London
correspondent:

"I was much pressed by many persons well affected in general to
consent to the election of Mr. Hancock (his connections being large),
which are strongly prejudiced against me for the frequent refusals to
accept of him in office. They assured me he wished to be separated from
Mr. Adams, . . . an incendiary equal to any at present in London; and,
if I would admit him to the Council, they had no doubt there could
be an end to the influence he has by means of his property in the town

* Thomas Flucker.

of Boston. As there had been no advances on his part, I could not think
it proper for me to follow their advice. I have now reason to think that,
before another election, he will alter his conduct so as to justify my
acceptance of him, which certainly will take off that sourness of temper
from many people which his negatives occasion; and . . . I believe I
shall accept of him. Having from year to year the general vote both of
Council and House, the constant refusal is more disagreeable to the
people." [31]

Hutchinson quoted Hancock on another occasion as expressing "dissatisfaction with the party and with their extending their designs further
than appeared to him warrantable," [32] which he took to indicate that
the inborn conservatism of the Beacon Hill patrician was reasserting
itself.

The governor had been prepared to believe that Hancock was ready
to bolt his party by the debate in the House of Representatives over the
locale of the General Court immediately after it reconvened in May
at Cambridge. Hancock had sided with the Crown and had carried
a majority of the House with him. So Hutchinson made overtures to
his seemingly most vulnerable, if not most dangerous, opponent soon
afterward. He thus recounts their interview, with its surprise ending:

"The Governor very willingly signified to him that the repeated
denials of consent to his election into public offices had not proceeded
from any degree of ill-will towards him or from any exception to his
general character, but altogether from the part which he had taken in
opposition to that authority which the Governor . . . was bound to
support; and that, upon a change of sentiments in Mr. Hancock, everything past would be entirely forgotten and it would be a pleasure to the
Governor to consent to his election to the Council. . . . This he declared
to be neither his object nor inclination; but he intended to quit all
active concern in public affairs and to attend to his private business,
which . . . had been too much neglected. The disunion, however, which
lasted several months, checked the progress of measures in opposition
to government." [33]

Hancock evidently was sincere in his expressed intention to retire
from public life, for as late as October he wrote to Haley & Hopkins
that illness since April had prevented his devoting any time to commercial interests, and that he expected to take another trip to London
in June, 1772.[34] But a sudden improvement in health in November
caused him to change his mind and to tell his agents joyfully: "I am so

surprisingly recovered that I have plunged myself into the business of life again." [35]

As for breaking with the Faction, he apparently had been bluffing all along. He seems merely to have been playing possum with his party to squelch an intolerable whispering campaign to the effect that he was Adams' tool. By December he had gone so far as to declare, according to Hutchinson, that he would "never again connect himself with the Adamses." [36] But the governor's inference that the Whigs were being weakened by division was entirely too sanguine. They were temporarily enfeebled—and the whole Revolutionary movement might have collapsed except for the assiduous inspirational letter writing of Adams and Major Joseph Hawley—but only by the twelve British warships that had been casting their awesome shadows upon the waters of Boston Harbor since August.

· 12 ·

At the end of January, 1772, Governor Hutchinson, after approving the choice of Hancock as speaker *pro tem,* fancied that he saw a definite breach in the heretofore solid ranks of the Whigs. He thus described his hallucination:

"Doctor Church . . . is now on the side of government. Hancock has not been with their club for two months past and seems to have a new set of acquaintance. . . . His [defection?] will be a great loss to them, as they support themselves with his money." [37]

The governor sought to exploit a gilt-edged opportunity by issuing a commission on April 1:

"His Excellency, the Captain-General, has been pleased to commission John Hancock, Esq., to be Captain of the Company of Cadets with the rank of Colonel." [38]

The attempt failed, according to Sam Adams, because it was a gesture under duress. Writing to Arthur Lee, London agent for Massachusetts, Adams thus outlined the circumstances:

"But it should be known it is not in the power of the Governor to give a commission for that company to whom he pleases, as their officers are chosen by themselves. Mr. Hancock was elected by an unanimous vote; and a reluctance at the idea of giving offense to an hundred gentlemen might very well account for the Governor giving the commission to Mr. H., without taking into consideration that most powerful of all other motives, *an instruction,* especially at a time when he vainly hoped he should gain him over." [39]

This tin-soldier status and the trappings that went with it must have been unalloyed bliss to John. One can readily picture him preening and strutting in his resplendent regimentals. Soon after the glory was thrust upon him he inserted this advertisement in a newspaper:

"Wanted. Immediately—For His Excellency's Company of Cadets. Two fifers that understand playing. Those that are masters of music and are inclined to engage with the Company are desired to apply to Col. John Hancock." [40]

Although the cadets, as the governor's honor guard, presumably were entitled to be equipped by the province, Hancock supplied his men with uniforms and ordnance at his own expense. He probably had a twofold purpose: to deck them out in accordance with his gorgeous fancy and to strengthen their allegiance to him. The second object proved to be especially well conceived.

The fallacy of Hutchinson's belief that the split in the Liberty party was widening into an unbridgeable gap became apparent to almost everybody else on election day, May 27. Just as if nothing had happened, John Hancock was reelected a representative, with Sam Adams as his running mate, on a ticket that also included Cushing and Phillips; and there was a genuine reconciliation after the returns came in. The successful silk-stocking candidate signalized it a few days later by commissioning Copley to paint companion portraits of Adams and himself, to be hung in his mansion.

Adams corroborated the ending of the three-year estrangement in a letter to Lee. He wrote that Hancock had not deserted the cause of liberty but had thumbed his nose at Hutchinson by declining the post of councilor, for which he again had been chosen—this time with the governor's ratification. He continued:

"Lord Hillsborough . . . wrote to the Governor that he had it in command from the *highest authority* to enjoin him to promote Mr. H. upon every occasion. Accordingly, . . . the latter . . . fawned and flattered one of the *heads of the faction* and at length approved of him when he was again chosen . . . a Councillor the last May. . . . But he had spirit enough to refuse a seat at the board and continue a member of the House, where he has . . . joined with the friends of the Constitution in opposition to the measures of a corrupt administration." [41]

Two weeks after the election, however, Hutchinson had written to Hillsborough, the Secretary of State for the Colonies: "You see, I accepted Hancock, who has, for many months, gone as far with the party as has been necessary to prevent a total breach, and no further; and his refusal to accept the place was not from any resentment for former negatives but from an apprehension that he should show to the people he had not been seeking after it. The measure will have good consequences and end in wholly detaching him from them or lessening his importance if he should put himself into their hands again." [42]

Since His Excellency Thomas Hutchinson lived up to the literal connotation of the title more closely than most of the men who held it in pre-Revolutionary America, the obtuseness of the royal governors in general to colonial psychology is painfully obvious.

VII

TEA AND DOUBTS ARE LIQUIDATED

JOHN HANCOCK was not content to be a political wheelhorse. Although willing to pull more than his share of the load, he refused to drag the Whig bandwagon in drudging obscurity back near the whiffletree. He insisted on being one of the lead team, so that his efforts would be noticed and applauded. If denied this privilege he would kick over the traces.

The desire to have his way and to bask in the limelight of the Revolutionary movement was the basic cause of almost all of John's feuds with Sam Adams and other Liberty party leaders. These gentlemen usually were glad to have him front for them, but they occasionally objected on the ground of inexpediency. Then he would sulk. His attitude was in sharp contrast to that of Adams, who was among the most selfless and self-effacing of the founding fathers. This humble philosophy may have been due in part to the hard blows rained upon him by the capricious jade, Fortune, who was as cruel to him as she was kind to John.

Adams, the elder by fifteen years, had experienced a fate diametrically opposite Hancock's. Born amid riches in 1722, he had been plunged into near-poverty at an early age. When he had come upon the scene his father, Deacon Samuel Adams, was a wealthy merchant, owner of a wharf, and proprietor of a brewery in Boston. But while his boy was enjoying the luxurious life of a "fifth placer" at Harvard the deacon met with a severe setback in the Land Bank collapse. The son was compelled to earn the rest of his tuition for a Master's degree as a student waiter.

On completing his studies he was forced into trade to help support his family. He first tried clerking but was soon discharged for spending more time putting two and two together in politics than in the counting-room. With the idea of setting up in business for himself, he then borrowed 1,000 of the precious pounds salvaged by Deacon Adams from the wreck of his banking venture. But he betrayed almost immediately the lack of monetary sense that was to get him into trouble repeatedly throughout his existence by loaning the loan to a friend, who never repaid it. As a last resort the senior Adams took his irresponsible offspring into the brewery, where it would be easier to keep an eye on him. This arrangement had worked out fairly well until the old man's death, when Sam let the enterprise go to pot as fast as the beer went down the throats of the customers—while he resumed his political pursuit.

Even in his favorite vocation young Adams was no world beater at the start. He was thirty-one before being elected to his first public office, town "scavenger"—equivalent to the modern street cleaner—and was in his forties when he became tax collector, with the almost disastrous results previously noted.

Sam already looked, as well as acted, the part of an aging failure. His hair was gray, his attire slovenly, and his hands and voice trembled with palsy.

But there was still one redeeming feature—his face. It radiated a luminous spirit and dauntless will which made his associates forget the pathetic physical figure. It reflected the conviction that freedom was not just an ideal to be aspired to but a Holy Grail to be pursued to the ends of the earth.

Unlike Hancock, however, Sam did not fancy himself a crusading knight whose mission it was to lead the hosts of righteousness into battle. He probably would have eschewed the role even if he had been fitted for it. He had the humility and sagacity of Abraham Lincoln, combined with the ruthlessness and amorality of John Brown. He preferred to remain in the background and manipulate the levers that controlled the Whig machine while Hancock, John Adams, James Otis, Ben Franklin, Patrick Henry, and the rest of the glamorous personages of eighteenth century America ostensibly ran it.

No more sincere patriot ever lived than Sam Adams. The purity of his motives was unquestioned. But the unscrupulousness of his methods was notorious. With a fanatic's zeal and bigotry he could justify the most dishonorable means by the glorious end—liberty. He idealized the cause with an almost religious fervor and placed it on a plane—in his own mind—entirely too high for the common man to comprehend. But he was practical enough to present it in workaday terms which the most hardheaded materialist could grasp and eventually accept as pragmatically desirable. He was almost inhumanly patient, too. He could wait for the lagging political thought of the period to catch up with him. When it did he acted—decisively and irrevocably.

· 2 ·

Hancock had no such power of sufferance. He craved constant action, although it was not always as drastic as Adams advocated. Probably that is why, throughout most of 1772 and the first half of 1773, when the pace of the Revolutionary movement slackened almost to a standstill, he sought outlets for his surplus energy in petty politics and public welfare activities. He seems to have lost considerable interest in his private business as it, too, sank into the doldrums under the weight of the increasingly heavy restrictions on overseas trade.

Months before playing hide-and-seek with Hutchinson in connection with the Council election and ratification the benefactor of Beacon Hill had added to his popular following by building a bandstand on the Common, by furnishing musicians for concerts on pleasant afternoons, and by planting a row of lime trees along the side of the huge recreation park nearest the mansion. He thus supplemented the civic improvements, including enclosure of the area with a fence and laying-out of additional walks, which the town had undertaken the year before.

He also had presented a fire engine to Boston, thereby increasing the number to the still inadequate total of seven. Either in reciprocation for his generosity or in accordance with the gift provisions, the community had decreed that the apparatus—bearing his name—should be placed near his wharf and that, whenever any of his buildings was ablaze, he should have prior use of it.

Still earlier in 1772 Hancock had become embroiled in his first fight with James Bowdoin—who would later be a political opponent of considerable stature. In fact, the animosity underlying the competition between the two politicians—a conflict which was to result in a temporary triumph for Bowdoin in 1786—probably had its origin in a contest over the privilege of making possible the construction of a new Brattle Street Church.

In a letter of February 6 John Hancock had offered to contribute handsomely to such a project, on condition that the building be erected on the site of the old meetinghouse which he and his foster family had long attended. On March 3 Bowdoin had notified the committee in charge that he would like to donate a piece of land for the purpose. Even though, in the opinion of the majority, this was the more desirable location, Hancock had had his way as usual by virtue of his influence with Dr. Cooper's congregation and the proffer of £1,000—five times as much as his rival had pledged—with which to furnish the house of worship. John eventually raised the amount to £7,500, with the characteristic reservation that he be allowed to dispose of the sum as he wished; to direct the installation of a mahogany pulpit, a deacons' seat, and a communion table; and to provide for the accommodation of poor widows "who are reputable persons." [1] He tossed in a bell for good measure.

While thus helping to dispel the darkness of men's souls, like his father and grandfather before him, Boston's benevolent dictator set about lighting up their terrestrial paths. It was high time, too; for the streets in the capital had been black at night since its settlement. In March he was appointed chairman of a committee "to consider of the expediency of fixing lamps in this town." [2] He and his colleagues must have canvassed the situation exhaustively, for it was a year later that they reached the momentous decision to import three hundred of the latest model—white globes—from England. Another twelvemonth elapsed before the illumination system went into effect. After miraculously surviving the wreck of one of the ships which occasioned the Boston Tea Party the lights were first used on the evening of March 2, 1774, and burned "tolerable well," according to Diarist Rowe.[3]

Hancock could not long confine his ambition to such relatively picayune projects. So when Hutchinson once more prorogued the General Court for recalcitrance on July 14, 1772, he jumped back into the lists with the governor. But he broke another lance with Sam Adams before turning his weapon against the King's officer.

"Let every town assemble," Adams wrote in the Boston Gazette at the beginning of October. "Let associations and combinations be everywhere set up to consult and recover our just rights." [4]

This was the genesis of the consummate rabble rouser's long pondered plan to unite America in opposition to Britain by means of his committees of correspondence, which constituted one of the most significant schemes of the pre-Revolutionary period. But Hancock, Cushing, Phillips, and the other comparatively conservative Whigs suffered a recurrence of the jitters when they heard of this treason-bordering proposal, and tried to induce the citizens to vote it down. When Sam attempted to outwit these backsliders at a town meeting by engineering their appointment to a committee to circularize the rest of the colonies in the interest of his unification idea, they refused to serve. He carried his point, however, with Otis acting as chairman and with the equally bold

spirits Dr. Warren and Dr. Church (who was not yet "on the side of
government," as Hutchinson had too optimistically assumed) in enthusiastic support.

The movement spread rapidly and spectacularly throughout the colonial councils. It brought about similar organizations in every town of any
consequence within the colony and laid a foundation of union that was
not to be shaken even by the stresses of a disheartening war.

So favorable was the reaction of the masses in the metropolis that
Hancock and his cohorts realized they were barking up the wrong
Liberty Tree. That, of course, would never do for the popularity hound,
who must always run with the pack.

In January, 1773, Governor Hutchinson, alarmed by the success of
the committees of correspondence and probably fancying that he perceived a new glimmer of dissension within the Faction as a result of
Hancock's brief opposition to its controlling clique, convened the Assembly for the first time in six months to deliver a speech on the theoreti-
cal power of Parliament. But at the May election the Liberty party
disillusioned him once more by putting Hancock and two of the other
ex-dissenters, Cushing and Phillips, on its ticket of delegates with Adams.
By polling every vote cast, the four candidates showed the governor that
his words had made no impression upon the people.

· 3 ·

During the three years intervening since the aftermath of the Boston
Massacre the shining light of Beacon Hill had been hidden under a
bushel of routine political pursuits. Except for tantalizing Hutchinson
and annoying Adams, he had had no major opportunity to attract attention. And even those flashes, emitted in the council chambers, had not
reached the masses. But now the great luminosity was to dazzle the
multitude again.

Ben Franklin set the stage for the beam to play upon. Then in London,
Franklin was deputy postmaster general for the colonies and at the
same time special advocate of more equitable treatment for them. A
person whose name he never revealed had given him a packet of letters
urging that more repressive measures be taken against the colonists. This
correspondence had been penned to English friends by Hutchinson and
Oliver before they became governor and lieutenant governor, and by
Customs Commissioner Charles Paxton, John Rowe, and other Loyalists.
Franklin sent the letters to Cushing, speaker of the Massachusetts House

of Representatives, enjoining him to show them only to the members of the committee of correspondence and a few other discreet gentlemen. He specified, too, that they were not to be printed or copied.

These epistles were not nearly so denunciatory or defamatory as the writings of the Sons of Liberty. In them Hutchinson asserted that the liberties usurped by the colonials should be curtailed, Oliver declared that the "incendiaries" should be dealt with, Paxton advocated dispatching two or three regiments to Boston; but Sam Adams seized upon these temperate statements to prod the conservatives into action close to his heart's desire.

What better man, he thought, than John Hancock, with his commanding presence, moving eloquence, and flair for the spectacular, could there be to dramatize the situation? So John on May 31, four days after being elected a councilor and again declining the post, arose majestically in the Assembly and announced that a momentous revelation would be made within forty-eight hours. Then on June 2, to render the occasion still more portentous, Sam Adams had the galleries cleared before the mysterious missives were revealed.

Sam then read them. When he had finished, John Hancock moved, and it was voted, that the writers were guilty of designing "to overthrow the government and to introduce arbitrary power into the Province." [5]

But Adams was not satisfied to let the affair die in the obscurity of the legislative hall. The great propagandist naturally took every advantage of this grand opportunity to embitter the people against Hutchinson and the other Crown sympathizers. He publicly circumvented the enjoinder against printing and copying by having Hancock tell the General Court that what appeared to be duplicates of letters addressed by the governor to the late Thomas Whately, former Tory member of Parliament, had been put into his hands by "somebody in the Common." [6] Since Franklin had forwarded only the original manuscripts, it must have been obvious to every one in the House that Sam already had broken faith by having copies made. But he induced another henchman to paint a legitimate face on the proceeding by moving that Hancock's "find" be compared with the communications in Cushing's possession and that, if identity should be established, the clerk (who, most conveniently, was Sam himself) should have the transcripts published, on the ground that the subject matter no longer would be private. The question was put and "proved" in the affirmative.

Needless to say, Adams followed the self-directed instructions with alacrity and on a wholesale scale. On June 16 he brought enough replicas, in pamphlet form, into the Assembly chamber for every legislator, and soon he broadcast hundreds more among the towns in the province.

The epistolary missiles with which Sam Adams hoped to wound the feelings of the colonists in general so deeply as to make them fighting-mad missed fire. But part of the barrage found its mark in the breasts of Hutchinson and Oliver, neither of whom ever recovered. Followed up by a petition (of Sam's authorship) to the King for their removal, the underhanded attack brought the governor's recall in favor of General Gage the next spring and probably hastened the death of the lieutenant governor about the same time. And, of course, Hancock scored another big hit with the masses, who credited him with noble intentions and true-blue patriotism.

One might suppose that he would feel embarrassed at leading the Independent Corps of Cadets in the annual review on the Common in honor of the King's birthday on June 4, during an interval in his assault upon the Crown officers and other supporters in the General Court. But straddling the fence fazed John Hancock no more than straddling his horse when the enraptured gaze of the populace was focused on him—especially since, as Rowe records: "Such a . . . multitude of . . . spectators I never saw before." [7] The colonel nonchalantly bestrode his charger not only on the thirty-fifth anniversary of His Majesty's coming into the world but also on the twelfth of his official accession to the throne on September 22.

· 4 ·

For some time Hancock had been a straddler on the politico-economic issue of nonimportation, too. He had been more and more "disposed to acquiesce" in the decision of most Boston merchants to drop their boycott of English goods. His apostasy was due partly to the suspicion that the Whigs were making a sacrificial goat of him and partly to his still dominant conviction that moderation was the wiser course for the resistance movement. So he had been bringing in tea, for which the people had developed an abnormal thirst simply because it had been denied them. But his withdrawal from open opposition to the British trade policy did not mean that he was cooperating with the government. He was continuing to help nullify its program surreptitiously by smuggling.

In September, 1773, Commissioner Hallowell reported to John

Pownall, now Undersecretary of State for the Colonies, that "into this port only there has been imported 1953 whole, and 106 half-, and seven quarter-chests of tea," and that "300 whole and fifty-five half-chests came in vessels belonging to Mr. Hancock, the patriot." [8]

Hancock could have found justification for evading the law (if his tough conscience had needed it) in the Tea Act passed during the early part of the year. It allowed the East India Company to sell tea to the colonists through agents of its own choosing without paying export duty. This would enable the huge corporation to dump the beverage upon America at greatly reduced prices and to drive importers like John out of the market, regardless of their success in eluding the customs barriers. The New England merchants were particularly incensed by the inclusion of Hutchinson's relatives and henchmen among the consignees.

To cope with this situation the Sons of Liberty summoned all "freemen" to assemble under the Liberty Tree on November 3. More than five hundred showed up—but not one of the East India factors. Thereupon it was resolved, in conformity with similar action taken by Philadelphia on October 8, that no tea should be landed. Furthermore, a committee was formed, with Molineux as chairman but with Sam Adams as the brains, to demand that Richard Clarke & Sons, the principal agents, resign. When Parliament had opened the way for the British concern to flood the province Adams immediately had sensed an excellent chance to win over the conservative merchants who had been left cold by the Tory letters. He also had come to the conclusion that the underlying purpose of this *carte blanche* legislation, designed ostensibly to help the company out of financial difficulties, was to bring about a showdown on the principle, embodied in the Declaratory Act, that the Crown had the right to tax the colonists without their consent. This issue, he felt, was the most important raised forcibly to date.

Accompanied by a large crowd of spectators, the Sons' representatives descended upon the Clarke store at the foot of King Street. The proprietor, Hutchinson's nephew, refused to surrender his agency and thereby gave the delegation—as Rowe phrases it—"much displeasure."

At a town meeting two days later Hancock was chosen to head another committee, with instructions to issue the same order to the governor's sons. Apparently it did not occur to him or the other violators of the trade laws that this was a case of the teapot calling the teakettle black. But before this ultimatum could be presented letters were received from all the East India factors saying that, because of prior obligations connected with five shiploads of tea already en route to Boston, they could not bow to the will of the people. These missives were voted to be "daringly affrontive." [9]

The "will" of the people, who in reality looked forward to lapping up the popular drink at half the price it brought in England, was dictated as usual by the Whigs. And such was their power that within two weeks they had brewed much hatred for the exporting trust. A mob attacked the Clarke home and smashed its windows. Next morning, the 18th, a second town meeting, with Hancock presiding, was called supposedly to deplore this violence but actually to discuss the strategy by which the impending torrent of tea was to be dammed.

For ten days the agents frantically petitioned the governor and the Council for protection against their high-handed adversaries. Just as feverishly these officials conferred on what should be done—without arriving at any conclusion. Finally, on the 29th, the Liberty boys again took matters into their own hands and plastered the town with hysterical posters reading:

"Friends, Brethren, Countrymen! That worst of plagues, the detestable tea shipped for this port by the East India Company, is now arrived in this harbor. The hour of destruction or manly opposition to the machinations of tyranny stares you in the face. Every friend to his country, to himself and posterity, is now called upon to meet at Faneuil Hall at 9 o'clock this day (at which time the bells will begin to ring) to make a united and successful resistance to this last, worst, and most destructive measure of administration." [10]

Hancock, still keeping one leg over the fence dividing the Loyalists from the rebels, declined to take the chair at this meeting. Jonathan Williams, nephew of Franklin, was chosen.

"A more determined spirit," Governor Hutchinson states, "was conspicuous in this body than in any of the former assemblies of the people." And he points out that the lower classes were as well represented as the upper, and that the gathering was a Boston town meeting in form only, for it was thrown open to the inhabitants of all the other settlements in the province.[11]

Sam Adams put the pregnant question as to whether the 114 chests of tea which had arrived in the *Dartmouth* on the previous day should be sent back as a challenge to the royal prerogative. Hancock must have laughed up his ruffled sleeve as he contemplated that the owner of the vessel was Francis Rotch, brother of his old archenemy William Rotch.

Before action was taken on the proposal it became apparent the hall was so crowded that business could not be conducted satisfactorily. So it was decided to adjourn and reassemble in a few hours at the Old South.

· 5 ·

At the afternoon session, which was attended by upwards of twenty-five hundred, Adams' motion was amended to include a provision that no duty should be paid on the tea to be returned to England. When it had been passed without a dissenting voice Dr. Thomas Young, one of the more rabid Whigs, issued the first invitation to the Boston Tea Party by declaring that the *Dartmouth's* cargo should be thrown overboard. But after another short adjournment cooler heads prevailed and carried a resolution that Rotch should be required to ship it back without unloading it. This measure was adopted over the vehement protests of that gentleman, who had belatedly appeared on the scene. It was also voted to set a watch on the wharf to see that the contents were not landed during the night.

Placing both feet on the Whig side of the fence once more and donning his uniform, Hancock immediately leaped into the saddle. Four days later the commandant of the Sixty-fourth Regiment of Redcoats stationed at the Castle reported to Lord Dartmouth, who had succeeded Hillsborough as Secretary of State for the Colonies, that the colonel of cadets was mounting guard with his men over the two tea ships then in port.[12]

The *Eleanor* had docked on December 2, and the *Beaver* was to drop anchor in Nantasket Road, "with the smallpox and part of the tea," according to Rowe's quaint juxtaposition, on the 18th.[13] Each carried exactly the same quantity of inflammatory leaves as the *Dartmouth*. The *William*, another vessel in this historic flotilla, foundered on a reef off Cape Cod with fifty-eight chests in its hold and the three hundred globes which Hancock and his lamp committee had ordered from London.

In inducing his Independent Corps to live up to their name by siding against Hutchinson, the unpredictable patriot of Beacon Hill gave his military superior a direct slap in the face. And its sting must have been rendered sharper by the governor's recollection that Hancock had refused to hold the cadets in readiness to defend the Crown in case of emergency when so ordered on November 12.

When the meeting at the Old South was resumed on the morning of the 30th Sheriff Stephen Greenleaf read a proclamation from the governor demanding that the conclave disperse. The words were greeted with "a loud and very general hiss, which continued during the stay of the sheriff and accompanied him in his retreat." [14]

Meanwhile the Loyalist Rowe, who was not mad at anybody, had inadvertently become involved in the controversy through business associations with James Bruce, master of the *Eleanor*. Of the leaders of the assemblage at the Old South, he writes in his diary: "I told them that I had purchased a cargo for Captain Bruce's ship . . . and that Captain Bruce . . . would apply to the Body and that I would endeavor to prevail on him to act with reason . . . and that I was very sorry he had any tea on board." Adams and his cohorts evidently had taken advantage of the diarist's meekness to place him in a compromising position, for he adds: "I was chose a committeeman much against my will but I dare not say a word. . . . After dinner, I was sent for by the Body. . . . This was at the motion of Mr. Hancock. I wish he had omitted it." [15]

Before the end of this eventful day the owners of the *Eleanor*, the *Beaver*, and the *William*, as well as the East India factors, were sternly warned to comply with the action taken in the case of the *Dartmouth*; all citizens were ordered to cease importation of the obnoxious beverage; a committee including Adams, Hancock, and the squirming Rowe was named to report this procedure to every part of Massachusetts, to New York, Philadelphia, and London. In a letter of December 1 John Andrews told his brother-in-law in Philadelphia that these goings-on amounted to considerably more than a tempest in a teapot. Hancock's man Palfrey, he wrote, "sets off express for New York and Philadelphia at 5 o'clock tomorrow morning to communicate the transactions of this town respecting the tea. It's not only the town but the country are unanimous against the landing it. . . . 'Twould puzzle any person to purchase a pair of p——ls in town, as they are all bought up with a full determination to repel force by force." [16]

Although greatly alarmed, Governor Hutchinson derived consolation from imagining that Hancock was hanging himself. He must have smacked his lips as he wrote to England two days later:

"Hancock, who had been moderator of the first meeting, took care to keep clear of this. . . . Hancock, notwithstanding, has exposed himself by his unguarded speeches more than ever before. . . . It is in everybody's mouth that Hancock said at the close of the meeting he would be willing to spend his fortune and life itself in so good a cause." [17]

· 6 ·

The Whigs concentrated on Rotch, probably because he owned the first tea ship to arrive and because he was most available, in attempting to enforce their dictum on consignments. Their committee of correspondence instructed him to dispatch the *Dartmouth* back to England at once, but he pleaded inability to obtain clearance. Thereupon another town meeting demanded the necessary papers from the customs but was refused. Then the "Body" tried to procure from the naval office a certificate that would enable the vessel to pass the Castle but failed. Finally Rotch was compelled to apply to Hutchinson in person for a sailing permit but again was turned down. In the evening of the day on which he visited the governor—the 16th—the harassed merchant announced his failure to a meeting which had been waiting at the Old South since morning to hear the verdict.

"Immediately thereupon," Hutchinson informed Lord Dartmouth, "numbers of the people cried out, 'A mob, a mob!'; left the house; repaired to the wharves, where three vessels lay aground, having on board 340 chests of tea, and in two hours' time it was wholly destroyed." [18]

Those are the unadorned facts of the Boston Tea Party. But the affair was much more picturesque—and portentous—than the governor's official report would indicate.

The generally accepted account is that of another contemporary, George Robert Twelvetrees Hewes. But this person's testimony is almost as incredible as his name. He was a scarcely literate jack-of-all-trades who worked at glue making, tanning, soap boiling, and tallow chandlery. He seems always to have been on hand when excitement was afoot. If he had written what he witnessed at the time it occurred, his words would carry more weight. But his observations have descended to posterity only through the pen of Benjamin B. Thatcher, who took them down from dictation in 1835, when Hewes was ninety-three years old. So they must be heavily discounted.

It is quite likely that Moderator Sam Adams gave the signal for the start of the Tea Party by declaring (according to an undocumented source) just before he adjourned the fateful assemblage: "This meeting can do nothing more to save the country." [19] It is also entirely plausible that Hancock previously should have made a speech in which (according to Hewes) he insisted, "The matter must be settled before 12 o'clock" that night, and should have shouted as the crowd rushed out of the building, "Let every man do what is right in his own eyes!" [20]

But Andrews' version of what followed, in a letter of the 18th to Philadelphia, appears to be much more reliable than Hewes'. With an imperturbability conducive to the truth he wrote:

"However precarious our situation may be, yet such is the calm composure of the people that a stranger would hardly think that £10,000 sterling of the East India Company's tea was destroyed the night . . . before last. . . . The house was so crowded that I could get no farther than the porch, when I found the moderator was just declaring the meeting to be dissolved, which caused another general shout, outdoors and in, and three cheers. . . . For my part, I went contentedly home and finished my tea but was soon informed what was going forward; but, still not crediting it without ocular demonstration, I went and was satisfied. They mustered, I'm told, upon Fort Hill to the number of about 200 and proceeded, two by two, to Griffin's Wharf* . . . and before 9 o'clock . . . every chest from on board the three vessels was knocked to pieces and flung over the sides.

"They say the actors were Indians from Narragansett. Whether they were or not, to a transient observer they appeared as such, being clothed in blankets with the heads muffled, and copper-colored countenances, being each armed with a hatchet or axe and pair pistols; nor was their dialect different from what I conceived these geniuses to speak, as their jargon was unintelligible to all but themselves. Not the least insult was offered to any person, save one Captain Conner, a letter of horses in this place . . . who had ripped up the lining of his coat and waistcoat under the arms and . . . had nearly filled 'em with tea. . . . They not only stripped him of his clothes but gave him a coat of mud, with a severe bruising into the bargain." [21]

The "Indians from Narragansett," or "Mohawks," were Whigs who had dressed up either at the Green Dragon or at the home of Benjamin Edes, publisher of the Boston *Gazette,* in accordance with a long matured plan. Led by Lendall Pitts, son of a prosperous merchant, and including Revere, Molineux, Young, and Hewes, they probably numbered about sixty. Rowe says that two thousand persons witnessed the spectacle.[22]

Thatcher quotes Hewes as claiming to have seen Adams and Hancock among the "Indians," and records that he "positively affirms, as of his own observation," that both men took part in the destruction of the tea; that he "was himself at one time engaged with" John Hancock "in the demolition of the same chest" and "recognized him not only by his ruffles . . . and by his figure and gait but by his features . . . and by his

* At the foot of the present Pearl Street.

voice, also, for he exchanged with him an Indian grunt and the expression, 'me know you,' which was a good deal used on that occasion for a countersign." But this statement strained even the credulity of the chronicler, who comments: "This is a curious reminiscence, but we believe it a mistake." [23]

Adams and Hancock had every reason for abstaining from direct participation in this high-handed attack upon private property and none at all for soiling their hands in it. They were too valuable to the cause to run the risk of being imprisoned at such a critical time.

This opinion seems to be corroborated by Hancock himself in a letter of the 21st to Haley & Hopkins, in whom he could safely confide. After outlining in one sentence what had happened he continued: "The particulars I must refer you to Captain Scott for; indeed, I am not acquainted with them myself, so as to give a detail. . . . No one circumstance could possibly have taken place more effectively to unite the colonies than this maneuvre of the tea. It is universally resented here." [24]

That the front man of the Whigs, however, had been behind the scenes when the plot of the tea drama was hatched at his own St. Andrews Lodge of Masons and at the headquarters of the North Caucus is indicated by Thompson Maxwell, who was a young teamster at the time. Although his recollections were not published until 1868—as written down by General James Miller, under whom he served as a major in the War of 1812—they have a more authentic ring than Hewes'.

"I had loaded at John Hancock's warehouse," Maxwell told General Miller, "and was about to leave town when Mr. Hancock requested me . . . to be on Long Wharf at 2 o'clock P. M. and informed me what was to be done. I went accordingly [and] joined the band under one Captain Hewes. We mounted the ships and made tea in a trice. This done, I took my team and went home, as an honest man should." [25]

For days after the Tea Party searching parties picked up chests that floated ashore as far away as Dorchester and burned them so that not a single drop should be tasted by a Tory. One group even went to the trouble of lugging a box from the South Boston beach to the Common and setting fire to it there with much fanfare near Hancock's mansion— no doubt to please the idol of the masses. On the Charlestown waterfront, too, a few pounds were scooped up and set afire, to the great delight of a thousand spectators. In January another band of "Mohawks" descended upon the ship that had rescued the precious street lights from the wreck off Cape Cod—and discovered not one leaf. In March the

Fortune, fifth and last of the tea carriers, was boarded, and its cargo demolished.

· 7 ·

Before the night of the main raid was over, Governor Hutchinson dispatched by express to his councilors instructions to meet with him in Boston at once; but he failed to collect a quorum. So he prudently spent the next night at the Castle on the pretense of visiting his sons, who had taken refuge there with the other consignees. On the morrow he sent off another summons to a conference at his Milton home, but with no better results. Finally, on the 21st, he managed to corral enough of his advisers at Cambridge to hold a legal session. But they were of no help. The hapless governor thus summarizes the cringing counsel they gave him:

"One of them declared against any step whatever. The people, he said, had taken the powers of government into their hands—any attempt to restrain them would only enrage them and render them more desperate. . . . So many of the actors and abettors were universally known that a proclamation, with a reward for discovery, would have been ridiculed. The attorney-general, therefore, was ordered to lay the matter before the grand jury; who, there was no room to expect, would ever find a bill for what they did not consider as an offence. This was the boldest stroke which had yet been struck in America. . . . Their leaders feared no consequences."

But just as paralyzed by the boldness of the Whigs was Admiral John Montague. This supposedly ferocious old sea dog watched the whole Tea Party in silence—except for a brief altercation with Pitts after its object had been accomplished—from the house of a friend at the head of Griffin's Wharf while his powerful fleet rode at anchor not a quarter of a mile distant. The "Indians" must have been surprised and moved to scorn when the vaunted British military raised no restraining hand from the time they took possession of the ships, with the passive cooperation of the crews, until they completed a victory march, to the strains of a fife, at the Town House. The Crown officers were afraid to budge until authorized by King or Parliament. Hutchinson admits as much:

"The tea could have been secured . . . in no other way than by landing marines from the men of war or bringing to town the regiment which was at the Castle. . . . This would have brought on a greater convulsion than there was any danger of in 1770, and it would not have been possible . . . for so small a body of troops to have kept possession of the town. Such a measure the governor had no reason to suppose would have been approved of in England. He was not sure of support from any one person in authority. . . . There was not a justice of peace, sheriff, constable . . . in the province who would venture to take cog-nizance of any breach of the law against the general bent of the people. The military authority . . . had been assumed by this body of the peo-ple, who appointed guards and officers, which appeared sometimes with firearms, though generally without them." [26]

But the House of Commons soon visited harsh retribution upon the insurgent town and province. Captain Scott, who had recently sailed one of Hancock's ships across the Atlantic in the fast time of twenty-eight days, with Francis Rotch and Captain James Hall of the *Dartmouth* on board, warned his employer of punishment to come:

"Mr. Rotch, with Hall and the other gentlemen passengers from Bos-ton, have been several times sent for to Lord Dartmouth's office and be-fore the Privy Council and . . . undergone a very strict examination, which is all committed to writing and their deposition taken. I don't know what plan the Ministry is going upon, but . . . it's generally thought the depositions will be sent over to Boston and the India Com-pany sue for damages to be tried there (a certain number of gentlemen, as I hear, are pitched upon as objects, of which number you have the honor to be one) in your own courts. When I first arrived I was im-mediately summoned up to Lord Dartmouth and asked a few questions; but very trifling, for I answered them very shortly. They have never sent for me since."

But the mere threat of another lawsuit could not shake Hancock loose from his Whig convictions now. He was at last on the Liberty party's side of the fence to stay. Between the beginning of the November 29–30 town meeting, when he had backed away from the chair that was offered him, and the end, when he had expressed a willingness to sacrifice his fortune and life for liberty, something had happened to turn him into a complete revolutionist. His heart had long embraced the cause of free-dom. From this time on, his mind also was to hold fast to it. But why?

This question brings up for consideration one of the most puzzling aspects of John's career. Why, when the issue of conservatism versus radicalism, embodied in the projected destruction of £10,000 worth of the East India Company's property, was put squarely up to him, did he choose to stand beside Adams and the other sworn enemies of the political and economic order? Why did he support a definitely iconoclastic act which horrified a great majority of his patrician class?

The answer lies buried with his bones. Perhaps even he did not know. But the best guess seems to be that he suddenly admitted to himself, when confronted with the inviting prospect of defying the power of the man he had come to hate above all others—King George III—the unpleasant truth that he was a failure as a merchant. He could find extenuation for his lack of business success in the troublous times and in his neglect of private affairs for public duty. But he could not blink the fact that some of his competitors—in similar, though somewhat less trying, circumstances—had managed to prosper.

At the beginning of 1774 Hancock owed Haley & Hopkins £11,000; his trade had been stagnating, and he had been disposing of his ships at a rapid rate. In the letter just quoted Captain Scott, intimating that his employer was regarded in England as a bad credit risk, nevertheless expressed his own affection:

"I hope you won't give up all your navigation, and . . . I am determined never to leave you while you please to employ me. In this way I assure you, Sir, it has given me much concern for some time past to see your credit and reputation suffering . . . ; but it has never been in my power to say more than I have done, though I have often wished I could have had more influence." [27]

The fate of the House of Hancock, however, was not nearly so important to its proprietor as his personal prestige. He would try to uphold it in politics, with virtual assurance of success, at the expense of the business structure. And now, on March 5, he buttressed his popularity among the masses with the strongest prop to come to hand thus far.

· 8 ·

Ever since the Boston Massacre the Whigs had commemorated the anniversary with an oration by a prominent patriot in the Old South Church. The principal purpose was to refresh the people's memories concerning what the Liberty party played up as a dastardly act of unmitigated cruelty on the part of the British government.

Now they selected Hancock as the speaker, and he—despite a siege of gout that had set in after the Tea Party—brought all the power of oratory to bear on the horrors of the bloody night. It was a spellbinding tirade of inflammatory rhetorical questions, extravagant accusations, gore-dripping passages, and passion-rousing apostrophes that was received, even by intellectuals, with reverberating plaudits and with tears. One excerpt reads:

"Did not our infants almost learn to lisp out curses before they knew their horrid import? Did not our youth forget they were Americans and . . . servilely copy from their tyrants those vices which must finally overthrow the Empire of Great Britain? And must I be compelled to acknowledge that even the noblest, fairest part of the lower creation did not entirely escape the cursed snare?

"When virtue has once erected her throne within the female breast it is upon so solid a basis that nothing is able to expel the heavenly inhabitant. But have there not been some—few, indeed, I hope—whose youth and inexperience have rendered them a prey to wretches whom, upon the least reflection, they would have despised and hated as foes to God and their country? I fear there have been such unhappy instances; or why have I seen an honest father clothed with shame? Or why a virtuous mother drowned in tears?

"But I forbear and come reluctantly to the transactions of that dismal night . . . , when Heaven, in anger for a dreadful moment, suffered Hell to take the reins; when Satan, with his chosen band, opened the sluices of New England's blood and sacrilegiously polluted our land with the dead bodies of her guiltless sons. . . . Let all America join in one common prayer to Heaven that the inhuman, unprovoked murders of the fifth of March, 1770, planned by Hillsborough and a knot of treacherous knaves in Boston and executed by the cruel hand of Preston and his sanguinary coadjutors, may ever stand on history without a parallel!"

The persuasive orator rose to heights of invective closely approaching sedition, and seldom heard even in that day of unbridled expression:

"Ye dark, designing knaves; ye murderers, parricides! How dare you tread upon the earth which has drank in the blood of slaughtered innocence shed by your wicked hands? How dare you breathe that air which wafted to the ear of Heaven the groans of those who fell a sacrifice to your accursed ambition? But if the laboring earth doth not expand her jaws; if the air you breathe is not commissioned to be the minister of death; yet hear it and tremble! The eye of Heaven penetrates the darkest chambers of the soul; . . . and you . . . must be arraigned, must lift your hands, red with the blood of those whose death you have procured, at the tremendous bar of God."

The richest man in Massachusetts even persuaded his auditors to accept, at face value, the following incongruous exhortation:

"Despise the glare of wealth. That people who pay greater respect to a wealthy villain than to an honest, upright man in poverty almost deserve to be enslaved; they plainly show that wealth, however it may be acquired, is, in their esteem, to be preferred to virtue."

And he dispelled any lingering doubt that he was reconciled with the Adamses and the Whigs by declaring:

"But I thank God that America abounds in men who are superior to all temptation. . . . And sure I am I should not incur your displeasure if I paid a respect so justly due to their much honored characters in this public place; but when I name an Adams such a numerous host of fellow-patriots rush upon my mind that I fear it would take up too much of your time should I attempt to call over the illustrious roll." [28]

John Adams, who might have been expected to comment sardonically, wrote in his diary:

"Heard the oration pronounced by Colonel Hancock in commemoration of the Massacre. An elegant, a pathetic, a spirited performance. A vast crowd, rainy eyes, etc. The composition, the pronunciation, the action—all exceeded the expectations of everybody. They exceeded even mine, which were very considerable. Many of the sentiments came with great propriety from him. His invective, particularly against a preference of riches to virtue, came from him with a singular dignity and grace." [29]

By means of this harangue the once wavering renegade patriot committed himself publicly to the Revolutionary movement. There could be no turning back now.

· 9 ·

Whether Hancock wrote the oration, which he read from manuscript, is open to question.

Wells, in his extremely partial biography of Sam Adams, attributes the declamation mainly to him; but the statement is based on a lost letter penned thirteen years after the event on the testimony of Adams' daughter and a nephew, who merely affirmed that Sam and John had conferred on the subject matter.

Stronger evidence that the speech was "ghost-written" is presented by Noah Webster, the lexicographer. This is in the form of an anecdote which Webster had heard from John Trumbull, poet and jurist, and which he retailed in 1840 to Ebenezer Thomas, son of Isaiah the printer:

"In the year 1774, Mr. Trumbull was a student of law in the office of John Adams. Mr. Hancock was, at that time, a wavering character. . . . It was a matter of no small importance to bring him to a decision as to the part he was to take in the crisis then approaching. To effect this object the more staunch, leading Whigs contrived to procure Mr. Hancock to be appointed to deliver an oration on the anniversary of the Massacre; and some of them wrote his oration for him, or a considerable part of it. This policy succeeded, and Mr. Hancock became a firm supporter of the American cause. Judge Trumbull related to me these facts as from his personal knowledge." [30]

Although John Adams thought the speech was Hancock's own work, the younger Thomas gives Dr. Cooper the credit. He comments most significantly: "Any man who ever heard Hancock address a public assembly, as I have, could not for a moment doubt his *ability* to write such an oration. The object was to get him committed beyond the hope of pardon, and that oration did it completely." [31]

Despite complete conversion into a rebel, the patriot in purple could not resist the temptation to bask in the social effulgence surrounding the leading Loyalists. With insouciant disregard of inconsistency and at the risk of becoming suspect again in the eyes of the Whigs, John offered to march at the head of his cadets in the funeral procession of Lieutenant Governor Oliver, who had died on March 3. So on the 8th, only three days after his scathing attack upon the official British family, there was "Colonel Hancock's company under arms," first in line ahead of the corpse as the long, impressive cortège wended its way toward the burying ground.[32] And the Independent Corps also fired the final salute over the grave.

In Parliament, meanwhile, oratorical salvos not so flattering to John Hancock were being discharged. On March 7 Prime Minister North had asked punitive legislation in retaliation for the Tea Party and other deeds of violence on the part of the Massachusetts insurgents. The Boston Port Bill, closing the harbor to all shipping until the town should reimburse the East India Company for its losses, was passed a week later. In the ensuing debate even the former friends of the Liberty party urged that its ringleaders be seized and brought to England for trial on charges of treason. The Privy Council recommended that warrants for the arrest of Sam Adams, Hancock, Cushing, and Warren be issued by the attorney general and the solicitor general. But when those officers, not wishing to accept the responsibility, demurred the agitation for this drastic step died down.

The government decided, instead, to take it out on the rebellious province by putting through two more retaliatory acts: one authorizing an appointive Council and abrogating the right of the people to select jurors; the other changing the venue of trials for capital offenses committed in support of the Crown to colonies outside Massachusetts or to Britain. And to enforce these measures they sent to Boston another formidable fleet, which arrived in midsummer.

The jubilation of the Whigs over returning their customary quartet —Adams, Hancock, Cushing, and Phillips—to office at the annual election for General Court representatives on May 10 was considerably dampened by news the same day about the Port Bill. It was to go into effect against outgoing vessels on June 1 and against incoming ones on the 14th.

This was particularly depressing to the head of the House of Hancock. But for once he acted promptly in the transatlantic field, and saved his financial hide, by speeding enough consignments to Haley & Hopkins to net £13,000—more than sufficient to liquidate his debt to that firm. He reduced his obligations to all his other foreign creditors to a pittance before the start of the Revolution, and established a balance in his favor before its close.

Hancock must have caused consternation among the Whigs and wonder among the Tories by ordering his cadets to assemble at the Bunch of Grapes on May 19 preparatory to meeting General Gage, who had returned from a short sojourn in England a week earlier to take over the reins from Hutchinson—another ceremonial occasion from which the colonel of the Independent Corps could not bear to absent himself. He and his command greeted Gage, who now bore the august and antagonizing title of "Vice-Admiral, Captain-General, and Governor-in-Chief of Massachusetts." They escorted him to the Town House, where he was officially inducted into office, and from there to Province House. Perhaps to create the impression that he was ushering in a regime of harmony between government and governed, or possibly to wean Hancock away from his Liberty party affiliations, the new governor presented to the corps a banner embroidered with his coat-of-arms. The socially acceptable political interloper from Beacon Hill then repaired, with most of the other leading functionaries, to Faneuil Hall for a feast and, as one of the speakers, probably gave lip service to King and governor without batting an eye.

But Hancock's "loyalty" went no deeper than words. Along with the rest of the all-powerful Faction he had refused to attend a meeting of the General Court summoned by Hutchinson before Gage's arrival for May 26. On that day the new governor adjourned the General Court to Salem, where it was to reassemble within two weeks. The purpose of the shift, as required by the Port Act, was the usual one of removing the seditious element from Boston; but by this time the Whigs cared not a whit. They had plans which would render it a matter of purely academic interest.

· 10 ·

On the first day of June, in accordance with the provisions of the Port Bill, an embargo was clamped upon outbound shipping. The town was placed virtually under martial law. Business soon was at a standstill. Food began to run short. The General Court convened at Salem on the date specified by Gage, but not to carry out the program he had in mind. On the 12th Sam Adams helped to make some of the most important political history of an era. He put through a motion that the Assembly choose five delegates to attend the First Continental Congress soon to be organized in Philadelphia at the joint instigation of Massachusetts and Virginia. All the colonies except Georgia agreed to take part in this project to consult on ways and means of gaining what they regarded as their rights.

Hancock was conspicuously missing from the delegation named by his own province—a group comprising both Adamses, Cushing, Bowdoin, and Robert Treat Paine. It is possible that the Whigs, after his recent hobnobbing with the Tories, still doubted their relatively new convert; but it is more likely that, next to Sam Adams, he was considered as the man most capable of keeping the fires of freedom burning at home. In strong support of this theory are his election to the presidency of the First Provincial Congress of Massachusetts and his appointment to the chairmanship of the committee of safety during the continental conference.

The manner of selecting the representatives was the most arbitrary proceeding as yet undertaken by the Liberty party. When Gage, who was not present at the time, learned what was going on he sent Secretary Flucker to the meeting hall with authority to prorogue the General Court. But Flucker discovered that Sam Adams had locked the door— from the inside—and had pocketed the key. Denied admittance, the secretary shouted his message through the closed portal and went away. After finishing their illegal business the Assembly graciously consented to be suspended.

Although forced to take a back seat while this dramatic defiance was in progress, Hancock was in the forefront of the King's thoughts at this period. Hutchinson, back in London, relates in his diary for July 1 the ensuing conversation with George III and Lord Dartmouth at the Court of St. James's:

"K.—'Pray, what does Hancock do now? How will the late affair affect him?'

"H.—'I don't know to what particular affair Your Majesty refers.'

"K.—'Oh, the late affair in the city—his bills being refused.' (Turning to Lord D.) 'Who is that in the city, My Lord?'

"Lord D. not recollecting—

"H.—'I have heard, Sir, that Mr. Haley, a merchant in the city, is Mr. Hancock's principal correspondent.'

"K.—'Ay, that's the name.'

"H.—'I heard, may it please Your Majesty, before I came from New England, that some small sums were returned but none of consequence.'

"K.—'Oh, no. I mean this month—large sums.'

"Lord D.—'I have heard such rumors but don't know the certainty.'

"H.—'Mr. Hancock, Sir, had a very large fortune left him by his uncle, and I believe his political engagements have taken off his attention from his private affairs. He was sensible not long ago of the damage it was to him and told me he was determined to quit all public business, but soon altered his mind.' " [33]

The "late affair in the city" to which the King referred was Haley's decision, conveyed to Hancock later in July while his ships were carrying their liquidating cargoes across the Atlantic, to stop honoring John's bills of exchange.[34] Probably noised about on 'change by the London agent, the news that he was on the point of cutting off the Boston merchant's credit had reached the regal ear. The "large sums" mentioned by the King were those constituting the £11,000 debt.

Considered by itself, the incident of the three-cornered confab at the royal palace is inconsequential. But it serves to show that the subject of the gossip was a person of lively interest to the most powerful monarch on earth.

· 11 ·

Another man especially interested in Hancock at this time was Henry Pelham, artist and half-brother of Copley. Pelham, it is believed, created an engraving used by Revere to stir up antipathy to the British in the early days of the Revolutionary movement; but he eventually turned Tory and sailed away with Lord Howe during the evacuation of Boston. He apparently had done some portrait work for the Beacon Hill connoisseur and now was dunning him for payment. Two letters written by the painter bring to light a failing for which his customer was notorious. The first, in July, complained sarcastically:

"I find it very difficult collecting money. . . . Colonel Hancock I have not yet been able to get an audience of, though he is so well as to talk of heading his company in a few days. I have always the misfortune to go there when he has a violent headache or when he is lying down."

Pelham was still more caustic in November. He noted also the extent to which the Whigs in general, and their potent partisan in particular, had gained the upper hand over the Loyalists:

"Your Honorable Colonel that was (for he is now dismissed) has scarcely behaved better than Mr. G., though much more complaisantly. Three times a day for a week together have I attended him, upon his appointment; as often disappoint[ed] either by his absence or business or having lost the account or some such trifling excuse.

"Here again the temper of the times forbids my doing other than taggle after his plaguy heels whenever he is pleased to appoint it. My tongue of[ten] itches to tell him that I think he is a very trifling fellow. I should certainly do it, was he a less man or I a greater or the times more favorable." [35]

The dismissal mentioned by Pelham had taken place on August 1. Ever since the ceremonial reception of May 19 Governor Gage had been brooding over a slight by Hancock's cadets. Sending for their colonel, he had asked why the men had not given the customary salute to the chief magistrate as he passed between their lines on entering Province House. Unconvinced by Hancock's explanation of the failure as an oversight, the governor had revoked his commission.

In this test the cadets stood stoutly by their colonel. Meeting on the 15th in Faneuil Hall, they named him chairman of a committee to notify Gage that they no longer would act as his bodyguard, and to return all the officers' certificates of rank, together with the embroidered banner. That very night Hancock carried out his mission, undoubtedly with keen relish—especially since it afforded him an opportunity to play the martyr in the executive mansion at Salem. In his best platform manner he declared:

"I shall always prefer retirement in a private station to being a tool, in the hand of power, to impress my countrymen." [36]

The corps then disbanded. But before doing so they turned over "their equipage, musical instruments, etc., into Colonel Hancock's keeping till some future time, being determined not to appear under any other leader while he lives." [37]

In 1787, the Massachusetts State legislature would reorganize the regiment; and the cadets would keep their vow conversely by serving under Hancock from his return to office that year as governor of the commonwealth until his death during the last of six consecutive terms.

John had now severed the sole remaining tie of fealty to His Majesty George III.

VIII

CUPID YIELDS TO MARS

*D*URING THAT seething summer of 1774, when Hancock's hostility toward England was crystallized into hatred by the news that the government had contemplated seizing him as a traitor and by the wound Gage inflicted upon his vanity in revoking his commission as colonel, he may have had a still more intimate reason for bitterness toward his mother country.

According to tradition, Earl Percy, who was placed in immediate command of all the British troops in Boston on his arrival early in July and was to take a prominent part in the opening battle of the Revolution a few months later, caught the fancy of Dorothy Quincy. He is supposed to have enthralled her as he drilled his forces on the Common within sight of her bedroom window in the Hancock mansion, where she was staying under the chaperonage of match-making Aunt Lydia.

The story may be apocryphal. But the delectable Dolly could not have helped being aware of Percy's presence, day and night, for he slept in a tent pitched among those of his men in the great green quadrangle and dined in the house formerly occupied by Governor Bernard on the side opposite Beacon Hill. There, he wrote to his father, the Duke of Northumberland, "I have always a table of 12 covers every day." [1]

There is no historical evidence, however, that Percy had even a nodding acquaintance with John Hancock's future lady. As the daughter of a stanch Whig, Edmund Quincy, and as the fiancée of an equally sound one—not to mention the restraining influence of her chaperon—Dorothy probably would hardly have encouraged a closer relationship—openly, at all events. But, in view of her reputation for coquetry, John may well have had cause to suspect her of desiring to fraternize with the undeclared enemy. No man could be sure of her undivided attachment up to the time when she became Mrs. Hancock about a year later

153

—and it is doubtful that her husband ever was certain of her love.

The shallowness of her affections may have been due to her being spoiled as the youngest of ten children—and the best-looking of five girls famous for their beauty throughout New England—born into one of the leading families in this land.[2] After a visit in 1628, the first Edmund Quincy arrived at Boston to stay on September 4, 1633, with the Reverend Mr. Hooker and the Reverend Mr. Cotton in the after-party of the Braintree company. There is some foundation, it will be recalled, for the belief that the first Hancock was in this group.

Dolly could trace her ancestry by inferential reasoning to Baron de Quincy, second Earl of Winchester, who was instrumental in forcing King John to sign Magna Carta. Although definite proof of this noble descent is lacking, Edmund Quincy of Wigsthorpe, Northamptonshire, the earliest Quincy of record in the American line, sported the same coat of arms as did the Baron. On the other hand, Edmund I may have scrupled no more about appropriating an escutcheon than Thomas Hancock.

However that may be, the Quincys, again matching the Hancocks, created an aristocratic tradition of their own after being transplanted to the New World. And they attained a preeminence that has lasted until modern times. They not only moved in the highest social circles of Boston and vicinity for three hundred years but contributed political leaders to the Colony and the Commonwealth of Massachusetts almost continuously down to the middle of the nineteenth century. On the distaff side they produced the sixth President of the United States—John Quincy Adams.

· 2 ·

Stemming from the same Puritan migration, the American branches of the Quincy and Hancock family trees were curiously intertwined. At the death of Dorothy's grandfather, Edmund III, in 1738, John's father preached the funeral sermon. North Braintree provided another point of contact. Dolly spent most of her girlhood in one of the two celebrated mansions still preserved in the part of Braintree later named Quincy in honor of Colonel Josiah, younger brother of Edmund IV; and the town, as previously indicated, was John's birthplace. The two families had a third common bond in the parsonage where the Reverend John Hancock II died in 1744—occupied by the colonel from about 1752 until it burned down in 1759. How Josiah happened to select it as his residence is explained by an anecdote which illustrates the similarity in sources of wealth accumulated by these illustrious New England clans.

In 1740, seven years before his youngest and most noted daughter was born, the fourth Edmund Quincy moved from the ancestral home in North Braintree to Boston, where he and Colonel Josiah went into the shipbuilding business with Edward Jackson, their brother-in-law. (Jackson's wife incidentally, about whom Oliver Wendell Holmes wrote the poem "Dorothy Q.," often is confused with her niece, the Dorothy Q. of this book.)

In 1748, during King George's War, the Quincy-Jackson firm operated the merchant ship *Bethell*. Although armed, she was not provided with letters of marque. She ran afoul of a Spanish privateer called the *Jesus, Maria, and Joseph* one night as both were emerging from the Straits of Gibraltar into the Atlantic. The American ship carried a crew of only thirty-seven and no more than fourteen guns, whereas the enemy vessel boasted one hundred and ten men and twenty-six cannon. Escape was out of the question, and the captain of the *Bethell* decided that offense, supported by an elaborate bluff, was the best defense. Fortunately, the darkness concealed from the Spaniards the extent of their foe's inferiority. The master of the weaker craft strung lanterns in the rigging; lined the rails with dummies decked out in all the spare clothing aboard; steered straight for the *Jesus, Maria, and Joseph* with every sail billowing, and called on her to surrender. She struck her colors without a shot.

The unexpected triumph brought the victors a windfall, in one hundred and sixty-one chests of silver, two of gold, a large quantity of cochineal, and many other items of great value. After throwing the vanquished into irons they sailed their prize home.

When the two vessels reached Boston a guard of the victorious sailors, brandishing pistols and cutlasses, convoyed the booty through curious crowds and deposited it in the wine cellar of Josiah's house on what now is Washington Street. The modern monetary equivalent of the swag, which the partners divided equally, would be more than $300,000.

Colonel Quincy and his brother-in-law retired with the hoard illegally acquired without letters of marque. Quincy invested his share in an ill starred venture with two of his sons. Within four or five years he was in such dire straits that he had to dispose of his Boston home and return to the country. In 1755 he was forced to sell that, also; but Jackson, the purchaser, generously permitted him to go on living there. That he was far from happy, however, is indicated by a letter in November of the following year to Sir Harry Frankland, collector of the port of Boston, whose chaise Thomas Hancock envied:

"The unhappy situation of my affairs has deprived me of . . . waiting upon yourself and lady. I have taken the freedom to send you a trifling collection of some of the fruits of the season produced on the place of my birth, on which (though mine no more!) I have yet a residence."[3]

· 3 ·

At this time Dorothy Quincy was nine years old. She had been born on May 10, 1747, in the spacious, gambrel-roofed, dormer-windowed frame house in Boston. Standing flush with the sidewalk on Summer Street, it was bounded on one wing by a roomy, square courtyard and several stables; on the other, by an equally large informal garden—the entire frontage measuring ninety-three feet. She must have had a happy childhood playing beneath numerous mulberry trees and an old English walnut, and in July, 1756, Edmund Quincy wrote to his wife, away from home, that "Daughter Dolly" had just gone to school, "where she seems to be very high in her mistress' graces."[4]

The favorable impression made by Dolly upon her teacher presumably was based chiefly on conduct, for girls in mid-eighteenth century Massachusetts were taught only the rudiments of reading, writing, arithmetic, and sewing, a smattering of music, and simple dance steps. Even this meager education was confined almost exclusively to daughters of the well-to-do and socially prominent. Designed primarily to fit them for marriage and motherhood, it was imparted by private tutors. Females were not admitted to Boston public schools until 1789.

But unmarried ladies did not lead the sheltered lives to which they traditionally have been doomed in European countries. Maidens in New England colonial days were allowed to mingle with men—of their own class—without much more restraint than is imposed upon them in America today. Chaperonage at parties was rare, probably because parents in the small, compact communities of the period knew all the gentlemen with whom their daughters associated, and had learned that there was more danger in the Puritan repression of past generations than in freedom.

Young Dorothy Quincy, of course, still would have been under strict surveillance in 1756 and also three years later when John Adams, at the age of twenty-two, committed to his diary the following remarks on a

New Year celebration at Colonel Quincy's home four months before it
was destroyed by fire:

"Here are two nights and one day and a half spent in a softening,
enervating, dissipating series of hustling, prattling, poetry, love, courtship, marriage. During all this time I was seduced into the course of
unmanly pleasures that Vice describes to Hercules, forgetful of the
glorious promises of fame, immortality, and a good conscience." [5]

Despite such occasional spells of remorse, Adams hearkened to the
counsel of "Vice" in North Braintree more often than he did to the
still, small voice. He put the quietus on his conscience by attributing to
stronger intellectual appeal—after the manner of romance-blinded youth
from time immemorial—his preference for Josiah's daughter Hannah
over Edmund's Esther.

It is no wonder that Dolly, after growing up in this atmosphere of
high-powered flirtation, became a coquette.

Adams' confidential chronicle gives a glimpse, too, into the exclusively
masculine aspect of existence among the Quincys. During the March
following that rollicking winter of 1758–1759 he wrote in this sarcastic
and sanctimonious vein:

"Two evenings I spent at Samuel Quincy's. . . . Doctor Gardiner,
Henry Quincy, Ned Quincy, and Samuel Quincy all playing cards the
whole evening. This is the wise and salutary amusement the young gentlemen take every evening in this town. Playing cards, drinking punch
and wine, smoking tobacco and swearing. . . . I know not how any
young fellow can study in this town." [6]

· 4 ·

Even when Adams and Hancock were boys—and Dorothy a babe of three
—the first families of North Braintree apparently flitted through life in a
social whirl. Captain Goelet, the New York merchant whose account of
an all-night revel in Boston during 1750 already has been quoted, also
included in his journal several vignettes of somewhat more decorous
diversions in company with the Quincy and the Wendell clans, who
had doubly intermarried. John Wendell, brother of Dolly's mother Elizabeth, had taken to wife Edmund Quincy's sister Elizabeth. During his
stay in the Massachusetts capital Goelet was a guest of the Wendells.

On the day which he had begun by tilting glasses with his hosts until
five o'clock in the morning the indefatigable captain drove young Betty
Wendell in a chaise to a Cambridge inn for an early afternoon "turtle

frolic" attended by about twenty couples, among whom were Katherine and Sarah Quincy. Afterwards they frolicked through "several minuets and country dances" and were "very merry" until dusk.

Among Goelet's engagements during this period were a dinner party at the Quincys', where he played the harpsichord with Katy and Sally, and an evening of whist with the Wendell ladies. But the New Yorker evidently was most impressed by a fish feast at the Quincy estate, for he describes it in greater detail than any other event on his social calendar:

"The country house is a neat . . . building and finely accommodated for company, with a fine hall and large rooms. About ten yards from the house is a beautiful canal, which is supplied by a brook . . . well stocked with fine silver eels. We caught a . . . parcel and . . . had them dressed for supper. The house has a beautiful pleasure garden adjoining it, and on the back part of the building is a beautiful orchard with fine fruit trees, etc."

Before his ship sailed on for London the visiting merchant repaid his sizable debt of hospitality with an all-night stag affair at a Boston tavern. Although he does not mention the younger generation of Quincys and Wendells, they probably were well represented.

"Gave them a good supper, with wine and arrack punch galore," he noted. "Were exceeding merry, drinking toasts, singing, roaring, etc., until morning, when could scarce see one another, being blinded by the wine, arrack, etc." [7]

It must have been obvious even at this time, while Dolly slept in her cradle, that the Quincys' youngest daughter was not destined to lead the simple life.

· 5 ·

There is no record as to just when the man who helped Dorothy to fulfill her destiny as a fine lady first met her. Lucy P. Higgins hazards the guess that the meeting occurred in 1764, when she was seventeen.[8] This conjecture is logical, for John Hancock inherited most of his uncle's fabulous fortune during that year and thereby gained the independence which enabled him to circulate at will in Boston society. Ever since consciousness had dawned upon him he undoubtedly had known the Quincy family by reason of their close association with his own in North Braintree. Before Dolly was born he probably had played with her older sisters Sarah and Esther, who were approximately his age.

But he would not have paid much attention to the Quincys' youngest daughter until she was grown up.

For another reason it is unlikely that John had given more than a passing thought to the girl whom he was to marry until—as the pretty but unverified tale has it—he was so captivated by her petite figure and tiny feet tripping down the church steps that he obtained an introduction to her. At that period he was enamoured of a lass named Sally Jackson. But on February 22, 1770, a printer's devil apprenticed to Richard Draper, publisher of the Boston *News Letter*, jotted in his private journal:

"Married—Mr. Henderson Inches, merchant, to Miss Sally Jackson, daughter of Joseph Jackson, Esq. Mr. Hancock hath paid his addresses to Miss Jackson for about ten years past but has lately sent her a letter of dismission." [9]

That Dolly was the cause of the jilting is not to be supposed, for there is no definite evidence that John became seriously interested in her until another year had passed. Then, on March 19, 1771, Samuel Salisbury, a prosperous hardware importer, wrote to his brother Stephen:

"'Tis said that John Hancock courts Dolly Quincy. 'Tis certain he visits her and has her company in private every evening." [10]

With the aid of Aunt Lydia, matchmaker extraordinary, his suit progressed rapidly. Presumably it reached the engagement stage by the end of August; for, writing from Bridgewater on the 31st, Richard Perkins reported to Ebenezer: "Aunt, Mr. Hancock, and Miss Dolly are here and all very agreeable." [11]

With due regard to the freedom of social intercourse between the sexes in those days, there is a strong presumption that enough of the old Puritan taboos remained in effect to prevent a respectable young lady from making an overnight or longer visit (as Dorothy obviously was doing) with a thirty-four-year-old gentleman friend, even though chaperoned, in the home of his relatives unless she was betrothed to him. They probably had an "understanding," at least, prior to being guests of the Perkinses. However, it might not have ripened into marriage four years later but for the constant nurture of John's foster mother, who seems to have adopted Dolly, too, in all except a legal sense. Aunt Lydia may have persuaded Edmund Quincy to consent to this step on the death of his wife in 1769. He may have agreed the more readily for the sake of relieving the burden assumed by his sister, Mrs. Edward Jackson, who had moved into the North Braintree mansion to keep house for him and his large family. In any event, Mrs. Hancock deserves greater credit (if that is the word for it) than her nephew for the success of his courtship. Dolly admitted in later life that she would have broken the engagement but for the steady pressure applied by Lydia.

And yet John was considered one of the best "catches" in Boston— not only because of his vast wealth but also because of his good looks, manners, bearing, and personableness in general. John Adams says of him and his fiancée:

"Mr. Hancock was the delight of the eyes of the whole town. There can be no doubt that he might have had his choice . . . of a companion; and that choice was very natural—a granddaughter of the great patron and most revered friend of his father. Beauty, politeness, and every domestic virtue justified his predilection." [12]

Two other factors may have decided Dorothy to stick to her bargain: the realization that, at twenty-four, she was fast approaching the age when women were talked about as prospectively permanent spinsters and when men also were inclined to regard them so; and the high esteem in which her father held her suitor. Quincy revealed this to his daughter in June, 1773, when she and Aunt Lydia were staying at Point Shirley, on the north shore of Boston Harbor, with the Reverend Phinehas Whitney and his wife Lydia, a cousin of John Hancock. In a letter delivered by John to his beloved Edmund wrote:

"You have the honor of Colonel Handcock's [sic] being the bearer. I wish him a pleasant journey and a happy meeting with his valuable aunt and you; and that you, with them, may have a safe and comfortable journey home. . . . Colonel Handcock and his associates have had a hard task respecting the G.'s, Lt.-G.'s, and other letters, of which you'll see the copies. But I think, notwithstanding, he appears to rise higher, the greater the burthens." [13]

· 6 ·

There is legal testimony in the Public Record Office at London to the effect that John Hancock gave something less than whole-souled devotion to his intended during the early part of their betrothal period. His "dismission" of Sally Jackson, which had terminated an apparently virtuous affair of the heart, had not quenched his ardor for intimate feminine companionship. He cultivated it less circumspectly for an indeterminate length of time prior to the opening of the Revolution, which was to monopolize both his sleeping and his waking hours.

In other words, John had a mistress. She was Mrs. Dorcas Griffiths, whose husband seems to have died or to have left her before she combined pleasure with business as a tenant of Hancock's Wharf. At the shop which she conducted in her home she sold liquor, groceries, tea, and linen drapery. But she had a side line of buxom beauty which probably accounted for a large share of the profits.

There is no positive indication in the annals as to when the versatile saleswoman started to deal in charm exclusively with her landlord. But their relations presumably antedated the fall of 1774, when the British seized the wharf.

It is not known, either, when Hancock broke loose from Mrs. Griffiths; but right after the battle of Bunker Hill on June 17, 1775, she extended the hospitality of her house to Captain David Johnston, a wounded British marine. She and her daughter fled with Johnston to England, where annual bounties of £50 each were awarded to them by General Howe—on the recommendation of none other than Dolly's alleged dream man, Lord Percy—for "loyalty" to the Crown and "sufferings" endured in its interests.

In 1782, however, when three payments had been made, the Commissioners for American Claims, tipped off by Flucker, persuaded the British authorities that Dorcas and her girl were Loyalists more by profession than by conviction, and the dole ceased abruptly. The lightsome ladies eventually petitioned for resumption of the gratuities, without success. Through the testimony given by the Tory informer—who naturally would jump at a chance to revenge himself upon a prominent Whig for being barred from the General Court at Salem as secretary in 1774—at a hearing in 1784 before the Commissioners of His Majesty's Treasury, Hancock's name was dragged into the case. But evidently this grating echo from his past did not reach America; if it had, his many ruthless political enemies would have amplified it with deadly effect when he rose to the vulnerable position of governor. The witness' implicating (and somewhat self-incriminating) words, as paraphrased in the commissioners' report, were:

"Mr. Flucker knows both the mother and the daughter extremely well. The mother was a common prostitute and bred up her daughter in the same way. She was kept by the famous Handcock [sic], and when he turned her off she lived with Captain Johnston." [14]

Age may have withered, if custom did not stale, the infinite variety of Dorcas' attractions in Hancock's eyes; for she was in her fifties when he "turned her off." His Dolly must have seemed incomparably more desirable, if less amiable, by that time.

Perhaps the wedding plans, although they proved to be abortive, had something to do with the prospective bridegroom's decision to dispense with the foibles of bachelorhood. Wild-oat sowing was more broadly condoned in colonial days than it is even in the present era of indulgence toward sexual promiscuity; but an extramarital liaison would have been fatal to the political ambitions, as well as to the cherished social standing, of the conspicuous Beacon Hill notable.

There remains to this day, in the north parlor of the Edmund Quincy mansion at North Braintree, colorful circumstantial evidence that John and Dorothy intended to tie the knot before the outbreak of the Revolution. It is in the form of wallpaper imported from Paris, with a pattern of blue Cupids and Venuses disporting among clusters of red flowers, which indicates that the room was redecorated in anticipation of nuptials to take place during the winter of 1774–1775. Postponement must have been caused by the country-wide crisis fast approaching, for even willful Dolly would not have dared to balk in defiance of two determined families when the plans had gone so far.

But all the Hancocks and all the Quincys and all the King's men could not stem the tide of history. John was swept into the maelstrom of feverish activities, both martial and political, leading up to Lexington; while his near-bride was left stranded for nine more months.

· 7 ·

Ever since the previous August the tidal wave had been rushing onward at a steadily accelerating pace. During the week before Hancock definitely cut himself adrift from the Crown by breaking up the Independent Corps of Cadets, Sam Adams and the other delegates to the First Continental Congress had set out upon the journey to Philadelphia. After attending a farewell dinner spiced with do-or-die speeches they had assembled on the Common in front of the Hancock mansion. Partly as a gesture of contempt toward the British troops bivouacked there, they had driven off in a coach-and-four preceded by two white flunkies, mounted and armed, and followed by four Negro outriders in livery.

The trip was a leisurely one even for those times. It consumed the better part of three weeks, including a six-day stopover in New York, where the feasting and lionizing reached a climax. Most of it, more than likely, was stage-managed by the Whigs to stress the importance of the representatives' mission.

Convening on September 5 at Carpenter's Hall, Philadelphia, the

First Continental Congress failed, by a considerable margin, to live up to the advertised significance of this initial attempt to create inter-colonial solidarity. Hortatory orations and framing of petitions con-sumed most of the session, which lasted until October 27. The appeals included one to the King for redress of grievances; another to the English people for support; a third to the Province of Quebec inviting it to send a delegation to the subsequent convention; and a fourth, urging unity of action, to every American colony. An agreement to consolidate the old provincial and municipal pacts against mercantile dealings with Britain into an all-embracing instrument, with an official association to back it and to punish violators, was the only salient definite step taken; but that alone justified the meeting. It laid the groundwork for the second, and far more momentous, congress, which was to assemble on May 10, 1775.

Although Hancock probably would have preferred to go on the original junket to Philadelphia, especially in view of the homage paid to the travelers on the way, he experienced much greater excitement in Boston throughout September. It consisted of threats against his life and those of other Liberty party leaders.

The Whigs' resentment and the Tories' gloating over the Port Bill were reflected in the press as their respective journalistic supporters opened a sniping campaign which lasted up to the firing of actual guns half a year later. Hancock was used by one side as a barricade; by the other as a target. Gage's revocation of his cadet commission seems to be the subject of a facetiously satirical jingle purporting to have been com-posed by George III, published in September, 1774, in the *Massa-chusetts Spy*, a patriot paper:

> Your Colonel H–n–k, by neglect,
> Has been deficient in respect;
> As he my Sovereign toe ne'er kissed,
> 'Twas proper he should be dismissed;
> I never was and never will
> By mortal man be treated ill!

* A more serious and vicious attack was made upon fifteen outstanding opponents of the Crown in the form of an anonymous letter printed in the Boston *Evening Post,* a Loyalist publication, reprinted in pamphlet size, and scattered among the British garrisons throughout the town. Addressed to "the officers and soldiers of His Majesty's troops," it in-cluded Hancock along with Sam Adams, Bowdoin, Cushing, Molineux,

and Church among "the authors . . . of all the misfortunes brought upon the province" and continued:

"The friends of your King and country and of America hope and expect it from you soldiers—the instant rebellion happens—that you will put the above persons to the sword, destroy their houses, and plunder their effects! It is just that they should be the first victims to the evils they brought upon us." [15]

On September 20, the day after this scare screed, Captain Scott sailed his ship into the port of Salem, because of the Boston blockade, with a cargo which probably would have aroused the writer to even more bloody exhortations if he had known of it—gunpowder. Its arrival was timely, for the Faction had been trying vainly for weeks to accumulate a supply to replace the province's biggest store, confiscated by Gage.

· 8 ·

While thus secretly getting ready for more decisive measures against the British the Whigs were openly employing obstructionist tactics. They now instructed the carpenters who were building badly needed barracks for the Redcoats to stop work in protest against the stringency of the embargo. On the 26th Andrews informed his brother-in-law that the governor had asked Hancock that day to use his influence to have the retaliatory injunction rescinded, and went on:

"The Colonel observed to him that he had taken every possible measure to distress us; that, notwithstanding it was the Solicitor's opinion that the act could be construed [not] to prevent goods . . . being transported within the bounds of the harbor, yet he had not suffered it to be done. . . . He likewise told him that he had been threatened and apprehended his person was in danger, as it had been gave out by some of his people that he deserved to be hanged; upon which the Governor told him he might have a guard, if he chose it, to attend him night and day. You will naturally conclude that he declined accepting."

Construction of the cantonments ceased as soon as this conference was over, according to another Andrews communication. Gage then sent a colonel and a major to bargain with the powerful politician on the basis that the workmen were to be put back on the job in return for consent to the free movement of merchandise in the harbor. But, suspecting that this concession would be withdrawn when the barracks were completed, Hancock turned down the proposition. Thereupon the governor dispatched a warship to Halifax to round up all available artisans.[16]

Meanwhile the Whigs had been planning a more positive course of action against constituted authority. Their scheme went into effect on October 5 right under Gage's eyes at Salem, where two hundred and sixty representatives from all parts of Massachusetts gathered to organize the First Provincial Congress. Together with its two successors this body, which was formed to fill the legislative vacuum created when the governor countermanded his call for the regular meeting of the General Court scheduled for June 1, was to be the guiding spirit of the Revolution in its early New England phase.

The new organism set its machinery in motion within two days and then adjourned to meet again October 11 at Concord. After pausing there just long enough to elect Hancock president it moved once more—this time to Cambridge. It changed locale constantly until the colonies were on the verge of open rebellion, probably with the object of confusing the spies of the now virtually defunct, but still militarily dangerous, royal government.

One of the first acts of the presiding officer was to send Revere to Philadelphia with letters outlining, for the benefit of the Continental Congress, the progress being made in Massachusetts toward promoting the common cause. This history-making messenger had instructions to report back concerning Congressional developments.

The Whigs now entrusted Hancock with more power than they ever had delegated to anybody. They appointed him chairman of the provincial committee of safety, which eventually gained almost absolute sway over the regional congress. Even at this relatively early stage in the usurpation of governmental functions the committee was authorized to raise militia, to call them up for active duty, and to procure martial supplies. When Gage heard this he denounced the parent body as being utterly subversive; but he did nothing to quash it—probably because he realized that his forces, concentrated in Boston, were not disposed strategically enough to risk a clash of arms. So, at a second meeting on November 23 in Cambridge, the congress threw down the gauntlet unequivocally by voting that 12,000 volunteers, soon to be known as Minutemen, be recruited immediately. Early in December the governor retaliated by ordering seizure of the military stores at Charlestown.

In the meantime Hancock, who had assumed, among other royal prerogatives, the minor one of issuing the annual Thanksgiving Day proclamation, had pointedly omitted the name of George III from the document. And before the Cambridge congress adjourned on December 10 he was selected as a delegate to the Second Continental Congress.

This office was to serve him as a steppingstone to heights from which he could assail the British monarch as an equal—in theory, at least.

· 9 ·

But early in the new year 1775 the King, or the Ministry, took steps to forestall such an eventuality. At just about the time when Hancock was being elected president of the Second Provincial Congress on February 1 at Cambridge orders were dispatched to Gage to seize the pesky patriot along with Sam Adams and several others. The long contemplated plan to ship them to England and try them for treason was at last to be carried out—if and when the propitious moment should arrive. This design came to light months later through publication of letters from Londoners who sympathized with the Revolutionary movement.

"Orders have now gone out," one letter reads, "to take up Messrs. Hancock, Adams, Williams, Otis, and six of the head men of Boston. . . . My heart aches for Mr. Hancock. Send off expresses immediately that they intend to seize his estate and have his fine house for General ———." [17] Another communication states that the King subsequently commanded that the culprits be hanged in Boston, but that Governor Gage stalled for fear of precipitating "an engagement, the event of which he had every reason to apprehend would be fatal to himself and the King's troops." [18]

A Tory newspaper published in the Massachusetts capital brought Hancock's peril home to him through the medium of verse more noteworthy for poetic license than for poetry:

> As for their King, that John Hancock,
> And Adams, if they're taken;
> Their heads for signs shall hang up high
> Upon the hill called Beacon! [19]

Hancock must have been apprised of the British government's intentions by Whig informers, but he probably was also aware of Gage's reluctance to carry them out. In any case, he not only circulated as freely as ever in Boston and vicinity but flaunted his newly acquired power in the governor's face with undiminished audacity.

The historical record discredits romantic stories to the effect that he used the Edmund Quincy homestead in North Braintree as a hide-out at this period. And yet there is presumptive evidence, etched on its window panes probably with the diamond of a ring, that he visited the house at some time. His initials, in what looks like the familiar copybook script, are cut in one piece of glass and Dolly's in another. A third inscription— also in handwriting resembling John's—reads: "Dear Cutte [Cutie?], You I love and you alone."

But Hancock could not have had much opportunity for wooing, either in person or in writing, during the first three months of 1775. Although the Second Provincial Congress recessed from February 16 to March 22, many matters of more materialistic import than love claimed the attention—and one of them menaced the life—of its head man.

There are three versions of the story concerning John's narrow escape. One has it that he, Sam Adams, Dr. Warren, and numerous other outstanding patriots were to be murdered (in the event of certain developments); another, that they were to be arrested and presumably hanged, in accordance with the Crown command received by Gage; a third, that they were nearly involved in a fire panic which quite likely would have caused their death.

The occasion was the annual Boston Massacre commemoration, which was held on March 6 because the 5th fell on a Sunday. Warren had been chosen to deliver the oration in the Old South Church.

In his usually reliable diary Hutchinson retailed the circumstances of the alleged assassination plot on the basis of hearsay evidence which detracts from the credibility of the account.

A British colonel named James, he wrote, "tells an odd story of the intention of the officers the 5th March; that 300 were in the meeting to hear Doctor Warren's oration; that if he had said anything against the King, etc., an officer was prepared, who stood near with an egg, to have thrown in his face; and that it was to have been a signal to draw swords; and they would have massacred Hancock, Adams, and hundreds more." [20]

A London newspaper article reprinted in the *Virginia Gazette* says that the extent of the designs against Hancock, Adams, and others was limited to seizure; and then elaborates on the egg episode. It relates that "this scheme was rendered abortive in the most whimsical manner, for he who was deputed to throw the egg fell in going to church . . . and broke the egg." [21]

The most authentic exposition of the affair seems to be that of Lieutenant John Barker, an English officer and diarist who either was on the scene or in the town when it took place:

"It was known for some days that this [Warren's oration] was to be delivered; accordingly, a great number of officers assembled at it; when, after he had finished a most seditious, inflammatory harangue, John Hancock stood up and made a short speech in the same strain; at the end of which some of the officers cried out, 'Fie, fie!', which, being mistaken for the cry of fire, an alarm immediately ensued which filled the people with such consternation that they were getting out as fast as they could by the doors and windows. It was imagined that there would have been a riot which . . . would . . . , in all probability, have proved fatal to Hancock, Adams, Warren, and the rest of those villains, as they were all up in the pulpit together and the meeting was crowded . . . in such manner that they could not have escaped."

At this point Barker makes it brutally plain that at least one "gentleman" of His Majesty's army would not have hesitated, like Gage, to work the sovereign will upon all patriots, whether in purple or in drab. He goes on:

"However, it luckily did not turn out so. It would, indeed, have been a pity for them to have made their exit in that way, as I hope we shall have the pleasure before long of seeing them do it by the hands of the hangman." [22]

· 10 ·

Hancock was undaunted by these unmistakable signs that his life might be snuffed out at any moment, either by authorized agents of the King or by men acting on their own initiative. He even provoked the wrath of the Redcoats afresh.

On March 8 a Billerica farmer visiting Boston was seized by British troops on a trumped-up charge that he had tried to induce a member of the Forty-seventh Regiment to desert. Without benefit of a trial he was stripped, tarred, feathered, and paraded on a wagon through the streets as a warning against tampering with the royal army. The procession was led by the regimental band playing, for the first time in public on these shores, a tune which soon was to become famous—"Yankee Doodle." These special words were set to it for the occasion and were sung by the military escort:

> Yankee Doodle came to town
>   For to buy a firelock;
> We will tar and feather him,
>   And so we will John Hancock.[23]

The principal object of this threat defied it by conducting an inquiry into the conspiracy against the man from Billerica. This set off a series of recriminatory actions against the people in general and their idol in particular that began on the 17th.

"In the evening Colonel Hancock's elegant seat . . . was attacked," according to an anonymous public letter, "by a number of officers who, with their swords, cut and hacked the fence before his house in a most scandalous manner." [24] Two days later, Andrews recounted that "four sergeants and as many men were sent to insult John Hancock under pretense of seeing if his stables would do for barracks." [25] They told him prophetically, as related by the unknown writer, that "his house, stables, etc., would soon be theirs, and then they would do as they pleased."

Hancock protested to Governor Gage, who responded with restraint and deference that seem extraordinary, even in view of John's influence over the masses, by sending "one of his aides-de-camp to the officer of the guard at the bottom of the Common to seize any officer or private who should molest Colonel Hancock or any inhabitant in their lawful calling," [26] and assuring the colonel that "if he was in any ways insulted again . . . he would immediately redress him." [27]

In spite of all these personal harassments and his official problems of how to cope with British arrogance by peaceful but strong means until the time should be ripe for armed resistance, John Hancock managed to find an opportunity on March 25 to write his first love letter of record to Dolly. She apparently was visiting the Whitneys again at Point Shirley, with her father, while John was attending the resumed session of the Second Provincial Congress at Concord as a plain, but still powerful, delegate. He had yielded the office of president to Dr. Warren, probably because his duties as chairman of the committe of safety had become too onerous for him to do justice to both offices. His letter sheds considerable light upon the evolution of his grand passion:

"I am necessitated to abide here to add my mite toward completing business of the utmost importance for a determination of the Congress on Monday, which prevents me the pleasure of seeing you so early as I expected. . . . I shall return as soon as possible, when I shall be with you; and, I hope, you will not be saucy. . . . My dear girl, I must close, as the room where I am writing is full of committeemen. I can only add that no person on earth can be possessed of greater affection and regard for any one than I have for the lady to whom I address this; and be fully convinced that no distance of time or place can ever erase the impressions made and the determinations I have formed, being forever yours." [28]

Within twenty-four hours after thus pouring out his soul the not-so-great lover dashed back to Boston to sit in on an important town meeting.

He put through a motion that had historically dramatic consequences illustrating what came to be known all over the world as Yankee resourcefulness. It decreed that four brass fieldpieces and a pair of mortars with which two of the local militia companies were equipped should be seized and turned over to the committee of safety.

This was an emergency measure prompted by a report that Major Adino Paddock, Loyalist commander of the artillery units, intended to surrender the guns to the British army. Two of the mounted cannon were kept in a small arsenal next to a school across the Common from the Hancock mansion. While the sergeant usually on guard was answering roll-call one day shortly after the confiscation vote had been taken a party of patriots slipped in, removed the barrels from their carriages, and put them into a large wood bin in the school. The precious weapons were spirited away none too soon, for the sergeant returned with a lieutenant a few moments later to carry out Paddock's plans. They rushed into the schoolhouse, only to find Master Samuel Holbrook nonchalantly resting his lame leg on the box containing the guns. Pretending that it would cause him great pain to touch his foot to the floor, Holbrook talked the military out of further investigation.

One night two weeks later the same group of Whigs transported the cannon by wheelbarrow in a trunk to a blacksmith's shop in the South End and buried them under a pile of coal, from which they eventually were transferred to the custody of the safety committee.

In honor of the master minds behind the seizure scheme these guns were christened "Hancock" and "Adams." Together with their companion pieces, which were acquired in a similar manner but fell subsequently into the hands of the enemy, they constituted the whole train of artillery at the disposal of the patriots when the Revolution opened.

Symbolically, the cannon named after Adams, most inflammatory leader of the cause, exploded; but the one bearing Hancock's cognomen endured through thick and thin.

· 11 ·

Events now were plunging headlong toward one of history's great climaxes. Both the British and the Americans must have felt, reluctantly, that the long-continued conflict of irreconcilable principles and interests would soon be resolved on the battlefield. There still was a possibility of compromise, but it was extremely remote. And each side proceeded on the theory that a clash of arms was inevitable.

When the Second Provincial Congress heard on April 2 that Gage was reenforcing his army it authorized the committee of safety under Chairman Hancock to recruit six additional companies of artillery, even though the ordnance was lacking, and cautioned the militia to be vigilant but to avoid overt acts. Sam Adams himself, despite his secret determination to bring the dissension to a head regardless of whether blood flowed as a consequence, was especially anxious that the lancing should be done by the Crown. He and the other shrewd members of the Liberty party saw the tremendous advantage of putting England in the wrong before the world by taunting her into becoming the aggressor.

That Hancock, Adams, and their fellow citizens as a whole were convinced it was only a matter of days before the boil would burst is indicated in a letter from James Warren, who eventually became one of Hancock's bitterest enemies, to his wife Mercy. In a postscript dated April 7 he wrote:

"The inhabitants of Boston are on the move. H and A go no more into that garrison. The female connections of the first come out early this morning, and measures are taken relative to those of the last." [29]

The "female connections" were Aunt Lydia and Dorothy, who had returned to Boston from Point Shirley during the previous fortnight. They had traveled in one of the Hancock carriages to the Clark parsonage in Lexington to join John and Adams, who were commuting between that place and Concord. All four guests of the Clarks remained in the original home of old Bishop Hancock until forced to flee in the historic dawn of April 19.

Warren's comments on the flight of Hancock's aunt and fiancée from Boston are supplemented in Helena Bayard's note of the 14th to her cousin Dolly:

"Your sudden departure gave me great uneasiness; and when I saw the furniture carried from the house and family leaving it, it appeared to me as though you were all dead. . . . I have taken my leave of Queen Street, as what I hold dear to me is gone." [30]

The house referred to must have been the Hancock homestead. Mrs. Bayard had paid a farewell call there before giving up her Queen Street boarding quarters, on her way to visit Katherine Quincy and Edmund at the residence of William Donnison, second husband of Mary Quincy.

While his nearest and dearest were thus looking out for themselves Hancock was jeopardizing his own physical welfare. In a speech supposed to have been delivered about this time he is reputed to have offered to sacrifice his magnificent mansion and numerous business buildings in the interest of the Revolutionary movement.

Although even the contemporary record is based on hearsay evidence, the words attributed to him are so closely in keeping with the spirit he displayed on many other occasions that their tenor, at least, may be accepted as factual. With characteristic bombast and exaggeration, but with patent sincerity, he is said to have declared before the North End caucus during a discussion as to how the British troops were to be driven from Boston:

"Burn Boston and make John Hancock a beggar if the public good requires it!" [31]

The man who stood to lose most by the burning never did himself more credit than by advocating it. In this purple passage, perhaps more forthrightly than in any of his other utterances on behalf of the great cause, the patriot in purple proved his right to the sobriquet.

· 12 ·

The Second Provincial Congress adjourned on April 15 to May 10, when it was to reassemble at Watertown after taking the most elaborate precautions to anticipate every move made by Gage's forces, to spread the word throughout the countryside, and to cope with any eventuality. These measures were effectuated through vigilance committees in Boston and surrounding towns.

Even the latest secret advices from England concerning the temper of Crown and Parliament were relayed to Hancock as head of the overall committee of safety, upon which the local preparedness groups were patterned. An hour after the Congress recessed John received one from the Cambridge coterie.

"We are certainly obliged to you, Gentlemen," he replied during the same evening, "for the early notice you gave us of the important intelligence. Our Congress have . . . determined upon measures which, under God . . . may work the salvation of this Province. . . . This intelligence from England ought, by no means, to occasion the least relaxation in measures here; but . . . every preparation [should be] made for an effectual opposition, if drove to that extremity. They that are best prepared for war are also best prepared for peace." [32]

The intelligence probably referred to Pitt's and Burke's eleventh-hour attempt to avert war in impassioned pleas before the House of Lords that such coercive acts as the Port Bill be repealed and that the inflaming Redcoats be removed from Boston. As Hancock and his committee evidently foresaw, the Prime Minister, Lord North, and the conservative majority which he controlled were deaf to these appeals. But news of the liberal statesmen's failure had not reached Massachusetts when the Cambridge correspondence was dispatched to Concord.

Meanwhile Gage, smarting under criticism from the Ministry for inaction and indecision, finally had made up his mind to take the bold step from which he had shrunk so long. He planned to launch, on the night of April 18–19, a swift surprise attack upon the military stores at Concord. But he had a less apparent purpose which overshadowed in importance the ostensible one, according to Dr. Warren, who had been put in charge of the Boston headquarters of the Whigs' espionage system. This was to put out of action the two most explosive elements in the rebel arsenal—Hancock and Adams.

However, they were apprised by Revere three days before the projected sortie that there was suspicious-looking activity in the British camp. One of his depositions describes it and what he did about it:

"In the winter, towards spring, we frequently took turns, two and two, to watch the soldiers by patrolling the streets all night. The Saturday night preceding the 19th of April, about 12 o'clock . . . , the boats belonging to the transports were all launched and carried under the sterns of the men-of-war. . . . We likewise found that the grenadiers and light infantry were all taken off duty. . . . On Tuesday evening . . . it was observed that a number of soldiers were marching towards the bottom of the Common. About 10 o'clock Doctor Warren sent in great haste for me and begged that I would immediately set off for Lexington, where Messrs. Hancock and Adams were, and acquaint them of the movement and that it was thought they were the objects. When I got to Doctor Warren's house I found he had sent an express by land to Lexington—a Mr. William Dawes. The Sunday before, by desire of Doctor Warren, I had been to Lexington to Messrs. Hancock and Adams." [33]

Thinking to prevent a forewarning of his scheme from leaking out of Boston during the day preceding the contemplated foray, Gage threw a cordon of officers across all the roads leading to Lexington and Concord; and to allay suspicion he sent them out in small parties, with their arms concealed, at widely separated intervals. This expedient, however, did not deceive the alert committee of safety, which was in session at Wetherby's Tavern in Menotomy (now Arlington) about six miles away in the direction of Boston and off the main highway. After its adjournment late in the afternoon Hancock and Adams went to the Clark parsonage, where Sam also had taken lodging. Most of the other members, including Richard Devens and Abraham Watson, who set out for Charlestown, scattered to their homes or temporary quarters; but Elbridge Gerry, one of the most prominent and capable, remained at the meeting place to spend the night preparatory to resumption of business on the morrow.

Riding to Charlestown in a chaise, Devens and Watson suddenly spied nine red-coated figures on horseback, dimly silhouetted against the darkening sky, advancing toward them. As the patriots started to pass they were asked by one of the horsemen where Clark's Tavern was. The questioner evidently had the parsonage confused with Buckman Tavern, also in Lexington, but left no doubt in the minds of the committeemen that the horsemen were seeking the former. Devens, by his quick-witted answer that it was on the Concord road, may have saved the lives of Hancock and Adams. He and his companion then either returned to Menotomy to notify Gerry of their encounter or continued to Charlestown and sent word from there.

In any event, Gerry passed on the tidings to the intended quarry of the British man hunt by an express messenger, who eluded and outdistanced the patrol by taking a bypath. In a message bearing the marginal notation "9 P.M." and carried by the same dispatch rider Hancock thus acknowledged receipt of the timely warning:

"I am much obliged for your notice. It is said the officers are gone Concord road, and I will send word thither. . . . I intend doing myself the pleasure of being with you tomorrow." [34]

But neither the word nor the sender reached the destination specified. Both were diverted by the stirring events connected with the midnight ride of Paul Revere.

IX

ALARUMS AND EXCURSIONS

AMONG THE military phases of the American Revolution most exhaustively discussed by historians are Paul Revere's ride and the battle of Lexington; but many of the writers have let their imaginations run so rampant that the conscientious chronicler is at his wit's end to unravel fact from fiction. The task has been further complicated by Henry Wadsworth Longfellow, who took unbridled license with historical truth in his poem about Revere's dramatic dash over the Middlesex countryside.

Since Hancock and Adams were so closely identified with the events leading up to the shot heard 'round the world—and were driven by these to a decision that could radically have altered the administrative conduct of the war—it seems especially incumbent upon a biographer to go to eyewitness sources for accounts of what actually happened. The graphic, straightforward depositions of the midnight rider and other actors in this momentous melodrama will be closely adhered to.

On the Sunday night preceding the grand climax Paul Revere returned from the Clark parsonage in Lexington to Boston—a distance of sixteen miles—by way of Charlestown. "There I agreed with a Colonel Conant and some other gentleman," he testifies, "that if the British went out by water we would show two lanterns in the North Church steeple and, if by land, one as a signal." Then he picks up the thread of the story at the point where he digressed after telling of being summoned by Warren on Tuesday evening:

"I left Doctor Warren, called upon a friend and desired him to make the signals. I then went home, took my boots and surtout, went to the north part of the town, where I had kept a boat. Two friends rowed me across the Charles River, a little to the eastward where the *Somerset* man-of-war lay. It was then young flood; the ship was winding, and the moon was rising. They landed me on the Charlestown side. When I got into town I met Colonel Conant and several others. They said they had seen our signals. I told them what was acting. . . . I got a horse of Deacon Larkin. . . . I set off. . . . It was then about 11 o'clock and very pleasant.

"After I had passed Charlestown Neck and got nearly opposite where Mark was hung in chains I saw two men on horseback under a tree. When I got near them I discovered they were British officers. . . . I turned my horse very quick and galloped towards Charlestown Neck and then pushed for the Medford road . . . and up to Menotomy. In Medford I awaked the captain of the Minute Men and after that I alarmed almost every house till I got to Lexington. I found Messrs. Hancock and Adams at the Reverend Mr. Clark's. I told them my errand and inquired for Mr. Dawes. They said he had not been there. . . . After . . . about half an hour Mr. Dawes came. We refreshed ourselves and set off for Concord to secure the stores." [1]

They had not been long on the road to Concord—six miles away—when Dr. Samuel Prescott overtook them, riding home after calling on his sweetheart in Lexington. Revere thus deposed:

"When we had got about half-way from Lexington to Concord the other two stopped at a house to wake the man. . . . When I had got about 200 yards ahead of them I saw two officers as before. . . . In an instant I saw four of them, who rode up to me with their pistols in their hands [and] said, 'G——d d——n you, stop! If you go an inch further you are a dead man.'

"Immediately Mr. Prescott came up we attempted to git through them, but they . . . swore, if we did not turn into that pasture, they would blow our brains out. . . . When we had got in Mr. Prescott said, 'Put on.' He took to the left, I to the right, towards a wood. . . . Just as I reached it, out started six officers, seized my bridle, put their pistols to my breast, ordered me to dismount, which I did."

He was questioned by several of the officers, particularly by Major Edward Mitchell, who was in command of the detachments fanning out on the roads leading to Concord. On hearing that the countryside had been aroused and five hundred men soon would be defending Lexington, the major decided to round up his charges before they could be cut off, and lead them back to the column advancing from Boston under Lieutenant Colonel Francis Smith.

"He then ordered me to mount my horse. They first searched me for pistols. When I was mounted the major took the reins out of my hand

. . . and gave them to an officer . . . to lead me. He then ordered four men out of the bushes and to mount their horses. They were countrymen * which they had stopped. Then ordered us to march. He said to me, 'We are now going towards your friends, and if you attempt to run, or we are insulted, we will blow your brains out.'

"When we had got into the road they formed a circle and ordered the prisoners in the center and to lead me in the front. We rid towards Lexington a quick pace. . . . When we got within about half a mile of the meeting-house we heard a gun fired. The major asked me what it was for. I told him, to alarm the country. He ordered the four prisoners to dismount. . . . Then one of the officers . . . told the men they might go about their business. . . . He then ordered us to march. When we got within sight of the meeting-house we heard a volley of guns fired, as I supposed, at the tavern as an alarm. The major ordered us to halt. . . . He then asked the sergeant if his horse was tired. He said, 'Yes.' He ordered him to take my horse. They cut the bridle and saddle of the sergeant's horse and rode off down the road. I then went to the house where I left Messrs. Adams and Hancock and told them what had happened. Their friends advised them to git out of the way. I went with them about two miles across road."

By "across road" Revere evidently meant across country. The meeting-house was on the Bedford road facing the common from the Boston side. Buckman Tavern, here referred to, still stands on the same highway at its junction with the one leading to Concord. The parsonage was then a few hundred yards up the Bedford turnpike. Paul continues:

"After resting myself I set off with another man † to go back to the tavern to enquire the news. When we got there we were told the troops were within two miles. We went into the tavern to git a trunk of papers belonging to Colonel Hancock. Before we left the house I saw the Ministerial troops from the chamber window. We made haste and had to pass through our militia, who were on a green behind the meeting-house to the number, as I supposed, about fifty or sixty. . . . As I passed I heard the commanding officer speak to his men to this purpose: 'Let the troops pass by and don't molest them without they begin first.' I had to go across road but had not got half . . . when the Ministerial troops appeared . . . behind the meeting-house. They made a short halt, when one gun was fired. I heard the report, turned my head, and saw the smoke in front of the troops. They immediately gave a great

* Including Hancock's messenger, Solomon Brown.
† Hancock's clerk, John Lowell.

shout, ran a few paces, and then the whole fired. . . . At this time I could not see our militia, for they were covered from me by a house at the bottom of the street." [2]

Although scholars and writers for popular consumption, in prose and poetry, have delved into the welter of conflicting evidence as to what took place at Lexington on the fateful night of April 18–19, 1775, Revere's matter-of-fact version—so far as it goes—seems to approach as close to the truth as possible. There is definite proof that eight of the Minutemen were killed and ten wounded, while one British private and the horse ridden by Major John Pitcairn at the head of the Redcoats were hit, in the little skirmish of great consequence. But who fired the shot that started it probably always will remain a mystery, obscured by the haze of time as effectually as the shooter's identity was hidden from Paul by the puff of smoke.

· 2 ·

For events at the Clark domicile just before and after Revere's first visit it is necessary to turn to Sergeant William Munroe, a survivor of the tragic, immortal conflict on Lexington Green. His testimony suggests that the inmates of the parsonage were not fully cognizant of their peril on this night of nights, despite the ominous advance information they had received:

"Early in the evening of the 18th . . . I was informed by Solomon Brown, who had just returned from Boston, that he had seen nine British officers on the road. . . . On learning this I supposed they had some design upon Hancock and Adams . . . and immediately assembled . . . eight men . . . to guard the house. About midnight . . . Paul Revere rode up and requested admittance. I told him the family had just retired and had requested that they might not be disturbed by any noise about the house.

" 'Noise!' said he. 'You'll have noise enough before long. The regulars are coming out.'

"We then permitted him to pass. Soon after Mr. Lincoln * came. These gentlemen . . . both brought letters from Doctor Warren . . . to Hancock and Adams, stating that a large body of British troops . . . were on their march to Lexington. On this it was thought advisable that Hancock and Adams should withdraw to some distant part of the town. To this Hancock consented with great reluctance and said as he went

* Munroe meant Dawes.

off, 'If I had my musket I would never turn my back on these troops.' " [3]

Concerning Hancock's gun Munroe flatly contradicts Dorothy Quincy's story, paraphrased by Sumner. This illustrates how unreliable even reports of contemporaries can be, when made half a century after the event.

"Mr. Hancock gave the alarm immediately," Sumner describes her as saying, "and the Lexington bell was rung all night; and before light about 150 men * were collected. Mr. H. was all night cleaning his gun and sword and putting his accouterments in order, and was determined to go out to the plain by the meetinghouse . . . to fight . . . ; and it was with very great difficulty that he was dissuaded from it by Mr. Clark and Mr. Adams. The latter, clapping him on the shoulder, said to him, 'That is not our business; we belong to the Cabinet.' " [4]

Despite the discrepancy between the statements regarding the weapons, it would seem to be fair, in the light of attestation by two witnesses, to assume that Hancock really was foolhardy enough to expose himself to British vengeance in the field, as he had done so often in the forum. Although later accused by politically prejudiced persons of cowardice, he demonstrated both physical and moral courage too many times to be adjudged faint-hearted. And a desire to play the swashbuckling hero would be consistent with his frustrated ambition, betrayed on several occasions, to distinguish himself in military circles. But it was well for the Revolutionary movement that Adams' discreet counsel prevailed.

Regardless of whether John reached for his gun, his sword, or merely his hat, the battle of Lexington was as sharp a turning point in his career as in the history of America. Heretofore, like most of the colonists, he had been bitterly resentful toward the mother country. He and they had flouted her authority politically, economically, and—as in connection with the *Liberty* seizure and the Boston Massacre—even physically. But neither he nor they had really wished to fight England. Now, at the instant when the green common was stained red by the first drop of blood to fall from a Minuteman's wound, Hancock became an outright revolutionary.

By heritage and environment, by nature and training, he had been a man of peace. He never had sought a quarrel, although he had been ever ready to stand up for his rights. A born compromiser, he always had been willing to go more than halfway in adjusting his differences with an opponent. He had secretly hoped, up to the sorry second when

* Against Revere's correct estimate of fifty or sixty.

the trigger was pulled by an unknown finger on the Lexington lawn, that actual war with Britain could be averted.

Henceforth he was convinced—and was reconciled to the conviction—that the deep cleavage between his *patria* and his principles must either be seared into an unhealable breach, or fused into a sound unit, in the heat of armed strife. He was now a sworn enemy of the King, the Ministry, and everything they represented. More wholeheartedly than all but a small minority of his fellow countrymen, he was resolved to keep the flame burning until it should accomplish the one result or the other.

· 3 ·

Revere does not state when he paid his second visit to the parsonage, or what Hancock was doing at the moment. But Munroe, who claims to have conducted Hancock and Adams (presumably together with Revere and the clerk, Lowell) to the northern part of the town, returned and went to the meetinghouse at about two o'clock. According to Dolly's recollection, the preeminent patriots did not leave until daybreak, which would have occurred after five o'clock. A letter written by Caesar Rodney, Delaware delegate to the Second Continental Congress, indicates that they made their getaway in Hancock's phaeton just before the fighting began:

"Mr. Hancock told me he had been to see that small company at Lexington exercise and had not left them more [than] ten minutes when the troops came up and that they had no suspicion of any." [5]

That would time Hancock's departure from the scene of battle about four-twenty, for Jonas Clark testified that he heard the alarm guns and drumbeat to arms at approximately four-thirty.

The "standard authorities" on the history of Lexington and surrounding localities differ almost as radically on the itinerary of the fugitives during the next two days as on the origin of the famous first shot. The consensus seems to be that they remained concealed until the British resumed their march at the point—probably a clump of woods—to which Munroe had taken them; that they then drove to the house of a Mr. Reed on the outskirts of Woburn (Burlington, not the present Woburn); that they moved on from there to the residence of the Reverend Thomas Jones' widow in the village proper and spent the night of the 20th at the home of Amos Wyman in Billerica.

It is not necessary to speculate on what happened in Lexington meanwhile. The vivid, detailed account of Elizabeth Clark, Jonas' daughter, has the ring of truth, even though it was written many years later. Addressing her niece from the parsonage, where she still lived, the spinster ruminated:

"Oh! Lucy, how many descendants can I count from the venerable Hancock down to this day, which is sixty-six years since the war began on the common, which I now can see from this window . . . and . . . in my mind just as plain—all the British troops marching off the common to Concord and the whole scene: how Aunt Hancock and Miss Dolly Quincy, with their cloaks and bonnets on; Aunt crying and wringing her hands and helping Mother dress the children; Dolly going round with Father to hide money, watches, and anything down in the potatoes and up garret. And then Grandfather Clark sent down men with carts, took *your* mother and all the children but Jonas and me and Sally, a babe six months old. Father sent Jonas down to Grandfather Cook's to see who was killed and what their condition was; and in the afternoon Father, Mother, with me and the baby, went to the meeting-house. There was the eight men that was killed, . . . all in boxes made of four large boards nailed up; and, after Pa had prayed, they were put into two horse carts and took into the graveyard." ⁰

This otherwise minute description of the scene in the Clark homestead omits one of the most dramatic incidents as retailed by Sumner from Hancock's widow:

"The ladies remained and saw the battle commence. . . . One of the first British bullets whizzed by old Mrs. Hancock's head as she was looking out of the door and struck the barn. She cried out, 'What is that?' They told her it was a bullet and she must take care of herself. Mrs. Scott * was at the chamber window looking at the fight. She says two of the wounded men were brought into the house."

Hancock's desertion of his aunt and his fiancée at such a time would not seem, on first consideration, to be the acme of gallantry. But to tag along through the woods, even in the extra carriage, would have exposed them to greater danger than to remain in the Clark home, under the protection of four men—for Revere and Lowell presumably had returned with the trunk to join the Reverend Jonas and his father. In the eighteenth century armies did not wage upon women and children the total war of our more enlightened century. But the ladies might have been subjected unavoidably to rough treatment, in the event of capture with the fleeing patriots. So John Hancock could hearken honorably to the pleading of Adams that they save their own hides.

* Dolly married Captain Scott three years after John Hancock's death.

He may not have worried about Aunt Lydia or Dorothy, but he became concerned about his stomach—always an object of the deepest solicitude with him—as soon as he and his companion were secure in the village. He dispatched a note to his womenfolk, "wishing them to get into the carriage and come over and bring the fine salmon that they had had sent to them for dinner." This they did and "had got it nicely cooked and were just sitting down to it when in came a man from Lexington. . . . Half frightened to death, he exclaimed, 'The British are coming! The British are coming! My wife's in eternity now.' Mr. H. and Mr. Adams . . . went into the swamp and stayed till the alarm was over."

When they had retraced their steps to the Jones domicile there occurred the previously mentioned near-rupture of Hancock's engagement. The lovers' quarrel, revealing the willfulness with which John would have to contend throughout his marital life, is thus reported by Sumner:

"Upon their return to the house Mrs. Scott told Mr. H. that, having left her father in Boston, she should return to him tomorrow. 'No, madam,' said he, 'you shall not return as long as there is a British bayonet in Boston.' She . . . said, 'Recollect, Mr. Hancock, I am not under your control yet. I *shall* go to my father'; for, . . . at that time, she should have been very glad to have got rid of him, but her aunt—as she afterwards was—would not let her go." [7]

· 4 ·

Why Gage's forces did not attempt to carry out the most important part of their mission by scouring the countryside in search of Hancock and Adams is another of the many mysteries connected with one of the most baffling episodes in American history. Perhaps it was because, realizing that hundreds of straight-shooting yeomen were converging upon Concord in response to Revere's rallying ride, they decided that no time was to be lost in seizing the stores and getting back to their base.

But the two Americans seem to have thought that it still was in progress after the British had moved on. There is no discoverable purpose in their continual shifting from one hide-out to another for two days except to throw pursuers off the scent.

The peripatetic patriots remained at the Wyman place, as already recorded, until morning. Then they returned to Woburn and escorted the ladies back to Billerica. Revere and Lowell probably completed the reunion of fugitives around Amos' hospitable hearth on the 20th. They would have delivered Adams' trunk to him for his journey to the Second Continental Congress at Philadelphia, on the following day.

"Oh! What a glorious morning is this!" Adams is said to have exclaimed as he and Hancock rolled away toward Worcester, to meet the other Massachusetts representatives—John Adams, Thomas Cushing, and Robert Treat Paine. It was indeed the beginning of a perfect day for Sam Adams, who now could see that his long-cherished hopes for independence from England were definitely closer to fulfillment.

Bidding farewell to Hancock's two clinging vines, who crept off to Point Shirley at approximately the same time, must have contributed materially to Adams' elation. But he and John were not to enjoy their freedom long, for the ladies were to rejoin them at Worcester.

In the meantime Aunt Lydia and Dolly traipsed about the province in a seemingly aimless manner. They went back to Point Shirley and then by the long way through Lancaster to Worcester, probably visiting the Whitneys and the Greenleafs. They stopped off at the home of Dolly's sister, Sarah Quincy Greenleaf, just long enough for dinner on the 25th. This was ten days before Edmund Quincy arrived there.

Quincy had left Boston on the 29th, for Gage had issued a proclamation granting the inhabitants permission to evacuate, with all their effects except firearms, on and after the 28th. He was well advised in speeding his departure, for the commander in chief went back on his word shortly afterward. His edict seems to have been a ruse to induce the citizens to surrender their weapons.

Quincy's diary of his journey to Lancaster brings up, by indirection, one of the saddest chapters in the annals of his family. It records that he spent a night in Cambridge with the Jonathan Sewells, who fled to England less than four months later to escape the senseless wrath visited upon the Tories. Sewell, one of the hardest-shelled of Tories, had felt this as far back as 1774, when the Boston rabble had rioted in an effort to force all Crown officers to resign and his home had been attacked. In 1788 the exiled daughter and son-in-law returned to America—to St. John, New Brunswick, where he died eight years afterward.

The only denier of the Whig faith in the Quincy clan, Sewell seems to have remained on good terms with all his direct in-laws. But a letter from the British capital in 1777 to John Lowell, Sr., his successor in the royal government of Massachusetts and the father of Mrs. Ebenezer Hancock, contains a tirade for John Hancock:

"Tell your Boston friend I remember his cautions and shall never fly to him for protection; but that a day is coming, with hasty strides, when his ill-gotten, pirated wealth must be refunded to the right owners with interest. When he wants my protection or friendship he shall find me ready to assist him so far as shall be consistent with my *loyalty*." [8]

· 5 ·

When they arrived at Worcester on April 24 Hancock and Adams began to question the loyalty (in a cooperative sense) of their fellow members on the committee of safety. The other delegates were not there; no word as to their whereabouts had been sent, and the guard of honor that apparently had been promised to the representatives by the liaison group back home was nowhere to be seen. Dr. Warren, chairman of the committee *pro tem*, and his hard-pressed cohorts probably were too busy figuring out how to cope with Gage's next move to concern themselves about anybody else, however important. But the sensitive seignior of the Beacon Hill manor, without taking that into consideration, sat down to impart his panicky, disconnected thoughts to the committeemen:

"Mr. S. Adams and myself . . . find no intelligence from you and no guard. We . . . hear an express has just passed through this place to you from New York, informing that Administration is bent upon pushing matters and that four regiments are expected there. How are we to proceed? Where are our brethren? Surely we ought to be supported. I had rather be with you, and at present am fully determined to be with you, before I proceed."

Revealing that he and Adams were as confused over the military developments at Lexington and Concord as most of those involved, but that they keenly appreciated the importance of proving that the enemy had been the aggressor, he went on:

"I . . . pray, furnish us with depositions of the conduct of the [British] troops, the certainty of their firing first, and every circumstance . . . from the 19th instant to this time, that we may be able to give some account of matters as we proceed, and especially at Philadelphia. And I beg you would order your secretary to make out a copy of your proceedings since—what has taken place and what your plan is; what prisoners we have and what they have of ours; who of note was killed on both sides; who commands our forces."

In the next paragraph the burgeoning statesman, probably with Adams at his elbow, advocated the siege of Boston and reasserted his willingness to be the chief sacrificial goat. He also showed an awareness that the

Revolutionary movement had passed from the purely political to the politico-martial phase as he continued inspirationally:

"Are our men in good spirits? For God's sake do not suffer the spirit to subside until they have perfected the reduction of our enemies. Boston must be entered; the troops must be sent away. . . . Our friends are valuable, but our country must be saved. I have an interest in that town. What can be the enjoyment of that to me if I am obliged to hold it at the will of General Gage or any one else? . . . We must have the Castle. . . . Stop up the harbor against large vessels coming."

Characteristically, he could not remain in such a rarefied atmosphere long. He had to come down to earth and claim the deference to which he considered himself entitled. The sense of dignity inherited from Bishop Hancock and the patrician pride infused by Uncle Thomas crop up in the concluding passage, which refers again, by implication, to the pledged military escort:

"Where is Cushing? Are Mr. Paine and Mr. John Adams to be with us? What are we to depend upon? We travel rather as deserters, which I will not submit to. I will return and join you if I cannot travel in reputation. . . . How goes on the Congress? Who is your President? God be with you." [9]

Hancock thought better of his threat to go back to where he had come from. He and Adams pushed on three days later with no other attendants than Aunt Lydia and Dolly, who had turned up meanwhile. When they reached Hartford on the 29th they called upon Governor Jonathan Trumbull and planned with him the first American counterattack of the war—the capture of Fort Ticonderoga on Lake Champlain by an expedition under Ethan Allen and Benedict Arnold. The consummation of the scheme on May 10 was a happy augury for the Second Continental Congress as it went into session.

Hancock was freed at last to devote himself exclusively to matters of state when he left his "female connections" behind at the home of Thaddeus Burr in Fairfield. At the average daily carriage pace of the period—twenty-five miles—they would have arrived May 5, for the male members were in New York the next day.

Fairfield was an ideal haven for Aunt Lydia and Dolly. Burr not only was an old friend of John's family but, as high sheriff of the county and one of the most zealous patriots in the colony, could be trusted implicitly to see that no harm came to his charges. Furthermore, he had considerable wealth and was in a position to provide them, in his commodious mansion, with the comforts and luxuries to which they were accustomed. This was Dolly's residence until her marriage there four months later, and the domicile of her aging guardian until her death in 1776.

· 6 ·

The reception at New York more than compensated for the neglect suffered at the hands of the Massachusetts committee of safety. With feigned modesty but obviously with supreme delight, John Hancock described it to Dolly in a letter which is one of his most revealing self-portraits. Dated the 7th, it reads:

"I arrived well, though fatigued, at King's Bridge at 50 minutes past 2 o'clock yesterday, where I found the delegates of Massachusetts and Connecticut, with a number of gentlemen from New York and a guard of the troop. I dined and then set out in procession for New York—the carriage of your humble servant, of course, being first in the procession. When we arrived within three miles of the city we were met by the Grenadier Company and a regiment of the city militia under arms, gentlemen in carriages and on horseback, and many thousand persons on foot—the roads filled with people and the greatest cloud of dust I ever saw. . . .

"When I got within a mile of the city my carriage was stopped and people, appearing with proper harnesses, insisted upon taking out my horses and dragging me into and through the city—a circumstance I would not have had taken place upon any consideration, not being fond of such parade. I begged and entreated they would suspend their design, and . . . the matter subsided. But when I got to the entrance of the city, and the number of spectators increased to perhaps 7000 or more, they declared they *would* have the horses out and *would drag me themselves* through the city. I repeated my request that they would so far oblige me as not to insist upon it. They would not hearken, and I was obliged to apply to the leading gentlemen in the procession to intercede with them. . . . They were at last prevailed upon, and I proceeded. I was much obliged to them for their good wishes and opinions—in short, no person could possibly be more noticed than myself."

The greatest egotist of all the founding fathers omitted to mention the fact, brought out by Silas Deane, one of the Connecticut representatives, that the populace had tried to pay the same homage to the entire party. But there is no reason to doubt that he was justified in interpreting the crowd's favor as being directed particularly at him, for the fame of his numerous gestures of defiance toward the British government had spread throughout the colonies.

As soon as the delegates, who now totaled fourteen, reached what presumably was Whig headquarters they "were visited by a great number of gentlemen of the first character in the city, who took up the evening." John sat down to a supper of fried oysters in Fraunces' Tavern at ten o'clock and went to bed in an inn at eleven. The next day, Sunday, he got up at five o'clock and went to meeting both in the morning and in the afternoon. "Tomorrow morning," he resumed, "propose to cross the ferry. We are to have a large guard in several boats. . . . I can't think they will dare attack us." He could not help feeling a bit sorry for himself and playing on Dolly's sympathy. "My poor face and eyes are in a most shocking situation; burnt up and much swelled and a little painful. I don't know how to manage with it. . . . Pray let me hear from you by every post," he concluded with a plaintiveness that was repeatedly to fall on deaf ears.[10]

That he did not exaggerate the enthusiasm with which the Congressional cortège was greeted on the outskirts of New York is attested by Silas Deane, who wrote to his wife that "a battalion of about 800 men in uniform and bayonets fixed, with a band of music, received us with the military salute" and "led us down the main street to the corner of Wall Street; up that and down the Broadway by the fort; then up to Fraunces' Tavern."

Hancock may still have been in the clouds Monday morning, when he journeyed on through New Jersey: "On our arrival within three miles of Newark," Deane recounted, "a troop of horse and a company of grenadiers met us; but, to Mr. Hancock's and the people's extreme disappointment, he—in his haste—took another road and passed the ferry direct to Elizabethtown."

He caught up with the cavalcade at that town, and must have soared on the wings of ecstasy all the way from there to Philadelphia. The delegates were lionized almost continuously, by military and civilian welcoming groups, as they drove through Woodbridge, New Brunswick, Princeton (where the president and students of the College of New Jersey, now Princeton University, joined in), Trenton, and Bristol.

"The next morning [May 10] set out for Philadelphia," Deane resumed, "and were met at about six miles on this side of the city by about 200 of the principal gentlemen on horseback, with their swords drawn. . . . Thence began a most lengthy procession; half the gentlemen on horseback in the van; . . . then Hancock and Adams. . . . Our rear

closed with the remainder of the gentlemen on horseback . . . and then
the carriages from the city. . . . At about two miles distance we were
met by a company on foot and then by a company of riflemen. . . .
Thus rolling and gathering like a snowball, we approached the city." [11]

This résumé of events leading up to the triumphal procession into
Philadelphia, which hardly could have been eclipsed if the participants
had been conquering military heroes instead of harried civilians, is an
understatement by comparison with that of Judge Samuel Curwen, another observer. And Curwen, as a former Boston merchant suspected of
Tory tendencies who had sought asylum among the Quakers, would have
been inclined to belittle rather than magnify the scene. He recorded in
his journal:

"Early in the morning a great number of persons rode out several
miles, . . . when, about 11 o'clock, the cavalcade appeared (I being
near the upper end of Fore Street); first, two or three hundred gentlemen on horseback, . . . followed by John Hancock and Samuel Adams
in a phaeton and pair, the former looking as if his journey and high
living, or solicitude to support the dignity of the first man in Massachusetts, had impaired his health. Next came John Adams and Thomas
Cushing in a single-horse chaise; behind followed Robert Treat Paine,
and after him the New York delegation and some from the province of
Connecticut. . . . The rear was brought up by a hundred carriages, the
streets crowded with people of all ages, sexes, and ranks. The procession
marched with a slow, solemn pace. On its entrance into the city all the
bells were set ringing . . . and every mark of respect that could be was
expressed; not much, I presume, to the secret liking of their fellow-
delegates from the other colonies, who doubtless had to digest the distinction as easily as they could." [12]

There was no rest for the weary delegates. They scarcely had time to
wash off the grime of the dusty roads and to eat dinner before the opening of the Second Continental Congress in Independence Hall. Hancock was so busy that a month elapsed before he wrote to Dolly. His
mind probably was occupied with politics—especially the phase affecting
the advancement of his personal interests—to the exclusion of virtually
everything else.

The next couple of weeks in the governmental chamber were devoted
mainly to procedural matters; but there was little peace or quiet. Deane
thus conveyed to his wife the pulsating impression made upon him by
the sounds of Philadelphia:

"The drum and fife are hourly sounding in every street, and my brain-pan is this moment echoing to the beat parading under my window." [13]

· 7 ·

Philadelphia had been a throbbing center—the only one in colonial America that could be dignified by the term "city" in the modern sense —for thirty-five years. By virtue of its extensive and variegated commerce its people were among the most cosmopolitan and sophisticated in the New World. Its population had increased from 13,000 in 1740 to almost 40,000 in 1775, making it the largest city in the British colonies.

Despite its Quaker origin and surface refinement, it was essentially a rowdy, roistering community of sharp contrasts. Indians wrapped in gaudy, dirty blankets and smoking clay pipes; Pennsylvania Dutch in wooden shoes; gawky Swedes from Delaware; hunters in filthy leather jackets, carrying six-foot rifles, from the back counties—all joined to form an incongruous substratum for a silk-and-satin society that was intensely aristocratic at the top. This made for much greater unrest than existed in Boston, which was far from democratic in a social sense but was more homogeneous in the composition of its inhabitants.

Slavery and the selling of slaves were practiced as heartlessly as any-where in the southern colonies. Auctions were conducted without the slightest regard for the feelings of the chattels. Miles Hennisy was notorious for the cynical disdain with which he used his silver-headed cane to prod Negro girls out of their pens and onto the block. While arousing the desire of the male customers with erotic descriptions of their bodies he would keep the wenches covered, but when the bidding reached a profitable level he would expose them in their nakedness. In giving a sales talk about the black men he would stress their breeding qualifications.

And yet life in the capital of Pennsylvania was good to those who could pay for its abundance. Fat pigs were raised in the neighboring German counties. Long-wooled sheep were pastured on the uplands north of the city. The near-by Alleghenies were teeming with deer.

This prosperity was reflected in the houses and streets. Set in neat rows, the solid-looking homes were constructed mainly of brick. Every important thoroughfare was cobbled. The buildings were safeguarded by the most up-to-date fire department of the colonial period. And the people's minds were protected from stultification by a public library and more freedom of thought than was to be found anywhere else on the continent.

But the smugness engendered by all these advantages stifled whatever good will toward the Revolutionary movement might have sprung from the Philadelphians' culture. The intellectuals on the whole were too absorbed in their comparatively insignificant new schools of literature and art to bother with the greatest experiment of an age.

The business leaders and moneyed men in general were ultraconservative, both economically and politically. They were completely satisfied with the basic principles of the existing order and had no sympathy with Sam Adams' iconoclastic ideas, even though the British trade restrictions cut heavily into their potential profits. Because of their infinitely richer resources for export they could stand the import duties much better than the hard-scrabbling New Englanders.

Such was the uncongenial and distracting atmosphere in which Hancock had to work for two years and a half. Both he and the Second Continental Congress as a whole were constantly made conscious of the indifference, if not actual hostility, toward their efforts of the community in which they struggled with some of the most difficult problems ever tackled by statesmen.[14]

· 8 ·

On May 24 the Congress unanimously elected Hancock President to succeed Peyton Randolph, who had left for Williamsburg to fulfill what he regarded as the more important duties of speaker of the Virginia Assembly, replacing the old House of Burgesses. The vacated post had been offered to Henry Middleton of South Carolina, but he had declined on account of poor health. The new incumbent plunged into his duties at once—undoubtedly in high fettle over receiving the greatest honor that could be conferred upon any American, but with little conception of the arduous and thankless labor it entailed.

This overwhelming tribute apparently was too much even for the poise of the urbane gentleman from Beacon Hill. He is said to have been ill at ease when Randolph's fellow Virginian, Benjamin Harrison, made the gracious gesture of escorting him to the chair. As the President took his seat Harrison is supposed to have declared: "We will show Great Britain how much we value her proscriptions."[15]

The Congress then resolved itself into a committee of the whole "to take into their farther consideration the state of America."[16] This vague wording covered a multitude of the sins—including interminable debates that wandered far from the subject, wrangling over inconsequential matters, and indecisiveness in general—which paralyzed for weeks what had been designed as an administrative body for the conduct of the war.

The main trouble was that the members lacked authority to legislate for the colonies in their entirety. Each of the thirteen provinces was jealous of its prerogatives and sovereign rights. None was willing to delegate executive power, even for levying taxes or borrowing money. The Congress was purely a deliberative and advisory body whose recommendations took effect only upon ratification by the colonial assemblies.

Any man who undertook the Presidency of this loose, dissident assemblage labored under a tremendous handicap, for the office carried little more weight than the chairmanship of a convention. Hancock toiled under the additional disadvantage of being intellectually inferior to many of the statesmen he presided over. Furthermore, most of these men of strong character and conviction held views at variance with those of the radical majority of the Massachusetts delegation. Few of the representatives from other colonies were willing, at first, to go along with the belief in independence from England which Sam Adams had inculcated in his followers.

Hancock's saving grace—and his greatest contribution to the founding of the nation—was his ability to mediate between bitterly antagonistic factions and maintain the semblance of unity until it could be made an actuality—in an official sense, at least—by the Declaration of Independence. For this service alone he is entitled to high esteem from his spiritual descendants.

Another important function he performed was to keep the colonial assemblies informed of Congressional actions, to wheedle them into complying with resolutions, and to pacify them when their pet projects were ignored or nullified. This involved laborious, unspectacular, voluminous daily correspondence. Governors, generals, and influential politicians also were on his mailing list for similar reasons.

Hancock was, in many respects, merely a glorified clerk. Nevertheless, he was an almost indispensable cog in the creaking governmental machinery.

· 9 ·

It was just as well for what remained of his peace of mind that John Hancock was too busy to moon about his Dolly during this—to her—

merry month of May. If he had had time to run up to Fairfield over a certain week end, he would have been considerably perturbed.

Aaron Burr, lady killer extraordinary, visited his uncle Thaddeus just a fortnight after Hancock deposited his fiancée in the supposedly safe custody of that patriot. On Monday the 15th, the senior Burr wrote to Tapping Reeve about the goings-on under his roof during the two preceding days:

"Burr came to us on Saturday evening; spent the Sabbath with us. Mrs. Hancock is vastly pleased with him. And, as to Miss Quincy, if Mr. H. was out of the way I don't know but she would court him. . . . Burr went off to Greenfield last night." [17]

Dolly's reminiscences, as recited to Sumner, diverge diametrically from Thaddeus' report of Aunt Lydia's reaction to Aaron. In her dotage Hancock's widow apparently romanticized her association with every prominent man for the sake of basking in reflected glory. Here is her version of what amounted to only a passing acquaintance:

"Aaron, she says, was very attentive to her, and her aunt was very jealous of him, lest he should gain her affections and defeat her purpose of connecting her with her nephew. Mr. Burr, she said, was a handsome young man of very pretty fortune, but her aunt would not leave them a moment together." [18]

Dorothy Dudley, a contemporary Cambridge diarist and correspondent, confirmed the other Dorothy's claim to young Burr's attentions in a letter to a Philadelphia friend:

"He is a young man of fascinating manners and many accomplishments. He was much charmed with Miss Quincy, I have heard, and she, in turn, was not insensible to his attractions; but Madame Hancock kept a jealous eye upon them both and would not allow any advances . . . toward the prize reserved for her nephew. When the knot was tied . . . she felt at liberty to breathe." [19]

All this Cupid's ointment would be very soothing to the romance-minded reader except for one annoying fly—the fact that Burr was a mere stripling of nineteen, whereas Mistress Quincy was a woman of twenty-eight, at the time of their alleged flirtation. To the eye of a male of Aaron's age—especially in the eighteenth century—a female of Dolly's years would appear to have one foot in the grave. It is probably true that Hancock's flighty fiancée "was not insensible" to the lure of the lusty lad as a prospective husband, even though he stood only five feet six. But it is highly improbable that she caused any matrimonial flutterings in his breast.

· 10 ·

Although living in blissful ignorance of what his girl was up to in Fair-field, Hancock was kept informed concerning his material possessions in Boston. Before leaving for Lexington he had commissioned a Captain Isaac Cazneau to watch over his property and smuggle as many of the valuable contents as possible out of the mansion, which Gage had com-mandeered for the use of his generals. Lord Howe, who had arrived from England on May 25 in command of reinforcements, is supposed (as previously mentioned) to have spotted from one of its windows, almost a year later, the Dorchester Heights fortifications which induced the British to evacuate the town. Earl Percy also is believed to have made his headquarters there for a while, and Clinton is known to have occu-pied it.

On June 5 John Lowell, Jr., who evidently had returned to his Charles-town home when his employer set out for Philadelphia, relayed to Aunt Lydia the first news from Cazneau concerning the big house on the hill:

"I am glad to inform you that all things remain safe as when I left them. He informs me that, as to getting anything more out of the house, it won't do, as all eyes are upon it; and that the goods I brought out was greatly magnified and soon after known at headquarters. . . . I hear those houses which are left is frequently . . . pillaged."

On the 17th, the day of the battle of Bunker Hill, the clerk rendered a second hearsay, roundabout accounting via Fairfield:

"Have only received two or three lines from Cazneau. Acknowledged a verbal account by Hopkins about a late attack upon the fences, some of which were again pulled down by soldiery; but, on complaint being made to the general, he has promised the fences shall be repaired and has sent an officer, with a guard of fifty men, to prevent any further damage." [20]

The second demonstration by Gage of solicitude for Hancock's prop-erty is particularly mysterious in view of his amnesty offer of the 12th, specifically and vengefully excluding the lord of Beacon Hill and Sam Adams:

"In this exigency of complicated calamities I avail myself of the last effort . . . to spare the effusion of blood; to offer, . . . in His Majesty's name, . . . his most gracious pardon to all persons who shall forthwith lay down their arms and return to their duties of peaceable subjects; excepting only . . . Samuel Adams and John Hancock, whose offenses are of too flagitious a nature to admit of any other consideration than that of condign punishment." [21]

It is understandable that Gage should have wished to preserve the mansion itself in habitable condition for his fellow officers; but why he should have been so concerned about the fences—especially since they were badly needed to replenish the besieged garrison's dwindling supply of firewood—is puzzling. There is a strong likelihood that he feared to have any harm whatsoever befall Hancock's estate, lest it should rally the idolizing masses to the cause. This explanation is no more fantastic than many other instances of the influence of the patriot in purple over those in homespun.

· 11 ·

But Hancock was being sorely neglected by his womenfolk, according to his letter of June 10 to Dolly:

"I am almost prevailed on to think that my letters to my aunt and you are not read, for I cannot obtain a reply. I have asked million questions, and not an answer to one. . . . I really take it extremely unkind. Pray, my dear, use not so much ceremony and reservedness. Why can't you use freedom in writing? Be not afraid of me. I want long letters."

This is the first suggestion on paper by the slighted swain that his sweetheart lacked enthusiasm for the betrothal she had been maneuvered into.

"I am glad the little things I sent you were agreeable. Why did you not write me of the top of the umbrella? I am so sorry it was spoiled, but I will send you another by my express. . . . How did my aunt like her gown? And do let me know if the stockings suited her. She had better send a pattern shoe and stocking."

The lorn lover asked nothing in return except a couple of "watch-strings"—one to be fashioned by each of the ladies. He made the request because "I wear them out fast" and "I want some little thing of your doing." It was a small enough favor to beg in reciprocation for the array of toggery which he had dispatched to Dolly by no less a personage than Dr. Church, who could not safely be trusted with much else since laying himself open to a charge of treason on the day after Lexington.

"I have sent you . . . the following things . . . , which I do insist you wear. (If you do not I shall think the donor is the objection): 2 pr. white silk, 4 pr. white thread stockings . . . ; 4 pr. black satin, 1 pr. black . . . shoes . . . ; 1 very pretty light hat; 1 neat, airy summer cloak; 2 caps; 1 fan." [22]

This epistle and most of the subsequent ones sent by the sentimental wooer to his beloved bear a seal representing Cupid plucking a heart from a thorn tree. Also imprinted in the wax is the pertinent motto which Thomas Hancock had used on his coat-of-arms, and which John had adopted for his own: *Nul plaisir sans peine.*

Within five days after posting this effusion the dreamy romanticist was rudely awakened by one of the bitterest disillusionments of his career. On June 15 the Congress passed over his name—which was in the political grab bag of candidates for the all-important and highly coveted appointment of commander in chief of the Continental army—in favor of George Washington.

It seems incredible that Hancock should have harbored, even for a moment, the notion that he was equal to such a responsibility. But it must be remembered that Washington, at the time, was distinguished only for his half-forgotten exploits as a colonel in the French and Indian War and was not nearly so well known throughout the colonies as his rival from Boston. Although the President had no other claim to military recognition than his service as a competent tin soldier in command of the Independent Corps of Cadets, he enjoyed much more political support at first. This was based on his wide renown, his ostensible leadership of the powerful Massachusetts Congressional delegation, and the fact that an overwhelming majority of the troops already raised hailed from New England. So the aristocrat of Beacon Hill had a sounder reason than mere egotism for considering himself the logical choice for the post.

Hancock could have swallowed his disappointment more easily if the two Adamses—of all people—had not turned against him and carried the torch for his opponent from Virginia. Although Thomas Johnson of Maryland made the official nomination, the President's fellow delegates delivered the deciding speeches a few days before the election.

"Mr. Washington, who happened to sit near the door," wrote John Adams, "as soon as he heard me allude to him—from his usual modesty—darted into the library room. Mr. Hancock, who was our President—which gave me an opportunity to observe his countenance while I was speaking on the state of the colonies, the army at Cambridge, and the enemy,—heard me with visible pleasure. But when I came to describe Washington for the commander I never remarked a more sudden and striking change of countenance. Mortification and resentment were expressed as forcibly as his face could exhibit them. Mr. Samuel Adams seconded the motion, and that did not soften the President's physiognomy at all." [23]

· 12 ·

John Adams admitted in after years that Hancock may have desired only an opportunity to decline the honor, and that the defeated candidate had good grounds for expecting to be accorded the post, "for at that time his exertions, sacrifices, and general merits in the cause of his country had been incomparably greater than those of Colonel Washington." But "the delicacy of his health and his entire want of experience in actual service, though an excellent militia officer, were decisive objections to him." [24]

The President took his medicine, on the whole, like a good soldier. While never forgiving the Adamses, he was magnanimous toward Washington—at least on the surface. Unaware that Dr. Warren had fallen at Bunker Hill, he wrote on the 18th to that brave and self-sacrificing patriot:

"The Congress have appointed George Washington, Esq., General and Commander-in-Chief of the Continental Army. His commission is made out, and I shall sign it tomorrow. He is a gentleman you will all like. I submit to you the propriety of providing a suitable place for his residence and the mode of his reception. Pray tell General Ward of this . . . and that we all expect to hear that the military movements of the day of his arrival will be such as to do . . . the Commander-in-Chief great honor." [25]

Under the same date he sent a similar note to Gerry, who was attending the Third Provincial Congress at Watertown. Referring to Washington as "a fine man," he urged that proper recognition be given him on his way through that town.[26]

The head of the Congress even humbled himself to the extent of asking the commander in chief to accept his enlistment as a common private. On July 10 he wrote: "I must beg the favor that you will reserve some berth for me in such department as you may judge proper; for I am determined to act under you, if it be to take a firelock and join the ranks as a volunteer." [27]

Thus to choke down his overweening pride, even though he probably did not expect Washington to interpret literally his offer to serve in the ranks, must have been painful for Hancock. And the evasive, although courteous and diplomatic, reply must have been still harder to take:

"I am particularly to acknowledge that part of your favor . . .

wherein you do me the honor of determining to join the army under my command. I need certainly make no professions of the pleasure I shall have in seeing you; at the same time I have to regret that so little is in my power to offer equal to Colonel Hancock's merits and worthy of his acceptance." [28]

In other words, the supreme commander did not consider the would-be warrior worthy of a staff commission. This plain implication must have rankled even more than the denial of his main aspiration.

The explanation of the visit mentioned is in a letter John Hancock wrote to Dolly in June. Although the fighting would not touch Philadelphia for two years, the Congress apparently foresaw that the British were planning to launch a campaign down the Hudson River valley and into Pennsylvania, for it contemplated moving to the relatively safe locality of Connecticut. Its President earnestly hoped for such a move so that he could call on his fiancée in Fairfield on the way to Cambridge for consultation with the commander in chief. She had finally deigned to write a few lines but had failed to acknowledge receipt of the pretty things he had sent by Dr. Church. And her letter had been far from satisfactory, as usual, in another respect.

"Pray write me one long letter," John pleaded in answer. "Fill the whole paper. You can do it if you only set about it. I verily think now we shall adjourn to Connecticut, as the seriousness of the times seems to call for it. . . . I heartily wish for it. I am greatly hurried. Have 500 commissions to sign for the officers of our army. I am now going to sign General Washington's commission. He will pass through Fairfield in four or five days." [29]

Fairfield nurses a tradition that Washington called on Aunt Lydia and Dolly when he passed through its precincts on the 28th. There is more than a legendary basis for this belief. He would have had a double incentive for pausing at the Burr mansion: to glean intelligence of the enemy's movements from its well informed owner and to mollify a powerful politician by paying respects to his ladies.

In any event, the commander in chief soon had occasion to do President Hancock a strange favor—that of helping him to heap coals of fire, doubtless unwittingly, upon the head of Aaron Burr. In July young Burr and his best friend, Matthias Ogden, turned up at Washington's headquarters with a written recommendation from Hancock that they be placed on his staff. Unable to get any action, Aaron joined Arnold's ill-fated expedition to Quebec but achieved his original object on his return.

Perhaps scheming Aunt Lydia had a hand in the intercession for Burr. She may have figured that the youthful Casanova would be less of a menace to her nuptial plans for her nephew and her ward under military discipline in Cambridge than loose in the vicinity of Fairfield. If so, she calculated correctly, for he went out of Dolly's life forever.

WHIGS ARE PARTED

*I*F HANCOCK had been compelled to render an accounting of his stewardship as President of the Second Continental Congress up to August 1, 1775, when it adjourned for about five weeks, he would have been hard pressed to find self-justifying words even in his own vocabulary, which was so rich in them. Its *Journals* are a sketchy record of speeches and debates touching chiefly on routine matters and shed little light on his leadership; but he must have done a prodigious amount of invaluable spadework during the two months. If this produced a minimum of immediately obvious results it was not his fault; but he was made the scapegoat by his enemies for most of the shortcomings of the numerous petty politicians in the governing body.

John Adams reciprocated the hostility he had aroused in the man whom he helped to defeat for commander in chief. He laid virtually the whole blame for Congressional ineptitude upon his shoulders in two thinly disguised and insinuating under-cover attacks delivered in July. One was in a letter addressed to James Warren:

"We are between hawk and buzzard. We ought to have had in our hands a month ago the executive, legislative, and judicial [control] of the whole continent and have completely modeled a constitution; to have raised a naval power and opened all our ports wide; to have arrested every friend of government on the continent and held them as hostages for the victims in Boston, and then opened the door as wide as possible for peace and reconciliation. . . . Is all this extravagant? Is it wild? Is it not the soundest policy?"[1]

This is so patently unfair that it scarcely needs comment. "Extravagant" and "wild," these Adams-conceived obligations most assuredly were. And his implied accusations against the President impugn his own judgment, for he and Sam Adams had been mainly instrumental in getting Hancock elected. While trying to turn the chaos that was Congress into an approximation of order during the embryonic days of the new government its leader did remarkably well to bring about partial fulfillment of one "ought" on this absurdly unreasonable list.

That was the "Olive Branch" petition signed on August 8 by President Hancock and a large majority of the delegates. It was the last attempt at appeasement by the conservatives who were willing to settle with Britain for dominion self-government in lieu of complete independence. While pledging loyalty to the King personally it besought him to induce the Ministry to abandon their policy of economic exploitation. But George III, still deeply affronted by the colonies' rebelliousness in the past and now entirely under the domination of Lord North, declined even to read the document.

Hancock and the rest of the left-wing Whigs probably had subscribed to this compromise proposal only under pressure. John Adams, it will be noted, had wished to extend the olive branch in an iron glove. But it had been proffered in a polished, Cambridge-calf, silk-lined box—quite likely with the hearty approval, if not at the suggestion, of the Beacon Hill hedonist. Once convinced of the necessity to yield, he always acted in accordance with the biblical injunction to go an extra mile if he thought Congressional harmony could thus be secured.

With an inconsistency typical of his comments on Hancock, Adams admitted by implication to his wife Abigail, on the very same day that he indirectly criticized the President for the Congress' defects, that he was deserving of sympathy:

"The business I have had upon my mind has been as great and important as can be entrusted to man, and the difficulty and intricacy of it prodigious. When fifty or sixty men have a constitution to form for a great empire at the same time that they have a country of 1500 miles' extent to fortify, millions to arm and train, a naval power to begin, an extensive commerce to regulate, numerous tribes of Indians to negotiate with, a standing army of 27,000 men to raise, pay, victual, and officer—I really shall pity those fifty or sixty men." [2]

· 2 ·

Although deserted by two of his oldest friends—the Adamses—the President had a new ally in Benjamin Harrison of Virginia, one of the many representatives who did not stoop to pull the chair from under the man whom they had seated unanimously. But John Adams, of course, saw an ulterior motive in Harrison's cultivation of Hancock's friendship.

"Mr. Samuel Adams and myself," he explained in the early part of 1776, "were very intimate with Mr. Lee, and he agreed perfectly with us in the great system of our policy; and by his means we kept a majority of the delegates of Virginia with us. But Harrison . . . and some others showed their jealousy. . . . Harrison . . . courted Mr. Hancock and some other of our colleagues, but we had now a majority and gave ourselves no trouble about their little intrigues." [3]

In July 1775, Harrison had confided to Washington: "Indeed, my friend, I do not know what to think of some of these men. They seem exceeding hearty in the cause but still wish to keep everything among themselves. Our President is quite of a different cast—noble, disinterested, and generous to a very great degree." [4]

But the disinterestedness of the now hardheaded politician from the silk-stocking district of Beacon Hill did not extend to the ruling clique of the patriot party. As soon as the Adamses had thrown down the gauntlet in opposing his ambition to be commander in chief he had picked it up, unostentatiously but determinedly. With Cushing as his first lieutenant, he had decided to wrest control of the Faction from Sam Adams.

This once all-powerful group had begun to disintegrate, anyway. Major Hawley had retired from public life. Dr. Warren had died at Bunker Hill; Bowdoin soon was to be rendered *hors de combat* by a long siege of illness; Dr. Church was about to be jailed for treason; and John Adams frequently steered an independent course through the turbulent sea of Revolutionary politics. James Warren and Gerry were the only outstanding members of the old guard on whom the boss of the Whigs still could count. Now Hancock began boring from within in a campaign which lasted for fifteen years and degenerated into a personal feud resulting in the utter discrediting of Sam Adams.

But the President subordinated to the public good his private antipathy toward the machine which had been running patriot politics for such a long time. He cooperated with the Adamses in supplying the wants of the army. To their great credit the three men, two of whom were so proud, pitched in at this desperate hour and saw to it that Washington's badly equipped forces received at least the essentials.

In June, John Adams had informed James Warren, successor of Dr. Joseph Warren as president of the Third Provincial Congress, that at one o'clock in the morning of the 25th he, Sam Adams, and Hancock had induced the Philadelphia committee of safety to ship ninety quarter-casks of powder to Washington before daybreak.[5] The same trio delivered $500,000 to the commander in chief on August 11 at Cambridge. With their fellow delegates they had started homeward shortly after the Continental Congress recessed. On their arrival they found that the new General Court of the "Territory of Massachusetts Bay," which had supplanted the Watertown congress on July 19, was in full swing.

· 3 ·

The President—who in May, before the dissolution of the old provisional government, had been named one of eighteen councilors in the Assembly —was not in the best of health.

Edmund Quincy wrote from Lancaster to his daughter about this time that her fiancé was suffering from one of his recurrent spells of gout and from eye trouble. He needed glasses, which the father regretted he could not supply because "I'm reduced to a single pair of temple spectacles and one pair of bows that I'm very sure can suit him in no respect." The best he could do was to "pray his health may be continued, as his present station calls for so great an exertion of every mental power, as well as bodily."

Dolly presumably was planning to visit her sister and brother-in-law, Elizabeth and Samuel Sewell, for he continued: "When circumstances will admit we shall be glad to come and see you at W[obur]n. One observation—by Mr. H.'s letter you are not to be seen there without change of name."[6] There may have been gossip to the effect that the Hancock-Quincy wedding would not come off. Reaching John's ears, it would have made him sensitive to the point of wishing to keep his bride-to-be in seclusion until he could take her out in public as his wife.

Whether Dolly heeded her fiancé's injunction to shun Woburn until she changed her name is not known; but he soon had the power to enforce obedience under the marriage vow at a period when it was taken seriously. Presumably he hurried from Cambridge to Fairfield, via Lancaster, as soon as he could break away and insisted that his lukewarm loved one make good her plighted troth. His success is attested by the Reverend Andrew Eliot, who perpetuated with these simple words in the records of his parish what probably was the most pretentious social event in the little Connecticut town up to that time:

"The Hon. John Hancock, Esq., and Miss Dorothy Quincy, both of Boston, were married at Fairfield August 28, 1775."[7]

In jarring contrast to this dignified statement is the attempt by a contemporary journalist to glorify the event:

"Florus informs us that 'in the Second Punic War, when Hannibal besieged Rome and was very near making himself master of it, a field upon which part of his army lay was offered for sale and was immediately purchased by a Roman in a strong assurance that the Roman valor and courage would soon raise the siege.' Equal to the conduct of that illustrious citizen was the marriage of the Hon. John Hancock, Esq., who, with his amiable lady, has paid as great a compliment to American valor and discovered equal patriotism by marrying now, while all the colonies are as much convulsed as Rome when Hannibal was at her gates." [8]

If Dolly read this masterpiece she must have bristled at being compared to a parcel of real estate. But if she was honest with herself she must have admitted that there was truth in the scribbler's unintentional implication that the marriage was fundamentally a mercenary transaction on her part.

These and similarly sketchy accounts of the union of the two famous families are all that have come down through the pages of history. Numerous members of the romantic school have essayed fanciful descriptions of the wedding, in the Burr mansion; but none contains any more authentic details.

It may be assumed that the nuptials were celebrated in the presence of all the political and social bigwigs within reasonable distance of Fairfield and that no expense was spared to make the occasion memorable. The vain and wealthy bridegroom would have seen to that.

Edmund Quincy understandably did not venture upon the long and tiresome journey from Lancaster to give his daughter away. The family was represented by Dolly's Aunt Dorothy Jackson.

There is well substantiated evidence that the bride declined the groom's offer to have her wedding dress cut out of some crimson velvet material, from which he was having a coat and vest tailored, because she thought it would obscure the sinuosity of her figure. But she was not so proud of her contours in later years, for she eventually had a set of ballroom chairs covered with the heavy damask used in the train of a matronly model.

A portrait painted about this time depicts the bride as having a high, intelligent forehead, dark, limpid eyes, a pointed, sharply defined nose, thin compressed lips, and a neatly molded chin—all combining to produce an effect of characterless prettiness. She is attired in a filmy gown, with a bodice fitted snugly over a flat chest but modestly revealing an exquisitely curved neck and gracefully sloping shoulders. Her arms are well rounded, and her hands delicately formed.

John and Dolly, at the ages of thirty-eight and twenty-eight, were married on a Monday. A letter from Edmund Quincy to his son Henry suggests that the pair spent at least their first forty-eight hours of wedded bliss with the Burrs:

"I haven't received any [letters] from you since mine after Colonel H. being here on the 26th ultimo; since which I have received a letter subscribed by him and your sister, Dorothy Hancock, acquainting me very kindly of their marriage . . . and their intention to set out for Philadelphia on the Thursday following. They proposed not to pass through New York, as the 'Asia' . . . had done much mischief by firing upon the city, and therefore proposed to cross the river above the city." [9] The couple did not carry out their plans to by-pass New York, for a social note of September 4 in the *New England Chronicle* states that they arrived there on Saturday.

The honeymoon (if that is the proper term for a trip of five or six days over alternately dusty and muddy, rock-strewn roads) ended on September 5 with the reopening of the Congress. And the bridal pair had little chance to coo over each other during the ensuing two years—a period that was among the most eventful in the history of America and one in which Hancock played a momentous role while his wife proved to be a worthy helpmeet.

· 4 ·

The Hancocks, however, did have a breathing spell after their arrival in Philadelphia. Although the President reported dutifully at Independence Hall on the 5th, a quorum was lacking; and the Congress did not hold its first official meeting until the 13th.

"Mr. Randolph, our former President, is here and sits very humbly in his seat while our new one continues in the chair without seeming to feel the impropriety," John Adams wrote in a letter; [10] and Dr. William Gordon, a contemporary, unscrupulous ministerial historian, states:

"When Mr. Hancock was first elected, in consequence of Mr. Peyton Randolph being under a necessity of returning to Virginia, it was expected that, as soon as the latter repaired again to Congress, the former would resign. Of this he was reminded by one of his Massachusetts brethren when Mr. Randolph got back; but the charms of Presidency made him deaf to the private advice of his colleague, and no one could, with propriety, move for his removal." [11]

What grounds, if any, Adams and Gordon had for charging the head of the Congress with being a usurper cannot be found either in the rules of parliamentary procedure or in the unwritten law of moral obligation. According to all available evidence, no strings were attached to his election. These insinuations are examples of the prejudice from which Hancock has suffered.

That President Hancock endured in silence the contumely leveled at him, besides usually holding his peace on controversial matters unless called upon to mediate, is implied by his severest critic. Adams quotes him only once in his "Notes of Debates." He records that during September, when Thomas Lynch, Jr., of South Carolina intimated that a Captain Dean was carrying supplies to the enemy, Hancock declared: "Dean belongs to Boston. He came from West Indies and was seized here. He loaded with flour and went out." [12]

By the first of October, Lynch had a real, major traitor to talk about. On that day, at a court-martial over which Washington presided, Dr. Church was convicted of "holding criminal correspondence with the enemy." [13]

The story of Church's betrayal of his country, right under the noses of his associates, goes back to 1774. Its first chapter is told by Revere in one of his depositions:

"In the fall of 1774 and the winter of 1775 I was one of upwards of thirty, chiefly mechanics, who formed ourselves into a committee for the purpose of watching the movements of the British soldiers and gaining every intelligence of the . . . Tories. We held our meetings at the Green Dragon Tavern. . . . Every time we met every person swore upon the Bible that they would not discover any of our transactions but to Messrs. Hancock, [Sam] Adams, Doctors Warren, Church, and one or two more.

"About November . . . a gentleman who had connections with the Tory party, but was a Whig at heart, acquainted me that our meetings were discovered and mentioned the identical words that were spoken among us the night before. We did not then distrust Doctor Church. . . . We removed to another place . . . but here we found that all our transactions were communicated to Governor Gage. . . . It was then a common opinion that there was a traitor in the Provincial Congress. . . .

"The day after the battle of Lexington I met him [Church] in Cambridge, when he showed me some blood on his stocking, which he said spurted on him from a man who was killed near him as he was urging the militia on. I well remember that I argued with myself, if a man will risk his life in a cause he must be a friend to that cause; and I never suspected him after till he was charged with being a traitor." [14]

He then recounts that on the following night, at a gathering of the committee of safety, Church had suddenly announced his intention of going to Boston on the morrow. Dr. Warren tried to dissuade him with a warning that he would be hanged, but he persisted. Finally it had been agreed that he should go and bring back medicaments for officers wounded in the Concord fight. He returned during the next evening with a tale that he had been arrested and examined by Gage.

Shortly after Washington assumed command of the army Church became surgeon general and established headquarters in Cambridge across the street from his superior. Writing from that town on October 3, the commander in chief notified Hancock that Dr. Church had been found guilty on the strength of a code letter and a confession made by his mistress. She had turned the message over to a Providence patriot, without knowing where his sympathies lay, and had asked him to deliver it to Major Caine, one of Gage's aides. Under questioning she had admitted that her paramour was the correspondent. But he was let off with a surprisingly soft sentence, pronounced by the General Court. He was merely jailed in Norwich, Connecticut, and "debarred the use of pen, ink, and paper." [15] The legislature, composed principally of his former associates, may have been inclined toward leniency by consideration for his earlier services to the cause.

· 5 ·

Hancock did not so easily escape the penalty of his fence-straddling on important issues—one of the most serious weaknesses of his character. He must have been roundly denounced by John Adams for withholding support from one of that statesman's pet projects—a powerful navy—when it first came up in the Congress during October. As time passed, Adams' opinion of his erstwhile enemy changed materially in most respects; but forty years later he still felt that the President had played politics with the fate of America in this connection, and wrote to Benjamin Rush, the Philadelphia physician and patriot:

"When armed ships came in question you can hardly imagine the opposition. . . . Even my colleagues, Mr. Paine, Mr. Cushing, were

JOHN HANCOCK SIGNING THE DECLARATION OF INDEPENDENCE ON JULY 4, 1776. FROM A MURAL BY JOHN TRUMBULL IN THE ROTUNDA OF THE CAPITOL AT WASHINGTON.

THE DECLARATION OF INDEPENDENCE, SHOWING FIFTY-SIX SIGNA-
TURES HEADED BY THAT OF HANCOCK. FACSIMILE OF THE ORIGINAL
DOCUMENT IN THE LIBRARY OF CONGRESS.

opposed to me. Mr. H. was . . . silent. After the business was established he became ambitious of stealing the glory of it." [16]

Adams' criticism seems to be justified in part, at least. The President did jump on the battle wagon with alacrity when the Congress decided on an organized navy policy and offered him the chairmanship of the Marine Committee, authorized to carry it out. Furthermore, he was as much interested in getting credit for his efforts as in getting the job done. But it must be said in extenuation that he achieved remarkable results.

Toward the close of October, Adams resumed harping on the shortcomings of the Massachusetts delegates. He wrote to Warren resignedly: "You wonder that certain *improprieties* are not felt. Well you may. But I have done finding fault. I content myself with blushing alone and mourning in secret the loss of reputation our colony suffers by giving such *samples* of her sons to the world." [17]

It must have been a great relief to the harried President to escape from the feverish and hostile atmosphere of the governmental chamber at the close of the daily sessions and to visit or entertain friends with his Dolly. On October 28 the Hancocks were guests of Benjamin Marshall, son of Christopher Marshall, a retired businessman of note, who records that he drank coffee with them and others. The presence of the Adamses probably did not enhance Hancock's enjoyment, but his dislike did not cause him to shun their company on this or any other social occasion. Both he and they presumably felt impelled to maintain a surface cordiality for politic reasons.

Within the next two weeks the Marshalls went to "Colonel Hancock's lodgings . . . to see the ensigns, or colors, taken at Fort Chambly; found him and his lady at home; spent an hour or two with him very agreeably." [18]

John Adams had called on the Hancocks a few days earlier to look at the British battle flags collected at Chambly—a consolation prize salvaged from Benedict Arnold's disastrous Quebec expedition. His antipathy, as indicated previously, did not extend to the President's lady. On the contrary, his liking for Dolly was strong, and he showed it unreservedly to Abigail:

"Two pair of colors belonging to the Seventh Regiment were brought here last night from Chambly and hung up in Mrs. H.'s chamber with great splendor and elegance. That lady sends her compliments and good wishes. Among a hundred men, almost, at this house she lives and behaves with modesty, decency, dignity, and discretion, I assure you. Her behavior is easy and genteel. She avoids talking upon politics. In large and mixed companies she is totally silent, as a lady ought to be.

"But whether her eyes are so penetrating and her attention so quick to the words, looks, gestures, sentiments, etc., of the company as yours would be—saucy as you are this way—I won't say."

In the view of an outsider, at least, love—whether true or not on Dolly's part—was running smoothly in the Hancock ménage at this time. Early in December, Adams declared enviously to his wife:

"I never will come here again without you if I can persuade you to come with me. . . . We will bring Master Johnny with us. You and he shall have the smallpox [inoculation] here, and we will be as happy as Mr. Hancock and his lady." [19]

Whether because of Mrs. Hancock's popularity or her husband's position as President, the Hancocks seem to have been recognized as the arbiters of Philadelphia society. This and the bad feeling between the transient Whigs and the native Tories are indicated by a strange incident.

A ball was planned for November 24 in honor of Martha Washington, on her way to join her husband at Cambridge; but it was called off, after the invitations had been issued, under pressure from a committee formed by Sam Adams. The cancellation is thus explained by Christopher Marshall:

"After dinner . . . I had heard some threats thrown out that, if the ball assembled this night, . . . they presumed that the New Tavern would cut but a poor figure tomorrow morning. These fears of some commotion's being made that would be very disagreeable at this melancholy time in disturbing the peace of the city I concluded . . . to prevent; in order to which I went to Colonel Hancock's lodgings and, finding he was not come from Congress, . . . I walked up to the State House in expectation of meeting him. That failing, I requested the doorkeeper to call Samuel Adams. . . . I then informed him . . . that Mrs. Washington and Colonel Hancock's wife were to be present. . . . I . . . requested he would give my respects to Colonel Hancock [and] desire him to wait on Lady Washington to request her not to attend. . . . This he promised. Thence I went and met the committee at the Philosophical Hall, . . . where it was then concluded . . . that there should be no such meeting held, not only this evening but in future while these troublous times continued." [20]

There was more than an official bond between the wives of the top military and civilian leaders of the country. They were on a friendly footing in a frankly personal sense as well, according to Martha A. Quincy, Dolly's grandniece. In her "Reminiscences of the Hancocks" she states: "Madam W. would say to Madam H., 'There is a great difference in our situations. Your husband is in the Cabinet, but mine is on the battlefield.' " [21] If Martha was inclined to be catty or Dolly sensitive, it would appear that this enigmatic remark could have put an end to the beautiful friendship. But it lasted until a much later period.

· 6 ·

If the tribute to Mrs. Washington had come off it would have been a rare interlude of gaiety for President and Mrs. Hancock. Except for quiet gatherings in their overcrowded lodging house or at the homes of friends, they enjoyed little relaxation during the first two years of the Revolution.

Three weeks after the banning of the ball Hancock undertook, in addition to his regular duties, the heavy responsibility of laying the foundation of the American navy. During the summer Washington had organized a force of converted merchant vessels to harass British sea communications with Boston, and in October the Congress had appropriated funds to acquire and arm eight similar ships, which Commodore Esek Hopkins sailed to Nassau in the Bahamas, in the spring of 1776, to seize a large store of powder. Steps also were taken to press into service more than two thousand privately owned craft that were to prey on enemy commerce throughout the great conflict.

Not until December 13, however, did the Congress sanction the construction of thirteen bona fide men-of-war—five of thirty-two guns, five of twenty-eight, and three of twenty-four. This nucleus of maritime power was virtually wiped out before the end of the war. But it inspired the colonists to build other fleets which could cope, in single combat, with the best that England had to offer. The most spectacular, if not the most significant, realization of this conviction was the victory of John Paul Jones' *Bon Homme Richard* over the *Serapis* in 1779.

On the day after the naval program was authorized Hancock was elected chairman of the Marine Committee. From that time he pushed the Massachusetts-sponsored warships—the *Hancock* and the *Boston*—to completion in the following fall with unremitting energy.

But the President still found time during the winter to prosecute the war vigorously on land. As his personal contribution he reiterated, in support of a resolution that Washington be empowered to attack Boston if he thought it advisable, his previously expressed willingness to sacrifice his possessions there. He is reputed to have declared on December 22: "It is true . . . nearly all of the property I have in the world is in houses and other real estate in the town of Boston; but if the expulsion of the British army from it—and the liberties of our country—require their being burnt to ashes, issue the order for that purpose immediately."

These words are not to be found in any contemporary source; but their tenor is typical of his public utterances, and there is definite authority for the assertion that he argued in favor of the proposed assault. Richard Smith, delegate from New Jersey, recorded in his diary: "Mr. Hancock spoke heartily for this measure." [22]

Dolly, however, was not quite so stoical over the prospect of being paupered for the sake of honor and glory. She is said to have sought the solitude of a Quaker meetinghouse and prayed for three hours that she would not have to bear such a cross.

Hancock was not talking for effect, either to the Congress or to his wife, when he laid his worldly goods on the block. He put himself on record in that respect privately, as well as publicly, in notifying Washington of the resolution:

"This passed after a most serious debate in a committee of the whole House, and the execution referred to you. And may God crown your attempt with success. I most heartily wish it, though individually I may be the greatest sufferer." [23]

· 7 ·

The patriot in purple may have had more than one motive when he acquiesced in the plan to attack Boston. His property was decidedly a liability during the British occupation, and his financial worries over it had been mounting. Shortly after his election to the presidency of the First Provincial Congress he had turned over the management of his business enterprises to William Bant, a lawyer-merchant whom he had set up in a subsidiary concern in 1767 on the basis of an equal division of the profits. Bant undertook conscientiously the difficult task of putting the parent firm's affairs in order and guarding the assets against looting British soldiery. He arranged to have the few remaining ships of its merchant fleet secreted from the enemy until they could be sold. He galloped about the countryside dunning the numerous debtors but reported that he could not collect £100 in five hundred miles. He finally was subjected to the humiliation of having the horse provided by the highly respectable merchant of Beacon Hill seized as stolen property.

The towering House of Hancock deteriorated gradually. At the close of the Revolution its head contemplated retiring from politics and shoring it up again, but the glamour of public life prevented him from doing anything to save the structure. After the death of Bant he merely commissioned a clerk, William Hoskins, to salvage as much as possible from the ruins.

John Hancock was not dependent on the income from his business. At the end of the war he still owned securities worth as much as £13,000. He possessed more real estate than ever before, by virtue of large grants on the frontier from the grateful young nation. Up to the day of his death there never was any doubt as to where his next meal—or his next lavish banquet, for that matter—would come from.

Why the great commercial edifice reared by Thomas Hancock decayed under the proprietorship of the nephew is explained clearly and authoritatively by Professor Baxter:

"The business had taken Thomas forty years to construct. In the next five John brought it to a standstill; in five more it had crumbled away.

"To blame John entirely for this abrupt ending would be unfair. He was heavily handicapped during his whole term of management. Few things stand out more clearly from the Hancocks' story than the strong rhythms that were imparted to trade by wars, and John was unlucky enough to take over the reins during a long down-swing. At their best, the postwar years seldom offered chances so golden as those which Thomas had enjoyed; at their worst, they were times during which trade was brought to a dead stop by political troubles.

"But the depression does not wholly explain John's failure. Nor do his defects of character; though these were many and grave—tardiness, spleen, and unreliability,—he also had merits (such as energy and boldness of design) that we might well have expected to offset his faults. Yet his grand schemes always seemed to go wrong. And, if we stop to analyze why this was so, I think that we see one of the main differences between uncle and nephew: Thomas made plans that fitted in with the conditions of the times; whereas John could not perceive what these conditions were and, as a result, exhausted himself in swimming against the current." *

* W. T. Baxter, *The House of Hancock* (Harvard University Press, Cambridge, 1945), 293–294. Reprinted by permission of the publishers.

• 8 •

As the momentous year 1775 merged into the still more significant 1776 President Hancock had to concentrate more and more on public business, to the increasing neglect of private concerns.

A counter-Revolutionary movement by a strong contingent of Tories must have perturbed him particularly. It was brought to his attention by William Alexander, Lord Stirling, one of the most ardent adherents of the patriot cause and colonel of the leading militia regiment of New Jersey, who thus outlined the dangerous situation in that province:

"The Tories in every part of it have of late assumed fresh courage and talk very daringly. I was yesterday evening informed . . . of a combination carrying on for opposing the measures of the Congress; that some of them are bold enough to assert that their list of association already amounts to about 4000 men and that they have had a supply of ammunition from on board the *Asia* man-of-war. On this foundation the Committee [of safety] have applied to me for a party of men to seize the two most active of the gang in this country, and I hope to surprise them tomorrow evening."

Early in January, Lord Stirling wrote to the President from Elizabethtown that he had arrested Governor William Franklin, the leader of the "gang." Because the governor "intended no longer to remain quiet, I thought it most prudent to secure him and bring him to this place. . . . I have provided good, genteel, private lodgings for him . . . where I intend he shall remain until I have directions from Congress what to do with him." [24] In accordance with instructions from the governing body, Franklin eventually was imprisoned for two years at Litchfield, Connecticut.

This was one of the numerous incidents that Hancock mentioned on the 10th, evidently in great vexation of spirit, in a letter to General Philip Schuyler, commander of the army in Canada:

"The distresses of this great continent, thrown into convulsions by an unnatural war; the unprepared state we were in when unjustly attacked; the enemies that have arisen up against us in different quarters and the horrid attempts of the Southern governors to excite domestic insurrections and bring the savages to desolate our frontiers; the necessity of providing armed vessels to prevent, if possible, the desolation threatened our seacoast—these and other matters of the highest importance . . . must apologize for your letters not having an earlier answer." [25]

A week later Hancock was still further depressed by the fate of the

Quebec expedition and by signs that New York was on the point of seceding from the so-called United Colonies. To Cushing, in Massachusetts at Washington's headquarters, he lamented:

"We have this day received disagreeable accounts from Canada; poor [Richard] Montgomery and several officers killed, Arnold wounded, etc. . . . I fear for the defection of New York. The spring will open before we are ready. However, we must bestir ourselves. . . ."

In the same communication there is an interesting commentary on Tom Paine's *Common Sense,* which had just been published. In the light of what ultimately was recognized as the incalculable inspirational effect of that work upon the discouraged colonists Hancock's remarks appear obtuse, but they typify the belittling attitude taken toward it in the beginning by many of the wisest founding fathers.

"I inclose you a pamphlet, which makes much talk here, said to be wrote by an English gentleman resident here by the name of Paine; and I believe him the author. I send it for your and friends' amusement."

Cushing, who according to John Adams was "famed for secrecy and . . . talent for procuring intelligence," had been replaced in the Continental Congress by Gerry because of his lack of enthusiasm for Sam Adams' independence policy and was safely seated in the Massachusetts Council. Hancock, as the leader of the patriot party's new wing, now sought to turn his faculties and his disaffection to account:

"I shall look on you as a stated friendly correspondent. I make offers of sincere attachment . . . to you and wish for a return of yours; and you may rely on every service in my power and that I am totally undisguised. . . . I will give you everything from hence, . . . and, pray, write me every occurrence with you."

He evidently suspected that the old guard at home, knowing he entertained ideas similar to Cushing's, were whetting their knives to use on him. He went on: "For a very particular reason do send me the state of the late election of members for Congress. . . . What is the Assembly about? I have received no orders to remain here." And he betrayed his thwarted, but still obsessive, aspiration toward martial glory by inquiring in a postscript: "How goes on the military matters in the Assembly? Am I to be noticed in the appointment of officers?" [26]

Cushing responded on January 30 in still more honeyed words, confirming Hancock's hunch that the daggers already were being sharpened behind his back:

"Am sincerely obliged to you for your kind offers of . . . friendship. Such offers, at a time when I am represented to you as deserted by all others, must be peculiarly acceptable . . . and fully confirm me in the opinion I always entertained of Mr. Hancock, that he was a gentleman of an amiable, humane, generous, and benevolent disposition. . . .

"Soon after I arrived here, I found you, as well as myself, had been placed in a disagreeable light and measures taken to hurt our influence. I instantly endeavored to remove every impression of this kind. I think I have succeeded and . . . I shall leave no stone unturned to serve you here. . . . I was treated with as much cordiality and friendship as ever. . . . It is true, I am informed, some few whom . . . you are well acquainted with . . . have endeavored by their little, low, dirty, and sly insinuating arts and machinations to destroy my influence among the new members of the House."

The letter closes with the welcome news that the Assembly had satisfied Hancock's military yearnings by appointing him "first major-general of the militia." [27] He was to be entitled to don his epaulets on May 8 after routine concurrence by the military board.

· 9 ·

On January 18, Hancock had been reelected to the Congress. Although his term as a delegate expired on the 30th, he was not apprised of its extension officially until after learning of it through the private advices of Cushing. His colleagues received the same inconsiderate treatment, but the situation was especially embarrassing to him because of his position as President. On the 31st he wrote to the Massachusetts Assembly with restrained asperity:

"On moving to Congress our situation and my proposing to resign in consequence of the expiration of our authority from you, the Congress, apprehending your intention to be that Massachusetts should be constantly represented . . . , desired us to attend as usual . . . until we could be honored with your further directions." [28]

On the following day he vented his feelings to Cushing more frankly:

"How can it happen that no account was forwarded? The Secretary* ought to know his duty. I cannot reconcile it but—. We go on as usual. I have been much hurried in giving out commissions, etc.; very little time to myself."

Continuing, he exhorted his right-hand man to speed up the naval program—in so far as it would enhance the reputation of one J. H.—through the launching of the *Hancock* and the *Boston*: "Pray, hurry the

* John Avery, who was acting in place of Sam Adams.

builders, etc. . . . . Let me know what article cannot be purchased with you. The iron cannot be got down. The river is froze. You must get the best you can." [29]

The President and marine chairman undoubtedly was busy; but he had exaggerated in making such a fuss over the time consumed in the distribution of officers' commissions. The burden of this task and some of his other official duties fell upon Dolly, according to the secondhand "Reminiscences" of Sumner:

"Mrs. Scott observed that she was busy all the time . . . packing up commissions to be sent off for the officers appointed by Congress. It was not till some months after this that Mr. Hancock kept a clerk, though all the business of Congress was done by the President. She herself was for months engaged with her scissors in trimming off the rough edges of the bills of credit issued by the Congress and signed by the President, and packing them up in saddle bags to be sent off to various quarters for the use of the army." [30]

Hancock, however, had enough on his mind, aside from his Presidential functions, to justify him in shifting the responsibility for these chores to his wife. He was perturbed by Cushing's verification of his worst fears concerning the underhanded tactics of his enemies back in Massachusetts. Under date of February 13 he replied to his confidant:

"Am glad to hear the reception you met with and have no doubt but you will ever acquit yourself the honest man and be superior to the arts and cunning of designing men. I am obliged to you for the hints you give respecting the designs of some against me." But their foes had been foiled temporarily. "By the state of the elections, neither you nor I were much neglected." Plans for his pet pair of warships and the $25,000 to be spent upon them were on the way to Cambridge. Praying Cushing to employ as many men as possible in their construction, he concluded: "Don't be behind any of the colonies."

Three days later the self-constituted naval expert dispatched another long message to his first lieutenant about the *Hancock* and the *Boston*. He had arranged to have two hundred pieces of duck for the sails shipped from New York, and now asked for a list of other requisites, so that he should "at least be on a footing with others of the committee." [31]

· 10 ·

Cushing signed a contract on March 1 with a Massachusetts firm for the construction of what President Hancock had come to regard as his private men-of-war. From that time until they were launched his desire to beat out the builders of the eleven other ships was a positive mania. That the *Hancock* and the *Boston* were among the earliest to slide down the ways is of no intrinsic significance; but the political importance attached to this achievement by its prime mover makes the steps leading up to it pertinent to an understanding of his character.

The shipwrights agreed to lay the keels "with the utmost dispatch" at Newburyport on the Merrimack River, in accordance with drafts and directions to be furnished by Hancock; to "do . . . all the carpenters' work in the finishing them off as a ship of war ought to be finished"; to have both of them "safely afloat" by the end of June—and even to "find rum for the laborer." [32] The *Hancock*, of course, was to be the larger of the two vessels. When finally ready for the sea she exceeded the original specifications—in keeping with the expansion of her sponsor's ego as she approached completion. Her over-all length was to be one hundred thirty-seven feet, and she was to carry fifty-two guns—twenty more than the maximum number provided for in the Congressional authorization.

On the 6th Hancock acknowledged receipt of a letter from Cushing notifying him that neither the plans nor the funds for the frigates had arrived. But this did not deter him from putting spurs to his harried henchman again:

"In the meantime I most earnestly entreat and beg of you that you exert every nerve in forwarding our two ships. . . . In short, spare no expense . . . ; for, *inter nos,* some *here* who are not very friendly to you and I (and, of our province, you know who) begin publicly to say that the Massachusetts ships will be the last finished."

Hancock cracked the whip once more over his docile follower on the very next day. Prefacing his laying-on by calling attention to the enclosed "dimensions of everything necessary for your guidance in matters respecting the ships," he goaded Cushing to "set every wheel in motion" and even insisted that the construction be artistic. "Let the heads and galleries . . . be neatly carved and executed" and "let ours be as good, handsome, strong, and as early completed as any that are building here or in any of the other colonies; for your reputation and mine are at stake, and there are not wanting those who are fond of prejudicing both." He importuned his henchman to "send me my commission as major-general, that I may appear in character," admitting that "this appointment pleases me," and concluded that, with the approval of the Congress, he had hired

Jacob Rush, brother of Dr. Rush, as a private secretary because of being overworked.

The first rift in the lute piped so harmoniously up to this time by the political duo appears in Hancock's next effusion concerning the ships. "Many oppor[tunities] and posts without even a line from you," he complained testily under date of April 27. "I did not think that *you* would have so soon fallen in with the common mode." He also took this occasion to send word that Captain William Manley had been named commander of the *Hancock* and Captain Cazneau, his caretaker, of the *Boston*.[33] But Cazneau declined the honor in favor of Captain Hector McNeill.

Hancock probably was in a generally carping mood now because his nerves were on edge to an even greater extent than usual. An open break between him and Sam Adams had occurred on March 15. John Adams, referring to the Congressional conniving of that day in his autobiography, relates:

"This is the first appearance of Mr. Harrison as chairman of the committee of the whole. The President, Mr. Hancock, had hitherto nominated Governor Ward of Rhode Island to that conspicuous distinction. Mr. Harrison had courted Mr. Hancock, and Mr. Hancock had courted Mr. [James] Duane, Mr. [John] Dickinson, and their party; and leaned so partially in their favor that Mr. Samuel Adams had become very bitter against Mr. Hancock and spoke of him with great asperity in private circles; and this alienation between them continued from this time till the year 1789 . . . when they were again reconciled. Governor Ward was become extremely obnoxious to Mr. Hancock's party by his zealous attachment to Mr. Samuel Adams and Mr. Richard Henry Lee. Such, I suppose, were the motives which excited Mr. Hancock to bring forward Mr. Harrison." [34]

These machinations may seem to indicate that Hancock was letting his private feud interfere with his public duty and was neglecting to maintain the harmony in government councils for which he has been given credit. But there is no evidence that the efficiency of the Congress (such as it was) suffered any diminution as a result of the President's political maneuvers. On the contrary, he appears to have made it function more smoothly by placing in key positions men who were in sympathy with him. Lacking the independence and power of the modern Chief Executive, he had the greater justification for adopting this policy, even though it happened to serve his personal ends.

· 11 ·

Although frequently remiss in foresight, Hancock and his Congressional colleagues had not failed to beware the Ides of March in the conduct of the war. On that ominous date they had anticipated Howe's evacuation of Boston by two days and his attack upon New York by almost five months.

The President had transmitted to Lord Stirling, now in command at the mouth of the Hudson, the resolutions that the fortification of the city should be strengthened. "Whatever may be the designs of General Howe, it appears . . . more than probable that the Ministry will make an effort to gain possession of New York," he warned. "It is therefore the desire of the Congress . . . to provide for the defense of that place." He also had conveyed the news that 8,000 men had been voted to supplement the forces already there and that the provinces of New York, New Jersey, and Connecticut had been instructed to hold their militia in readiness.[35] In consequence of these prudent decisions Forts Lee and Washington, together with several other strongholds, were erected along the northern and eastern approaches to the town in time to confront Howe (who had supplanted Gage as the supreme British commander) when he landed with 10,000 troops and forty guns near Gravesend, Long Island, on August 22.

In the midst of so much anxiety, political conflict, and vexations of all sorts it must have been a tremendous relief to receive from General Washington the following letter—remarkable for its deference to, and consideration for, a man so generally unappreciated—a few days after the enemy abandoned the Massachusetts capital:

"It is with the greatest pleasure I inform you that, on Sunday last, the 17th . . . , about 9 o'clock in the forenoon, the Ministerial army evacuated the town of Boston and that the forces of the United Colonies are now in actual possession thereof. . . . The town, although it has suffered greatly, is not in so bad a state as I expected to find it; and I have a particular pleasure in being able to inform you, Sir, that your house has received no damage worth mentioning. Your furniture is in tolerable order, and the family pictures are all left entire and untouched. Captain Cazneau takes charge of the whole until he shall receive further orders from you."[36]

On April 4 Cazneau submitted a much more detailed report on the condition of the Beacon Hill mansion. But it deepens, rather than dissipates, the mystery as to why the English were so solicitous of property belonging to one of the two patriots whom they hated above all others: "The mansion house was thought by most people a place devoted to destruction; [but it] has escaped a scouring in more than one sense. The best furniture I put into the chamber back of the great chamber and kept the key till about three weeks before General Clinton left the house; then was sent for, and they demanded to search for papers. . . . When we came to open the door the key would not turn. . . . On this he seemed much displeased and said would break it open. . . . He kept the key and wished me good morning, which I took as a signal to depart. . . .

"A few days before he left the house he sent for me and desired I would look about and see if anything was wanting. I told him the great settee was not in the house and desired he would see [it] returned, which he did. The backgammon table in the library was wanting, but none knew anything of it. He desired one of the captains to purchase one as good and send it up, but I never saw it yet. The china and glassware was found out, unpacked, and put into the great room. I was sent for, and Mr. Clinton was very angry that I did not acquaint him 'twas secreted. . . . Said I had not used him well. If his servants had been dishonest it might been sold and given suspicion that 'twas done by his orders. He put it into the back chamber with the other things and . . . gave me the key." [97]

The stable and the coach house had been used as hospitals; the garden was in fair shape, but most of the fences enclosing the two pastures behind the mansion were gone. Ebenezer Hancock had been in town for a week, cleaning his combination home and shop in preparation for the return of his family. The scuttling of the "new ship" was the only serious damage done to John Hancock's commercial holdings. Ironically the patriot who was celebrated for his self-sacrificing offer to have his property in Boston burned while the enemy was within its gates had unwittingly helped the British troops in their departure: they had affixed ladders to Hancock's Wharf for embarking. The next paragraph of Cazneau's letter illustrates the striking inconsistency of the foe's attitude toward Hancock—or the difference between that of the officers and that of the enlisted men:

"The town in general is shockingly defaced, especially the places of public worship. Your name on the cornerstone of Dr. Cooper's church is mangled out with an axe."

Other records of the over-all devastation wrought by the English garrison tend to substantiate this statement. A majority of the trees—

including the huge elm dedicated to liberty—which had made the Massachusetts metropolis one of the most beautiful in America had been cut down to meet the crying need for fuel. Almost all the ramshackle stores and warehouses that had marred the mercantile district had been torn apart for the same purpose. Old North Meetinghouse had been razed; and Old South, stripped of all its pews except one preserved for use as a pigsty, had been turned into a riding academy for Burgoyne's crack regiment, the Queen's Light Dragoons. Virtually every dwelling deserted by the common, ordinary Whigs had been pillaged; but the homes of the socially and financially important had been left intact to provide quarters for Howe's high-ranking officers. Disease was rampant, and food had become so scarce that even the twenty-year-old town bull had been slaughtered.

Boston probably made Hancock feel like weeping into his Madeira the next time he laid eyes upon it.[38]

$\mathcal{C}\!\!\mathcal{D}$ XI $\mathcal{Q}$

WHAT'S IN A NAME

$\mathcal{J}$N THE SPRING of 1776 the tide in the affairs of men which periodically churns up the sluggish stream of history was rising fast in the American colonies. Taken at the flood, it led on to fortune, in accordance with Shakespeare's sage observation. For one man in particular, among the forty-six who seized their opportunity, it insured immortality. First patriot leader to sign the Declaration of Independence and the only subscriber for almost a month after it was drawn up, John Hancock achieved, with the bold strokes of his pen, a fame which his numerous detractors have not been able to dim.

A grave crisis in the military situation also was approaching. The probability, pointed out by Hancock in March, that Howe would attack New York had become a certainty. In the middle of May, under instructions from the Congress, he asked Washington to come to Philadelphia for a consultation on means of coping with the prospective British campaign. The message also contained a personal invitation:

"I request . . . that you will . . . honor me with your and your lady's company at my house, where I have a bed at your service . . . and where every endeavor of mine and Mrs. Hancock's shall be exerted to make your abode agreeable. I reside in an airy, open part of the city, in Arch and Fourth Streets." [1]

This was not the lodging house where, according to John Adams, Dolly had lived with her husband so discreetly among a hundred men during the preceding fall. The Hancocks were now in the establishment of a Mrs. Yard. Even a couple in moderate circumstances could well have afforded to put up guests there, for a suite of furnished rooms—exclusive of firewood and candles—with board, cost only three pounds per week.

Washington wrote on May 20 that he planned to set out for Philadelphia within the next two days and thanked the President for his offer of hospitality, but without committing himself as to acceptance. So Hancock repeated his overture more insistently. "I . . . cannot help expressing the very great pleasure it would afford Mrs. Hancock and myself," he importuned, "to have the happiness of accommodating you during your stay in this city. As the house I live in is large and roomy, it will be entirely in your power to live in that manner you should wish." Washington apparently had told of being invited to stay with his fellow Virginian, Peyton Randolph, who had preceded Hancock in office. This may have annoyed the President if he thought Randolph was at the bottom of the usurpation charges circulated by John Adams and Gordon. At all events, he continued obsequiously: "Mrs. Washington may be as retired as she pleases while under inoculation, and Mrs. Hancock will esteem it an honor to have Mrs. Washington inoculated in her house; and, as I am informed Mr. Randolph has not any lady about his house to take the necessary care of Mrs. Washington, I flatter myself she will be as well attended in my family. In short, Sir, I . . . repeat my wish that you would be pleased to condescend to dwell under my roof." [2]

The commander in chief finally elected to lodge with Randolph or somebody else—and may thereby have brought on the first of the attacks of political gout from which Hancock suffered to the end of his days; for this was not an isolated instance, and one is justified in suspecting that the ailment was more mental than physical.

On June 3, when Washington was about to return to New York, Hancock wrote: "I am extremely sorry it is not in my power to wait on you in person to execute the commands of Congress but, being deprived of that pleasure by a severe fit of the gout, I am . . . taking this method to acquaint you that the Congress have directed me . . . to make the thanks of that body to you for the unremitted attention you have paid to your important trust." The always urbane politician went on to wish that "you may be crowned with success equal to your merit and the righteousness of our cause," and closed with the "highest esteem and regards." [3] But the communication contains not a single intimate touch like the former effusions. The verbiage is typical of that employed to sugar-coat the bitterest feelings in correspondence of the eighteenth century.

· 2 ·

To Hancock's credit, he refrained, as usual, from letting any private resentment toward Washington decrease his ardor or exertions for the high emprise to which he had dedicated himself. On the day after his excuses to the commander in chief he composed a long, thoughtful letter on the state of the burgeoning nation. Circularized in Massachusetts, Connecticut, New Hampshire, New York, New Jersey, Maryland, and Delaware, it sets forth frankly the critical situation faced by the United Colonies but glows with faith in the eventual realization of their ideals. Its most salient passage follows:

"Our affairs are hastening fast to a crisis, and the approaching campaign will, in all probability, determine forever the fate of America. Such is the unrelenting spirit which possesses the Tyrant of Britain and his Parliament that they have left no measure unessayed that had a tendency to accomplish our destruction. . . . Should the Canadians and Indians take up arms against us (which there is too much reason to fear), we shall then have the whole force of that country to contend with. . . . Our continental troops alone are unable to stem the torrent; nor is it possible at this day to raise and discipline men ready to take the field by the time they will be needed. . . .

"Should the United Colonies be able to keep their ground this campaign, I am under no apprehensions on account of any future one. We have many disadvantages at present to struggle with, which time and progress in the art of war will remove. But this circumstance should rouse us to superior exertions. . . . The militia of the United Colonies . . . may be depended upon. . . . They are called upon to say whether they will live slaves or die free men. . . . The cause is certainly a glorious one. . . . In short, on your exertions . . . together with those of the other colonies . . . the salvation of America now evidently depends. . . . Quicken your preparations and stimulate the good people of your government—and there is no danger, notwithstanding the mighty armament with which we are threatened, but you will be able to lead them to victory, to liberty, and to happiness." [4]

Many of Hancock's contemporaries contended—and historians have parroted them ever since—that he was incapable of writing a good speech; that most of those he made were ghost-written. The second statement was true in certain instances; but the foregoing Presidential message, of which he unquestionably was the author, proves that he could express himself clearly, forcefully, and inspirationally. He did not lack the gifts of tongue or pen.

There is no doubt, either, that these sentiments came from his heart—a heart rendered heavy by personal grief as well as by public concern. Aunt Lydia had died on April 25 at the age of sixty-two, in Fairfield.

Ten days before her death she had suffered, like her husband, a stroke of apoplexy; but apparently she had recovered. "The quick approach of death," stated the Boston *Gazette*, "would not allow her to be attended in her last moments by her nephew, who was . . . the object of her fondest affection on this side heaven. In her last illness, before she was thought dangerous, she suddenly grew insensible and spoke but little. This is the less to be regretted, since her life spoke so much." [5]

So humane was Hancock's nature that his absence hardly could have been due to callousness. He did neglect, however, to have a headstone placed on her grave until 1792, a year before he was laid away in his own. And then he was shamed into doing his duty by a request from Eunice, wife of Thaddeus Burr, for permission to erect the marker.

That he put his obligations to the United Colonies above all others and above self-interest is indicated by the fact that he postponed the probate of Mrs. Hancock's will until his return to Boston in November, 1777, on his first leave of absence from the Congress. As executor and principal heir he would have been eager to settle up the estate, from which he inherited £10,000 and much valuable real property.

Dolly was not at the obsequies of the woman who had been so good to her. Her excuse may have been that she was pregnant and would have run the risk of a miscarriage by traveling over the rough roads. Katherine Quincy had left Lancaster and after a visit to her friend Dorothy Dudley, in Cambridge, was coming under Bant's escort to Philadelphia to be with her sister during the lying-in period. Until the 4th of July the prospective father would have little leisure for dispelling the fears of an expectant mother—fears that were very real in that day of comparatively crude obstetrical methods and high infant mortality.

· 3 ·

The movement for independence had been gaining momentum rapidly ever since England, by the Prohibitory Act of December 22, 1775, clamped a blockade upon all colonial ports. Initiated by Sam Adams and the rest of the redder Whigs; pounded into the public's consciousness by John Adams and the other more articulate dyed-in-the-wool patriots, and brought to a head by circumstances, this issue quickly became paramount during the first half of 1776.

The conservatives, particularly in powerful Pennsylvania, still clung to the thread of hope that a reconciliation with the mother country might be effected. But Tom Paine's *Common Sense* was fast bringing

the Quaker colony and the whole of America to the realization that
the only way out for liberty-loving men was self-assertion. In dynamic
words that clarioned their stirring message throughout the land Paine
brushed aside all half-measures and arguments for loyalty to the Crown
and boldly challenged his compatriots to cast off the shackles of tyranny.
By spring 100,000 copies of his pamphlet were in circulation and were
reaching the remotest readers.

When the Congress, in retaliation against the British embargo, declared on April 6 that the colonies would trade with every nation except Great Britain it added a very practical, compelling reason to the
idealistic one for making the break. To wage war, thereby putting a
crimp in the commerce so badly needed, was now obviously senseless
unless its object was freedom from mercantile, as well as political, restrictions of any kind whatsoever.

Although Massachusetts, earlier in the year, had informed its representatives in Philadelphia that the province favored independence,
North Carolina was the first to give its delegates specific authority to
vote affirmatively on the question. It did so six days after passage of the
Congressional resolution on commercial intercourse. Virginia went a
step further on May 15 by directing its agents to propose a declaration
of separation from England.

Meanwhile the Congress had given additional impetus to the agitation
by recommending that all colonies which had no governments of their
own should form them. One after another, in quick succession, they acted
accordingly. Even Pennsylvania, which had been among the most
reluctant to cast off the royal yoke, yielded to popular pressure by granting its representatives, on July 14, a free hand in the matter of independence and by organizing, soon after the old governing body adjourned,
county committees to take over the legislative reins.

By this time the irresistible drive for severance from the Crown
was well under way. On the 7th Richard Henry Lee had carried out
Virginia's directive by introducing the famous, world-shaking resolution, the crux of which was:

"That these United Colonies are, and of right ought to be, free and
independent states; that they are absolved from all allegiance to the
British Crown and that all political connection between them and the
State of Great Britain is, and ought to be, totally dissolved." [6]

Seconded by John Adams and referred to a committee of the whole on
the 8th, it was debated hotly on the 10th as the still strong conservative
minority faction of the Whig party came to a preliminary showdown

with the radical element. It was put to a vote on the same day and approved by the narrow margin of seven colonies to five. The thirteenth, Delaware, had no delegate in attendance at the moment. Both sides agreed to reconsider Lee's motion on July 1—the proponents, in anticipation of gaining enough converts to make adoption unanimous; the opponents, in the hope of mustering sufficient strength to defeat it. A condition of the deal was that Thomas Jefferson, Ben Franklin, John Adams, Roger Sherman, and Robert R. Livingston—who had been appointed by Hancock to draw up the Declaration of Independence, embodying the resolve—should complete their work in the interim. To implement this document the Congress authorized the President to name another group, consisting of one representative from each province, to prepare Articles of Confederation—an assignment he performed within twenty-four hours.

While setting in motion all this history-making machinery with one hand Hancock had to dash off reams of correspondence about the conduct of the war with the other, for the situation in New York had become acute. On the 11th, also, he notified New Jersey: "The Congress have this day received advices . . . that it is the design of General Howe to . . . attack . . . the City of New York. . . . The attack, they have reason to believe, will be made within ten days. I am therefore most earnestly to request you . . . to call forth your militia . . . and to forward them with all dispatch. . . . The important day is at hand that will decide not only the fate of . . . New York but, in all probability, the whole continent." [7]

These diversified duties did not comprise the full extent of Hancock's labors between dawn and dark. On that busy day likewise he found time to forward a letter from Martha Washington to her husband, with an accompanying note acquainting him that she was in good spirits and would visit him the following week.[8] And before tumbling into bed that night he set a precedent followed by publicity-conscious Chief Executives to this day. He consented to adoption by an Indian tribe, whose chief conferred upon him the name Karonduaan, or Great Tree.

The alert President did not forget to look out for "me and mine" during the feverish month of June. Even in the ethereal realm of idealism he always managed to glance down his long nose at what was taking place on the mundane level where all the Hancocks, for generations, had had their feet firmly planted. On this occasion he was concerned about his personal military aspirations, his political fortunes back in

Massachusetts, and the means of putting Ebenezer on the government pay roll. On the 12th he wrote to Cushing:

"Do send me my commission as major-general. I find I am left out of both House and Council. I can't help it. They have a right to do as they please. I think I do not merit such treatment; but my exertions and my life are, and shall be, at their service." [9]

He called forth his highest powers of manipulation in getting access to the public purse for his brother. He saw to it that his weak-kneed relative would have a solid citizen to prop him up if he should sag under the weight of responsibility. By the end of April he had wangled out of the Congress an appointment for William Palfrey, his former clerk, to succeed Warren, who had resigned from the post of paymaster general for the eastern department. Six weeks later he had Ebenezer installed as deputy under Palfrey, with headquarters in Boston. This job carried a salary of only $50 per month, but the new incumbent proved to be no bargain even at that figure.

· 4 ·

When Congressional bargaining over Lee's independence resolution was reopened on July 1 its supporters and adversaries haggled for two days about the now familiar, but still magical and thrilling, words that brought hope to oppressed peoples everywhere in the world. The main body of the Declaration, to which they were appended, is merely a public justification of their purport. But mankind has aspired to no loftier ideals than those expressed in the eloquent introductory clauses of the preamble: "That all men are created equal, that they are endowed by their Creator with certain unalienable rights, that among these are life, liberty, and the pursuit of happiness."

On the 1st the resounding resolve was again thrown into a committee of the whole—a parliamentary device that enabled the President to add his yea to those of his Massachusetts colleagues—and was passed by a margin of two more delegation votes than previously. But the Congress, sitting in regular session, to which the decision was then reported, still did not come to grips with the issue because the leaders of the separatist movement insisted on postponing final action until the next day in the belief that they could win at least approximate unanimity of ratification. They were vindicated by the capitulation of Pennsylvania and South Carolina and by the dramatic appearance of Caesar Rodney, who had galloped from Dover, Delaware, to Philadelphia just in time to weight the balanced scales of his colony on the side of adoption. New York's representatives alone continued to hold out by the negative process of abstaining on the ground that, although they themselves favored the motion, they were bound by year-old instructions to keep the door open for reconciliation.

So, as is not generally realized, July 2, 1776, is the date on which the American nation was born, to all intents and purposes, rather than on the 4th, when its birth is commemorated.

Even well informed persons need not feel ashamed for being confused about what occurred in Independence Hall on the Fourth of July. Jefferson himself, author of the Declaration and one of those present when it was adopted, made a glaring misstatement forty-three years later concerning what took place, although he had notes to refresh his memory. Furthermore, the *Journals* of the Congress are utterly misleading.

No sooner had the revolutionary resolution been disposed of than the Declaration proper was taken under consideration, in the usual committee of the whole. For three days impassioned oratory, pro and con, echoed throughout the governmental chamber. At last, about two o'clock in the afternoon of the 4th, the great white paper was reported out of committee to the House with a recommendation for approval, and was immediately ratified. Hancock and Secretary Charles Thomson then were ordered to authenticate it with their signatures, in the customary manner of handling all Congressional measures. They also were directed to have copies printed for dispatching to the colonial assemblies and to the army. The printing was done by the next morning.

Thus far the record is clear. But whether a lost final draft of the much corrected original manuscript, preserved in the Library of Congress to this day, contained anything except the text is a question that puzzled scholars for more than half a century. In 1819 Jefferson wrote that every delegate on hand when the Declaration was ratified, except John Dickinson of Pennsylvania, had signed it. But the public *Journal* makes no mention of any signing on the 4th, and the duplicates which came off the press that night—many of which still are in existence—include no signature other than those of the President and the Secretary. The secret *Journal*, published in 1821, reveals no entry at all for the historic day. So the experts are convinced, on the basis of circumstantial evidence, that no name besides those required for authentication was attached to any document concerning independence on the 4th of July, 1776.

· 5 ·

Specialists on this complicated phase of American history—not to mention ordinary laymen—were further mystified at first by the insertion, in the public *Journal* of July 4, of the Declaration in print, followed by the statement that it was engrossed and signed by the members whose names were appended—also in type. The natural inference was that the signing took place on the same day. But the engrossing was not ordered until two weeks later. Besides, it has been proved that one-fourth of the delegates on the list were absent on the 4th.

It is recorded in the secret *Journal* that on the 19th, four days after the news that New York had fallen into line was announced to the Congress, the governing body decreed that the Declaration be "fairly engrossed on parchment, with the title and style of 'The Unanimous Declaration of the Thirteen United States of America'; and that the same . . . be signed by every member of Congress." [10] Not until the 2nd of August is there an entry definitely asserting that this or any other such pronouncement was subscribed by the general membership.

Even when the colonies registered, in black and white, their consent to be enrolled in the independence movement the procedure was highly irregular. Many of the individual delegates who voted to join never attested to that act in writing; not all who did attach their signatures were accredited representatives at the time; and Thomas McKean of Delaware, who in 1814 stirred up the controversy over the seemingly erroneous accounts of the affair in the *Journals,* did not get around to adding his endorsement the fifty sixth and last—until 1781.

But there is no doubt that the signing ceremony glamorized by pen and brush as having been performed on Independence Day actually came off almost a month later. Just where Hancock, the first signer on two occasions, fits into the true picture, however, still is open to argument. Comments, both prejudiced and judicious, have been made on the significance of the fact that his name stood alone, except for Thomson's, for nearly thirty days on what was tantamount to a confession of treason to Great Britain. All commentators are agreed that the Secretary probably would not have been held accountable in his subordinate, purely clerical capacity even if the rebellion had been crushed.

One of the most biased interpretations of the splendid isolation in which the President's signature adorned the Declaration during this period is that of Stephen Higginson. With the possible exception of John Adams, Higginson flung more vitriol from his pen into the face of the first signer than any other contemporary. But a high percentage of it must be diluted in the interest of veracity, for the writer was a political propagandist of the most partisan type. Hiding behind the pseudonym "Laco," he attacked Hancock unmercifully in a series of articles published in the *Massachusetts Centinel* during the campaign for the governorship of the Bay State in 1789. In one of these he sneered: "The Secretary of Congress has as good a title to superior respect for having certified the copy as Mr. H. has for having signed the original. They were both mere official, mechanical acts without any responsibility, such as the most timid man upon the continent, in their situations, would not have hesitated to perform. . ◆ . Having been opposed to it until it became inevitable and reluctantly drawn in with his vote at the last moment, we ought to resent his vanity and assurance in claiming our first esteem and respect on that occasion."[11]

There may be a half-truth in Higginson's concluding sentence, for Hancock often did wait to see which way the political straws were bending before he committed himself on a controversial matter. But there is no indication that he held back when it became evident—let alone "inevitable"—that independence was indispensable to the fulfillment of his country's destiny. The extent of his responsibility will be discussed later, but it was indubitably greater than "Laco" contends. Whether he claimed undue credit for his act is not revealed in the written record; but, in view of the egotism he exhibited on many occasions, his detractor must be given the benefit of the doubt.

Mellen Chamberlain, after a special study of the authentication episode, offers a more balanced judgment of the President's part in it. He states:

"For more than six months [until January 8, 1777] Congress had withheld the names of those signing the Declaration. This may have been from prudential considerations. Unless the Declaration was made good by arms, every party signing it might have been held personally responsible for an overt act of treason. Whether this would have been the case in respect to Hancock and Thomson, who were not acting in any personal capacity, and possibly even in opposition to their own convictions, in an accordance with an express direction of Congress, may be a matter of question."[12]

Chamberlain, however, appears to be unwarranted in placing Hancock in the same category as Thomson. The head of the Congress, as an old offender against the Crown, was in a much more vulnerable position than the Secretary. And the historian's skepticism concerning the President's convictions is certainly unjustified in the light of his aggressiveness at the time of the general signing.

In a sense Higginson is right in maintaining that the certification was merely an official act. It must be admitted, also, that Hancock was more or less obligated, as the leader of the body which did the declaring, to corroborate that action in writing. Yet he must have been long forewarned that he might be placed in this situation as public opinion, crystallizing into an overwhelming desire for independence, was reflected in the Congressional chamber. So he had ample opportunity and timely justification—in legitimate concern for his private interests in Boston—for resigning or insisting on a leave of absence. But, instead of turning a deaf ear, he hearkened to the higher call of patriotism enthusiastically.

The assertion in the "Laco" screed that Hancock assumed no more responsibility than "the most timid man upon the continent" is entirely indefensible. If the Revolution had collapsed the King would have delighted in pouncing upon the man who had defied him on numerous occasions and had always managed to elude his grasp. George III would not have hesitated, in deference to the mere legalism that that gentleman had acted as a servant of the people in this particular instance, to string up such an arch rebel. On the contrary, he probably would have singled the President out for specially Draconian treatment and let off most of the other members of the Congress with prison sentences on the conciliatory ground that they had added their signatures tardily and reluctantly when no longer able to withstand the pressure of mass hysteria. And if England had succeeded in beating down America's resistance before the ensuing January, the king might not even have discovered the identity of the other subscribing patriots.

Although it cannot reasonably be claimed that Hancock was solely responsible for the Declaration from July 4 until August 2, there is sound basis for the contention that he bore the main part of the onus attached to that traitorous manifesto. Whether or not he was a victim of circumstance, the fact remains that he was in a ticklish spot for a month and in a decidedly uncomfortable one for five months more.

· 6 ·

Why did this man of peace take upon himself the lion's share of liability for his country's awe-inspiring apostasy? It may be answered that he felt duty-bound, as head of the insurrectionist government, to set an example to the faint-hearted among his fellow revolutionists. But even when convinced that there was no way for the colonies to gain political and economic freedom short of arrogating it to themselves he might have hung back, without dishonor, until the more vociferous advocates of rebellion should be willing to put their preachments into practice.

Up to the time when this conviction took hold of him he had been lukewarm, if not downright cold, toward the idea of independence. If the aims expounded in the Declaration could have been achieved within the framework of the British Empire he would infinitely have preferred to continue giving allegiance to the Crown; for he was, as has been demonstrated, inherently conservative. What, then, turned him from a laggard into a leader?

Although genuine sympathy with the spirit of the momentous manifesto probably contributed largely to Hancock's decision to play a lone hand during the first month of declared independence, his consuming desire for notoriety was, more than likely, the determining factor. Popular acclaim, the ruling passion of his life, appears to have been the magnet that drew pen to paper when discretion dictated delay. Exhibitionism—so obvious even to an amateur chirographer in his flamboyant handwriting—seems to have been the dominant influence in inducing him to invite foremost attention from the hangman.

This line of reasoning leads back to the fundamental question as to what converted Hancock into a separatist sympathizer. How did he arrive at the conclusion that independence was essential to the exercise of free enterprise in all phases of existence?

This mental metamorphosis had started as early as 1765, when he was fulminating against the Stamp Act. It was first expressed in the fall of that year to Barnard & Harrison: "I will not be a slave. I have a right to the liberties and privileges of the English Constitution and I, as an Englishman, will enjoy them." As he became more and more of an American and less and less of a Briton in his thought, his determination stiffened.

Basically this conviction, like most of those underlying patriotism, was selfish. This is not to say that Hancock was exceptionally so. On the contrary, his love of his native land was stronger and more constant than that of the great majority of the founding fathers. But he was motivated inherently by what is called today enlightened self-interest. Therefore, his private concerns were of paramount importance to him. True, he virtually abandoned his business to go into politics. But at that time he undoubtedly considered this step as a temporary expedient to accomplish permanent improvement in trade and intended to resume active proprietorship of the House of Hancock as soon as possible.

Gradually he came to enjoy a political career for its own sake. But even when the Revolution had been under way for a year he continued to show lively solicitude for his mercantile interests, as is evidenced by his hiring of Bant and Cazneau to look after them. He probably hoped secretly that the Congress would not take seriously his sacrificial gesture of willingness to have Boston burned in 1775. So when the shortsighted English Ministry made it clear in 1776 that they were bent on forcing the colonists into unconditional surrender, which would have brought about still harsher restrictions on commerce, he realized that if he ever was to prosper again as a merchant it would be necessary to make a clean break with Great Britain.

But another and, quite likely, a stronger incentive moved Hancock to throw in his lot with the independence advocates. Unless the proposed purpose of the rebellion should be achieved he would have no outlet for his passionate yearning to be famous. Without any prospect of regaining his prestige as a business magnate, he would fade into obscurity; for his future as a politician—if his life were spared by the King—would be dark as a result of the overshadowing power of the British ruler and his ministers. Even if, by some remote chance, he should rise to the governorship of Massachusetts he would be only a colonial governor. He would not be the sovereign potentate of the great commonwealth that obviously was to develop into one of the most important components of a free United States.

· 7 ·

On the very day when he exposed his neck to the noose in theory by subscribing to the Declaration alone, the President was given reason to fear that he soon might be hanged in reality. Philadelphia itself was in danger of attack from Howe, as he pointed out to the Maryland Convention in a letter bearing the same date as the great document:

"The Congress have this day received intelligence which renders it absolutely necessary that the greatest exertions should be made to save our country from being desolated by the hand of tyranny. General Howe having taken possession of Staten Island, and the Jerseys being drained of their militia for the defense of New York, I am directed by Congress to request you will proceed immediately to embody your militia for the establishment of the flying camp [presumably a mobile reserve] and march them with all possible expedition . . . to the City of Philadelphia." [13]

Within forty-eight hours the versatile Mr. Hancock, who must have derived much vicarious satisfaction from the opportunity to act the part of a military strategist, had resumed his more suitable role of administrative go-between. In a message of the 6th to Washington he enclosed a copy of the Declaration, with the request that the commander in chief "have it proclaimed at the head of the army in the way you shall think most proper." [14] Simultaneously he sent replicas of the document, with similar instructions, to all the colonial legislatures.

In a more personal note of the same date he dispatched a fifth transcript to his old friend William Cooper, Boston town clerk. After hinting that he would like Cooper to make sure it was read to the home folks he told of Katy Quincy's arrival in Philadelphia and said that Dolly was in a "tolerable good way." But the most interesting paragraph concerns a gory incident off the coast of New Jersey. This passage puts gentle John in the new light of posing as a gloating avenger:

"Two days ago a brig of ours . . . arrived off these capes and was chased by a man-of-war. They ran her on shore at Egg Harbor, and our people . . . after taking out some arms and . . . powder . . . discovered a number of boats full of men . . . approaching them. Our people, finding it necessary to quit the vessel . . . laid a long train whereby to blow her up. The men from the boats boarded her, gave three cheers, and immediately the ship blew up and destroyed in a moment fifty or sixty of the man-of-war's men and sent them to—Heaven, I hope. . . . Thus they see it is dangerous to be too meddling in other men's affairs. They had better quit; but if they will be so foolish they must abide the consequences." [15]

When New York at last came into the independence fold on the 9th Philadelphia, too, exploded. The Whigs in the Quaker city could not wait for official notification in their eagerness to publicize the news of their great political victory. With implied disapproval of an undignified ceremony, John Adams thus described it to Samuel Chase of Maryland:

"The Declaration was yesterday published and proclaimed from that awful stage in the State House yard. By whom do you think? By the Committee of Safety, the Committee of Inspection, and a great crowd of people. Three cheers rended the welkin. The battalion paraded the common. . . . The bells * rung all day and almost all night. Even the chimers chimed away." [16]

* But *not* the Liberty Bell, contrary to tradition.

This celebration was duplicated, in various forms, throughout what the colonists proclaimed, somewhat prematurely, to be the sovereign and independent United States of America. In spectacular contrast to the matter-of-fact, almost casual manner in which their leaders theoretically had cut all ties with England, the people in every city, town, and hamlet that dotted their jubilant land signalized the historic event with an abandon never before witnessed in the New World.

Wherever artillery was available they fired thirteen cannon or thirteen volleys from one gun in symbolic salute to the corresponding number of states that comprised the new nation. The unthinking populace, on the whole, did not stop to consider the terrifying implications of the great decision, although many copies of the Declaration broadcast by the thousands were read in churches and the occasion was solemnized with prayer. While the masses gave vent to their feelings in characteristically "vulgar" ways, such as tearing down a statue of George III in New York, the classes did so more genteelly by indulging in a "collation" or attending an "elegant entertainment." The exultation reached fanatical heights in Rhode Island, where it was decreed that anybody who prayed for the King would be subject to a fine of £1,000.

In the evening of the day on which the enthralling pronunciamento was released in Philadelphia the military inhabitants of New York welcomed it just as enthusiastically as the civilians but, of course, in a more disciplined manner. Washington reported that "the measure seemed to have their most hearty assent; the expressions and behavior, both of officers and men, testifying their warmest approbation of it." [17] Strangely enough, the news was not published officially in the President's home town until the 25th, in spite of the special pains taken by Boston's first citizen to have it announced there as soon as possible. But it was finally done with fitting fanfare as the high point of a ceremony on the Statehouse balcony. The Massachusetts metropolis made up in longevity for what it lacked in promptness of recognition; for as late as August 11 the renowned Dr. Cooper was intoning the majestic periods of the political masterpiece before his Brattle Street congregation, which "attended . . . with great solemnity and satisfaction." [18]

· 8 ·

But Cooper's parishioners could not have derived as much satisfaction from listening to the Declaration as did the first signer from affixing his "John Hancock" to the engrossed copy on August 2. He must have glowed with pride in the seat where he had squirmed through so many tedious hours as the little men of the Congress wrangled over matters of no significance or pertinence while one of the greatest issues in the annals of humanity cried out for the most thoughtful consideration that mortal man could give it.

In front of the President was a plain mahogany table, cleared for action except for an impressive silver inkstand from which projected several quill pens, like plumes. Near by sat Thomson, keeping the *Journal*. Ranged in a semicircle behind desks in the center of the chamber were the expectant delegates. This was the most dramatic and gratifying moment—even more so than the instant of the original signing because this occurred in the presence of such an august assemblage—in the career of a statesman whose life teemed with stirring experiences.

Rising from his chair and—as can readily be imagined—pulling himself up to the full extent of his imposing stature, Hancock wrote, for the second time, what might have been his death warrant in the firm, beautiful, challenging script so well known and so greatly admired to this day. After inscribing beneath his name the elaborate flourish which symbolized the manner of all his public acts he is supposed by numerous historians to have made two statements. The initial one, variously reported, was to this effect:

"There! John Bull can read my name without spectacles and may now double his reward of £500 for my head. *That* is my defiance." [19]

The president may have been thinking in these terms, but it is doubtful that he would have quipped under such sobering circumstances. There is less reason to question, although no more evidence to buttress, the historical foundation for his next alleged assertion:

"We must be unanimous; there must be no pulling different ways; we must all hang together."

This remark and the famous pun Ben Franklin is said to have perpetrated in reply were inserted by Jared Sparks, admittedly as anecdotal quotations, while he was editing Franklin's works almost a hundred years ago. It seems unlikely that even such a witty phrase maker as "Poor Richard" would have spoken in a vein so foreign to the spirit of the occasion as:

"Yes, we must indeed all hang together, or most assuredly we shall all hang separately." [20]

Although there is nothing but tradition to support what Hancock said —if anything—when he wrote his name in characters twice as large as any other signer, and at the top center of the list, there is authority for what ran through his mind then or on subsequent calm reflection. He revealed that he was fully aware of the document's significance for posterity in a circular letter to all the states on January 31, 1777, three weeks after the Congress finally decided to disclose the identity of the delegates who had endorsed the parchment version. Accompanying each copy was the following explanatory comment:

"As there is not a more distinguished event in the history of America than the Declaration of her Independence—nor any that, in all probability, will so much excite the attention of future ages,—it is highly proper that the memory of that transaction, together with the causes that gave rise to it, should be preserved in the most careful manner that can be devised . . . that it may henceforth form a part of the archives of your state and remain a lasting testimony of your approbation of that necessary and important measure." [21]

· 9 ·

The Congress apparently did not attach as much importance to the means of achieving independence as to the paper enunciating it. One of the most serious charges brought against the governing body by historians is that it failed to supply Washington with the sinews of war—men, arms, and money. But this organization, which "governed" the "United States" from 1775 to 1789 only by sufferance of the capricious colonial legislatures, was not as much at fault as they; and its President was almost entirely blameless in regard to cooperation. He did virtually everything within his limited power (which consisted mainly of personal influence) to persuade, cajole, and goad the ruggedly individualistic assemblies into supporting the commander in chief.

An instance of this is the series of letters Hancock wrote during 1776 to the General Court of Massachusetts, pleading that its militia be rushed to the defense of New York. He evidently received no response to his appeals of the 4th and 11th of June, for on the 16th he exhorted Cushing to "impress the Assembly with the importance of answering letters from Congress," and added: "We are in the dark whether matters are carried into execution." In despair he then decided to seek information about the doings of the Bay Colony legislators through the columns of the *Continental Journal,* a Boston newspaper that had been taken over recently by John Gill, former associate of Benjamin Edes in the publication of the *Gazette.* In closing the above communication he requested his henchman to "ask him to enter me for a paper and to send it me regularly here every week." [22]

On July 16 the distraught President made a final attempt to convince Massachusetts of the pressing need for more troops not only in New York but also on the Canadian border. Desperation is manifest in every line of this message, duplicates of which he dispatched to Connecticut and New Jersey:

"If we turn our attention towards the Northern Department we behold an army reduced by sickness and obliged to flee before an enemy of vastly superior force. If we cast our eyes to headquarters we see the British army reinforced under Lord Howe and ready to strike a blow which may be attended with the most fatal consequences if not timely resisted. . . . The intelligence received this day from General Washington points out the absolute, the indispensable, necessity of sending forward all the troops that can possibly be collected to strengthen both the army in New York and that on this side of Canada." [23]

The patriot who was without a peer as a mediator rendered another generally unrecognized service of considerable import to his country in July—possibly against his private inclinations.

Aaron Burr had joined Washington's staff in May, shortly after returning from the Quebec expedition, and had spent about six weeks as his guest at Richmond Hill on the Hudson. But their strong personalities had clashed over the commander in chief's refusal or failure to obtain a more advantageous post for the fiery, glory-seeking young officer. So Burr finally had notified Hancock that he was contemplating retirement to civil life. Thereupon the man with whose wife's affections he is reputed to have toyed procured for him an appointment as aide-de-camp to General Israel Putnam. In doing so he insured to the fighting forces for three more years the skill and courage of a soldier who performed many notable feats. These included preserving a whole brigade from capture during the retreat from Long Island, guarding a pass through which the British might have attacked the freezing and starving remnants of Washington's army at Valley Forge, and preventing a rout at Monmouth.

Such extra undertakings as interceding for Burr, piled upon the countless routine duties of his office, had so overburdened the President by the end of July that he planned to resign from the Marine Committee. On the 30th he asked Cushing for an accounting of the moneys expended on the Massachusetts men-of-war, so that he might leave the affairs of the chairmanship in order. He urged speed in compliance with

THE "HANCOCK" AND THE "BOSTON," FRIGATES BUILT UNDER THE
DIRECTION OF HANCOCK, CAPTURING THE BRITISH FRIGATE "FOX" ON
JUNE 7, 1777. FROM A WATER COLOR IN THE MARINERS' MUSEUM
AT NEWPORT NEWS, VA.

ENGLISH FRIGATE "RAINBOW" CAPTURING THE "HANCOCK" ON JULY
7, 1777, WHILE THE "FOX" STANDS BY IN THE BACKGROUND. FROM
A WATER COLOR IN THE NAVY DEPARTMENT BUILDING
AT WASHINGTON.

THE "HANCOCK," AIRCRAFT CARRIER WHICH SAW ACTION IN THE
PACIFIC DURING THE SECOND WORLD WAR. FROM A PAINTING BY
ANTON OTTO FISCHER.

this request, "for I have determined to move my family to Boston the beginning of September and propose being there myself in all that month." [24]

The load of care resting upon Hancock is confirmed by Representative Josiah Bartlett of New Hampshire, who confided to a friend in October: "I believe (*inter nos*) your letters to the President concerning marine affairs have not been laid before the committee nor much attention been paid to them. The great and important business in which he is constantly employed and the almost immense number of letters which he is constantly receiving . . . makes it impossible for him to attend to them all. . . . I sincerely wish he did not belong to the Marine Committee but would confine himself to the affairs of Congress, which is business abundantly sufficient to employ the time of any one human being." [25]

· 10 ·

It is not known exactly when either the *Hancock* or the *Boston* hoisted sail, but neither could have been the first of the Congressional fleet to do so. In communicating to Cushing his intention to withdraw from maritime circles Hancock commanded his henchman to get "the two frigates . . . ready for the sea—I mean, to be furnished with every necessary that is to be had with you. Cannon are casting, but when we shall have a sufficiency I know not." [26] And as late as the middle of October the Congress recommended to the General Court of Massachusetts that it "give the continental agent the full weight of their influence to make the frigate *Hancock* ready for the sea immediately." [27] There is no indication that the *Boston* was any further advanced.

On August 6 the Marine chairman signed an order directing John Paul Jones to "proceed immediately on a cruise against our enemies." [28] Impatient to prove his mettle, Jones had gone over the head of Commodore Hopkins to the leader of the Congress with a request to be given command of one of the new ships and had promptly been assigned to the *Providence*, sponsored by Rhode Island. Two days after complying, the President confirmed the captaincy which John Paul received in May by issuing a second commission.

This incident belies another charge made against Hancock by his vilifiers: that he deliberately destroyed the original document testifying to the captain's rank. He may well have been tempted thus to delay the sailing of the *Providence* until his personally superintended men-of-war could be finished; but the paper still was in existence in 1840. [29]

He could have saved face by stalling while Jones' reappointment was going through the Congressional mill and then could have used his influence to have the brilliant naval tactician put in command of the *Hancock*. In declining to stoop to such a political trick he lost the benefit of having his name borne by the first of the thirteen frigates to embark upon a fighting expedition. Almost a year elapsed before the *Hancock* and the *Boston* were dispatched on their maiden mission— and that a disastrous one.

Another illustration of Hancock's dominant desire to prosecute the war to the utmost, regardless of his private interests, is his attitude toward a peace feeler that had been tickling the more timid patriots for six months. In January the Maryland Tory Lord Drummond, who had just returned from England, had approached Congressman Lynch, the suspicious South Carolina delegate slapped down by the President for aspersing a Boston shipmaster, with an offer of mediation purporting to come from the Ministry. The principal provisions were that the Americans should be relieved of direct taxation by Britain, that all duties levied on overseas trade should be paid to the colony in which the participating merchants operated, and that each province should contribute to the general support of the Empire annual sums in proportion to the amount of business it did with the mother country.

Lynch had forwarded these proposals to Washington from Philadelphia, with the comment that he was definitely opposed to considering them. In February Drummond also had mailed a copy to the commander in chief, who had sent it on to the Congress. Soon afterward His Lordship had been taken into custody by the New York committee of safety and had been paroled on his word of honor. Toward the end of April he had sailed, ostensibly for Bermuda, but had been picked up on the high seas by the *Asia,* the British warship which had supplied the New Jersey Tories with ammunition for their abortive counter revolt. Now, in August, he had turned up in New York Harbor again—this time with the enemy fleet—and had made new overtures, under a flag of truce, to Washington. After rejecting the terms of the proposition the General enclosed it, for the perusal of the governing body, in this puzzled note of the 18th to Hancock:

"I am exceedingly at a loss to know the motives and causes inducing a proceeding of such a nature at this time, and why Lord Howe has not attempted some plan of negotiation before, as he seems so desirous of it. . . . It may be that part of the Hessians have not arrived, . . . or that General Burgoyne has not made such progress as was expected to form a junction of their two armies, or . . . they mean to procrastinate . . . trusting that the militia who have come to our succor will soon become tired and return home." [30]

The President replied scornfully a week later: "Congress highly approve of the manner in which you have checked the officious and intemperate zeal of His Lordship. . . . I hope . . . he will be convinced that it is highly imprudent to attract the attention of the public to a character which will only pass without censure when it passes without notice." [31]

Hancock stood to gain as much as any merchant in America by a resumption of trade with England under the terms proffered by Drummond. But he, like Washington and his own Congressional colleagues, apparently realized that the olive branch was rotten with propaganda designed to weaken the colonists' singleness of purpose.

· 11 ·

The President now was diverted briefly from duties attendant upon the birth of a nation by becoming a father in his own household. A daughter, Lydia Henchman, was born to him at about this time—probably in November. The only evidence as to the date is a badly mutilated scrap of foolscap on which one of Dolly's nephews or nieces scrawled a note at her request a few weeks after her husband's death in 1793. There is no indication of the person to whom it was addressed, but the context suggests that the "Sir" of the salutation was a jeweler. It lists the exact death dates of Hancock and his aunt but only the month and year— August, 1777—of the baby's demise. This is inserted above "was born November, 1776"—the words before "1776" being scratched out but still legible. The message is an order to inscribe a ring with the facts concerning the infant girl and a boy, John George Washington, who came into the world on May 21, 1778, and went out of it on January 27, 1787; and to engrave similar data respecting Uncle Thomas and Aunt Lydia on a bracelet. [32]

For an account of the circumstances surrounding the advent of the first child it is necessary to rely on Bant. In a series of four letters (one of which contains possibly Rabelaisian implications) Hancock's intimate, who had returned to Boston after accompanying Katherine Quincy to Philadelphia, refers to the impending arrival of what he virtually took for granted would be a male heir. He was kept in ignorance of its materialization, however, until the middle of December, at least.

Edmund Quincy, who was staying in Boston with his daughter, Mrs. Donnison, expected a visit from Dolly and Katy. This indicates that his youngest daughter originally planned to have her child there. He may have scared the prospective father out of permitting his wife to take the journey by warning him on October 6 that the roads in the vicinity of New York were unsafe—probably on account of war hazards; or John may have decided against it because he could not fulfill his earlier intention to go along. In any event, the trip did not take place. On the 19th Bant wrote:

"In your last letter I observe that your town and the State are not to be favored with a visit this season. For my part I begin to fear, if we are to wait until you are at leisure before we see you here, that both you and your *boy* (for I suppose he cannot be parted with) will stay in Philadelphia until the war is ended; though I hope the young gentleman will, in due time, become more visible than he has lately been . . . unless the happy genius of his papa has pushed him into place rather sooner than was expected. If so, I give you joy, Sir, and hope that Madam is comfortable."

Curiosity must have been killing the Boston correspondent, for he took quill in hand again two days later to continue his prodding:

"All your friends, Sir,—that is to say, every man I meet—are frequently inquiring after your health and welfare; and since the report that there is a prospect of an important addition to your family I have many questions asked me that are of a new and particular kind as they respect you, Sir, and more especially by the ladies. I hope soon to be able to answer them in a more positive style than at present."

Early in December Bant spurred his unresponsive friend from a different and more compelling quarter: "On my return from Bedford, I called at Mr. Perkins' in Bridgewater. . . . The good lady's eyes were in tears upon saying that it seemed to her she never should see you again. She is particularly anxious to hear if Mrs. Hancock is yet abed and earnestly hopes she will bring you a brave boy. . . . My being out of town last week prevented me the pleasure of seeing the *Hancock* man-of-war make her first entrance into our harbor. She arrived last Friday. She is a fine ship. Makes a most war-like appearance. She lays off the end of your wharf."

On December 16 the inquisitive Bant still was probing and pulling for a Hancock son. Business-minded William made this final stab in the dark: "We hope that Mrs. Hancock . . . has blessed you with a fine boy. If so, Mrs. Bant begs the favor of his mama to give him a thousand kisses of welcome and charge them to her account." [33]

Hancock probably was as disappointed as his attorney when his first-born had turned out to be a girl. That may have been the reason for his presumptive failure to record the date on which she came upon the scene—in marked contrast to his meticulous notations concerning his boy's birth.

The Boston lawyer must have waited considerably longer to hear of the arrival and the sex of the child, for the parents were in Baltimore. Sam Adams, writing to his wife Elizabeth on the 19th from the Maryland town—whither the Congress, without its President, had fled on the 12th because the Hessians had taken Burlington, New Jersey—reported that John Hancock and his family had just come. [34]

This means that John had exposed Dolly and their newborn babe for several days to possible capture by the enemy, who were only twenty miles from Philadelphia. It would not have required a week to travel to Baltimore even in that era. Perhaps he had not been able to get his large ménage, including Katy and a staff of servants, packed up and under way any sooner; for the style in which his household moved necessitated elaborate preparation, regardless of the danger involved.

· 12 ·

It was against President Hancock's better judgment, anyway, that the Congress had removed to Baltimore. He thought that such a precipitate flight had a bad psychological effect upon the United Colonies, and expressed that opinion in a letter of January 14, 1777, to Robert Morris, famous financier of the Revolution, whose acquaintance he was cultivating. Morris, who was among the most public-spirited of the founding fathers, had remained in Philadelphia as head of a committee appointed at his own suggestion to take care of government business that could not be handled by remote control. The Continental army might have disintegrated but for his loyal support through the purchase of supplies under great difficulties. Hancock apparently recognized in him a valuable adjunct to the new wing of the Whig party:

"The marks of regard you . . . mentioned as contained in the few hasty lines I sent you are very far short of what I early expressed after I had the pleasure of a connection with you; and be assured, Sir, . . . it will be . . . pleasurable . . . to continue . . . a correspondence, not only in the commercial and public line, but in a solid, friendly, and free intercourse . . . and . . . hereafter I . . . shall be ambitious of being reckoned among the list of your real friends. . . . I can assure you your whole conduct since our flight is highly approved. . . .

"I have got to housekeeping, but really, my friend, in a very poor house and but just furniture sufficient to live tolerably decent; though when I tell you I give £25 . . . you would judge it to be amply furnished. I have only two rooms below, and one of them I am obliged to let my servants occupy. In point of convenience I wish to return to Philadelphia, which brings me to the hint in your letter."

The hint was that the government printing presses, which were turning out rapidly depreciating currency by the bale and which had been carried along to Baltimore, should be shipped back to Philadelphia. The President, however, disapproved of the suggestion on the ground that the manufacture of this fiat, but urgently needed, money should not be interrupted. "As things have turned out, I am very sorry we removed at all and . . . I think we were full hasty enough. It damped people much."

The landed proprietor of Beacon Hill, of course, would have regarded anything short of a mansion as a shanty for the housing of his entourage. And the idea of having to get along with "only two rooms below," even though he probably had half a dozen above, would depress him to the point of wishing to drown his self-pity in the Madeira Morris had given him—possibly for safe-keeping. "I have some of your wine left for you," he said in conclusion. "I wish to have one sitdown with you in my poor habitation." [35]

Three days later he sat down to give further encouragement to the "free intercourse of letters" with his new ally. He began by reminiscing about life in the once inhospitable Quaker capital, which now seemed glamorous in retrospect:

"Do you go to the Oyster Club as usual? . . . or are your evenings taken up with business? I long to be with you but I must submit to my present fate. I think our public affairs wear a very favorable aspect. *General Washington has certainly outgeneraled How[e].* These movements of his will tell."

It required implicit faith in Washington to recognize then the greatness of his generalship. To be sure, he had recently performed three remarkable military feats: crossing the Delaware under the nose of the enemy on December 8; recrossing it to surprise the wassailing Hessians at Trenton and seize a thousand of them on the night after Christmas; and attacking the British in the rear for another victory at Princeton on January 3 just before going into winter quarters at Morristown. But these had been his only successful major operations in six months, during which Howe had driven the American forces out of New York, had captured Fort Washington and three thousand prisoners, and had pushed on down through New Jersey to threaten Philadelphia.

After approving the man whom he would be expected to envy Hancock went on to praise the spirit of one whom historians have accused him of wronging:

"I admire the spirited conduct of little Jones. Pray push him out again. I know he does not love to be idle and I am as certain you wish him to be constantly active. He is a fine fellow, and he shall meet with every notice of mine." [36]

Meanwhile Massachusetts had reaffirmed its faith in the President of the Congress, which had reconvened on December 20 at Baltimore, by reelecting him a Congressional representative on the 10th for another year. The General Court also had given a semblance of meaning to his rank as major general of militia three days earlier by appointing him commander of an independent company formed for the defense of Boston. This apparently was merely a token of appreciation, however, for he obviously would be tied down in his Presidential office for some time to come; but it was well calculated to soothe his martial urge.

Ebenezer Hancock had joined in the back-scratching by anticipating his brother in naming a son after Washington. The deputy paymaster may have done this to mollify his superior, who had been appealing in vain for funds to be used in recruiting. After replying on January 30 that the treasury was very low he added irrelevantly: "I now take the liberty to acquaint Your Excellency that I have lately named a child after you for the very great respect and regard I have for Your Excellency and the glorious cause in which you are engaged." [37]

· 13 ·

For John Hancock, however, this period of good will could not long endure. His political foes had sheathed their knives temporarily but were just waiting for a pretext to use them again. He furnished it in February by talking about taking his deferred trip to Boston. John Adams whipped out his blade immediately, as is indicated by this comment in his diary for the 17th:

"Mr. Hancock told C. W. yesterday that he had determined to go to Boston in April. Mrs. Hancock was not willing to go till May, but Mr. Hancock was determined upon April. Perhaps the choice of a Governor may come on in May. What aspiring little creatures we are! How subtle, sagacious, and judicious this passion is! How clearly it sees its object, how constantly it pursues it, and what wise plans it devises for obtaining it!" [38]

Although the Massachusetts House had recommended during the previous September that after the next election the legislature should be empowered to form a state government, nothing definite was done for almost four years. It is quite possible, however, that Adams was right in thinking the President's decision to go home was prompted by a desire to be on hand when the political plums growing out of the new regime should be passed around. The aspiring politician, who always took the long view, probably figured that the governorship of his own powerful bailiwick might be a steppingstone to leadership of the nation in a real sense if independence should be won from Great Britain. He was to get himself elected first chief executive of the commonwealth in 1780 and was to run against Washington for the Presidency of the United States in 1789. But Adams' sarcasm over such legitimate ambitions can be explained only by spleen.

Hancock advanced his plans for returning to Boston to the stage of inducing the General Court to agree that he should be released from his duties as a Congressional delegate in March. But in the meantime his Presidential responsibilities increased to such an extent that he felt constrained to put off the trip once more. His most pressing problem at the moment was posed by the projected removal of the Congress back to Philadelphia on February 25, now that Washington had checked the progress of the British army by pinning down its flank in northern New Jersey.

On the 18th Hancock requested Morris to "issue orders . . . for four good covered wagons, with four good horses and a sober driver to each, to . . . convey down to Philadelphia the public papers, etc." [39] Later in the same day he used his freshly developed friendship to write that he was sending William Taylor (who apparently had replaced Rush as his private secretary) "to procure a suitable house, well furnished, for me"; and he asked his new friend to advise Taylor in selecting it, and urged him: "Pray do hurry on the wagons I wrote you for this morning. I cannot move without them, nor can Thompson [Thomson, Secretary of the Congress]. . . . I hope soon to join you at the Oyster Club." [40]

On the 20th Samuel Purviance gave a farewell dinner for his friends the Hancocks. In addition to the guests of honor about fifteen people were present, including Katherine Quincy, John Adams, Richard

Henry Lee, and several colonels with their wives. Describing it, Adams could not resist taking a sly dig at Hancock's pride. After listing two women ahead of Dolly and Katy he wrote: "If this letter, like some other wise ones, should be intercepted I suppose I shall be called to account for not adjusting the ranks of these ladies a little better." [41]

Adams's confidential record of the 21st reveals that the President had had a falling-out with the commander in chief. Attributing their differences to politics, he notes: "This morning received a long card from Mr. H. expressing great resentment about fixing the magazine at Brookfield, against the bookbinder [General Henry Knox] and the General. The complaisance to me and the jealousy for the Massachusetts in this message indicate . . . the same passion and the same design with the journey to Boston in April." [42]

Hancock wanted the powder magazine to be built at Brookfield in Worcester County, whereas Washington and Knox preferred to have it at Springfield in Hampshire County. By "complaisance" Adams probably meant flattery intended to wheedle him into supporting his political antagonist, and by "jealousy for the Massachusetts" he may have been referring to solicitude for the voters in the more conservative eastern part of the state, where—except for Boston—the Hancock party was relatively weak.

· 14 ·

But disturbing news from Morris soon gave Hancock something of greater importance to the general welfare to worry about. It was a warning that the Congress should delay its departure from Baltimore because the British front at New Brunswick, New Jersey, had been strengthened by reinforcements and because the American army at Morristown was in poor condition. On Wednesday February 26 the President, still writing from Maryland, replied that the governing body had decided to heed this advice; but he personally had no fear of the enemy. Determination and optimism radiate from this letter:

"We must give these fellows a trimming. If we can but subdue the present force in the Jerseys I think the day is ours. One noble exertion by a large body flying to the support of the General . . . would effect the business; and before any reinforcements could arrive from Europe we should be in such readiness as soon to give a good account of them, though I believe they will soon be tired of their game. We have got the trumps. Let us play the game well. . . . I am almost hurried to death but must keep at it." [43]

The pace was getting on Hancock's nerves. He even became annoyed at his cooperative correspondent in Philadelphia. On the day after composing his inspirational message he wailed:

"My dear friend, you have reduced me to a most distressed situation, as I find by a letter this moment received from Mr. Taylor . . . that you had counter-ordered my wagons. What I shall do I know not. I can't get away here. Congress is adjourned to Philadelphia, and I must be there on Wednesday next . . . and I cannot remove my papers and . . . am obliged to leave the whole of my family behind. For God's sake hurry the wagons along. . . . Thomson is obliged to stay behind for want of those wagons. I shall set off on Saturday alone, to my great mortification, and hope to meet the wagons on the road." [44]

The President did "mortify" himself by setting out alone in his own conveyance, probably pulled by half a dozen horses and attended by as many liveried outriders. He arrived on the 3rd at a Maryland village (not now on the map) called appropriately God's Graces, of which he was in sore need. The epistolary effort he made there for Dolly's benefit includes an almost bite-by-bite account of his dinner:

"Through much bad road I arrived here at 1 o'clock in good order. . . . I met Governor Johnston [sic], who is just come from the General. Things look well, and I judge we shall remain at Philadelphia if I find it so on my arrival there. You may depend I shall immediately send for you. . . .

"Dinner is coming. I have just taken up the vinegar bottle. Poor stuff. . . . ½ after 2. I have got up from dinner and standing at the window. Dinner served up. Boiled beef, roast turkey, ham, roast beef, greens salad, gooseberry and apple tarts, cheese, apples, etc.; Baltimore punch, wine, etc. . . .

"P. S.—The turkey was so tough that I broke out one of my teeth." [45]

On the morrow the bedeviled traveler addressed his wife from a tavern in Susquehannah, a now extinct hamlet near the Pennsylvania-Maryland line:

"After I wrote you from God's Graces yesterday I proceeded on through bad roads to Mr. Stele's at Bush, where I arrived at sunset, supped well, and lay well—that is, as well as I could alone,—and after breakfast this morning set out for this place through intolerable bad roads and got here at 11 o'clock. But, to my great mortification, cannot pass the ferry. They are now cutting the ice, and hope to get over in the morning.

"My boy Joe has treated me very ill. He drank a deal of my wine in the wagon; broke and lost several bottles; dropped out my trunk, which was luckily found; and was brought to the tavern drunk and put to bed. I shall turn him adrift at Philadelphia. . . . Tomorrow morning I intend to set out on horseback. . . . God bless you. Take care of yourself. There is wine in the closet. When that is gone get more. Live reputably. Keep up the part of a family." [46]

Despite all his mortifications Hancock reached Philadelphia on schedule, March 5. But if he could have seen John Adams' letter of the 7th to Abigail, with its cavalier comments on moving, he probably would have felt more than ever like punching that gentleman in the nose—especially after picking up en route a communication written by Mrs. Adams and placing it in her husband's hands.

"The President, who is just arrived from Baltimore," Adams replied, "came in a few minutes ago and delivered me yours of February 8, which he found at Susquehannah River on its way to Baltimore. . . . We may possibly remove again from hence, perhaps to Lancaster or Reading. It is good to change place. It promotes health and spirits. It does good many ways. It does good to the place we remove from, as well as that we remove to, and it does good to those who move." [47]

XII

PRIDE AND PREJUDICE

*I*N COMPARISON WITH the year 1777 Hancock's previous tenure as President of the Second Continental Congress had been a sinecure. After the governing body returned from Baltimore to Philadelphia on March 5 the high-sounding name—United States of America—conferred upon the colonies by the authors of the Declaration of Independence, became a mockery. The thirteen subscribing provinces were disunited as never before. Most of them were still more reluctant than heretofore to surrender one iota of their sovereignty, and some even suspected the Congress of harboring imperialistic designs.

The small states feared the large ones. Pennsylvania fought—physically in several instances—with Maryland, Virginia, Delaware, New York, and Connecticut over ill defined boundary lines. Its feud with the last-mentioned colony over the rich Wyoming Valley territory, whither numerous Connecticut families had recently migrated, was especially bitter and long. New York and New Hampshire engaged in a similar squabble over the Green Mountain area. The sections of these two colonies which later combined to form Vermont declared their independence and insisted on being admitted as a sovereign entity to the "Union" under the projected Articles of Confederation.

The disorganization of the country was reflected in the Congress. Necessity, self-interest, and apathy caused wholesale resignations. Several sessions were attended by as few as twelve delegates. Many withdrew to carry out important foreign missions; others, to accept governorships; some, to go home in disgust. Their successors arrived with chips of still more obstinate individualism on their shoulders. Even veterans like Benjamin Harrison grew cantankerous under the protracted strain of bringing a new nation into being while waging war upon the mightiest empire in the world. Harrison accused the New Englanders—

250

presumably with reservations respecting his friend Hancock—of trying to domineer everybody in the manner of the "Grand Turk." Edward Rutledge of South Carolina made just as scathing attacks upon the northern delegates.

The consummate tact and compromising ability of the President were barely equal to the occasion. More than any other person he prevented the disintegration of the organization which held the only hope for achievement of genuine unity. His correspondence during the first half of this ultracritical year shows what he had to contend with outside, as well as inside, Independence Hall. Early in January he warned Archibald Bullock, head of the Georgia Convention, against treasonable dealings between George McIntosh, one of its leading members, and the Loyalist province of East Florida. At the beginning of February he urged the Maryland Assembly to use its militia for the suppression of an insurrection in two of its counties. Later in the month he requested it to appoint commissioners for a meeting with those of New York, Pennsylvania, Delaware, and Virginia in an effort to regulate prices and curb inflation.[1]

Unsound currency was one of the most serious and baffling problems posed by the Revolutionary movement. Shortly after the battle of Bunker Hill the Congress had authorized the issuance of $2,000,000 in virtually worthless bills of credit. In rapidly mounting desperation the governing body resorted to this demoralizing but inescapable expedient on an ever increasing scale. By the end of 1779 the total of printing-press money had risen to $241,000,000. Meanwhile the colonies, independently, had turned out $209,000,000. The value of Congressional and provincial paper depreciated to the vanishing point. Efforts to make it legal tender by fiat failed utterly. Except for advances—and outright contributions—of sterling by a few wealthy men, including Hancock, the Revolution was not financed in the ordinary sense until loans aggregating approximately $7,830,000 were obtained from France, Spain, and private banking sources in Holland.

· 2 ·

Between the lines of two long letters John Hancock wrote to Dolly on successive days in March may be read the effect of those trying times upon him as President. The communications, however, are significant chiefly for the light they shed upon the writer's nature—depression over domestic discomforts, detailed interest in comestibles, and longing for his wife in the midst of public responsibilities calculated to preoccupy most men. The first, begun on the evening of the 10th, told of his arrival in Philadelphia and then continued:

"I put my things into Mr. Williams' house and went in pursuit of lodgings. Neither Mrs. Yard nor Lucy could accommodate me. I then went to Smith and borrowed two blankets and returned to my own house; soon after which Mrs. S. sent me up a very handsome supper, with a tablecloth, knives, and forks; plates, salt, a print of butter, tea, double-refined sugar, a bowl of cream, a loaf of bread, etc., etc.; and there I have remained and shall do so, waiting your arrival. . . . I, however, lead a doleful, lonesome life. . . . Last night Miss Lucy came to see me, and this morning, while I was at breakfast on tea, with a pewter teaspoon, Mrs. Yard came in. . . .

"I spend my evenings at home, snuff my candles with a pair of scissors, which, Lucy seeing, sent me a pair of snuffers and, dipping the gravy out of the dish with my pewter teaspoon, she sent me a large silver spoon and two silver teaspoons—that I am now quite rich. I shall make out as well as I can but I assure you, my dear soul, I long to have you here. . . . When I part from you again it must be a very extraordinary occasion.

"I have sent everywhere to get a gold or silver rattle for the child, with a coral, . . . but cannot get one. . . . I have sent a sash for her and two little papers of pins for you. . . . However unsettled things may be, I could not help sending for you, as I cannot live this way."

Digressing for a moment, the husband and father became a military seer—but not a very good one, for his two negative predictions turned out to be wrong:

"We have an abundance of lies. The current report is, General Howe is bent on coming here. Another report is that the merchants at New York are packing their goods and putting them on board ships and that the [American] troops are going away, neither of which do I believe. We must, however, take our chances. This you may depend on: that you will be ever the object of my utmost care and attention."

He then instructed his helpmeet to give enclosed directions to a Baltimore wagoner with whom he had contracted to move his family to Philadelphia; cautioned her to be careful in packing, with the help of Katy, and not to forget anything; notified her that he was sending a Mr. McClosky to assist in the preparations for the journey; told her what inns to put up at, and advised her not to stop at Wilmington, Delaware, because that town was infected with smallpox.

In a postscript penned the next morning the man of many cares informed his wife that he had arranged to have little Lydia inoculated on arrival. Then, before tacking on more suggestions concerning the trip, he inserted this social note:

"Mrs. Washington got here on Saturday. I went to see her. She told me she drank tea with you." [2] Martha, too, apparently had taken refuge in Baltimore while the commander in chief endured the privations of the Morristown winter quarters.

At the end of the day on which he posted this letter John Hancock resumed the correspondence on what he evidently regarded as a veritable expedition, although the distance to be covered was only a hundred miles. According to his plans, which now included the dispatching of two men besides McClosky "with horses and a wagon as winged messengers to bring you along," Dolly was to be attended by an entourage befitting a queen. He began in the same melancholy strain that runs through his previous communication:

"No Congress today, and I have been as busily employed as you can conceive; quite lonesome and in a domestic situation that ought to be relieved as speedily as possible. This relief depends upon you."

The First Lady must not only travel in a style suitable to her position but treat her escorts with regal munificence. "Should any gentlemen and ladies accompany you out of town, do send McClosky forward to order a handsome dinner, and I beg you will pay every expense. Order McClosky to direct the landlord not to receive a single farthing from any one but by your direction. . . . If Mr. Thomson cannot be ready with his wagons as soon as you are, do not wait. But part of the guard, with an officer, must attend yours and part be left to guard his."

Dolly's foresighted provider apparently even anticipated the wear and tear of the journey upon her attire and was determined she should not look disheveled on her grand entrance into the capital of the country: "I shall send off Mr. Rush, a tailor, tomorrow or next day to meet you. I wish I could do better for you, but we must rough it."

Probably by an association of ideas he, at this point, was reminded of the rough going in his Presidential office:

"I am so harassed with applications for funds [to pay the army] and have been sending off expresses to call all the members here that I have as much as I can turn my hand to. I don't get down to dinner; catch a bit, I write, and then at it again. . . . Do beg Mr. Hillegas * to send some money by my wagons. . . . Pray him to take pity on me. I have lent my own stock already to stop some mouths."

* Michael Hillegas, "Continental Treasurer of the United States."

But John Hancock was feeling too sorry for himself to dwell long on the hunger of others, and soon reverted to his own:

"Joe comes in with a plate of minced veal, that I must stop. I shall take the plate in one hand, the knife in the other, without cloth or any comfort, and eat a little and then to writing, for I have not room on the table to put a plate. I am up to the eyes in papers. . . .

"Supper is over—no relish, nor shall I till I have you here; and I wish Mr. and Mrs. Hillegas to join us at supper on Tuesday evening, when I shall expect you. I shall have fires made and everything ready for your reception."

He concluded the letter proper with more military speculation but in a somewhat less certain vein than formerly:

"The opinion of some seems to be that the troops will leave New York—where bound, none yet knows. One thing I know: that they can't at present come here. Perhaps they are going to Boston or up North River. . . . Never fear; we shall get the day finally, with the smiles of Heaven."

Before the epistle was sealed the gourmet again got the better of the statesman:

"Do let Harry buy and bring me one or two bushels of parsnips. Bring all the wine—none to be got here." [3]

· 3 ·

Not long after regaining his domestic happiness through Dolly's return Hancock was placed in an unhappy position in his official family through his efforts to preserve harmony. He yielded to the temptation he had resisted during the preceding summer. He played politics—for what he thought was the good of his country—with John Paul Jones' commission.

Toward the end of April, shortly before Jones returned from Philadelphia to Boston to embark upon another of his innumerable cruises, the President summoned him to a conference. The naval genius thus recounts what occurred:

"He requested me to show him the captain's commission he had given me the year before. I did so. He then desired me to leave it with him a day or two till he could find a leisure moment to fill up a new commission. I made no difficulty. When I waited on him the day before my departure—to my great surprise—he put into my hands a commission dated the 10th day of October, 1776, and numbered *eighteen* on the margin. I told him that was not what I expected and requested my former commission. He turned over various papers on the table and at last told me he was sorry to have lost or mislaid it. I shall here make no remark on such conduct in a President of Congress. Perhaps it needs none.

"He paid me many compliments on the services I had performed in vessels of little force and assured me no officer stood higher in the opinion of Congress than I. . . . That the table of naval rank that had been adopted the 10th of October, 1776, had been drawn up in a hurry and without well knowing the different merits and qualifications of the officers; but it was the intention of Congress to render impartial justice. . . . And, as to myself, that I might depend on receiving a very agreeable appointment soon after my return to Boston; and, until I was perfectly satisfied respecting my rank, I should have a separate command."

Commenting on Hancock's actions, Jones' most authoritative biographer, Lincoln Lorenz, states:

"His opinion of the captain continued to be highly favorable, but neither his character nor his political associations were of such independence as to withstand freely the influence of sectionalism and other prejudice. He had to reconcile such powerful advocates for favored officers as John Adams . . . and Richard Henry Lee. . . . Unbecoming as the subterfuge of Hancock appears, his explanation of the circumstances under which Jones received his standing from Congress is the more reasonable in view of the stress of political forces which the President undoubtedly had to reconcile." [4]

Even though he treats the great naval commander sympathetically, Lorenz is in the small category of writers who have made a determined effort to be fair to Hancock. He has peered through the ruffles on John's shirt front into the heart of one of the most misunderstood figures in history and finds it sound, while recognizing that the brain which controlled its impulses did not always function perfectly. In this particular instance, however, the reasoning appears to have been logical and justifiable.

With reference to Hancock's conduct at this time Dr. Gordon, who accused him of usurping the Presidency and attacked him on many other occasions, in person as well as in writing, quotes an unnamed member of the Congress on Hancock's announced intention of returning to Boston:

" 'I am much concerned, though his great fatigue and long attendance entitle him to some relaxation. How we shall do without him I know not, for we have never yet put in a chairman on a committee of the whole House that could, in any measure, fill his place. He has not only dignity and impartiality, which are the great requisites of a president of such a body; but has alertness, attention, readiness to conceive of any motion and its tendency and of every alteration proposed in the course of debate, which greatly tends to facilitate and expedite business.' "

Having thrown this sop to historical integrity, Gordon cannot resist flinging a few barbed comments at the man for whom he had a spiteful dislike based on a private feud:

"The chair is known to be his forte. As chairman of a committee or any other body he presides with much advantage to himself; but it has been . . . observed that the number at the head of whom he is . . . makes a wide difference in him. When great he appears to be in his own element and is all animation. If small, it is otherwise. This is common to public characters, especially where there is a fondness for popularity." [5]

One of President Hancock's strongest bids for popularity came to naught in a manner that must have delighted his enemies. On May 21 the *Hancock* and the *Boston,* on which he had lavished so much thought and time in the hope of sending them into battle before any of the eleven other ships in the embryonic Congressional fleet, set sail at last from Boston in search of the foe, at the head of a squadron including nine privateers. The converted merchantmen, poorly adapted to cruising, dispersed either by the choice of their commanders or by force of circumstance, within the first six days. On June 7 the two bona-fide men-of-war engaged the British frigate *Fox* and overpowered her.

Their next—and disastrous—encounter began on the anniversary of Hancock's great day, July 4. In the evening, while they were convoying their prize toward the New England coast, three of His Majesty's ships— the *Rainbow,* the *Flora,* and the *Victor*—sighted them and gave chase. The pursuit lasted until the 7th, when Captain Manley surrendered the *Hancock* and the captured vessel to Sir George Collier of the *Rainbow.* Meanwhile the *Boston* escaped, and eventually found her way back to Boston.

Thus the fine frigate, which the chairman of the Marine Committee had fondly fancied as the first full-fledged American sea fighter to go into action, became the first to go down to defeat. This news must have staggered him when it reached him about a month later, although there is no record of his reaction.

As a matter of fact, however, the seizure of the *Hancock* (which the

British renamed *Iris* and put into their own service) was not due to any fault of construction. She might have come off victorious if the *Boston* had not run away. Captain McNeill evidently disobeyed orders, for he was subordinate to Manley. A court-martial resulted in the acquittal of the superior officer and either a suspended sentence or dismissal in the case of the inferior.

In a posthumous sense the luck of the Hancocks stood by the most illustrious member of the family, even with respect to the naval phase of his career. Two more war vessels and two merchantmen were to bear his name. The latest fighting ship is an Essex-class aircraft carrier which saw eight months' service in the Pacific during World War II. A Japanese bomb exploded on her flight deck, causing one hundred and forty casualties and destroying sixteen planes; but she survived and still is one of the stoutest bulwarks in the nation's first line of defense.[6]

· 4 ·

However mortifying to President Hancock was the loss of the frigate he had fathered, it was a minor matter in comparison with other setbacks sustained by the patriot cause during the summer and fall of 1777.

On July 6 the withdrawal of the Continental garrison from New York under Howe's pressure proved the President to be a poor prophet. On the 29th, Burgoyne drove General Arthur St. Clair out of Ticonderoga. Meanwhile Howe, abandoning his plan to effect a junction with Burgoyne in the Hudson River valley, had moved his troops by sea to the head of Chesapeake Bay. He defeated Washington, who rushed south to intercept him, at Brandywine Creek, Pennsylvania, on September 11 and thus cleared the way for the taking of Philadelphia two weeks later. Howe repulsed a counterattack by his adversary on October 4 at near-by Germantown and made inevitable the eventual retirement of the badly battered American army to Valley Forge for the winter. Two compensatory events occurred during this disheartening period: Arnold's victory over Colonel Barry St. Leger on August 22 at Fort Schuyler; and Burgoyne's far more significant surrender to Gates, with almost one-fourth of the English expeditionary forces, on October 17 at Saratoga. This was the turning point of the war.

The Congress and its President apparently had not kept in close touch with the rapidly changing military situation prior to September 9, for on that day it was resolved that "General Washington be requested to appoint a proper person at headquarters to write to the President twice a day, or oftener if necessary, advising the position and movements of the armies; and that the Board of War appoint proper expresses for conveying the said letters with the utmost expedition." [7] The general complied promptly after the Germantown reverse, reports of which reached Philadelphia at four o'clock next morning.

It must have been with a heavy heart that Hancock, still sorrowing over the death of his daughter during the preceding month, attempted to console Washington:

"I am sorry for the unfortunate issue of the day but, from the troops keeping up their spirits, I flatter myself it will still be in our power to retrieve the loss of yesterday. I have thought proper . . . to call the Congress together at 6 o'clock." [8]

Realizing that there now was nothing to prevent Howe from advancing into Philadelphia, the Congress decided at this special session to move to Lancaster—sixty miles almost due west—and did so on the 18th. Its presiding officer was free to go along, for Dolly—probably to grieve in a quieter atmosphere—had returned to Baltimore after little Lydia passed away, and Sister Katy had gone to visit Uncle Josiah Quincy in Medford.

For some unexplained reason the governing body did not reconvene until the 27th, and in the interim Hancock, Sam Adams, and fourteen other representatives turned up in Bethlehem—sixty-five miles northeast of Lancaster and forty-five miles northwest of Philadelphia—on the 22nd. Presumably they could not forget that they were politicians even in this crucial hour, for they felt obliged to show their interest in the religious training of the younger generation.

"Many of the delegates," writes a contemporary diarist, "attended the children's meeting in the chapel. After the service John Hancock took up the Text Book, which was on the table and, with several others, examined its contents." [9]

With a recklessness and an effrontery that are still harder to account for than their journey to Bethlehem, President Hancock and some of his traveling companions slipped into Philadelphia—almost into the jaws of the British—on another mysterious mission on the 25th, the eve of Howe's arrival, according to the private record of Christopher Marshall.[10] They returned to Lancaster on the 27th in time to transact only one day's business before the Congress hopped off again to the safer locality of York—twenty-five miles to the southwest—where it reassembled on the 30th.

It may easily be imagined that John Hancock's tongue was hanging out at this juncture, and it is no wonder that he wrote to Morris a few days later: "My good friend, I should esteem it a very particular favor if you could . . . spare me a little Madeira, if it was only three dozen. I care not for price, for I feel awkward not to have it in my power to ask a friend to take a glass. If you can oblige me I will send my light wagon." [11]

· 5 ·

Hancock not only was thirsty but was hungering for the sight of his beloved Boston. Dolly had already set out from Baltimore to visit Katy in Medford on the way home, and he longed to follow her. Now that Howe apparently had settled down in Philadelphia for the winter, the President was more justified than heretofore in entrusting the Congress to other hands for a short time. His health, which had shown signs of a serious breakdown recently, was another strong inducement to the long-deferred trip. And not least weighty was his desire to reestablish political contacts in Massachusetts, which had reelected him a councilor in May.

So, on October 15, Hancock asked the governing body for a two months' leave of absence and was given until the first of the ensuing year. But the complaisance with which his request was received and the alacrity with which it was granted must have been a severe shock to him. In a letter to a friend on the following day Henry Laurens, who was to be elected on November 1 to fill his office *pro tem*, expressed astonishment that must have been redoubled in the President's mind:

"Our President gave notice yesterday of his purpose to quit the chair and Congress next week. I moved the House to entreat and solicit his continuance. To my surprise, I was seconded—and *no more*." [12]

On the 17th Hancock outlined to Washington his reasons for leaving his post and sought, rather pathetically, from the commander in chief the recognition of indispensability so pointedly withheld by Congress:

"It is now above two years since I have had the honor of presiding in Congress, and I should esteem myself happy to . . . render further service to my country in that department. But the decline of health occasioned by so long and unremitting an application to the duties of my office, both in Congress and out of Congress, joined to the situation of my own private affairs, has at length taught me to think of retiring for two or three months. . . . Upon the review . . . of the intercourse . . . between us . . . I feel a great degree of pleasure in having . . .

endeavored to execute the business committed to my care and, in a particular manner, with regard to the army under your command. I flatter myself my conduct . . . will meet with your approbation. The politeness and attention I have ever experienced from you . . . will always be a source of the most pleasant satisfaction to me."

These protestations of tender regard may have been designed, in part, to soften up the war-hardened general in preparation for the presumptuous claim upon his indulgence referred to in the prologue of this book. In the next paragraph the writer begged for an escort of light horse to protect him while passing through the Tory-infested towns skirting the North River.[13]

As has also been pointed out, the man who braved so many dangers, to the extent of foolhardiness, could not have been cowed by the prospect of running the gantlet of mere Tories—especially with the protection of the numerous personal attendants who always accompanied him on his journeys. He must have been actuated almost solely by the overweening vanity that demanded a display of the symbols of power, particularly while he was traveling through strange country.

But if Hancock imposed upon people in the interest of his ego he was ever ready to reciprocate. On the very day when he burdened Washington with this appeal he did his best to forestall the sufferings of the army during that terrible winter at Valley Forge. He earnestly besought the Pennsylvania Assembly to collect as much clothing as possible for the troops.[14]

The sybarite of Beacon Hill, however, was thinking of his own comfort, too, at this time. In a letter of the 18th, directed to Dolly "at Worcester or Boston," he said:

"You will . . . please . . . to tell Mr. Sprigs to prepare the light carriage and four horses and himself to be ready to proceed on to Hartford or Fairfield, as I shall hereafter direct, to meet me on the road. If my old black horses are not able to perform the journey he must hire two. . . . My present intention is to leave Congress in eight days. . . . I . . . must desire that you will take a seat in the carriage and meet me on the road, which will much advance your health. . . . And I have desired Mr. Bant to accompany you . . . and when we meet he can take my sulkey and I return with you in the carriage to town. Mr. Bant must hire or borrow a servant to attend you on horseback. . . . I long to see you. . . . I have much to say, which I leave to a cheerful evening with you in person. God bless you, my dear Dolly." [15]

· 6 ·

Washington returned Hancock's compliments on the 22nd from his headquarters "near Philadelphia":

"It gives me real pain to learn that the declining state of your health
. . . oblige[s] you to relinquish a station . . . which you have so long
filled with acknowledged propriety. Motives, as well of a personal as of a
general concern, make me regret the necessity that compels you to retire
and to wish your absence from office may be of as short a duration as
possible. In the progress of that intercourse which has necessarily sub-
sisted between us the manner in which you have conducted it . . . accompanied with every expression of politeness and regard to me, gives
you a claim to my warmest acknowledgements."

He confirmed the President's professed misgivings about crossing the
North River and advised him to delay his trip until conditions were more
settled, but added that, on being apprised of Hancock's departure, he
would order an escort of horse to accompany him from Bethlehem to
General Putnam's camp at Fishkill, New York, where another would
take over and carry on to the end of his journey.[16]

On the 25th Hancock notified Washington that he was planning to
set out two days later, although his conscience was uneasy over deserting
his post during "the present critical state of our affairs." [17] He was not
to get under way, however, until the 29th or 30th.

Whatever obligation there may have been for the President to stick
to his job was strictly moral, because he drew no salary for services
stretching over a period of almost two years and a half. Shortly before
he left York the Congress ordered Hillegas to pay him, in recompense
for personal advances to the treasury, the sum of $1,392. But not until
1783 was he reimbursed, in the amount of $3,248, for household and in-
cidental expenses. Although he could well afford to work for nothing,
the devotion with which he did so, to the unquestioned detriment of
his health, should be entered among the larger items in the historical
ledger showing where his country stands in debt to him.

Hancock modestly refrained—for once—from claiming credit for his
labors, but hinted wistfully that he longed for it, in a farewell speech
before the governing body on Wednesday the 29th. Appealing prayer-
fully for unity, steadfastness, and forbearance in the stupendous effort
to make the American dream come true, he said:

"Friday last completed two years and five months since you did me
the honor of electing me to fill this chair. As I could never flatter myself

your choice proceeded from any idea of my abilities, but rather from a partial opinion of my attachment to the liberties of America, I felt myself under the strongest obligations to discharge the duties of the office . . . in the best manner I was able. . . . As to my conduct, both in and out of Congress, in the execution of your business, it is improper for me to say anything. You are the best judges. But I think I shall be forgiven if I say I have spared no pains, expense, or labor to gratify your wishes and to accomplish the views of Congress.

"My health being much impaired, I find some relaxation absolutely necessary after such constant application. I must therefore request your indulgence for leave of absence for two months. But I cannot take my departure, Gentlemen, without expressing my thanks for the civility and politeness I have experienced from you. . . . If . . . any expressions have dropped from me that may have given the least offense to any member, as it was not intentional, so I hope his candor will pass it over.

"May every happiness, Gentlemen, attend you, both as members of this House and as individuals; and I pray Heaven that unanimity and perseverance may go hand-in-hand in this House and that everything which may tend to distract or divide your councils be forever banished." [18]

But Hancock's hopes for unanimity—not to mention reciprocal magnanimity—on the part of his fellow members were dashed, chiefly because of Sam Adams' vindictiveness. Writing to Warren on the 30th, Adams summarized the President's speech and went on to indicate what was in the wind:

"But it is not improbable that you may have a copy of it, for a motion was made in the afternoon by Mr. D. of New York * that a copy should be requested [for the *Journal*] and thanks returned for his great services and a request that he would return and take the chair. This motion was opposed by several members but it obtained so far as to request the copy, and this day the latter part of the motion will be considered. I have given you this merely as a piece of news, leaving you to judge of the tendency and probable effect of the speech and motion. We have had two Presidents before, neither of whom made a parting speech or received the thanks of Congress." [19]

The President probably started for Boston either on the afternoon of the 29th or on the following morning, without entering the House again; for he had too keen a sense of propriety to be present while his address was being discussed. More than likely he was well on the road by the 31st, when it was moved that "the thanks of Congress be presented

* Either James Duane or William Duer.

to John Hancock, Esq., for the unremitted attention and steady impartiality which he has manifested in discharge of the various duties of his office as President."

In any event, consideration of the motion to thank Hancock was postponed "till the sense of Congress be taken on the general proposition." A resolution was then proposed that, in "the opinion of this Congress, . . . it is improper to thank any President for the discharge of the duties of that office." [20] The voting on this proposal eventuated in an even division of the ten states officially represented as Massachusetts cast its ballot in the affirmative. Finally, when the question was put on the first motion it was carried by a majority of six to four; but the President's provincial colleagues were in the dissenting minority.

It is almost unbelievable that any body of public men would consider withholding a mere gesture of gratitude, under such circumstances, from a leader who had been so faithful to his trust as Hancock, whether or not they privately regarded him as incompetent. But Sam Adams, whose great influence undoubtedly accounted for the raising of the issue and for the opposition vote, would stop at nothing to defend his peculiarly narrow conception of democracy—including the belief that no special homage should be paid to any human being, lest he get ideas similar to the royal prerogative. Even if Adams' prime motive in this case was impersonal and patriotic, the most charitable conclusion to be drawn from his action is that he was dangerously fanatical.

It was natural that Hancock, in the light of past performance, should interpret his estranged patron's attempt to deprive him of well merited gratification as a purely personal rebuke. After this affair—and for years to come—their enmity was as stinging as the blow administered in the chamber of Congress.

· 7 ·

In his relations with the President, as in many other instances, Washington proved himself to be a bigger man than the majority of those under whose direction he served. The commander in chief was true to his promise that he would provide an escort for Hancock and apparently had no fears that the pomp of a military convoy would give him a kingly complex. In a letter of November 2, probably sent by express to Fishkill, he gave notice that Cornet Buckmer and twelve dragoons were on their way despite an acute shortage of horses needed for patrol duty, and apologized for the smallness of the detachment. This seems to have been the relief guard referred to in his earlier communication.

William Ellery, delegate from Rhode Island, considered it more than sufficient even for the head of the Congress. In his diary under date of the 7th he maliciously describes the impression made upon him by an encounter with the Presidential party at White Plains, near Putnam's headquarters:

"In our way to the ferry we met President Hancock in a sulky, escorted by one of his secretaries and two or three other gentlemen and one light horseman. This escort surprised us, as it seemed inadequate to the purpose either of defense or parade. But our surprise was not of long continuance; for we had not rode far before we met six or eight light horsemen on the canter and, just as we reached the ferry, a boat arrived with as many more. . . .

"Who would not be a great man? I verily believe that the President, as he passes through the country thus escorted, feels a more triumphant satisfaction than the colonel of the Queen's Regiment of Light Dragoons, attended by his whole army and an escort of a thousand militia." [21]

Hancock did not even pay for the maintenance of his convoy, according to John Adams, who had headed for Massachusetts with Sam Adams shortly after. The troopers apparently were supposed to defray the cost of board and lodging out of their own pockets and to draw on the government for compensation; but they tried to beat the game, after the manner of their ilk since the dawn of paid soldiery. The younger Adams noted privately:

"The taverners, all along, are complaining of the guard of light horse which attended Mr. H. They did not pay, and the taverners were obliged to go after them to demand their dues. The expense, which is supposed to be the country's, is unpopular. The Tories laugh at the tavern-keepers, who have often turned them out of their houses for abusing Mr. H. They now scoff at them for being imposed upon by their king, as they call him. Vanity is always mean; vanity is never rich enough to be generous." [22]

Despite the front he put up in public, John Hancock seems not to have felt like a conquering hero when he sat down to write to Dolly on Saturday the 8th in his tavern room at Dover, "within sixty miles of Hartford." Realizing, as a wise man does, that it is impossible to pretend before one's wife, he revealed himself to be a weary, gouty, prematurely aging gentleman of forty in need of sympathy and companionship:

"I am thus far on my journey to meet you, thank luck for it. I have gone through many difficulties on the road but that I shall not mind. The remembrance of these difficulties will vanish when I have the happiness of seeing you. I am still obliged to have my foot wrapped up in baize but I brave all these things. I hire this person to carry you this letter in confidence it will meet you at Hartford. I shall get along as fast as I can but, having a party of eight horse with me and a wagon, I do not travel so fast as I otherwise should. What if you should, on Monday morning, set out to meet me on the Litchfield road, and then, if I am not able to reach Hartford on that day, I shall have the satisfaction of seeing you on the road. If you think the ride will be too much I would not have you undertake it, but I hope you will . . . as I trust Mr. Bant is with you." [23]

It was on the 14th that the Hancocks actually passed through the Connecticut capital according to a newspaper published there. Within another week, however, they were back in their dear Boston.

Accounts differ as to the date of their arrival. General William Heath, commandant of the eastern department and a stanch Hancockonian, placed it on the 19th; whereas a local journal fixes it on the 21st. But the two sources agree as to the thundering welcome accorded the President and the First Lady. The paper pictures it thus:

"We have only time to inform the public that last Wednesday arrived here, under the escort of light dragoons, His Excellency John Hancock, Esq. . . . By his coming into town sooner than was expected he avoided some public marks of respect. . . . His arrival was made known by the ringing of bells, the discharge of thirteen cannon . . . on the Common, the cannon from the fortress on the hill, and the ships in the harbor. The independent and light infantry companies paid him their military salutes. He received the compliments of gentlemen of all orders, and recent indication was given of the sense the public has of his important services to the American cause."

The beaker of joy poured out for Hancock by his fellow citizens must have overflowed when Sam Adams entered the metropolis and John Adams reached North Braintree on the 30th—both entirely unheralded. The publication that had reported the President's advent in such glowing terms devoted only one sentence each to the coming of the Adamses.[24] And, of course, the contrast with the reception tendered his enemy was not lost upon the elder Adams—or the younger, either, it is safe to assume. To a letter from Sam after his return to York, James

Lovell, a member of the Congressional Committee for Foreign Affairs then residing in Boston, replied:

"Duly notice your history of the different entry made into the capital by three travelers. . . . Risible faculties were given to man for wise purposes, without doubt. I have let them have full exercise on this occasion, let who will be vexed or sorry." [25]

But the idol of Massachusetts was to have the last laugh on Lovell and all the rest of the old guard. He probably chortled more heartily than Adams' follower as he started to patch up his political fences simultaneously with the renovation of his mansion in December. Besides repairing the damage caused by the British occupation he rehabilitated the big house on the hill in several other ways and added a wing with the grand banquet hall in which he was to entertain so lavishly after becoming governor. Meanwhile the Hancocks lived in their rented summer home at Jamaica Plain.

Although reelected to Congress on the 4th, President Hancock was not above serving as moderator of the town meeting four days later. And he had not forgotten the people on whose good will his career as a public man depended. He was given a vote of thanks for his gift of 150 cords of firewood to the poor.

His remarkable flair for cultivating the favor of the masses excited the admiration of a German officer in Boston who had been captured with Burgoyne at Saratoga. Writing on the 10th to his family in the Old World, he related:

"President Hancock has now been several weeks in Boston. . . . This man, whom the most zealous Republicans call the 'American King' in order to provoke us, looks . . . worthy of the position he holds as the first man in America. Moreover, he is so frank and condescending to the lowest that one would think he was talking to a brother or relative. He visits the coffee-houses of Boston, where are congregated the poorest of the inhabitants—men who get their living by bringing wood and vegetables to the city. Indeed, he who desires to advance in popularity must understand the art of making himself popular. In no country does wealth and birth count for so little as in this; and yet one can maintain the position given him by fate without being in the least familiar with the lowest." [26]

· 8 ·

At the moment, however, Hancock was distinctly unpopular with the authorities of Harvard College.

Whenever the name of this founding father comes up in a conversation about the nation's beginnings at least one participant—often one whose historical background should guard him against being duped by a common fallacy—is apt to smile knowingly and voice some such utterance as: "Oh, yes, good old John Hancock—the man who absconded with the Harvard funds." Why such an exaggerated statement of his culpability should be taken at face value to this day, and why the misconception should be uppermost in the minds of the few who pretend to any knowledge of the victim, can be explained only by the perverse human tendency to believe and stress the worst of a famous character. Even reputable historians have perpetuated the canard started by his bitterest foes.

On July 30, 1773, subject to the approval of the board of overseers, the Harvard corporation elected the budding celebrity treasurer succeeding Thomas Hubbard—mainly because this prominent alumnus' huge fortune and reputation for integrity would be the safest possible security for more than £15,400 in bonds and notes to be entrusted to him.

In November, 1774, the Reverend Samuel Langdon, president of the institution, wrote to Hancock the first of a series of dunning letters in an effort to obtain an accounting. He ignored this appeal and another of the following January. Finally he deigned to reply to a third communication of March 7, 1775, that he was too busy to comply—as, of course, was true—but that he would soon appoint another day for a settlement. Two dates for a meeting during the same month were then successively agreed upon, but the procrastinating party failed to show up.

After neglecting to respond to a fourth request for a reckoning Hancock was confronted with a demand, issued a week before the battle of Lexington, that he deliver the securities, together with the balance of the cash into which he had converted some of them for the payment of professors' salaries, to a committee selected by the corporation. Writing in the chilly third person on April 11 from Concord, he answered:

"Mr. Hancock presents his compliments to the Reverend President and the other gentlemen who were present yesterday at the meeting and acquaints them that he has at heart the interest of the college as much as any one and will pursue it. He is much surprised . . . at the contents of the President's letter, *as well as at the doings of the gentlemen present, which he very seriously resents;* and, however great the gentlemen may think the burden upon his mind may be, Mr. Hancock is not disposed to look upon it in that light . . . but if the gentlemen choose to make *a public choice* of a gentleman to the displacing him, they will please to act their pleasure. Mr. Hancock . . . shall write very particularly or be at Cambridge in person as soon as the [Second Provincial] Congress rises. *He leaves all his matters in the hands of a gentleman of approved integrity* during his absence [at the Continental Congress], which he is not disposed to alter."

The Harvard authorities dismounted from their high horse as soon as Hancock mounted his. And the following months of war discouraged the academicians from striking an equestrian attitude again. The college buildings were requisitioned by the British as barracks and storehouses, with the result, of course, that the students had to leave. At the enemy's evacuation a year later the institution was teetering on the verge of financial ruin. So, on March 18, 1776—the day after Howe had moved his forces out of Boston and vicinity—President Langdon was in a much humbler frame of mind as he resumed his correspondence with the man who had become President of the Continental Congress.

Beginning obsequiously to the effect that he was "reluctant to interrupt Mr. Hancock, engaged in momentous affairs on which the salvation of the United Colonies depends," he expressed hope "for a moment's attention just to mention the difficulties of the seminary of learning" and asked: "Will you give me leave to depend upon your employing a few thoughts on our circumstances?" [27]

The chicken-hearted Harvard administrators thus continued alternately to threaten and to wheedle Hancock, even after dismissing him from the treasurership, until he was elected governor. Then they fawned upon him because he controlled the state appropriations for education upon which the college was compelled to rely. Whatever may be said about his high-handedness, he hardly can be blamed for despising such a vacillating and pusillanimous policy.

· 9 ·

Hancock paid no attention to Langdon's latest overture but replied, in a conciliatory tone, to another dated a month afterward. Revealing that he had had the Harvard account books and securities transported to Philadelphia, he offered two alternatives: either to give William Winthrop (probably a brother of John Winthrop, well-known Harvard astronomer) power to act for him or to resign. Back bounced an answer in little more than two weeks, at the end of May, diplomatically calling his bluff at resignation. But he did not reveal his hand.

Meanwhile the board of overseers had taken direct charge of the proceedings and had appointed a committee, including such eminent members of the old Faction as Bowdoin and Phillips, to investigate the state of the college and the treasury. But these practical men of affairs, like the academic authorities, shilly-shallied until fall. At last, on November 13, they delegated Tutor Stephen Hall to rescue the financial papers from the enemy-menaced Pennsylvania capital. Although Hall was compelled to pursue his quarry to Baltimore, he returned not only with the "stolen goods" but with instructions from Hancock to James Sullivan, a Boston attorney who apparently had relieved Bant of the bulk of the treasurer's legal business, to deliver officially into the hands of the corporation approximately £16,000 worth of bonds and other obligations. This sum, it will be noted, was £600 more than had been put into the possession of the "absconder" in the first place, despite the salary disbursements. But the Harvard emissary did not succeed in bringing back an accounting for the remainder.[28]

Finally, on March 25, 1777, the overseers committee recommended to the corporation that it elect a successor to Hancock. Two days later Dr. Gordon, who was a member of the board, wrote to John Adams an exposition of the pussyfooting manner in which the action had been taken and suggested that Adams—of all people—"make a prudent use of this early information so as to guard Mr H against showing any intemperate heat to the hurt of his character." Here is Gordon's story:

"The necessity of our college affairs has obliged the board of overseers to advise the corporation to choose a treasurer that shall constantly reside in the state. I believe they all . . . thought that the Hon. Mr. Hancock expressed himself in some of his letters . . . with too great asperity and that they should have been treated rather with more decency had not Hancock been warmed by mistaking the propriety of their proceedings. However, they professed the highest regards for him and took care so to word their vote as that he should not be reflected upon." [29]

But the corporation was reluctant to follow its superiors' advice. After three fruitless meetings it drew up, on April 22, a twenty-eight-page letter designed to prepare Hancock for the news that he was to be superseded and to justify the institution's conduct toward him in general. He disregarded the warning.

Eventually, on July 14, the subordinate administrative body worked up sufficient gumption to name Ebenezer Storer as treasurer. Josiah Quincy (VI), who later became president of Harvard, thus describes the reaction of the ousted bursar:

"This act was regarded by Mr. Hancock as personal and intended to injure his popularity and was never forgiven. His subsequent intercourse with the corporation was in language respectful but, in fact, defying and embarrassing. . . . The balance of the securities in his hands was unknown to the corporation, and he showed no disposition to give them any satisfaction on the subject. Yet, being aware of his political influence and the great dependence of the college upon the annual grants of the legislature . . . for the support of its president and professors, they made a bold attempt to conciliate him." [30]

The peace offering, made on January 22, 1778, is such a pretty piece of toadyism that it bears citation. In the form of a resolution, it reminds Hancock that the college, in 1772, had his portrait painted and placed in the library which he had helped to restore after the fire of 1764, and that he removed it for safe keeping when the war broke out. Then follows a request that he permit it to be "placed in the philosophy chamber by that of his late honorable uncle . . . or . . . that he would grant us leave to have another taken by some masterly hand, as we are very desirous to perpetuate the memory of so great a benefactor." [31]

Despite this flattery the Harvard authorities did not give up their attempt to extract an accounting from the ex-treasurer. Under the leadership of Storer, who evidently was more aggressive than the other officers of the institution, the corporation solicited him for a settlement at intervals during the next seven years. Finally, just before the end of his first administration as governor in February, 1785, he submitted a financial statement indicating that he owed £1,054. But he still did not evince any intention to pay up and was threatened with legal action once more. This eventually turned out, however, to be another empty gesture. In November, 1789, Storer protested that the college could not get along without income from its investments. His Excellency retorted verbally and blandly, according to Quincy's paraphrase, "It was very well." [32]

Hancock, now more firmly seated in the gubernatorial chair than ever before, continued to duck the lawsuit that was constantly dangled over his head until death removed him from its menace in 1793. His heirs paid nine years' balance of interest out of his still sizable estate in 1795 and made good the principal at the turn of the century. Combined, these amounts totaled about £1,500 nine months before his demise. [33] But Harvard is whistling, down to the present time, for a claim of $526 compound interest, which his beneficiaries refused to recognize.

· 10 ·

The foregoing review of the celebrated Hancock-versus-Harvard comedy of low finance may seem unduly partial to the villain of the piece, but it is not so intended. He unquestionably was unfair, unreasonable, stubborn, and high-handed with his alma mater at a period when she was in dire need of funds. In fact, he may justly be charged with inadvertent embezzlement by default. But that is as far as the evidence allows one to go in assessing blame. The most meticulous research has not revealed even an implication that he had a dishonorable purpose in retaining the institution's securities or in declining to account for them.

James Truslow Adams, one of Hancock's severest modern critics, asserts in this connection: "It would seem that there were little escape from the unpleasant admission that Hancock had been living beyond his means—what with his lavish expenditure for show and popularity—and that it was inconvenient for him to restore the funds." [34]

There is a categorical refutation of this statement in the official inventory and appraisal of Hancock's estate filed in 1794. They show that he had cash, securities, and Boston real estate valued at almost £27,000; notes of hand and balances due on account amounting to more than £10,000; vast tracts of woodland in Massachusetts, Maine, and New Hampshire. It may be argued, in support of Adams' contention, that he was property-poor. That was true to a certain extent; but the price placed by a conservative probate court on his negotiable stock alone was nearly £30,000. [35] Why, then, would it have been "inconvenient" for him to honor a debt of only £1,500?

Josiah Quincy was twenty-one years old at the time of Hancock's death. He therefore should know when he writes:

"The marked neglect with which Mr. Hancock treated the requests, complaints of embarrassment, and even threats of prosecution from the overseers and corporation has no sufficient apology in the circumstances, either of the country or of the individual. The corporation were at all times disposed to grant him every indulgence, . . . and during nearly twenty years . . . there probably was not a week in which it [the account] might not have been closed . . . by a simple order to his clerk. . . . The great estate which he left at his death shows that his resources were always ample." [36]

Testimony which seems to exonerate the accused of deliberate dishonesty, beyond all doubt, is contained in Langdon's letter to him of April 22, 1777, which in Quincy's paraphrase states that "a considerable number of persons indebted to the college had applied to make payment and were uneasy that they were obliged to keep the money by them and pay interest." [37]

Kenneth B. Umbreit, in a comparatively recent work which often excoriates Hancock, contends that this communication definitely proves his innocence of fraudulent intent:

"Hancock's conduct is hardly evidence that he had embezzled any college funds. The endowment which he carried to Philadelphia . . . was in securities, not cash. It would have been very difficult to raise cash on it; and, in any event, if he was in want of ready money he had ample property of his own for collateral—much more than the seventeen-thousand-pound endowment of Harvard. But the conclusive bit of evidence is that among the letters from the college which he refused to answer was one asking him to make arrangements to collect from mortgagees who had expressed a desire to pay off their obligations. He would neither pay nor receive payment." *

No, John Hancock was not crooked, however great were his faults. If he had been, his chief villifier, Higginson, assuredly would have ferreted out some concrete proof to that effect for use in his journalistic diatribe of 1789. Such damning data, of course, would have ruined the governor's public and private life. Yet there is not a single reference to his connections with Harvard in any of the ten articles.

The relations between Hancock and the Cambridge institution gave rise to many political repercussions during his last fifteen years. They will be discussed in their proper place. For the present they must yield precedence to numerous other developments in the crowded and colorful career of the patriot in purple.[38]

* K. B. Umbreit, *The Founding Fathers* (Harper & Bros., New York, 1941), 173. Reprinted by permission of the publishers.

$$\mathcal{QD} XIII \mathcal{QD}$$

VIRTUE AND VOTE-GETTING TRIUMPH

*W*HEN HANCOCK RETURNED to Boston in the autumn of 1777 the nuclei of the two great parties destined to dominate American politics for generations were in an amorphous stage throughout Massachusetts. Under various labels and in varying degrees of consistency these groupings have retained until modern times the distinguishing characteristics they acquired during the germinative phase. Counterparts were beginning to spring up in the twelve other states, but the directions of their growth were not so clearly indicated as in the Bay State.

The seeds from which grew the factions known as Federalist and Antifederalist were products of the disintegration of the old Whig party. They were, respectively, the conservative and the liberal elements of the organism which gave life to the Revolutionary movement. The first eventually became the support of a strong central government; the second, of a less dominant, decentralized ruling power.

But at the period under discussion their differences were along lines of democratic social philosophy, rather than of governmental organization. The split paralleled the cleavage between Sam Adams and Hancock. Although ultimately the one coterie, currently led by Adams, would espouse the Antifederal cause under Warren and Gerry, it now sided with Bowdoin (later, titular head of the Federal party bossed by Theophilus Parsons, an eminent jurist), against the Hancockonians. The fundamental issue was uncompromising, down-to-earth, Puritanical democracy—every man standing on his own feet—versus, as the Bowdoinites saw it, the easy-going, unstable, amoral, corrupting paternalism and demagogy of the Beacon Hill plutocrat.

Principles, however, were secondary to personalities, ax grinding, and nest feathering as factors in Massachusetts politics during the decade before ratification of the Federal Constitution in 1788. Personal magnetism had more influence than definite convictions upon the continuously fluctuating allegiance of professional politicos, and of the people in general. This was due partly to the lack of clear-cut conceptions as to how democratic ideals should be put into practice—conceptions which crystallized during the ratifying convention in the course of the controversy over national and state sovereignty—and partly to the dearth of political machinery.

The situation was made to order for Hancock. He had only to rely on his popular appeal, which was so much greater than that of any rival, for success in a contest at the polls. As he began executing his long considered plan to reinvigorate the lame liberal wing of the once all-powerful Whig organization and to crush the Adamses—particularly the elder—he received new assurance of his popularity. Gloatingly he wrote to Morris on January 12, 1778: "I am received with every mark of respect and have the great satisfaction to find my friends retain the same disposition towards me they formerly did; of which more hereafter when I have the pleasure of seeing you, which will be by the 6th of March if no unfortunate accident prevents."

Several political "accidents" of a very fortunate nature precluded this meeting until June 18, when President Hancock returned to the Congress at York as an ordinary delegate. In the meantime Laurens had been formally installed in his place; and he was not reelected to the Presidency until 1785, when poor health compelled him to resign without taking office.

In his letter the Boston Croesus told of entertaining Baron Friedrich von Steuben, famous German disciplinarian who soon was to help Washington make an army out of the pitiful, disorganized Continentals at Valley Forge, and then revealed one important source of his tremendous prestige: "I have advanced the baron $1000, besides paying for horses and saddles, etc. I will send the account. I charge no commission. Congress surely will reimburse me." [1] Whether or not Hancock was reimbursed, it is certain that he received high recompense from the populace in the coin of admiration when his patriotic act was noised abroad.

It was approximately at this time, too, that the politician *par excellence* made the endearing gesture of settling with his penurious debtors on the basis of the fiat currency pouring out of the Congressional printing presses—then at the ratio of about four to one in terms of gold. His motives, as usual, soon became suspect. Within six months William Pynchon, a conservative lawyer of Warren's home town, questioned them in his diary: "Does Mr. H., in fact, mean to give his debtors the difference;

or to induce his own creditors to take of him their dues at that rate. . . . or to become popular and obtain votes at the choice of governor next May? See the newspapers." [2]

But it was not only among the indigent that Hancock enjoyed esteem. Even the well-to-do Newburyport owners of a privateer, which had picked up an "elegant coach" on one of her raids, had presented it to him "as a token of their respect for that gentleman who has so nobly distinguished himself in the present contest with Great Britain," according to the New York *Gazette* of February 2. In the words of the *Pennsylvania Ledger,* apparently an opposition paper, under date of March 11:

"John Hancock of Boston appears in public with all the state and pageantry of an Oriental prince. He rides in an elegant chariot, which was taken in a prize to the *Civil Usage* pirate vessel and by the owners presented to him. He is attended by four servants dressed in superb livery, mounted on fine horses richly caparisoned, and escorted by fifty horsemen with drawn sabres—the one half of whom precede, and the other follow, his carriage." [3]

While using this generous gift to the fullest advantage Hancock was treated in princely fashion by the State of Massachusetts. On the 13th the General Court resolved that he be paid £2,335.15 for services and expenses as a Congressional delegate from the day before his departure from Worcester for Philadelphia with Sam Adams to the date of his return to Boston—April 26, 1775, to November 19, 1777. [4] This sum was almost four times as much as he would collect, as compensation for expenditures alone, for the corresponding period from the Continental Congress. The difference may have been the measure of his rapidly increasing influence with the Bay State legislature, as well as with private individuals, rich and poor.

· 2 ·

Hancock was gaining in prestige at home despite the efforts of his enemies to connect him with a political scandal in high places. This was the Conway Cabal to oust Washington from the supreme military command and to replace him with Gates. It was organized by Thomas Conway, an Irish adventurer who had wormed his way into the office of inspector general of the army in 1777, when the commander in chief was sustaining the long series of reverses that culminated in the disheartening withdrawal into winter quarters at Valley Forge. Gates himself seems to have been only the cat's-paw of a disgruntled faction both within and outside the Congress. Washington quickly put a stop to the machinations by exposing Conway's treachery, but repercussions still were felt in many sections of the country during the spring of 1778.

As early as January one of Hancock's most nettlesome foes, Dr. Gordon, attempted to implicate him in the plot by writing to General Washington: "Mr. Hancock reports that Your Excellency designs quitting the command of the army. . . . I am not so mistaken in Mr. Hancock as the generality and therefore *can* easily suppose, if he has any particular end to answer, that he will propagate such a report upon the slightest foundation." By March 2, however, he backed down completely, writing to Washington—this time to retract categorically his previous insinuations: "Do not find out, in any way whatsoever, that he hath concerned himself at all about the late subject of conversation." [5]

Sam Adams, too, jumped to conclusions. He unburdened himself to Warren, on May 25:

"I recollect that your election of councillors will come on the day after tomorrow. Has Mr. [Hancock] waited for the event of that important day? Or is he on his journey to this place? . . . Was he present here he might, if he pleased, vindicate me against a report . . . that I have been called to account and severely reprehended at a Boston town meeting for being in a conspiracy against a very great man [Washington]. . . . It is easy for me to conjecture by what means it extended itself from Manheim, where I first heard it, to York town; and it may not be difficult to guess how it came from Boston to that place. Manheim is about twelve miles east of the Susquehanna. There lives Mr. R. M. [Robert Morris], a very intimate acquaintance of *my* excellent friend. Mr. H. *is said* to be on the road, but no one makes it *certain*. When he arrives Messrs. Gerry and Dana propose to set off for New England. I shall be mortified at their leaving us, for I verily think that the accession even of *that* gentleman will not make up for the absence of the other two." [6]

Three years later he confessed to his wife:

"James Rivington has published in his *Royal Gazette* that the acrimony between Mr. Hancock and me was owing to his attachment to General Washington and my being . . . desirous of his removal. This is an old story which men have believed and disbelieved as they pleased without much concern of mine. . . . Mr. Hancock never thought me an enemy to General Washington. He never thought that I was desirous of his being removed, and therefore could never treat me with acrimony on that account." [7]

Adams' jaundiced suspicion of Hancock on the eve of the Massachusetts election in 1778 was symptomatic of an ailment brought on in the process of committing political suicide. Sam had taken slow poison while a Congressional delegate. Although one of the prime movers for the Declaration of Independence at the start of the agitation, he had done little to promote its adoption. In fact, he had delayed ratification by attacks upon its opponents that degenerated into personalities. And he had accelerated his political eclipse by his attempt to defeat the motion of thanks to the President.

He may have realized this; else he probably would not have gone back to York and turned over the leadership of the faction he had once dominated to Warren, who then occupied the key post of speaker of the Massachusetts House. Under the provisional government that had succeeded the royal regime the powers of the governor formerly appointed by the Crown were scattered among the twenty-eight councilors, and the office Warren held was the only one which approached, in individual prestige, the old gubernatorial portfolio. Hancock, therefore, concentrated upon him his effort to beat the Adams "gang" in the fight for control of the General Court; for he knew he could push his own man, John Pickering, into the speakership if the incumbent should lose his seat in the House.

Warren may have seen what lay before him when he wrote wonderingly to Adams on May 10, three days before the balloting: "I was yesterday at an elegant entertainment made at Marston's House by our Council for the officers of the French frigate and other strangers. . . . The representatives of your town were all present except General Hancock. . . . Why he did not [attend] is a subject for conjecture for you and others." Evidently sensing that Adams' influence was on the wane, he added: "Had you been present you might not have appeared as the greatest man in company . . . though you might actually have been so." Then he reverted to his favorite topic, with a veiled charge that Hancock was trying to break up the Franco-American alliance concluded on February 6:

"The Tories are very industrious in instilling prejudices into the minds of the people against our connections with France. . . . This may be more excusable in some people; but what will you think of a member of Congress who, for the sake of establishing his own popularity or for any other reason, should express his . . . opinion that this connection will ruin America? When such an opinion was given in the hearing of one Tory lady you may easily conceive it is told to others and quoted by the great numbers with which your dear town abounds."

· 3 ·

Warren's misgivings concerning his political future were confirmed by
the election results on May 13. He was not returned to the Assembly by
his own town of Salem; but Hancock was voted in by Boston—for an
eleventh term—along with Pickering, who was chosen speaker. This
marked the eclipse of the Adams crowd, who were not to emerge from
the shadows until after their archenemy's death fifteen years later. On
the 31st the defeated candidate resentfully recounted the sad story to his
intimate:

"Your curiosity will lead you to inquire how my town came to leave
me out and how the interest I used to have in the House vanished . . .
on this occasion. It may not satisfy you to carry it to the account only of
the versatility and caprice of mankind. They have had their effects but
they would not do alone. Envy and the ambition of some people has
aided them, and the . . . cunning of a party here, who have set up an
idol they are determined to worship . . . has had the greatest. . . . The
partiality of you and the rest of my friends has made me an object of
great importance with this party, and everything is done to get me out
of sight. In short, the plan is to sacrifice you and me to the shrine of their
idol."

In the same letter he informed Adams that Hancock intended to take
his delayed departure for York within twenty-four hours, and gave an
illustration of the popularity still enjoyed in Boston by the former President of the Congress:

"General Hancock, . . . I hear, took a pompous leave of the House
yesterday by going up and shaking hands with the speaker, etc., after
moving for leave to return soon if his health would not admit of his
tarrying long [in York]. I suppose a cavalcade will attend him, subscrip-
tions for that purpose having been circulated for a week. I believe he
will go tomorrow. You will provide for his reception as you think fit." [8]

Hancock, after originally planning to leave on the 18th, postponed his
journey again for the very good reason that Dolly was momentarily expecting her second child. Now he apparently was waiting to make sure
that John George Washington, the long desired son—born on the 21st—
and his mother could do without him.

The proud father finally got under way on June 3. Samuel Holten,
a Danvers physician going to the Congress as a delegate for the first
time, kept a daily account of the trip and recorded with obvious gratification that he rode in Hancock's carriage, as well as Dr. Cooper and

General Heath. His notations for the day of departure substantiate Warren's supposition, for "a large number of gentlemen, with their servants and carriages, accompanied us to Watertown, where an elegant dinner was provided"; many toasts were drunk, guns were fired in salute, and three cheers were given by the populace as the party proceeded toward West Town, where they spent the night.

The two-week jaunt to York, however, was relatively uneventful. Hancock was "much indisposed with the gout" at Springfield but must have been temporarily reinvigorated by a salvo of welcome from an artillery company. The travelers visited with General Putnam at Hartford and, after crossing the North River at Fishkill, were "handsomely entertained without charge" at the house of a man named Townsend; but, on the whole, it was a dispiriting trek over the usual rocky route.[9]

On the 20th Hancock, who affected to be unimpressed by the wayside hospitality, could not resist complaining to his wife about his own discomfort while she was still recuperating from the eighteenth century ordeal of childbirth. He had reached his destination two days previously "after a most fatiguing journey, bad roads, and miserable entertainment; but, thank God, I am in tolerable health." After beseeching her to write often for the sake of his delicate constitution he gave her the gladdening news that the British had evacuated Philadelphia and the American troops were reoccupying it.[10]

General Clinton, who had been elevated to the supreme command of the enemy forces because of Howe's do-nothing policy and reports that he had idled away the preceding winter in luxurious living, had withdrawn the garrison on the 18th with the idea of concentrating his strength at New York. But Washington, with a hardy, well-trained army that had survived the rigors of Valley Forge, overtook him ten days later at Monmouth, New Jersey, where he inflicted as heavy losses as he sustained in an indecisive engagement. He followed Clinton northward and intrenched himself so securely at West Point on the Hudson that the English did not dare to attack and therefore were pinned down in New York all the rest of the year. The rebels made the most of this time by cementing their entente with France and planning, in conjunction with the French navy, the campaign that was to encompass Britain's defeat at Yorktown, Virginia, in 1781.

· 4 ·

Even the prospect of soon reentering Philadelphia did not make it easier for Hancock to put up with York. "I can by no means, in justice to myself," he wailed to Dolly on the 23rd, "continue long under such disagreeable circumstances. . . . The mode is so very different from what I have been always accustomed to that to continue it long would prejudice my health exceedingly.

"This moment the post arrived, and, to my very great surprise and disappointment, not a single line from Boston. I am not much disposed to resent, but it feels exceeding hard to be slighted . . . by those from whom I have a . . . right to expect different conduct. . . . I shall write no more till I hear from you." He hoped she had recovered from her confinement and urged her to improve her health with horseback-riding, although cautioning her in words that look strange in the light of the source: "Be as frugal and prudent in other matters as is consistent with our situation."

No longer in the Presidential chair, the once high and mighty Massachusetts delegate apparently felt out of place in the Congressional chamber. "As soon as we have got over the important business now before Congress" (ratification of the Articles of Confederation) he expected to return home, because his services would not then be needed. And he concluded his letter "with the utmost affection and love." [11]

The committee named by Hancock on June 12, 1776, had submitted the first draft of twenty-one Articles just a month later. But no action had been taken on it for more than a year, partly because the Congress was preoccupied with the prosecution of the Revolution and partly because the states were so jealous of their sovereignty that ratification obviously could not be obtained. Finally, in November, 1777, the governing body had adopted a revised version and had sent it to the various assemblies for consideration. The document provided for a loose confederacy with scarcely more real power than was already conceded to the Congressional delegates, who were to retain their functions and to appoint a Council of State primarily for the purpose of carrying on when the parent organization was not in session. Among the rights granted under this agreement were to wage war and make peace, to direct diplomatic dealings, to coin and borrow money—but not to levy taxes. And nine of the thirteen delegation votes were required for enactment of any important measure.

The Articles were the first business of any significance undertaken after the Congress adjourned from York to Philadelphia on June 27, 1778, and reconvened on July 2. On the 9th they were signed in Independence Hall by eight states, including Massachusetts, which had approved them in January at a convention presided over by Hancock. The smaller states—New Hampshire, Rhode Island, New Jersey, Delaware, and Maryland— held out until assured that the claims of the larger ones to western territory would not be recognized. Unanimous consent was not procured until 1781, when Maryland finally yielded on condition that this land gradually be admitted to the Union independently as the various sections should qualify for statehood.

Having helped his country to achieve as great a degree of political unity as possible during the summer of 1778, Hancock felt free to go home and gratify a long cherished wish to take an active part in advancing its military aims: he would make his commission as major general of militia mean something. So, on the day when the Articles were rendered virtually certain of eventual ratification, he obtained leave of absence from the Congress. He had more personal reasons, too, for returning to Boston, as Sam Adams confided to Elizabeth: "Mr. H. . . . is going home on account of his ill state of health and the circumstances of his family. He tells me his wife is dangerously ill." [12]

John Adams may have picked up a telepathic emanation from his cousin; for he was writing to Sam on that same day from Passy, France, headquarters of the American mission, about their mutual enemy. He related that a letter containing plans for a project to undermine the Revolution had been thrown through a grated doorway in their building, probably with the knowledge and approval of King George. It proposed that the patriot leaders should be bribed with peerages and set up as a congress to govern America under the ultimate authority of the Crown. Adding that Franklin, Washington, Sam Adams, and Hancock were among those mentioned as being in line for these honors, John Adams concluded: "Ask our friend if he should like to be a peer." [13]

The most susceptible candidate for the peerage was back in his Beacon Hill castle by the 26th or 27th, ready to fare forth in knightly quest of martial glory.

On July 8 Count de Rochambeau had arrived in Delaware Bay with the first fleet ordered by Louis XVI to go to the assistance of the Americans under their treaty with France. Rochambeau had dispatched Admiral d'Estaing with a small squadron to attack Howe's supporting men-of-war, which were stationed off Sandy Hook, New Jersey, preparatory to cooperating with Clinton's forces advancing from Philadelphia to New York. But D'Estaing, whose ships were too big to engage the British vessels in the shallow waters within the arm of the Jersey cape, had been compelled to anchor outside.

Seeing that his ally was stalemated, Washington had appealed to the

Congress, under whose direction the French were operating, to instruct him to sail for Newport and work with General John Sullivan, who was organizing an expedition to drive the enemy out of Rhode Island. It was so arranged, and D'Estaing appeared in Narragansett Bay on the 29th. He at once agreed with Sullivan on a maneuver embracing a land and sea attack upon Sir Robert Pigott's English garrison of 6,000 at the northern tip of the island on which Newport was situated. The assault was to be conducted under the immediate joint command of General Nathanael Greene and the Marquis de Lafayette, who had been serving with Washington for almost a year. The Franco-American troop contingent was composed of 14,000 men—4,000 of D'Estaing's marines, 5,000 Continentals, and 5,000 militia supplied by Rhode Island, Connecticut, and Massachusetts. That was where Hancock came in.

· 5 ·

As Ezekiel Price, Boston selectman, phrased it in his diary entry for August 8: "General Hancock set out with his suite on the expedition against Newport." [14] What the "suite" comprised is not stated; but that it was sizable and ostentatious goes without saying. The general must have reached his post by the 10th, for he was in command of the right flank of the second line under Greene on that date, when the movement was launched from the mainland town of Tiverton in eighty-six flat-bottomed boats. The former tin soldier, whose only pretense to gallantry had been to lead the Independent Corps of Cadets on a charge through the friendly streets of Boston, must have felt like a red-blooded warrior when the British, greatly outnumbered, retreated southward toward strong intrenchments on the outskirts of the Rhode Island capital.

Meanwhile, however, the grand strategy of the invaders went awry. On the 9th Howe turned up unexpectedly, with twenty-five sail, off the port now defended by the English troops. Next morning D'Estaing, without notifying Sullivan, had sailed forth—with his marines still on board —to challenge the enemy fleet. A gale was blowing up, and on the following day it reached hurricane proportions. For forty-eight hours both squadrons had all they could do to cope with the storm—let alone with each other. Three of the French craft, including the admiral's flagship, were dismasted by the wind and then attacked by the British as the tempest subsided, but without incurring any more serious damage. Finally, on the 14th, D'Estaing made contact with a few of his battered vessels and retired with them to Newport. About a week later he sailed for

Boston, picking up the remainder of his widely scattered command along the way, while Howe headed back toward New York.

Hancock's experiences in the interim had better be told in his own words. On the 12th, with a presumption which indicates that his new military authority had inflated his ego, he reported directly to Washington over the heads of Lafayette, Greene, and Sullivan—just as if he were in charge of the expedition. After expressing "mortification" over the suffering of his men in consequence of insufficient tents and over the leavetaking of three hundred at the end of their fifteen-day enlistment period, "notwithstanding all my desires and entreaties," he assured the supreme commander: "As soon as the weather clears up I hope to have account of the French fleet. Nothing material will be attempted but in conjunction with Count D'Estaing." [15]

After waiting until the 15th for the weather to relent Sullivan, expecting his naval allies soon to return and support him, ordered his three divisions to pursue the enemy. On the morning of the 18th, when they were within two miles of the British lines, he gave the signal to open fire. In the midst of this bombardment Hancock was principally concerned about his wet feet and a pain in his head as he complained to his thoughtless wife: "Yesterday Mr. J. Lusher arrived with the things, but you forgot to send any gaiters or black cloth short boots. Pray send them by any person. I had yesterday a bad turn of the headache but am better this morning." [16]

On the same day Warren was sniping at the distressed warrior behind his back. He wrote to Sam Adams: "I am told he solicited the Council to be ordered on this business. . . . What a noble example of heroism, as well as patriotism, does this conduct exhibit! We want a Homer or a Virgil to celebrate it, and surely Congress itself must be the Maecenas to prompt and encourage them." [17] This heavy-handed satire came with peculiarly bad grace from a man who, together with Hancock and Sullivan, had been appointed a major general to lead the Massachusetts militia into Rhode Island but had resigned during the previous year on feigned grounds of illness. His real reason was unwillingness to bemean himself, as paymaster general for the state, by serving under the commander of the expedition, whose rank was slightly inferior.

Catching the martial spirit at last, General Hancock reported optimistically to domestic headquarters on the 19th: "We yesterday morning opened one battery on the enemy. They cannonaded the whole day, with no other loss to us but one man killed and two wounded. As soon as the fog clears away this morning we shall open another battery. We have a strong report that the French fleet is seen off [Newport]. If they arrive our business will soon be over, and hope we shall soon enter Newport. . . . Hope soon to be with you." [18]

· 6 ·

It was on the following night that D'Estaing appeared off the Rhode Island capital. At a council of war aboard his flagship, Lafayette and Greene tried to persuade him to put into the harbor, to land the marines, and to shell the English position. The admiral was willing at first but was dissuaded by his half-hearted officers, who argued that he should obey the instructions of their government to return to Boston for repairs in case any of the vessels should be injured. So he set sail on the 22nd —but not before Sullivan, Lafayette, and Hancock had done their best to change his mind, as our disillusioned hero informed Jeremiah Powell, president of the Massachusetts Council, on the day of D'Estaing's departure:

"At 12 o'clock this morning General Sullivan, Marquis de Lafayette, and myself sent an express boat to the admiral and each of us wrote very pressing letters to him, entreating him to tarry with his fleet . . . only for two days; and if he would land his troops in the rear of the enemy the general [Washington] would send 2000 of his troops to join them . . . and we would . . . make the attack this very coming night."

Characteristically the civilian-minded soldier was wondering how the failure of the expedition would affect his political fortunes. He decided to forestall criticism by disclaiming responsibility, and continued:

"If we fail the censure must not fall upon us, for the expedition was undertaken in full confidence that the fleet and troops would co-operate with us. . . . What effect the departure of the fleet will have on our troops you can judge. In short, in that situation we have but one alternative left, and that is to—I cannot bring myself to write it. I am exceedingly mortified . . . at the prospect and could almost wish I had not been here to undergo such feelings, which I scarce ever before experienced."

As usual, however, higher motives were contending with lower beneath the cloak of the patriot in purple. He concluded:

"I write thus particular to you in full confidence that it will by no means be suffered to go into the newspapers. Any persons you may be pleased to show the letter to I have no objection, nor do I regard how publicly it is talked of, for the failure must center with the fleet. But I beg that my name may not be annexed to these particulars in the paper in so early stage of the alliance with France, as it might prejudice me with some French gentlemen with whom I wish to stand fair."

The doom foreshadowed in this letter loomed before the Americans in the twilight of the 24th. Wholesale desertions to the number of almost 3,000 had set in, reducing Sullivan's forces approximately to the size of Pigott's and rendering hopeless an attack upon the strong enemy position. In the belief that Howe would return with reinforcements and cut off their line of retreat, the patriot leaders decided to withdraw to the northern part of the island and make a stand behind fortifications to be erected there. In a melancholy mood Hancock agreed that this decision was wise; but he deplored it in another message to Powell next morning:

"This is the only step that we could take under our deserted situation. It is exceedingly chagrining after the favorable prospect we had of success, but the good of the service induced us to adopt the measure. As soon as I see the troops under my command safe through their retreat and well lodged on their new ground . . . I shall . . . return to Boston. Having exerted myself to the extent of my slender constitution, I must, with your leave, enjoy the quiet of retirement in my own house and, after recruiting a little, shall be ready to obey your further commands."

That he was sincere in his expressed solicitude for his men is indicated in a postscript reading: "Poor Ross, the drum major of Colonel Craft's regiment, was most badly burnt by a box of cartridges which yesterday took fire from one of the enemy's shells. I fear he will not live."

In the same communication Hancock predicted confidently that the Americans could defend themselves "on their new ground" against any British assault.[19] But even the consolation of fighting a successful defensive action was denied them when Sullivan—receiving word on the 29th, the second day of the retreat, that Howe was on his way back—ordered an immediate evacuation of the state. This signalized the miserable collapse of the Rhode Island expedition, which had been undertaken with such rosy expectations on the part of all and with such lofty aspirations toward military renown on the part of the frustrated self-fancied fighter from the peaceful purlieus of Beacon Hill.

But by the time he reached the always cheering environs of Boston this inveterate optimist had rebounded from the depths of depression and was living in a fool's paradise. Price entered in his diary, on the 26th:

"In the evening General Hancock came to town. He is in high

spirits and says the troops there are determined not to leave . . . and that the advanced works are still supported by our brave soldiers; that he is to return in a few days and doubts not but our troops will still . . . get possession of Newport." [20]

Hancock's political foes, of course, gleefully made capital of the fiasco —and especially of the general's withdrawal from the field four days before the other officers of corresponding rank. On the 27th Warren seized his pen and indulged in a bit of sardonic commentary for Sam Adams' benefit:

"General Hancock returned last evening to this town. It is reported and believed, I suppose, that he is come to order back the French squadron. If it was reported that he came to arrest the course of nature or reverse the decrees of Providence, there are enough to believe it practicable." [21]

· 7 ·

But Warren's animadversions on his hated adversary were mild by comparison with what Higginson ("Laco") said about him, in regard to this episode, during the heat of the 1789 campaign for the governorship. In one of the most vicious verbal onslaughts ever directed at Hancock he wrote:

"When he got to Rhode Island he took an eligible situation for his quarters. He appeared on the parade *en militaire*. He sailed out often for air and exercise and he sometimes approached so near to the enemy . . . as to distinguish . . . that the British flag was still flying at some miles' distance. . . . Never was the fire of military ambition so conspicuous in any man's countenance and conduct. . . . But this flame was of short duration. The severe cannonade at the arrival of the French fleet . . . disordered his nerves; the sound of the drum disturbed his muscles by alarming his fears; and his nightly slumbers were short and uncertain from lively scenes of blood and carnage which a heated imagination was continually presenting to his view.

"This situation was too painful and humiliating for the Man of the People long to endure. He grew peevish and uneasy; he complained of the length of the campaign; and he talked frequently of quitting the field. This his aides . . . were fearful would soon happen. . . . They used every argument to allay his fears. . . . But the departure of the fleet, the roar of the cannon, and the smell of powder was too much for our hero to support. He resolved to return home . . . and he flattered himself that, by urging his great anxiety for the safety of the fleet as the

cause of his flight, he might save his reputation. . . . Having good cattle, he reached home in a few hours . . . but after . . . finding himself
safe in his own house his fears subsided, his solicitude for the fleet
abated, and he enjoyed his pleasures as well as ever. . . . It is well
worthy of observation that Mr. H., after his return from Rhode Island,
had a grant of $40,000, I think it was; while the gentlemen volunteers
who . . . raised companies . . . for that expedition received nothing
from the government." [22]

As usual, there is a modicum of truth in Higginson's charges. But, for
the most part, they are an outrageous libel upon the man who did more
than any other to prevent a serious diplomatic breach from eventuating
out of this bungled affair.

That Hancock strutted and plumed himself in the heady martial atmosphere of the Rhode Island camp probably is true, although not to
the extent pictured by his slanderer. It would have been inconsistent
with his nature for him to behave otherwise. The cannonading may have
got on his nerves, for he was high-strung almost to the point of neuroti-
cism. This strain, in turn, would have made him irritable and impatient.
And the rigors of military life must have been especially hard on an
epicure of such a delicate constitution.

But the accusations of cowardice are entirely unwarranted. As has
been demonstrated in several instances, Hancock had met every other
verifiable test of physical courage in a manly manner. Why, then, should
he quail at the sights and sounds of war?

That he was eager to "save his reputation," there can be no doubt.
And yet he must have realized that, by deserting his men in the field,
he was committing the unpardonable sin for an officer and thereby was
running the risk of pulling down the prestige he had built up over the
years. So patriotism—in this case, as in every one involving the Hamlet
of the Revolution—must have been mingled with self-interest as he hastened to be the first to insure continuance of the Franco-American alliance.

Higginson is right in maintaining that Hancock collected money from
the State of Massachusetts for his part in the expedition. In 1779 the
General Court awarded him £12,000; but that sum included reimbursement for expenses, which must necessarily have been large, as well as
compensation for services.[23] And this grant, which could not have been
disproportionate to those voted to the other general officers of militia
without raising a fuss over discrimination, at least constituted official recognition that he had been faithful to his trust.

The worst that can be said truthfully about Hancock's ill advised venture is that it was inspired chiefly by vanity. He may have convinced himself that it was his duty to exchange the gavel of the born administrator for the sword of the miscast soldier; but subconsciously he probably was driven by consummate conceit to essay an utterly unsuitable role.

America's foremost mediator had been home only four days when he put his extraordinary talent to use. He induced Council President Powell and General Heath to accompany him on a good-will mission to D'Estaing's flagship, anchored in Boston Harbor, and made considerable progress toward smoothing down the admiral's feelings, which had been further ruffled by insulting comments in Sullivan's report on the Rhode Island debacle.

Up to the time when the French sailed, early in November, to join Rochambeau's main fleet, Hancock devoted a great deal of thought and effort to restoring amicable relations with D'Estaing in the face of several provocative incidents on the part of the metropolitan rabble. For the duration of the war he spent his own funds on entertainment to keep other sensitive Gallic functionaries happy—and incidentally, of course, to enhance his standing with the impressionable masses. He may not have saved the alliance which assured the success of the Revolution; but he certainly made it doubly effective by preserving the spirit, in addition to the letter, of the treaty.

· 8 ·

Lafayette was the first of many—enemies as well as friends—to commend this smart and unremitting diplomacy. On September 1 he called it to Washington's attention:

"The Count D'Estaing arrived the day before in Boston. I found him much displeased at a protest [Sullivan's] . . . and many other circumstances which I have reported to you. . . . We waited together on the Council, General Heath, and General Hancock, and were very well satisfied with them. The last one distinguished himself very much by his zeal upon the occasion." [24]

Hancock's concern for his reputation was proved baseless by a Congressional resolution. But he was not to be trusted, in the opinion of Sam Adams, who still was imbued with the suspicions aroused by Warren. On the 12th, only a day after the self-appointed diplomat had given a dinner for D'Estaing, his staff, and the Council at Marston's Tavern, Adams confided:

"Congress has approved the retreat, thanked General Sullivan and his brave troops, and applauded the patriotic exertions of New England. Major-General Hancock . . . unluckily . . . missed the laurel! In my opinion it is . . . impolitic, at this juncture, to suffer an odium to be cast on the Count D'Estaing. . . . And he who, not long ago, expressed his opinion that 'a connection with France will ruin America' will not fail to promote a jealousy if he can thereby establish his popularity. Such a man should be critically watched." [25]

The absurdity of these misgivings soon was made manifest by Hancock's further cultivation of the *entente cordiale*. Not only General Greene but such unlikely persons as Warren and Mrs. John Adams acknowledged his invaluable contributions to this end. On the 16th Greene reported to Washington: "The admiral and all the French officers are now upon an exceeding good footing with the gentlemen of the town. General Hancock takes unwearied pains to promote a good understanding. . . . His house is full from morning till night." [26]

On the 22nd, five days after a group of French sailors had been mobbed in Boston, the big house on the hill was more crowded than at any other time in its history. Its master's hospitality was imposed upon to such an extent as to cause an emergency, which the mistress handled most resourcefully. Sumner gives her recollections of the occasion:

"When the French fleet were in Boston in 1778, under the Count D'Estaing, Mr. Hancock ordered a breakfast to be provided for thirty of the officers. . . . But the Count brought up almost all the officers . . . and the whole Common (to use Mrs. Scott's expression) 'was bedizened with lace.' Mr. H. sent word for her to get breakfast for 120 more. . . . They [the servants] . . . sent to the guard on the Common to *milk all the cows and bring her the milk*. She sent to all the neighbors for cake but could not get much brought into the room, for the little midshipmen . . . made prize of it as the servants passed through the entry. . . . The Frenchmen, she said, ate voraciously and one of them drank seventeen cups of tea. . . . The midshipmen . . . made sad destruction with the fruit in the garden."

When Admiral d'Estaing returned the hospitality by inviting Dolly to visit the fleet with all her friends she took him at his word and descended with five hundred people, who spent a whole day aboard his flagship. Sumner thus paraphrases her reminiscences:

"The Count was an elegant man. He asked her to pull a string to fire a gun—which, half frightened to death, she did . . . and found that she had given the signal for a *feu de joie* to the fleet, the whole of which immediately commenced firing; and they were all enveloped in smoke and stunned with the noise. . . .

"Mr. Codman [a friend of Dolly who was present as she told the story] said (sotto voce) the party . . . suspected the French had played a trick on them by giving them something to eat which operated on them as a violent cathartic, with which the ladies, as well as the men, were seized in the boats; where, having no accommodations for relief, they were obliged, ex necessitate rei, to do as they could. . . . Mrs. Scott, observing Mr. C. telling me something which convulsed me with laughter, . . . corroborated the . . . story by laughing most heartily and crying out: 'What a horrid time we had!'" [27]

In a long effusion to Sam Adams on the 30th Warren testified to the round of banquets tendered to the French by Hancock, and indirectly gave him credit for reviving the weakened bond between the Americans and their comrades in arms:

"The disposition that at first appeared to cast an odium on the Count and to discredit our new allies seems to have entirely subsided and has been succeeded by the most perfect good humor. . . . General Hancock has made the most magnificent entertainments for the Count and his officers, both at his own and the public houses." [28]

At about this time Abigail Adams, writing to her husband, gave Heath and Hancock much credit for fostering cordial relations with the foreign auxiliaries:

"Count D'Estaing has been exceedingly polite to me. . . . I have been the more desirous to take notice of them [the French], as . . . they have been neglected in the town of Boston. Generals Heath and Hancock have done their part; but few, if any, private families have any acquaintance with them." [29]

· 9 ·

In October, Hancock himself was one object of an attempt at mediation. Samuel Phillips Savage, a meddling member of the old Whig party, expressed to Sam Adams a strong desire, for the sake of America, to patch up the feud between the two patriots. Adams' belittling, contemptuous, and satiric reply is one of his most candid revelations:

"But . . . can a difference between Mr. —— and me . . . be of any consequence to the world? I think not. Tories, you say, triumph . . . but . . . it is too unimportant a matter for a sensible Whig to weep and break his heart about. I am desirous of making you easy; and I do assure you that, so far from brooding . . . an unfriendly disposition towards that man, I seldom think of him unless I happen to take up a Boston newspaper or hear his name mentioned in chit-chat conversation.

"You call upon me . . . to forgive him. Do you think *he* has injured *me?* If he has, should he not ask for forgiveness? . . . If he is conscious of having done or designed me an injury, let him do so no more, and I will promise to forgive and forget him, too; or . . . to do him all the service in my power. But this is needless. It is not in my power to serve him. *He* is above it." [30]

While these abortive peace negotiations were in progress Warren directed to the other Adams a letter which clearly indicates his state of mind concerning Hancock:

"The eyes of many people are open and see his views and motives; and some of the judicious think nothing necessary but to veer away rope. Last week this day was assigned for the choice of delegates [to Congress]. . . . If the great man fails he will be mortified, indeed." [31]

Warren's hopes were disappointed. The balloting actually took place a week later, and Hancock was voted back into his seat in Independence Hall. He did not occupy it until May 26, and then only for a fortnight.

Warren was in high company when he underestimated the reelected Congressman toward the end of 1778. Far across the sea at the Court of St. James's, King George discussed Hancock with Ex Governor Hutchinson, who summarizes the interview in his diary under date of December 17:

"At Court—the Queen not there—confined with a cold. The King said somewhat about the weather. Observed that I was more affected by the State of America. . . . I hoped they [political conditions] looked more favorably than they had done a year or two past. He thought so, . . . and particularly in New England. I did not know but they might in Connecticut, but in Massachusetts I thought the leaders had as much sway as ever. He asked if they had not changed their leaders. No: they had the same men as at first, particularly Hancock and Adams. Hancock, he said, was but a weak man. Adams, he had heard, was very able. I agreed with him." [32]

Warren shared the King's opinion of Hancock. He wrote to Sam Adams in February, 1779:

"Your old friend figures away in his usual style. Sometimes the pendulum swings one way and sometimes the other—I mean with regard to Whigism or Toryism—but never fails to swing uniformly against all who won't bow down and worship a very silly image." [33]

In reality this seeming weakness was one of the principal sources of the Beacon Hill politician's strength. His laisser-faire policy attracted all the people repelled by the Adams-Bowdoin type of democracy, which was losing its appeal as political philosophy went through a revolution in consonance with military rebellion.

· 10 ·

In May Dr. Gordon made a similar false judgment of Hancock. He predicted confidently to John Adams, who still was in France: "The *man* whom you thought would be governor, I apprehend, never will be. He sinks daily, and the world begins to know a little more of him." And on June 8 this obtuse soothsayer wrote to General Gates, of his short, late attendance at Congress:

"The H. party weaken apace. The head had a severe basting in the House by two able speakers for not going nor declining; and one of his friends had no other way of getting him off but by desiring that the matter in hand [presumably electing a successor] might be waived." [34]

Hancock cut short his stay in Philadelphia apparently because he had been chosen speaker of the Massachusetts House on June 3 after being reinstalled as a member about a month earlier. Mindful of the fall convention for adoption of a state constitution, he evidently regarded the speakership as a springboard to the governorship. He still had an astonishing hold on the electorate back home. In the face of the fact that he could not serve actively at the same time in Boston and Philadelphia, the voters continued to heap mutually exclusive offices upon him. On November 18 they tried to draft him for another term in Congress under a new three-months-rotation plan. He pretended to acquiesce before the election but afterwards found it inexpedient to assume his duties.

In July of this year the idol of the masses had betrayed evidence of being drunk with power by riding roughshod over the man who had once saved his life—Paul Revere. After returning to Boston, Hancock was put on a committee to strengthen the fortifications of Castle William. Revere, in command of an artillery regiment stationed there, was ordered on the 19th, with one hundred of his gunners, to join the Penobscot expedition against the British at Castine, Maine. About a week later Hancock inspected the fort, and the hero of the midnight ride reported to General Heath on October 24 after his return from the mismanaged campaign:

"He found fault with everything there. . . . When he went to Boston he told in all companies that none but Colonel Revere would have left the Castle in such a situation. . . . At the time I came home a number of the inhabitants of Boston had begun work at the Castle. . . . The Council arrested me and ordered me to my house. . . . They gave the command to Captain Cushing for the time being, since which General Hancock is appointed captain." [35]

Perhaps Revere had been guilty of neglect, but he had had all he could do since the start of the Revolution to keep his men from running off to sea in the more adventurous and rewarding privateer service. So the autocrat of Beacon Hill seems to have been unduly harsh in his treatment of a patriot to whom he was deeply indebted.

· 11 ·

The records for the last half of 1779 and the first half of 1780 are strangely reticent concerning Hancock's activities. Apparently he was quietly making plans for the bitter governorship struggle which loomed ahead. A constitution drawn up by a joint committee of the Council and the House and submitted to the voters for ratification in February, 1778, had been decisively rejected. In June of the following year, a call had been issued for a convention to draft a new instrument at Cambridge on September 1. Hancock was chosen one of twelve Boston delegates and one of three hundred state representatives. After exhaustive debates on a proposed bill of rights and after as many adjournments a revised constitution was agreed upon. Finally, on June 15, 1780, the people adopted this and brought the great commonwealth into being.

Meanwhile the name of the outstanding aspirant to the chief magistracy had been on the lips of thousands as constantly in old England as in New England. On this period George O. Trevelyan writes:

"Morning after morning the citizens of London were dosed and, for the most part, sickened with scurrilous attacks upon American statesmen and warriors for whom they entertained the respect due to eminent adversaries. . . . It was deliberately announced that there was in existence a secret correspondence, between John Hancock and George Washington, . . . indicating that the Commander-in-Chief of the American army had been privy to the conspiracy for burning down London, which had so narrowly failed of success at the time of the Gordon riots. Hancock was represented as condoling with Washington about the capture of Charleston by the royal fleet and army. 'But the victory of Britain' (so the ex-President of Congress was made to say) 'will be short-lived. We have friends who are working such a mine as will blow up all their triumphal schemes; and, if Providence favors us, the news of the surrender will come to their ears a day too late for their rejoicing in London.' " [36]

In a letter to Dolly at Point Shirley probably written as the campaign for governor warmed up in the spring of 1780, Hancock indicated that he was too busy to bother his head about Tory propaganda on the other side of the water: "Am going to Council. This forenoon I delivered my speech to the Court. . . . I am now so confined by the Court that I know not when I shall see you. . . . I thank you for the birds but I do not eat anything." [37]

On July 11, less than two months before the election, the outcome of the contest between Hancock and Bowdoin seemed doubtful to the prejudiced Warren, who thus summarized the situation for the enlightenment of John Adams:

"Mr. B. has again come into public life that he may . . . stand as a candidate in competition with H. for the highest honor and rank in this state. Who will carry the election is very uncertain. . . . The vanity of one of them will sting like an adder if it is disappointed; and the advancements made by the other, if they don't succeed, will hurt his *modest* pride. . . . I don't hear who is to be lieutenant [governor]; . . . only that an interest is making for C[ushing] in this town. If H. is chief why will not C. make an excellent second?" [38]

Gordon joined in the speculation with even nastier comments for the information of the same Adams. On the 22nd he insinuated that Hancock might sell out to the opposition—a contingency which the good doctor intended to promote underhandedly:

"It is thought that Mr. Bowdoin or Mr. Hancock will be chosen governor. Heaven grant that it may be . . . not the latter, who is one of the most egregious triflers I know! . . . A hint has been given me that he would serve as lieutenant-governor under Mr. Bowdoin . . . and this is not a little stoop for his ambition. . . . He can't, as lieutenant-governor, do much hurt. I mean, therefore, to propagate the hint . . . and possibly some may, by that, be taken off from voting for him as governor." [39]

But Warren's hopes and Gordon's machinations came to naught. Hancock was elected first governor of the new Commonwealth of Massachusetts by a majority that must have surprised even his most optimistic adherents and must have stunned his most fearful antagonists. He polled 9,475 votes out of the 10,383 cast; Bowdoin ran a bad second with only 888, and a few of the fifteen independent candidates divided the rest.

Although the balloting took place on September 4 in the various town meetings, the official totals were not announced until October 25. The initial term was to last but seven months, for the constitution provided that henceforth the local voting should be on the first Monday in April and the state-wide tally should be at the "general election" on the last Wednesday in May, when governor, lieutenant governor, and senators (replacing the old Council) were to be installed.

Hancock simply had cashed in on the popularity he had built up slowly and carefully from the time of the *Liberty* seizure. His election was due almost alone to personal attributes, supplemented by genuine sympathy with, and thorough understanding of, the people. They appreciated his gifts of money, firewood, and recreational projects. They admired his sacrificial patriotism as expressed in the "Burn Boston" speeches. They thrilled to tales of his eagerness to join the Minutemen on the green at Lexington. They looked upon him as the glamorous man of the hour who had led the Congress through the most desperate days of the Revolution. They liked his very vanity and showmanship because those traits restored color to an existence made drab by the departure of the picturesque Crown functionaries. And, above all, they loved him for turning against his own class politically to side with them, without condescension, while upholding the social standards of the aristocratic tradition; for they were not yet educated to accept the democratic principle in all its aspects.

The great issue of a strong central government versus states' rights, over which the Federalists and Antifederalists were to struggle for years, had not arisen, of course, because there was no real national executive or legislative authority. So this first governorship campaign in Massachusetts was primarily a clash of personalities. And the most personable of all public men in the country was the inevitable victor.

Thus did the idol of the masses enter upon a new phase of his fabulous career at the age of forty-three. It was just as spectacular, in a sense, as the stage during which he had been thrust into the forefront of the Revolutionary movement, and it opened up still broader opportunities for service to the young republic.

✠ XIV ✠

ADVANCEMENT BY RETIREMENT

 s THE INSIDERS among Hancock's foes faced the fact, long before his overwhelming triumph became public, that he was the governor elect Sam Adams executed a startling about-face. Warren remained hostile and resentful. Gordon, realizing that his underhand efforts to make his enemy a stalking-horse for the candidacy of Bowdoin had failed, attempted to undermine the new administration by the reverse stratagem of urging the beaten candidate to seek the lieutenant governorship, which was to be filled by the General Court because no aspirant to that office had polled a majority vote. But Adams turned right around and approved the popular choice for chief magistrate.

These various reactions are contained in letters written between the middle of September and the end of October, 1780. Two weeks after the general balloting began Warren glumly condoled with Adams over the already obvious result. Conceding defeat, he pointed out that "the votes of your own *beloved* town will give you at once an idea of the majority in favor of Mr. Hancock." He thought the selection of several of the senators who were to constitute the Upper House would be thrown into the Assembly along with that of lieutenant governor, and added that in most instances the outcome of the voting was calculated "to render their idol as uncontrollable as possible"—in other words, to place in power dyed-in-the-wool Hancockonians who would grant their leader a completely free hand. The influence of those who "don't worship devoutly may be very small, and you and I may have none at all." [1]

There is no record of a reply by Adams; but on October 10 he wrote to his wife that nothing except divergent political convictions stood between him and Hancock, and that he viewed with an open mind his adversary's elevation to the governorship:

"Is not Mr. —— my friend? He professes to be such, and I do verily believe he is as much so as he can be. Could I always adjust my ideas of politics to his views, I might perhaps insure the most flattering expressions of his friendship. I expect soon to see it announced in the papers that Mr. Hancock is elected governor of the Commonwealth of Massachusetts. I confess I did not foresee that Boston would have been so united . . . when two such competitors as he and Mr. Bowdoin were set up. Their respective characters, abilities, and merit were well known to the electors. . . . It is to be presumed that they have been influenced to this choice by the pure motives of public affection. A due attention to the administration of government, I fancy, will soon determine whether they have acted with wisdom or not."

A week later Adams was actually giving the governor elect his blessing, although not quite certain whether he was worthy of it. There is no doubt, however, as to the sincerity of the sanction, for he conferred it in a second letter to Mrs. Adams:

"I am disposed to think that my fellow-citizens had upright views in giving him their suffrages. Many circumstances have combined to make his election appear to be politically necessary; and if the people . . . will exercise their watchfulness over men whom they exalt to places of power . . . his will prove a happy choice. You may wonder at my saying so, but I think I am not misguided in my judgment. . . . If they have now chosen a wise and virtuous governor a few only will be disappointed, if otherwise, many will see their error and will be induced to greater vigilance for the future."

Here again may be discerned the almost religious fervor with which Adams believed in democracy. His faith in the wisdom of the people and in their capacity for learning by experience amounted to a fetish. It was destroyed by evidence of their folly in later years, and he died an embittered old man.

In his next paragraph he returned to the subject now apparently uppermost in his thoughts: renewal of friendship with his erstwhile protégé. He had accepted—for the time being—the Christian precept of forgiveness. The words of his confession, which stem from whole-souled patriotism, are a striking commentary on the emotional transformation of a wondrous character:

"I am far from being an enemy to that gentleman, though he has been prevailed upon to mark me as such. I have so much friendship for him as to wish with all my heart that . . . he may distinguish between . . . the real friends of the country and those who will be ready to offer the incense of flattery to him who is the first man in it. . . . If . . . he is able to hold the reins of government with dignity I wish him a continuance of the honor. If he renders our country secure . . . I will never be so partial and unjust as to withhold my tribute of applause." [2]

On October 19, two days after the man who could be so diabolic on occasion had penned these charitable sentiments, one who spoke by profession in the name of God informed John Adams malevolently of his latest scheme to tie the hands of the governor elect. Possibly with wishful thinking behind his opening sentence, the Reverend Dr. Gordon confided:

"Mr. Hancock will be governor unless death should prevent it. I was employed by a Boston representative *under the rose* to plead with Mr. Bowdoin that, *pro bono publico,* he condescend to serve as lieutenant-governor. I urged that plea and encourage the expectation, from his not declaring off, that if the General Court are pretty well agreed he will not decline. He will be a good poise and prevent undue influence and eccentric motions." [3]

· 2 ·

Although Gordon thus tried to kill off Governor Hancock at the height of his career, posterity is indebted to him for the most comprehensive eye-witness account of the inauguration on the 25th. With the help of a few details from Pynchon's diary, it is possible to set forth the main events of the most dazzling day in the life of the patriot in purple.

Not to be outdone by Sam Adams, even the weather warmed up to Hancock on the occasion of the handsomest tribute ever paid to him while he was alive. "Remarkably fair and pleasant," Pynchon noted in Salem—but added significantly that "at noon no cannon is heard . . . as formerly on election days." [4] Thus obliquely did the diarist record the failure of his friend Warren to regain a seat in the House.

The great day "was ushered in by the ringing of bells, firing of cannon, and other demonstrations of public rejoicing." When the new legislature assembled at the Statehouse to take over the duties of the General Court, which had been dissolved two days before, a committee was appointed to go through the formality of counting the ballots sent in by the several towns, "though it was before known on whom the choice had fallen." [5] After this foregone conclusion had been confirmed a committee representing both branches of the Assembly called upon the governor elect at his mansion. A military company, probably blaring forth in brass the purpose of the parade, led the way as the committee escorted him to the council chamber, seated in his chariot and wearing "a suit of crimson velvet, plain." [6] With pardonable pride in the fact that his election was so decisive as to render a formal announcement unnecessary, he presumed upon the situation by making the following extemporaneous remarks to the "Honorable Gentlemen":

"It would have ill become me at so early a moment after being notified of my appointment . . . to appear here to comply with the qualifying requisitions of the constitution, had not the circumstances of the returns made the choice a matter of public notoriety some weeks past . . . and, although fully sensible of my inability to the important purposes of the appointment, . . . I venture to offer myself, ready to comply . . . and regularly . . . attend to the duties of the department in which my country has been pleased to place me." [7]

In using the word "country" he may still have been thinking in terms of the Presidency of the Congress—or possibly in subconscious anticipation of occupying the yet to be created supreme seat at the head of the nation. On the other hand, he may have chosen this way to express his glorified conception of the Commonwealth of Massachusetts.

After his brief speech Hancock took the oath of office. Then Secretary John Avery, addressing the expectant crowd outside from the balcony opening off the inauguration hall, proclaimed him to be "His Excellency John Hancock, Esq., Governor of the Massachusetts Commonwealth."

These electric words, which the adulating people so long had yearned to hear, touched off the customary ceremonial gunfire throughout the town. The now traditional, symbolic routine of discharging thirteen cannon was performed by the artillery while all available ordnance on Fort Hill, at the Castle, and aboard the ships in the harbor joined in thunderous salute to the first citizen of Boston, of Massachusetts, and—in his idolaters' opinion—of the United States of America.

It was now three o'clock in the afternoon and time to thank God, "agreeable to ancient established custom," for conferring such a great blessing upon the state and to pray—also in accord with a ritual dating from the investiture of the original royal governor—that it would not prove to be a curse in disguise. Governor Hancock, accompanied by the Council, the Senate, and the House, repaired to the Old Brick Meetinghouse, where Dr. Cooper "delivered a suitable and acceptable discourse." After the service they proceeded through humanity-packed streets to Faneuil Hall, where the proverbial "elegant entertainment" was provided.[8] The hungry functionaries sat down to dinner at sunset and may not have got up until sunrise. At least, the drinking of thirteen toasts, each punctuated by cannonading, must have put the company in a convivial and wakeful frame of mind. And Hancock would not have gone home, even to his dear Dolly, before the last glass of Madeira had been spilled on the tablecloth or blended with the crimson of his velvet suit.

· 3 ·

Nine days after his induction Hancock had the more sober, and still more gratifying, pleasure of seeing Cushing elected lieutenant governor. Bowdoin had been chosen for the post by the General Court on the 30th but had declined because he had not been accorded the popular suffrage. Hancock's henchman, the next most logical candidate as president of the old Council, was offered the portfolio on November 3 and accepted with alacrity the chance to become the official right-hand man of his unofficial boss. Since Secretary Avery was Cushing's son-in-law, there was not a crevice of disunity in the foundation of the governmental household. Thus the already impregnable position of the Hancockonians was further solidified.

Hancock himself was now unquestionably the most powerful political leader on the continent. In all other states that had adopted constitutions (except Pennsylvania, which had no governor) the chief executive was dominated by the legislature or was narrowly circumscribed as to authority by a council. He enjoyed few appointive rights and no veto privilege such as the first officer of Massachusetts exercised.

In his inaugural address, delivered before the Assembly on the 31st, Governor Hancock showed that he was just as interested in strengthening his administration—and, indirectly, the country at large—by military means as in riveting his hold upon the electorate. In the most emphatic passage of his speech he declared:

"Gentlemen, of all the weighty business that lies before you a point of the first importance and most pressing necessity is the establishment of the army in such consistency and force . . . as may render it . . . an effectual defense to the free constitutions and independence of the United States."

As if in rebuttal to his opponents' campaign charges that he encouraged high living and free spending he advocated tightening the laws "for the suppression of idleness, dissipation, extravagancy, and all those vices that are peculiarly inimical to free republics." He also tried apparently to reassure those who mistrusted his financial philosophy: "No expedient should be unexplored to maintain our credit and remove all just ground of complaint from the army that protects us or from those who have relied on public engagements." The legislature's failure to adopt this policy was largely responsible for his only loss of power and retirement from public life.

The rest of the opening message to the General Court concerned the desirability of working out a system of postwar trade with England; taking precautions against secret enemies; making the seacoast and the western frontier secure; promoting education; guaranteeing religious liberty but enforcing observance of the Sabbath and fostering Christian piety in every respect. His peroration indicates he foresaw that the people might be expecting too much of him, and that their blind worship might turn to denunciation if he should fail to achieve the impossible. Yet the passage before the closing supplication for Providential aid is hopeful and confident:

"May the new government diffuse a new animation through the whole political body. The people expect much from it—perhaps more, in some points, than circumstances will allow it to perform;—but, standing as we do upon their choice and affections and strenuously exerting ourselves as we ought for their interest, they may find it happily advanced." [9]

Hancock took occasion, in the same oration, to pacify the Harvard faction that was demanding he be sued for the college funds remaining in his possession. At its last meeting on this matter in May, 1779, the corporation had voted down the overseers' recommendation of a suit, probably in anticipation of his election to the governorship, which carried power over the allotment of money for educational purposes. The two Harvard bodies still were deadlocked over the issue when the ex-treasurer became governor, with the prerogative to serve, *ex officio*, as head of the advisory board. So he was in a highly strategic position to relieve the pressure for a final accounting.

This he did with a gentle touch by saying he wished "warmly to commend" the college to the state legislators' "care and patronage." In reply a representative of the corporation who was in the audience expressed "their happiness that a gentleman is placed at the head of the General Court and of the overseers who has given such substantial evidence of his love of letters and affection to the college by the generous and repeated benefactions with which he hath endowed it." [10] Thus was staged one of the side shows of the Cambridge circus, and its star performer extricated from a situation that could have become very embarrassing at the start of his first term as chief executive of the Massachusetts Commonwealth.

· 4 ·

The general conditions under which Hancock assumed office were distressing enough. It is no wonder that he had misgivings as to his ability to measure up to the expectations of his constituents. The year 1780 was one of the most disastrous militarily in the whole course of the Revolution.

After General Benjamin Lincoln had surrendered Charleston to Clinton in May, with the loss of 5,000 men, a new American army was organized under Gates to check the threatened British sweep through the Carolinas. In August it encountered the enemy force under Cornwallis, whom Clinton had placed in command before returning to New York; and was thoroughly defeated at Camden, where Baron Johann de Kalb, the Bavarian tactician who had come over with Lafayette from France to help the patriots, was killed in action. Cornwallis then overran North Carolina at will. In September the brilliant Benedict Arnold was lost to the cause through his attempt to betray West Point, gateway to the Hudson River valley, and his flight to the English lines.

But these setbacks in the field, bad as they were, did not weaken the Revolutionary movement so seriously as developments on the financial front. Inflation was rampant in Massachusetts, as throughout the country. Ten paper dollars were equivalent to only one cent in hard money. In Boston beef was selling wholesale at $8 a pound, sugar at $10, butter at $12, tea at $90, corn at $150 per bushel, and a barrel of flour at $1,575. Sam Adams paid $2,000 for a suit of clothes.

The resulting civilian discontent, piled on top of the discouraging news from the war, was breaking New England's spirit. Some sections were insisting that peace without victory be made with Britain. Massachusetts was not among the backsliders but was rent with equally dangerous dissension. The masses resented the privateering, speculation, and profiteering war contracts on which the upper classes were battening in the name of patriotism.

Such was Governor Hancock's unenviable heritage of office. The weight of it probably would have dragged him down to oblivion by the end of his first term but for the still stronger counterpull of popularity which buoyed him up. Warren, who might be expected to have exhausted his capacity for surprise at the might of the Hancock political machine, was more deeply impressed than before by its manifestations after the election. He was at a loss for words to do it justice in writing to Sam Adams on November 2:

HANCOCK MAKING THE SPEECH WHICH CLINCHED RATIFICATION OF THE FEDERAL CONSTITUTION IN MASSACHUSETTS. FROM A MURAL BY ALBERT HERTER IN THE STATE-HOUSE, BOSTON. BY COURTESY OF U.S. REPRESENTATIVE CHRISTIAN A. HERTER.

"It is impossible to describe to you, in its full extent, the prevalence of a certain influence here. The papers will at least show you that it exceeds any that ever took place in any country and, if it be as lasting as it is violent and extensive, will be a singular phenomenon. . . . Nothing excited my resentment so much as the neglect you are treated with. Neither your beloved town, the county, the state, or the two Houses have shown any gratitude for your many and great services; and the man who had the greatest hand in the greatest revolution in the world, in the choice of a secretary, could not be supported in competition with Mr. Avery. . . . Everything past is forgot, and everybody that will not worship the great image is to be treated in that way."

But Warren was temperate in his strictures on the new administration by comparison with his wife—a sister of James Otis. A pungent writer and militant behind-the-scenes politician, Mercy was a feminist in advance of her time. She was the female counterpart of Sam Adams in her devotion to pure democratic principles, social as well as political, and zealously abetted her husband in hatred of Hancock. Enmity blazes from almost every line in her letter of the 15th to John Adams:

"Of course, the daily incense is offered in the capital; and the gilded puppet placed on the public theater a few years ago (for certain purposes) is become the idol to whom the supple homage of adulation is paid by a people once disinterested, firm, discerning, and tenacious of their rights. . . . Yet the image whose feet are of clay may, in a short time, become as the chaff of the summer threshing-floor unless, like another Pisastratus [sic], for the sake of prolonging his power, he should govern according to the minutest forms of the constitution." [11]

By the end of the year Sam Adams had again lost faith in Hancock. In a long screed to the Boston merchant John Scollay, alluding to the new administration, he asserted:

"I am afraid there is more pomp and parade than is consistent with those sober republican principles upon which the framers of it thought they had founded it. Why should this new era be introduced with entertainments expensive and tending to dissipate the minds of the people? Does it become us to lead the people to such public diversions as promote superfluity of dress and ornament when it is as much as they can bear to support the expense of clothing a naked army? Will vanity and levity ever be the stability of government?"

After throwing back into the governor's teeth the passages in his inaugural address recommending "suppression of idleness, dissipation, and extravagancy," the dour Puritan indicated he shared Warren's suspicions that Hancock intended to make the people subservient with a deliberate attempt to break their Spartan spirit by encouraging soft living:

"Pownal . . . ventured to have his riots and routs at his own house to please a few boys and girls. Sober people were disgusted at it, and his privy councillors never thought it prudent to venture so far as expensive balls. Our Bradfords, Winslows, and Winthrops would have revolted at . . . scenes of dissipation and folly. . . .

"I love the people of Boston. I once thought that city would be the Christian Sparta. But alas! Will men never be free! . . . Sidney tells us there are times when people are not worth saving, meaning when they have lost their virtue. I pray God this may never be truly said of my beloved town." [12]

· 5 ·

This piece of correspondence outlines more clearly than any other the basis of the Adams-Hancock feud. Adams, the most practical of politicians, could overlook differences of belief, respect the opinions of opponents on matters of governmental policy, and rise above all such considerations to cooperate with foe and friend alike for the good of his country. But he could not reconcile himself to what he regarded as disloyalty to the first social principles of republicanism—simple, modest, frugal living. In his eyes the governor was guilty of such infidelity.

There is no doubt that the apostle of asceticism was right—according to his lights. But they were growing dimmer as old age crept upon him. They no longer enabled him to perceive that the temper of the times was changing. Puritanism had served an invaluable purpose in giving men the stanchness and resoluteness to conquer a wilderness; but it had outlived its usefulness. Although the Americans were in the most critical stage of a war which called for as much daring and fortitude as the establishment of a foothold on a desolate continent, a new generation had sprung up without being inured to the hardships suffered by their forebears. The current crop of New Englanders was just as sound at the core, but it needed an outlet for long repressed emotions. This was provided in Massachusetts by Hancock. His gala entertainments, begun largely at his own expense before a meager salary of £1,000 was voted him four months after he took office, relieved the tension among the leaders of society directly and did likewise for the common men vicariously.[13] These diversions helped all classes to bear up under the terrific strain of the

Revolution. And most of the affairs were indispensable to the maintenance of cordial relations with the many representatives of foreign governments who received their initial impression of America while entering the country through Boston.

Sam Adams and Warren mistook the shadow for the substance. They suspected the governor of nefarious scheming that was entirely alien to his nature. He loved the people and the town where he had been brought up, fully as much as Adams. It is inconceivable that, after deserting his class to fight throughout adult life for the liberties of the masses—as well as for his own personal freedom—he should have tried to curb them now.

History can produce numerous instances of liberators turned tyrant, but few if any with a background like Hancock's. An aristocrat with the instincts of a democrat seldom proves recreant to his inherent convictions. There is no evidence that the people were deprived of a single constitutional right, save in the case of a justifying emergency, while he was governor during eleven of thirteen years. In his first administration the underprivileged were victims of economic inequities which eventually gave rise to Shays' Rebellion; but the injustices were not of his making or within his power to remedy. If the legislature had hearkened to his advocacy of sound currency they might have been alleviated without violence.

That he doted on authority and prestige has often been demonstrated in this book. But he usually used both for what he thought were the best interests of the greatest number.

Yet Governor Hancock cracked down hard upon disloyal malcontents. Military necessity warranted it. Neither the state nor the nation could tolerate troublemakers at this crucial point in the war. He ordered all justices of the peace early in 1781 to jail any person whom they considered dangerous to the commonwealth. In March, Pynchon noted three arrests in Deerfield, under this arbitrary decree, for the issuance of "instructions to the representatives of the town as to a speedy peace" and the voicing of "sentiments and expressions about taxes being insupportable by many of the people." Two days later the Salem chronicler recorded that one of the seized men, after being imprisoned in Boston, had been "committed to close confinement in a low, dark room; denied pen, ink, etc., and all conversation with any but jailer," and had even been refused medical attention. But when Pynchon protested in person "Governor Hancock . . . humanely ordered that the prisoners should have a physician and all necessaries and conveniences." [14]

· 6 ·

Although there is no reason to believe that Hancock's ruthless suppression of free speech was due to a rush of power to the head, a series of letters written by Washington indicates that he suffered during the following summer from this common ailment of popular politicians—a disorder aggravated by his reelection on May 30. Eight times in ten weeks the commander in chief wrote to the governor asking to have 600 militiamen sent to Albany, without even receiving an acknowledgment. An army was being formed near the headwaters of the Hudson to attack Cornwallis in conjunction with French land and sea forces at Yorktown, Virginia, in what proved to be the decisive engagement of the Revolution. The Massachusetts troops were to be part of a defensive contingent guarding the New York border when the Continental regulars should depart for the south.

On July 8 Washington pointed out to the governor, with astonishing restraint: "I . . . am . . . unable to form any certain estimate of what may be expected in consequence of my requisitions. This puts me in rather an awkward situation, as I cannot give . . . Count Rochambeau . . . that official insurance of support which I had promised upon the faith of the States." In desperation, on August 2, the general complained to Thomas McKean, who had been elected President of the Congress about a month previously, that "not a single militia man from any State has joined the army except . . . about 80 levies of New York and about 200 . . . troops of Connecticut." Three days later he wrote to General George Clinton, governor of New York, who was doubling as commandant of the frontier replacements: "It is not a little distressing to find that the States will not or cannot . . . afford the aids of militia required of them; . . . instead of an active and decisive campaign . . . we must end our operations in languor and disgrace and perhaps protract the war to the hazard of our final ruin." Within the next twenty-four hours he took matters into his own hands by asking General Lincoln to round up the missing militia sought from the Bay State and to speed them on their way.[15]

Obviously Hancock was no more remiss in his duty to the cause than most of the other northern governors. But that does not excuse him or explain his failure to cooperate with the man whom he professed to admire so much. Some time before July 30 he finally ordered the raising of the militia, according to Washington, but had not issued instructions for the march to Albany. These presumably were the troops which Lincoln was requested to dispatch to their destination.

Inability, rather than unwillingness, may have been the reason for the delay in responding to the first part of the supreme commander's appeal. While six hundred men would not seem to have been a disproportionate requisition to make upon a state the size of Massachusetts, New England's apathy toward the war rendered recruiting difficult; but that does not absolve the chief executive from blame for neglect to provide for their disposition when enlisted or for keeping Washington in the dark.

So there is no apparent explanation for Governor Hancock's strange conduct other than sheer determination to do as he pleased—when he pleased. In this instance he is open to strong suspicion of being obsessed with his own importance and with a desire to impress upon one of his few serious rivals for the highest homage of the nation that he did not intend to brook any such competition. This episode may have been another phase in the struggle between the two patriots for the paramount allegiance of the people—a struggle which culminated in a showdown after the father of the country became its first President.

The records are curiously bare of significant events involving Hancock for about a year from this time. There is not even any indication that he took cognizance of the thrilling news, brought to Boston by Lafayette in December, 1781, of Cornwallis' surrender at Yorktown on October 19.

Toward the end of April the British general had marched from Wilmington, North Carolina, to Petersburg, Virginia, where he had picked up 2,000 reinforcements in charge of the traitorous Arnold. Thereupon he had proceeded to envelop most of the Old Dominion and then had retired to Yorktown early in August to fortify the place in anticipation of the Franco-American attack from the north.

Meanwhile Washington, on learning that Count de Grasse was holding a large squadron near the West Indies in readiness to cooperate with the allied soldiery, had induced Rochambeau to order all the rest of the naval units under his supreme command to join in besieging the Virginia seaport. English Admiral Thomas Graves had tried to forestall this scheme by sailing from New York and engaging De Grasse in Chesapeake Bay at the beginning of September, but had been driven off. The siege, which pitted about 16,000 troops and a formidable armada against a stronghold defended by a garrison of approximately 7,000, had opened on the 28th. Cornwallis had held out until October 17 and then had asked for the terms of the surrender which, to all intents and purposes, gloriously terminated the earth-shaking American Revolution two days later.

Hancock's neglect to make political capital of this epochal event may have been due partly to the need of concentrating on the internal affairs of his administration. But probably the principal cause was the bad health he mentioned in a letter of May 22, 1782, to Dolly's cousin John Wendell, about a tax investigation on land he owned in New Hampshire which Wendell was conducting for him: "I have only strength . . . to acknowledge receipt of your several letters and to thank you for your very great readiness to serve me. . . . By flattering myself that I had . . . recovered my health . . . I exerted myself to too great a degree and have taken such a cold as to give me such a nervous pain in my head as has confined me to my chamber, unfit for business, for several days past." [16]

This tends to show that the governor had had a long siege of illness which prevented him from being as active as usual in politics. That an increasing invalidism was the main cause of his mysterious disappearance from the world of men is implicit in the writings of William Sullivan, a contemporary Boston lawyer and historian, who describes a visit which he made to the Beacon Hill mansion in the next month at the age of eight:

"In June 1782 Governor Hancock had the appearance of advanced age, though only forty-five. He had been repeatedly and severely afflicted with the gout. . . . As recollected, . . . Mr. Hancock was nearly six feet in stature and of slender person, stooping a little and apparently enfeebled by disease. His manners were very gracious, of the old style of dignified complaisance. His face had been very handsome. . . . At this time . . . about noon, Hancock was dressed in a red velvet cap, within which was one of fine linen. . . . He wore a blue damask gown lined with silk; a white stock; a white satin, embroidered waistcoat; black satin smallclothes; white silk stockings, and red morocco slippers.

"It was a general practice in genteel families to have a tankard of punch made in the morning and placed in a cooler when the season required it. . . . At this visit Hancock took . . . a full tankard and drank first himself and then offered it to those present." [17]

While the governor was quietly tippling at home—and thereby hastening the day when gout should take him off—the people did not forget him. In fact, his semiretirement apparently made them more eager to get a glimpse of him; for when he showed up at the Harvard commencement in July their flattering attention caused the facetious Pynchon to exclaim in his diary: "All eyes, addresses, all compliments are directed toward thee, Handcocky, O rare Handcocky! Not a word of thee, stout first mover, Adams." [18]

It is not surprising that the probably graying head under the red velvet cap was turned by this constant idolatry. Many a less susceptible man than Hancock would have been affected by it.

· 7 ·

A situation calculated to increase the number of silver threads on the governor's pate was developing at this time. The Congress was crying for money and more money with which to bring the Revolution to a financially sound conclusion, and in September, when Massachusetts still was feeling the strain of raising almost £4,000,000 for this purpose, it levied an assessment of $1,200,000 (about £250,000) upon the state as its share of interest due on the national debt. Toward the close of October, Governor Hancock announced to the legislature that more than $1,000,000 had been paid; but by then the ante had been jumped up to $2,000,000 per month.

To collect this staggering sum the General Court resorted, at his urging, to the extraordinary taxation which was a contributing cause of Shays' Rebellion of 1786–1787. In November, 1782, Hancock told the Assembly: "Experience has taught us that we cannot avail ourselves of money sufficient to carry on the war solely by the common mode of taxation. It is, then, of great importance that we should obtain all we can by duties and excises." But by stressing the advisability of distributing the burden evenly he did his best to ward off the conditions that led to the civil strife: "The more important this measure appears to be, the more necessary it is that it should be done in such a way as to render it effectual and permanent, as well as conducted in such a manner as to make it an equal tax and thereby render it agreeable to the people in general." [19]

There are indications that Hancock now was finding it as difficult to pay his own bills as to meet those of the commonwealth. His diplomatic entertainments apparently had been a severe drain even upon his huge resources.

At intervals for several years, individuals, as well as Harvard College, had been threatening to prosecute him for failure to discharge his financial obligations; and in the midst of the public economic crisis Wendell seems to have demanded compensation for his work on the New Hampshire tax matter. Catherine Wendell Davis, telling her brother that she had received £15 on account, went to the defense of Hancock: "You do the governor injustice. . . . He has not been able to hold a pen since I've been from Portsmouth. He desired me to inform you . . . whatever you were in advance he is willing to refund." [20]

Hancock may have been stalling off his creditors on the theory that he was more sinned against than sinning, for numerous former customers of the House of Hancock still owed him large sums. While winding up its affairs Hoskins wrote about eighty dunning letters in an effort to collect debts, some of which dated back nearly two decades.

And yet the fancy financier of Beacon Hill was sufficiently well heeled at this period to invest heavily in depreciated paper. It will be recalled that as early as 1778 he had started to settle with poor borrowers on the basis of the fiat currency which even then was flooding the country. Shortly after the preliminary peace treaty with England was ratified on April 15, 1783, to signalize the cessation of hostilities on the 11th, he gave the Massachusetts militia hard money in exchange for the virtually worthless "continentals" which they had received as discharge pay. As on the occasion of his previous seemingly foolish trading, he was suspected of being motivated more by speculation than by soft-heartedness.

A century later, William C. Todd wrote that all, including Hancock, who had faith in the government were fortunate in their purchases of this highly inflated medium; and he pointed out that the refunding scheme put into effect by Alexander Hamilton, while Secretary of the Treasury under Washington, restored it to par value.[21] On the other hand, Martha Quincy maintains in her reminiscences that the governor "expressed his opinion in favor of the poor soldiers"; gave them "dollar for dollar in good money and took in return their valueless paper, for which he received only one cent for a dollar when he came to dispose of it." Friends of the family, she adds, warned Dolly that the trunk in which her prodigal husband kept his sterling "must be removed from the house, or she and her child would be penniless; and, without consulting the governor, it was removed." [22]

It would seem advisable to discount this story of strictly noble intentions, told by a relative of the astute plutocratic politician, as liberally as the continentals were discounted on Boston 'change in 1783.

· 8 ·

Now that the Revolution was over, Hancock attempted to hitch his bandwagon to the star of the great drama. In a gushing letter of October

15 he extended best wishes to Washington for a happy retirement: "After such services, which consecrate your name to all posterity, with what home-felt satisfaction must your future days be blest! Heaven crown them with every favor! May you long live, my dear General, and long have the joy to see the increasing splendor and prosperity of a rising nation, aided by your counsels and defended by your sword! Indulge me the pleasure to believe that I have a place in your recollection and still honor and make me happy in your friendship." [23]

The governor himself had been talking since April about retiring. General Heath, writing to Hancock that he had heard it rumored he would decline a fourth term if returned to office at the May election, had urged him to reconsider.[24] Although he deferred his decision, after retaining his seat with somewhat more difficulty than heretofore, he toyed with the notion as late as November and formulated plans for going back into private business in the spring. In a long letter of November 14 he revealed to Captain Scott, then in London, that he was experiencing one of his rare compulsions to account for his stewardship of public trust and to defend himself against the criticism of his enemies:

"I have, for ten years past, devoted myself to the concern of the public. I have not the vanity to think that I have been of very extensive service in our late unhappy contest, but one thing I can truly boast: I set out upon honest principles and strictly adhered to them to the close of the contest, and this I defy malice itself to controvert. I have lost many thousand sterling but, thank God, my country is saved and, by the smile of Heaven, I am a free and independent man. And now, my friend, I can pleasantly congratulate you on the return of peace, which gives a countenance to retire from public life and enjoy the sweets of calm domestic retirement and pursue business merely for my own amusement."

Three months earlier he had commissioned Hoskins to make advances to his prewar agents and customers in England. "Governor Hancock hopes yet to see," his manager had written to one British firm, "all disjointment and alienation among former friends reunited, made permanent, and reciprocally happy." [25]

Although the head of the House of Hancock probably did have a deep-seated desire, such as takes possession of most men who have been embroiled in politics for many years, to withdraw into the comparative peace and quiet of a commercial career, he must have been influenced by expediency. Politics had so permeated his blood that he could not seriously have considered it unless the prevalent economic unrest had warned him

to avoid the danger menacing his prestige. But the time to take this precaution had not yet arrived.

· 9 ·

However, apparently depressed by long continued poor health, and with
a trace of bitterness at signs that the idolatry of the people was less fervid
than before, Hancock intended when he wrote to Captain Scott to
withdraw from the governorship almost at once: "I am determined, in
the course of this month, to resign my command of this Commonwealth
and return to private life after the many fatigues I have gone through.
I leave the government under the public conviction that a much better
man may be my successor."

Hoskins was to sail for London within three weeks "to examine accounts in England that have been settled, for I rather think I shall be a
gainer," and to have power of attorney jointly with Scott, who was to
approach Harrison with "the offer of my business." But his trade was to
be resumed on the modest basis of only one ship, which the captain was
to acquire and command if he would "consent to go into the old line."

Enclosed in this letter was a long memorandum concerning a post-
chaise or chariot and numerous house furnishings to be purchased by the
shipmaster—presumably to make the governor's declining years of relative
leisure as luxurious and comfortable as possible.* The carriage was to
conform to the following specifications, reminiscent of Uncle Thomas'
for a similar vehicle:

"Elegantly neat, not made expensive by external tawdry ornaments.
The coachman's seat to unship and ship . . . so as occasionally to have
the servants on the seat or to ride postillion; the box inside . . . to draw
out . . . a lamp at each side of the carriage. A handsome traveling
trunk, made exactly to fit. . . . To be lined with crimson velvet. . . .
Captain Scott will find inclosed Mr. Hancock's arms, which he would
have neatly introduced . . . and the motto subjoined. The ground paint-
work of the carriage to be stone yellow, that being the color all his carriages bear."

The coat-of-arms undoubtedly was Hancock's own creation, for it
bore no resemblance to that of the family recorded in the Heraldry Office

---

* According to the inventory of his estate, Hancock owned ten conveyances: the
chariot and the chaise inherited from his uncle; a smaller chariot, a coach, a kit-
tereen, a sulky, a booby-hut (enclosed sleigh); a double and a single open sleigh,
and a horse cart. He also had four horses. (Probate Records, File No. 20215.)

at London. Inventing the hallmark of a noble lineage was a common practice among early American aristocrats; and the governor adopted the obviously appropriate pattern of an upraised hand (to represent the first syllable in the original spelling of his surname), surmounted by three cocks in line and a larger chanticleer, with the tail of a dragon, poised above—the whole superimposed on a shield. Inscribed beneath the design was the family motto: *Nul plaisir sans peine.*

The Beacon Hill hedonist intended to restore his mansion in all its pre-Revolutionary magnificence and to live more regally as a private citizen than as a public figure. His memorandum continues:

"Six dozen very best pewter plates . . . oval or long dishes for Saturday's salt fish. You know how it used to be. My crest to be engraved in each dish and plate. . . . The furniture has stood from the finishing of the room to the present moment but is now much worn and stands in need of a recruit. At least, Mr. Hancock's son will want it. . . . I think a silk and worsted furniture will be good enough. The window curtains to be made to draw up. The window cushions . . . and twelve stuff-back chairs . . . and a sophia [sofa] of the same."

Wilton carpets for the two principal bedchambers—to replace those defaced by the British officers—and a silver tea urn completed the order.[26] But the last mentioned article must have been included for Dolly's benefit alone. Her husband seldom, if ever, tasted of its contents. He stuck to good old "Solomon Townsend," a gallon tankard named after a drinking companion.

The governor had a practical reason for specifying that his new dining utensils should be made of pewter. As his gout became more acute with advancing age his nerves were frayed almost to the breaking point, so that he could not stand even the clatter of chinaware as the servants cleared the banquet table. One day while he was confined upstairs by a particularly severe attack, Dolly told Sumner, he jumped at the sound of the slight impact between dish and tray. He shouted for Cato to bring the offending but highly valuable piece, imported from India, and commanded him to throw it out the window. The negro, shocked at the willful destruction of such an expensive object, tossed it upon the grass with the idea of retrieving it later. His now enraged employer, however, forced him to go down and smash it against a wall within hearing distance to prove that the intent of the order had been carried out.[27]

It was not only as a semi-invalid, but as an active governor, that Hancock went on making life miserable for everybody in his household—and many on the outside. He let it be known publicly in December, 1783, that he purposed to tender his resignation to the Council and led his foes to believe that they were to receive a Christmas present in such form. But after summoning his official family ostensibly to hear his farewell address he announced that he had changed his mind. Gordon disgustedly described the workings of that remarkable intellect in a letter to Gerry:

"His Excellency the Governor has been playing over again the childish trick of the preceding year. He would resign. Yes, he would resign; that he would. . . . The Council was summoned . . . to hear his big speech upon the occasion. They came, and the mouse appeared upon the green cloth. His friends had persuaded him not to resign." [28]

Urgent counsel from trusted advisers must, indeed, have caused this sudden mental flip-flop, for the gubernatorial gymnast certainly had been sincere in expressing to Captain Scott a month previously his intention to surrender his portfolio. Perhaps his intimates convinced him that it would be politically unwise to desert his post in mid-term, especially during this winter of discontent. They may have argued, too, that if he should remain in office until the next election he could quit not only with better grace but with higher hope of bequeathing a greatly aggravated situation, which would boomerang upon his successor.

Nobody thought any the worse of Hancock for reversing his decision except his adversaries, as Warren acidly admitted to John Adams in February: "His character is neither stained with ridicule or contempt—a privilege peculiar to himself." [29] The governor had yet to make his first political mistake.

· 10 ·

The year 1784 was as uneventful in Hancock annals as the period spanning the summers of 1781 and 1782. Unable to check the avalanche of economic chaos that was fast engulfing Massachusetts, the governor may have coasted with it while offering just enough token resistance in recommended remedial legislation to avert the stigma of personal responsibility and to get himself reelected in May. On the other hand, this second hiatus in his ordinarily bustling existence may have been caused by circumstances beyond his control. The imperative task of converting the commonwealth from a war to a peace basis, and of rehabilitating it after eight years of deterioration from concentration upon martial objectives, was enough to keep the most exhibitionistic politician preoccupied with the everyday business of government.

In any event, Hancock apparently had little opportunity to attract attention during this interval. He had only two recorded chances to act the part of the social lion in which he reveled. A celebration on March 4 to mark the signing of the definitive treaty that officially ended the Revolution provided the first occasion. In the evening of a day made clamorous by the inevitable bell clanging and cannon booming the governor entertained at his mansion all the other leading functionaries, headed by Lieutenant Governor Cushing, who had remained in office by clinging to the governor's coat tails; "and at seven o'clock," according to the *Continental Journal*, "a grand exhibition of fireworks were displayed on the Common, such as were never before equalled in this place." [30]

Lafayette visited Boston August 19 on his return from a sojourn in France, and Hancock seized upon the event to swagger as master of ceremonies at a welcoming festival. He greeted the distinguished French guest and five hundred leading citizens at Faneuil Hall after a parade through the town and a banquet at the Bunch of Grapes; then topped off the program by disporting himself—probably in the most conspicuous manner possible—at a ball in honor of the marquis.

Although the rank-and-file inhabitants of the Massachusetts capital rarely caught sight of their idol during the remainder of the year, his penetrating political mind must have been working overtime. Having failed to insist on the collection of long overdue and badly needed taxes for fear of antagonizing the heavily burdened lower classes, he must have seen that the day of reckoning was close at hand and may have decided not to be around, in an official sense, when it should come.

An opportune, though excruciatingly painful, seizure of gout early in 1785 furnished Hancock with a plausible pretext for resigning from the governorship. Shortly before taking the fateful step he suffered such a devastating attack that he had to be carried from his carriage to his home by servants, who placed him on a sofa in the great parlor and cut a new suit off him to relieve the torture of his swollen joints before bearing him upstairs to bed.

On January 29 he tendered to the Assembly a preliminary, informal resignation in these carefully weighed words:

"Sensible of my infirm state of health and of my incapacity to render that service . . . which is expected from a person in my station, justice to the public and myself loudly call upon me not to prejudice the community but rather to promote its benefit; to effect which I am obliged, Gentlemen, to inform you that some relaxation is absolutely necessary for me and that I must at present give up all attention to public business

and pursue the means of regaining my health. Under these circumstances I must request to be indulged with a resignation of the chair;
and . . . I hope I shall be able, in a few days, to meet the General Court
. . . and take my leave in a formal manner." [31]

The phrase "at present" suggests that he had no thought of divesting
himself of his gubernatorial robes for good. It lends validity to the theory
that he was sliding out of office on the undertow of dissatisfaction, with
the idea of riding back on a wave of reaction. Prejudiced persons were
confident that Hancock did not really wish to retire at all, and that his
speech was merely a trial balloon to determine whether the wind of popularity still was blowing in his direction.

The great political meteorologist may, for once, have misinterpreted the
cross currents that constantly agitated public life in eighteenth century
Massachusetts.

· 11 ·

Governor Hancock waited until February 18 to follow up his test flight
of oratory with an official resignation. It caused an emotional orgy in the
Statehouse according to Charles Gore, a Bowdoin supporter, who described the scene in a letter to Rufus King:

"The late Governor's resignation was a source of great joy to his opponents and much grief to his friends. When he attended on the floor
of the House . . . to take leave of the legislature his enemies discovered
marks of indecent joy, while his admirers chose to display their sorrow
by unmanly blubbering and sycophantic speeches."

But Hancock must have known that his supporters were wasting their
tears. Gerry wrote to King, on excellent authority, that their enemy realized he had been taken at his word two days after notifying the legislators of his intentions and that he had made his tentative decision
without benefit of counsel:

"I find by a person who conferred with the Lieutenant-Governor that
the Governor, in a freak, without consulting . . . even his most intimate friends, sent his first message to the Court. He expected they would
be unhappy . . . be silent for some time . . . and then request him to
continue in the chair and pursue measures to recover his health while
the duties of the office should devolve on the Lieutenant-Governor. But
when the Governor found that his message was taken up the second day
after it was made and that his proposition to resign was, in polite terms,
encouraged by the legislature he was much chagrined and disgusted;

but he delayed his resignation three weeks and was then under the necessity of proffering it, as all sources failed him for making retreat." [32]

The lid was off the furiously boiling political pot, and the campaign for the chief magistracy was the hottest of all those fought during Hancock's lifetime. Furthermore, it became involved in a bitter controversy over public dancing and gambling.

As an upshot of the anti-Puritan agitation that had been going on in Boston social circles ever since the start of the Hancock era the "Tea Assembly," or "Sans Souci Club," had been organized during the winter of 1784–1785 to supplement such dignified diversions as the Thursday lectures and the fortnightly dances at Concert Hall. The Sans Soucians afforded devotees of Terpsichore and Fortune an opportunity to combine their pleasures in a somewhat less circumspect, though still quite proper, manner at the same recreation center. In addition to dancing there was card playing and betting—to the limit of twenty-five cents. Tea, coffee, and hot chocolate were served gratis; punch, wine, negus, and lemonade, at a slight extra charge. All such assemblages terminated at midnight.

But even this decorous dissipation offended the moral sensibilities of such Whig purists as Sam Adams. It is believed that he was the author of a series of denunciatory articles, the first of which appeared under the pseudonym of "Observer" in the January 15 issue of the *Massachusetts Centinel*. The writer implied that the new club was Tory-inspired and advocated indirectly that it be suppressed by force, like a similar assembly in New York. These tirades called forth answers in the same paper from several defenders of the organization, most influential of whom was Harrison Gray Otis, who used the pen name "Sans Souci."

Underlying this social squabble were the fundamental principles that divided the conservative Whigs, carrying on under Bowdoin, from the liberal wing which had broken away under Hancock. Both parties found the Sans Souci affair—in which the retired governor's followers naturally lined up on the side of more freedom for the socially inclined—a convenient battleground for the governorship. As the conflict of killjoys versus fun lovers merged into that of politicians the journalistic recriminations were printed under the new aliases of "Candidus" and "Truth," respectively. These scribes narrowed the issue down to the old personal vendetta between Adams and Hancock.

As a matter of fact, it was one phase of the struggle. Adams was running for lieutenant governor against his antagonist's close friend and

compliant wheelhorse, General Heath. But this was just a skirmish incidental to the main action, which centered in the fierce conflict for the
governorship between Bowdoin and Cushing. Like a good general, Hancock was shooting for maximum and minimum objectives. The first was
to keep his party in power through his aide. With this purpose in mind
he had resigned early enough to accustom the people to the idea of Cushing—filling out the unexpired term—in the role of chief magistrate. His
secondary aim was to maintain partial control of the government by maneuvering his man into the lieutenant governorship.

After the opening clash on April 4 the outcome still remained in
doubt. Neither Bowdoin nor Cushing received a majority vote, and the
fight had to be rejoined in the legislative chamber. The Senate plumped
for the conservative candidate; the House, for the liberal standard bearer.
Finally, within four days, the more representative but less forceful body
yielded under pressure and swung over to Bowdoin. Cushing, however,
polled sufficient write-in ballots in the two branches of the Assembly to
beat both Adams and Heath for the post of lieutenant governor, which
he retained until his death three years later.

Thus did Hancock establish himself in a position from which to
launch an overwhelming counterattack in 1787.

After the ex-governor had withdrawn from the field in good order
Gerry fired a pot-shot in his direction. Writing to King on May 27, he
whipped out what he considered a high-powered prank played at their
foe's expense. It had been perpetrated at the "general election" on the
previous day when Hancock was occupying the House seat in which he
had been reinstalled by his loyal Boston adherents on the 16th and the
General Court was on the point of taking a belated vote on the secretary-
ship. The sniper thus let go with both barrels:

"'I move,' says Mr. H., 'Sir, that a message be sent to the Senate to
inform them we are ready to proceed to the choice of a secretary.' The
motion passed, and the speaker [Nathaniel Gorham] desired Mr. H. to
do the message; but the latter did not incline to hear until the request
was repeated and then said: 'Sir, I hear you and *can do the message.*'
What little mortifications *great* men are liable to!" [33]

Gerry meant that Hancock, conscious of the unjust charge that he
could not write even the simplest statement and that all his speeches
were ghost-written, had been provoked into implying the report had some
basis. The ex-governor, however, was to enjoy the last—and most lasting
laugh.

XV

WORDS MAKE A NATION

*T*HE EXHILARATION produced by the rough-and-tumble political fight
that he had just been through apparently drove out of Hancock's mind
all thought of retiring from public life. It even made him insensible to
the pangs of gout, for when he was reelected to the Congress on June
16, 1785, he began hatching plans to regain the Presidency and to keep
his name before the people until the governorship of the Bay State should
open up to him again.

In July, John Quincy Adams, inheriting his father's animosity,
wrote to his sister Abigail: "Mr. Hancock, being too infirm to act as
governor of Massachusetts, is chosen a member of Congress for the next
year and will probably take his rest in the President's seat next November. This is escaping Scylla to fall into Charybdis." [1] He underestimated the ability of the master politician to steer a safe course between
the treacherous shoals toward which popularity and ambition beckoned
him.

Gordon and Warren, as usual, read a Machiavellian meaning into the
rumor that Hancock was angling for the Congressional leadership.

"Mr. Hancock . . . is chosen one of our delegates," Gordon wrote
in August to John Adams, now minister to the Court of St. James's.
"Politicians conjecture he is laying out for the President's chair; that
there will be all the apparatus of his coming on and that, if chosen during absence, he will answer to appearances; but that, if not chosen, illness real or feigned will prevent it."

"H—— has got the gout," Warren wrote to Gerry in October. "Whether
it is a political or natural fit I don't know. If the former, he may have
some reason to despair of the Presidency and may wrap up in baize as a
preparatory to a resignation when the Court meets. If everybody loves
him as I do they would save him that trouble and excuse without the
expense of a single piece of baize."

319

On the same day Gordon confided to John Adams that he suspected Hancock of even deeper machinations in connection with his prospective return to the seat of national government. After charging him with favoritism while still in office through appointing Francis Dana to the superior court, ridding his lawyer friends of the able attorney's competition at the bar, the clerical politico continued: "Upon the same principle, should the aforementioned gentleman go to Congress . . . he would use all his interest in *favor* of you to keep you abroad, should he have hopes of getting again into the chair unless you should return." [2]

And so the speculation went on while the object of it remained calmly at home and confidently waited for the central governing body, currently sitting at New York, to put him at its head *in absentia*. Even though the election was scheduled to take place in November, he still was in Boston on October 25 and had not signified whether he would, or could, attend the session. That he was eager to do so if chosen President is indicated by Judge Sullivan, one of the most eminent exemplars of the legal profession in Massachusetts. Three years later Sullivan was to promote Hancock's candidacy for the Vice Presidency of the United States; but he seems to have been on friendly terms with the anti-Hancockonians as well, for he wrote to King, the Secretary of the Congress:

"Our friend Hancock has been very sick at his country seat. He came into town last evening. I called upon him. He will soon be better. He has not yet given his answer respecting going to Congress, but I believe he will go. I told him I thought he would be President if he went. He smiled and said that it would give him great pleasure to meet his old compatriots . . . and should be glad to serve his country . . . so far as his health would admit of. By the by, I think the President's chair the easiest in the Union for an invalid and told him so. You may expect him before you will have the representation of all the States." [3]

Although the judge was wrong in his last prediction, it was true that the Congress had trouble collecting a quorum. The majority of seven delegations required for selecting a President did not materialize until November 23. On that day Hancock, still nursing his gout in Boston, was chosen. His ability to reestablish himself by remote control is one of the most remarkable testimonials to his nation-wide repute.

· 2 ·

By mail, on the 30th, Hancock accepted the call to the post which he never was to occupy. Until the turn of the year, he was eager to serve again as titular head of the country; but his flesh was not as willing as his spirit. By January, 1786, it had become evident that his puffy legs were not equal to a journey even to New York, although he would have to use them only to get into and out of a carriage. When David Ramsay of South Carolina, who had been picked to act as chairman of the Congress until the elected incumbent should report, gave up the seat at the expiration of his term as delegate, the national legislature chose Gorham on May 15 to carry on with the same status and waited until June 6, the day after the still unsolicited resignation finally arrived, to install the interim President as the official one.

In the meantime political circles continued to buzz with the prospects. One might almost say that whenever Hancock turned over on his sickbed a bulletin was issued by sympathizers and adversaries alike.

In his letter of November 30 he had gratefully acknowledged notice of his election from King, expressing himself to that gentleman as being "exceedingly honored by its contents," and asserting that he hoped to leave for the Congress within ten or twelve days, when "I shall in person express my obligation to you." He could not, however, "think of residing at [New] York without Mrs. Hancock," for "I have scarcely yet recovered from a late very severe fit of the gout so as to have the free use of my hands." [4]

King replied just as graciously that he derived "very sincere pleasure" from Hancock's acceptance, and that he had made living arrangements for the presidential family: "The house is good and, although the furniture is not such as it should be, it will be within your direction, at the public charge, to make such dispositions and amendments as may be convenient. The servants, carriages, horses, etc., of the late President are retained and wait your coming. The carriage is very ordinary." [5]

Just why the two political opponents thus buttered up their correspondence is not clear. They may have hoped that some of the grease would drip upon the machinery of government, and Secretary King may have figured that if the President was comfortable in New York he would refrain from throwing a monkey-wrench among the wheels of the Bowdoin administration in Massachusetts.

Hancock's adherents, too, wished him on his way in letters written throughout the winter of 1785–1786. Among those especially interested in seeing him profit by the new opportunity were Henry Knox, Secretary of War and one of the most celebrated generals in the Revolution, and General Henry Jackson, his business agent. On December 12 Jackson informed his associate that their friend planned to set out within a week.[6]

But on January 2 Nathan Dane, Congressman from New York, communicated with Bowdoin on the absorbing subject of Hancock's intentions, evidently in an effort to confirm a rumor that he still was confined by illness.[7] From then until they were relieved of their anxiety the curious politicos contented themselves with watchful waiting.

And so the "image whose feet are of clay" kept all factions on tenterhooks for six months, during which his swollen legs might as well have been made of putty.

· 3 ·

Disappointed though he was at being unable to resume his place as nominal head of the nation, Hancock must have been thankful that he was not the responsible leader of his state during 1786. By the end of August, the economic cancer from which Massachusetts had been suffering was too far advanced to be arrested by palliatives.

Small property holders were losing their land through seizure for overdue debts and delinquent taxes, and faced the prospect of additional assessments so that the commonwealth might pay off its obligations over a period of fifteen years at the rate of $330,000 annually. The situation had not been ameliorated by imprisonment of debtors who had bought and mortgaged farms on the basis of continental currency but were being required to sell or amortize in terms of hard money, almost nonexistent in the western counties. These desperate men had been demanding relief through revision of the constitution but lacked property qualifications to effectuate their will by means of the ballot. So they decided to close up the courts by force and thus bring about a moratorium on indebtedness.

They rallied around Daniel Shays of Pelham, who had fought at Lexington, Bunker Hill, Ticonderoga, Saratoga, and Stony Point. Cited for bravery, he had been commissioned a captain in 1777. On August 29, with a few hundred untrained and inadequately equipped rebels, Shays intimidated the court at Northampton into suspending business. Courts at Taunton, Great Barrington, and Concord, yielded to similar pressure in the days following. Emboldened by this success, which the weak government headed by Bowdoin did nothing to prevent, Shays marched his pitiful little band to Springfield on September 26 and lined them up in front of the supreme court building. By this time the state had dispatched a contingent of militia under General William Shepard. Even now, however, through its military representative, it temporized and made a "compromise" with Shays whereby both sides agreed to disperse and the court to adjourn.

The bloodless insurrection continued as the General Court refrained from taking any firmer stand than to suspend the right of habeas corpus. Finally, on January 25, 1787, Shays led an attack upon the Springfield arsenal in the hope of capturing badly needed munitions. The effort proved abortive when communications with his first lieutenant, Luke Day, broke down. Four days later General Lincoln, with a greatly superior force of Massachusetts "regulars," routed Day's isolated command and offered to recommend for pardon all insurgents who would take an oath of allegiance to the state. They asked for an armistice, during which petitions for redress of grievances could be presented to the legislature, but obtained no satisfaction. The administration now was determined to crush the rebellion without further ado, and Lincoln did so in a blizzard on the night of February 2 by shattering Shays' main body at Petersham.

The leader of the revolt fled to Vermont, but several of his subordinates were imprisoned and sentenced to death. Their disposition became a major issue in the next gubernatorial campaign, and Hancock, back in the running, promised pardon for those convicted of treason if he should be elected. Largely on the strength of this offer, supplemented by pledges of reformation along the lines desired by the rebels, he climbed back into the governor's seat. He deserves credit for making good on all counts and for rectifying inequities which, although perhaps not justifying a resort to arms, had warranted drastic measures to arouse Bowdoin's government from its timorous lethargy.

Long before the outbreak was quelled, there had been a clamorous demand that Hancock be reinstalled in the governorship. His strategic withdrawal two years earlier to saddle upon his successor the blame for the economic anarchy had worked out perfectly. Bowdoin did not even receive recognition for his eventual firm stand against the insurrectionists or the improvement in conditions that followed. He had acted too late to win his campaign for reelection.

So, on April 2, the former governor surged back into power with the momentum of the mass movement that had reached its violent climax during the preceding summer, and the impetus of his own reform drive. The 18,000 votes for Hancock against 6,000 for Bowdoin represented partly protest and partly renewed faith in the liberal principles of a man whom the populace still loved.

In the meantime Hancock had received a blow which put him in greater need of affection than ever before. On January 27 he had lost his nine-year-old son. Having just turned fifty, he now was doomed to die without any descendants to carry on the name of which he was justly proud.

John George Washington Hancock, walking with his father and another man in Milton, Massachusetts, spied a pair of skates in a store window, and asked for them. When Hancock senior refused the companion gratified the boy's wish. Tempted by an icy sidewalk, young John tried out his steel blades immediately and fell on his head. The accident proved fatal.

The funeral took place in Boston, and the *Independent Chronicle* of February 1, recorded that "the corpse was carried in Mr. Hancock's own coach" and the "worthy gentleman and his amiable lady, in great affliction, followed in another coach." In an editorial it stated:

"We are certain that Mr. H. wished to avoid . . . the too common parade at funerals; yet a number of his friends . . . attended with their own carriages. This honorable gentleman hath set an example, in his strict observance of the regulations of the town respecting funerals, which we wish may be followed by every class of people. . . . He hath guarded against every unnecessary expense . . . in the article of mourning, by which many families . . . have been greatly injured. . . . It is to be hoped, therefore, that . . . a gentleman who hath filled the highest places in government with dignity and who now stands high in the esteem of his fellow-citizens will have a prevailing influence." [8]

Hancock could curb his desire for display at a time when political wisdom dictated economy to avoid giving offense to the financially distressed—even though the ceremony in honor of his son's memory had to be the occasion for the retrenchment. That he was deeply grieved by the loss, however, is indicated in his pathetic letter of March 14 to General Knox:

"The obtainment of health is now my pursuit. Journeying is much recommended to me; and, as my situation is totally deranged by the untimely death of my dear and promising boy, I have no affectionate object to promise myself the enjoyment of what I leave. I . . . am now only waiting the roads to be good to set out with Mrs. Hancock . . . to New York and Philadelphia."

Mingling with his erstwhile Congressional associates in the stimulating atmosphere of New York, the new capital of the country, also was calculated to be salubrious—and so was a chance to splurge in the old way, out of sight of the home folks:

"I take the liberty, my friend, to request of you . . . to engage such lodgings in an airy place as . . . will be suitable for Mrs. Hancock and myself and three servants. I wish for a decent parlor or two parlors; an handsome, well-furnished chamber for us, and decent rooms for my servants, for they lodge and eat at home as well as I do myself." [9]

King, informing Gerry on the 25th of their adversary's request to Knox, inquired suspiciously: "What is the meaning of this movement?" [10]

Whether the proposed trip came off is not revealed in the annals. But on April 14 the reinstalled governor thanked the Secretary of War for attending to the accommodations and said he expected to set out within a few days.

Whatever Hancock may have done for the "obtainment of health," his ailments probably would have been complicated by shock if he could have peered over Warren's shoulder on May 18 as that once relentless antagonist wrote to John Adams. Warren, like Sam Adams on one occasion, admitted that he had changed his mind—although the effort apparently had pained him considerably—about the unspeakable resident of Beacon Hill:

"Mr. H. is undoubtedly chose the first magistrate. I do not regret the change so much as I once should, though I am sorry for it. If I used to despise the administration of H., I am disappointed in that of B." [11]

Almost immediately after his second inauguration the governor fulfilled the main part of his campaign vow to have the Shays insurgents pardoned. On June 1 he induced the General Court to nullify all penalties and citizenship disqualifications to which the rank and file were liable. The amnesty did not apply at first to the ringleaders; but they, too, were restored to good standing within a year by repeal of the law under which they had been arrested.

This exoneration of a few hotheads, however, was the lesser of Hancock's contributions to the cause of human rights. Through his influence with the Assembly he obtained legislation which set a precedent for national laws that eliminated one of the grossest injustices suffered by the poor and downtrodden. He put through a bill providing that no person's clothing, household goods, or tools of trade should be seized as security for debt—although imprisoned debtors would have to take a pauper's oath to gain freedom.

Even before his election was assured he had enhanced his popularity by advocating that the governor's salary be reduced from £1,100 to £800. A statute to that effect had been enacted in March and had been put into force when he took office. He had intended that this self-invited slash— an almost unheard-of sacrifice for a politician to make—should be a temporary measure for the advertised purpose of encouraging economy among the people as a whole. But when he tried to have the stipend reestablished on the original level at the start of his next term the legislature refused to loosen the purse strings.

As usual, the governor's enemies attributed his startling altruism entirely to sordid motives. John Quincy Adams, in a letter to his father, interpreted it not only as a bid for votes but as a design to lay the governorship on the auction block:

"The salaries of all civil officers, which are now too small, will . . . be reduced still lower. Mr. Hancock, who has a peculiar talent of pleasing the multitude, has compounded this matter by offering to make a present to the public of £300. But I consider this as a pernicious precedent. . . . For if one man gives up £300 another, fishing equally for popularity, may give more, and the chair of government may finally be offered to the lowest bidder." [12]

Although the renunciation probably was not completely disinterested, it could not have been as venal as Adams contended. Such a preeminent politician would not have had to undersell his competitors.

· 5 ·

Governor Hancock now was about to undertake one of the biggest and most important selling campaigns in the history of America, after being first "sold" on the proposition himself. He was to win over to the Constitution of the United States the Massachusetts ratifying convention and, indirectly, the nation.

The movement for a governmental instrument that would bind together the thirteen loosely federated states, still intensely individualistic under the Articles of Confederation, had been initiated during the summer of 1786, when delegates from eight of them met at Annapolis, Maryland, to discuss their common problems. But they disbanded after wrangling for months without even an approximation of unanimity. Finally, on May 14, 1787, representatives from all the provinces convened in Independence Hall at Philadelphia and hammered out a new frame of government which reasonably reconciled the numerous conflicting interests. After affixing their signatures on September 17 they forwarded it to the Congress, which dispatched copies to the various legislatures for acceptance or rejection.

At the first session of the Massachusetts Assembly under his second administration Hancock ordered Secretary Avery to lay "this momentous affair" before the legislators, and made a noncommittal speech calling attention to the "truly respectable" characters of the framers.[13] It was then decided to have the commonwealth act upon the great charter at a convention to open at Boston on January 9, 1788.

Under the cold analysis to which the proposed Constitution was subjected during this conclave the factions that had been gradually splitting the conservative element of the old Whig party for a decade crystallized, in the main, into full-fledged Federalists and Antifederalists. The Bowdoinites, who naturally favored any medium through which the national government might be made strong enough to effectuate their reactionary principles, threw their support solidly behind ratification. This group, composed chiefly of men of money and property, was influenced more by selfish interests than by objective political convictions. The wealthy—and therefore most powerful—classes throughout the country accounted for the success of the Constitutional movement. Those with fewer material possessions at stake, including the irresponsible masses, opposed it. Both classifications, of course, embraced many persons who were actuated by desire for the welfare of the nation.

Although the members of the Adams-Warren-Gerry coterie were no more idealistic, on the whole, than the ratificationists, they parted company with Bowdoin and his followers to form the opposition in Massachusetts. In spite of their sympathy with the social and economic policies of the Bowdoinites, as contrasted with the Hancock theories and the vested interests of some, they were against centralization of power lest it should curb the liberties of the people. Being, for the most part, extreme individualists, they also were swayed by considerations of personal prestige and freedom of political action, which they feared would be curtailed by concentration of authority.

Hancock, as usual, seems to have assumed a noncommittal attitude at first, although Judge Sullivan insists that he was in favor of the Constitution from the start, with reservations. Possessing the most extensive real estate holdings in the commonwealth, the governor had good reason for siding with the Federalists on this issue. But, although he finally went along with them to the extent of giving his invaluable approval to ratification, he remained a firm believer in states' rights.

Greatly outnumbered by their opponents, the Federalists realized that they would have to win over a large percentage of them, by agreeing to projected amendments such as the governor had in mind. And what more effective means could there be, they argued, than to steer the most popular and influential man in Massachusetts to the chair of the convention? So Theophilus Parsons, who will be recalled as the boss of the Bowdoinites, went to work.

But Hancock, one of the Boston delegates along with Bowdoin, Adams, Sullivan, and Higginson, proved to be coy as usual. He came down with a timely attack of gout as the opening day for the constitutional deliberations approached. He was accused of waiting to see in which direction the sentiment of the populace was inclined so that he could be sure of heading that way. He also was charged with procrastinating in anticipation of an offer from the Federalists to back him for the Presidency of the Union in return for his support of their cause.

Thomas C. Amory quotes Judge Sullivan, who was Hancock's closest adviser throughout the ratification proceedings, as giving the lie to these imputations:

" 'When the plan was offered . . . for consideration it was realized that the part which Governor Hancock should take would decide the fate of the important business as to this state. He had objections to the system . . . but he considered a general government to be the salvation of his country . . . therefore, *before* the convention was assembled he prepared his proposals for amendments and resolved to give the constitution his decided support.' "

Even Amory, however, admits that Parsons may have drafted the modifying addenda, and that the copy read by Hancock before the assemblage may have been in Sullivan's handwriting.[14]

The governor had no need for haste, except to appear on the 9th for election as chairman. The rest of the two hundred eighty representatives required more than a week to find a suitable meeting place. Dr. Jeremy Belknap, minister-secretary of the convention, renders a day-by-day account of this farcical procedure in his minutes. The opening session was at the Statehouse, as originally planned; on the 10th the assemblage repaired to the Brattle Street Church (where the Hancock family had owned a pew for more than a century); this was too large for adequate audibility, and on the 12th the delegates returned to the original location. Finding it too crowded, they appointed a committee on the 15th to solve the problem, and finally, on the 17th, settled down in Dr. Belknap's house of worship in the part of Long Lane that was to become Federal Street.

· 6 ·

Even after the place of the convention had been agreed upon Hancock stayed away—whether by choice or by compulsion is not definitely known. His enemies, of course, accused him of feigning illness in order to avoid a commitment on the Constitution: "Hancock is still confined or, rather, he has not yet taken his seat; as soon as the majority is exhibited on either side I think his health will suffice him to be abroad." [15]

Some time between the 20th and the end of the month the Federalists succeeded in persuading the allegedly vacillating governor to sponsor their views. There are differing versions of the means employed.

James T. Austin, a contemporary and prejudiced commentator, states that they played on Hancock's vanity by presenting to him a series of amendments which not only would overcome the objections of the Anti-federalists but could be attached to the confirmation measure as recommendations to the national delegates, with an excellent chance that the immense influence of Massachusetts would secure their incorporation in the federal instrument: "They tendered to His Excellency the honor of proposing them in Convention. The reputation of having devised this middle course, the credit of announcing it, the imperishable glory of its success, they had deemed it respectful to offer to him, that to the fame of having given his official sanction to the declaration of his country's independence might be added that of securing for it a permanent constitution of government."

Another measure to gain Hancock's acquiescence possibly was a political deal guaranteeing him support in the imminent gubernatorial campaign, and in the first Presidential contest under the Constitution a year hence. Three days after a speech by the governor in behalf of affirmative action, accompanied by the suggested reservations, King confided to General Knox: "Hancock will hereafter receive the universal support of Bowdoin's friends; and we tell him that if Virginia does not unite [on Washington], which is problematical, . . . he is considered the only fair candidate for President."

Whatever the inducement, "the charm was irresistible," according to Austin. "Wrapped in his flannels, Hancock . . . took the chair of the Convention, and a scene ensued more in the character of a dramatic presentation than of that serious and important business. . . . In a speech, wise and plausible enough in itself but sufficiently ludicrous to those behind the scenes, the governor . . . announced the anxiety of his mind, his doubts, his wishes, his conciliatory plans." [16]

Colonel Joseph May—who had married Mrs. Hancock's niece Dorothy Sewell—described the episode of the 31st more vividly in his journal, quoted by Wells:

"So when the day arrived Mr. Hancock was helped out of his house into his coach and driven down to the place where the convention was held . . . and thence carried into the convention by several young gentlemen who were friends of the family and in the secret. He rose in his place and apologized for his absence, for his feebleness. . . . He hoped they would pardon him for *reading* a speech which he had carefully prepared, not being well enough to make it in any other manner. Then he read the speech which Parsons had written for him, and from Parsons' manuscript, and sat down. One of his friends took the manuscript from him, afraid that the looker-on might see that it was not in Hancock's hand."

Wells asserts that May, in the capacity of administrator of the Hancock estate, found the original draft, in the handwriting of the Federalist boss, among the private papers of the deceased.[17] It is no longer there, so far as thorough research has been able to determine.

It is not necessary to rely on secondhand sources for the context of Governor Hancock's oration, which unquestionably was one of the most momentous in American annals, regardless of its authorship. Summarized in the third person, in the *Debates and Proceedings* of the Convention it loses force and sounds tentative—almost neutral. But it brings out clearly that the speaker had conferred with the Antifederalists and probably with the Federalists. In the official paraphrase, Hancock said:

"His situation . . . had not permitted him to enter into the debates of this Convention. It, however, appeared to him necessary, from what had been advanced in them, to adopt the form of government proposed; but, observing the diversity of sentiment in the gentlemen of the Convention, he had frequently had conversation with them on the subject; and . . . he was induced to propose to them whether the introduction of some general amendments would not be attended with the happiest consequences. For that purpose he should . . . submit . . . a proposition in order to remove the doubts and quiet the apprehensions of these gentlemen." [18]

Thereupon, he read the nine proposed amendments—lumped together by historians as the celebrated Conciliatory Proposition—which made possible the establishment of the Constitution and the creation of the Union. The gist of it—recognizable in the wording of the Bill of Rights appended to the immortal document—was that all powers not expressly delegated by the Constitution should be reserved to the several states; that indictment by a grand jury should precede trial for a capital offense; that all civil actions between citizens of different states should be tried by a jury at the request of either party, and that no person holding federal office should accept a title from a foreign power.

· 7 ·

The reaction of Sam Adams, one of the most confirmed opponents of ratification, was enigmatic. As soon as Hancock sat down Adams jumped up and moved that the proposition be taken under consideration. Yet on February 6, the balloting day, he introduced some amendments of his own concerning freedom of conscience and the press, the right to possess firearms, protection of persons and property from seizure, which caused so much consternation, even in his own party, that he withdrew them. Belknap suspected him of a sinister design to wreck the entire constitutional movement by stirring up again the factional differences that had been reconciled by such judicious compromise. In his confidential correspondence the secretary wrote that Adams "almost overset the apple-cart," that it was feared "this maneuver lost the Constitution several votes," and that some of the delegates thought "his intention was to overset the whole." [19]

On the 2nd the ratifying motion had been referred to a committee with instructions to make whatever changes were deemed advisable, but had been reported back to the convention essentially unaltered. It was carried by a majority of only 187 to 168 votes; but that small margin of 19 was a tremendous testimonial to Hancock's amazing power of persuasion.

In a penetrating study of this whole episode George H. Haynes, although generally unsympathetic, admits by implication that the service which the governor rendered to his country at the convention was inestimable: "Great doors often turn upon small hinges. But for our Convention's adoption of that 'Conciliatory Proposition,' it would seem that the [nation-wide] ratification of the Constitution would have been impossible. The only alternative, so Washington declared, would have been 'a recurrence to an unqualified state of anarchy.'" [20]

George Bancroft, the historian, unreservedly approves of Hancock's handling of a profoundly difficult situation. Maintaining that he favored ratification from the start, Bancroft writes that his "conduct . . . in support of the Constitution was, from beginning to end, consistent and so wise that the after-thought of the most skilful caviller cannot point out where it can be improved." [21]

Samuel B. Harding, another writer on Massachusetts' much mooted part in the establishment of the Constitution, brands as "a deliberate attempt to falsify the facts" [22] Judge Sullivan's insistence that Hancock originated the proposed amendments and made up his mind to work for approval of the basic document, with those modifications, prior to the opening of the convention. This contention is defensible, for Sullivan was biased. But King, Austin, and the others who accused the governor of playing politics also were actuated by partisanship.

The truth, as usual, probably lies somewhere between. That Hancock was swayed somewhat by ulterior motives is quite likely; but that he would forward his own interests at the expense of his country is unthinkable. That the Conciliatory Proposition was not entirely the product of his brain also is a sound conclusion, for great ideas seldom are conceived by one person. That he did not even write the tide-turning speech is a strong possibility, because phrasing a public paper and the mere mechanical manipulation of a pen would have cost him considerable effort at a period when he was chronically subject to genuine physical pain, although he sometimes exaggerated its intensity for a purpose. And that he had not formed a definite conviction as to whether the Constitution should be ratified, before wisely studying the opinions of more analytical statesmen, is logical.

How Hancock reached his vital decision, and how he impressed his will upon the convention, are academic questions so far as the development of America is concerned. Discussion of them is justified only as a means of probing into his character. The all-important fact is that he *did* assure national ratification of the instrument which welded together a group of independent-minded, self-sufficient, and mutually antagonistic principalities into a union that was to become one of the wonders of the world. But for the recommended amendments which made the Constitution acceptable to the eight additional states whose assent was required to render it effective, Massachusetts would have rejected it. And if the great commonwealth had spurned it there would have been no chance of bringing the United States into being through the clinching approval of New Hampshire on June 21—or within the foreseeable future.

This achievement put Hancock in the select company of American patriots—Washington, John Adams, Jefferson, Hamilton, Franklin, and a few others—who served their country as well in post-Revolutionary peace as before and during the struggle for independence. Many of the ablest actors faded into the background at the close of the conflict which had called forth their best talents for the founding of the United States. They had little or nothing to contribute to the equally important establishment of the nation on a sure and lasting foundation. Sam Adams, perhaps the most effective all-around performer during the prologue of the drama; Patrick Henry, the most eloquent inspirational character; and Tom Paine, the most persuasive pamphleteer—all passed into comparative obscurity. They could not adapt themselves to change. But Hancock, like the rest of the great cast who carried on at a high level of excellence until death rang down the curtain, played his part up to the hilt until he made his exit.

· 8 ·

The Massachusetts Federalists paid a heavy penalty for entering into a compact with the devil of Beacon Hill. Although willing to make common cause with them for the sake of preserving his country from dissolution, Hancock was no more in sympathy with their fundamental principles now than he ever had been, and he had no more intention of allying himself with them in state politics than with the Antifederalists. He was in accord with the latter on limitation of the federal power, but he still could not take Warren or Gerry to his bosom.

The effect of the Constitutional convention within the commonwealth was to render the Hancock forces immeasurably stronger and their adversaries proportionately weaker; for the people knew that the original pro-ratification party owed its success in setting up a central government to Hancock's cooperation. Besides, the Federalist whips felt constrained—probably by fear of retaliation if they should fail in their agreement to support the governor—to lash their wheelhorses into line in front of his bandwagon.

The election of April 7 was a landslide for Hancock. His previous triumphs were minor by comparison with this. He was elected virtually by acclamation, for he polled 17,841 votes out of a possible total of 22,157. Bowdoin ran against him, but only for the sake of appearances. So did Gerry, as the representative of the Antifederalists.

General Lincoln, capitalizing on his reputation as crusher of Shays' Rebellion, salvaged the lieutenant governorship for the Federalists, most of whom did not feel obligated to turn apostate beyond the extent of their personal pledge to Hancock. But Lincoln probably would not have won if Cushing had been alive. The governor's loyal henchman had passed on early in the spring; and Sam Adams, presumably with the consent of the all-powerful leader of the party, had leaped into the breach as a substitute. To get a decision over even this makeshift rival the conservative party had to rely, in default of a popular majority, on the like-minded Senate. As in the case of the gubernatorial contest, the Anti-federalists, with Warren carrying the torch, ran last.

Hancock, by accepting such a once formidable foe as Adams for a running mate, displayed supreme confidence in the impregnability of his position. The rupture in their friendship was gradually healing, anyway, as Adams recognized that the governor's political beliefs were not so divergent as they had seemed to be during his first administration and were more in harmony than the Bowdoin-Parsons system with his own governmental philosophy. Besides, the old Whig had to admit that Massachusetts was prospering under its present chief magistrate—a consideration which outweighed all others in the eyes of this really devoted public servant.

Economic conditions had been improving rapidly ever since the suppression of the insurrection at the beginning of 1787. Renewed respect for law and a restored sense of security had started the state on the road to recovery from its wartime disorganization. The pace of its recuperation was quickened by the prospect of a stable federal government. Backbreaking taxes were lightened in anticipation of reimbursement for advances made to the Congress during the years close after the Revolution. Veterans of the great struggle received long overdue pay, with interest, in sound currency. The credit of the commonwealth consequently improved, and trade picked up. Boston's population, which had shrunk to less than 10,000 during the decade 1770–1780 because of bad times and the wholesale migration of Loyalists, was now nearly double that figure. Not only the capital but the entire Bay State was bursting with optimism.

Hancock, of course, was the chief beneficiary of the upturn. Although not directly responsible for it, he had helped incalculably to bring it about by smoothing the way for an authoritative and dependable national governing body. He was justified in expecting a more tangible reward than the adoration of the populace, to which he was so accustomed that it must have lost some of its savor.

The prize which he had in mind was the Presidency; but, realizing that Washington had an almost preemptive right to it, he was prepared to settle for the Vice Presidency. Friendly newspapers throughout New England had started to boom him for the second highest office in the

HANCOCK MANSION IN 1789. FROM AN ENGRAVING IN THE BOSTONIAN SOCIETY COLLECTION.

nation as early as February—long before the Congress had the authority to decree that the choice of electors should be made in January, 1789, and that the election should be held a month later. The *New Hampshire Gazette*, published in a state where the Massachusetts candidate was better known than in any other except his own, had confidently predicted: "Should the new Constitution be adopted, General Washington will undoubtedly be President and Governor Hancock Vice-President of the Union." [23]

By July the drive was gaining fast both in momentum and in extent. A Philadelphia backer wrote on the 2nd: "We drink some excellent wine to Massachusetts patriots. Hancock is the deity for Vice-President." The Bay State press, of course, was climbing on the band wagon enthusiastically. One journal blew the horn to the effect that "the two spoken of generally in Massachusetts for Vice-President" were "His Excellency, our worthy Governor, and Hon. John Adams." Another tooted cockily: "Undoubtedly Hancock for Vice-President and Adams for Chief Justice Federal Judiciary." [24]

· 9 ·

John Adams himself, who returned from England in time to take part in the campaign, analyzed the interplay of political forces more dispassionately from the vantage point of nearly nineteen years after the event. His exposition, in a letter to Mercy Warren answering derogatory statements she had made about him in her history of the Revolution, probably is as accurate as any that could be obtained from one of the participants, partisan as they were:

"Mr. Hancock was ambitious of being President or Vice-President. I stood in the way. Hamilton was afraid of me; and General Knox, over whom Hamilton at that time had great influence, came to Boston with a view of promoting Hancock to the Vice-Presidency. . . . Knox, however, . . . found he was upon a wrong scent and that Mr. Hancock could not be carried; and, indeed, he . . . decided in my favor, though he had previously gone so far with Mr. Hancock . . . that he was under embarrassment about declaring it openly. . . . From this time some of Mr. Hancock's intimates began to insinuate, in secret whispers, prejudices and calumnies against me."

Disclosing that the former hand-in-glove Whig triumvirate had broken up, with Warren shaking a clenched fist at the Adamses, he went on: "Samuel Adams . . . told me that General Warren had said that

'John Adams had been corrupted by his residence in England.' Astonished as I was, I said nothing. But I remembered a letter from General Warren . . . in which he said, 'Samuel Adams has become, contrary to all his former principles and professions, the most arbitrary man in the State.'" [25]

When the younger Adams arrived from London on July 19 Hancock gave him an unctuous welcome. This would have been virtually incumbent upon him as governor; but he probably reasoned, anyway, that there was no sense in aggravating old wounds at a time when he needed tolerance from his enemies as well as good will from his friends. In any case, the minister to the Court of St. James's, according to a press report, "was met by the Secretary of State in the Governor's carriage and rode to his house, the streets filled with thousands. He remained at the Governor's and there received the congratulations of the Lieutenant-Governor and the Council." [26]

Three weeks after this ceremony Governor Hancock embarked upon an electioneering tour of New England. He did not take the stump directly but made sure that he was seen as guest of honor at dinners, reviewer of troops, and leader of parades. Probably referring to this junket, Higginson ("Laco") maintained that the seemingly spontaneous tributes were solicited and prearranged:

"We all have heard of his very whimsical conduct when the Roxbury horse . . . was to be reviewed . . . and almost every one recollects the various freaks that marked his conduct as to the review at Braintree. The county of Essex will not soon forget his pompous entrance and passage through their towns and the previous pains which were taken, by circulating letters and by active messengers, to notify his coming and to solicit attention." [27]

Accompanied by Dolly, Hancock first visited Portsmouth, the capital of his political stronghold in New Hampshire. The *Independent Chronicle*, reporting his arrival on August 12, stated, "The patriotism which this worthy character has ever discovered . . . and the great sacrifices he has made . . . call for the love of every virtuous American." His departure on the 17th was recorded by the *New Hampshire Gazette* with even more outspoken propaganda for his Vice Presidential candidacy: "This illustrious patriot . . . appears to be selected . . . for the second seat in the new federal government. . . . He was escorted as far as Greenland by His Excellency President [Governor] Langdon and lady, by the consul of France and others; and Colonel [Joshua] Wentworth, with his elegant independent company of light horse." [28]

On the following day Hancock stopped over at Newburyport, where John Quincy Adams was visiting, and that unsympathetic observer recorded in his diary: "This morning I perceived a deal of stirring in the streets and was finally informed that the Governor was reviewing the troops of this town; after which a number of officers and other gentlemen escorted His Excellency to Haverhill, where he intends to dine; and then, I suppose, he means to show himself somewhere else." [29] Before returning to Boston on the 19th he showed himself, to similarly good advantage, at Salem and Marblehead.

This vote-seeking jaunt was summarized more caustically by Christopher Gore, brother of Charles and an equally stanch Federalist, in a letter of the 31st to the speaker of the Massachusetts House:

"I . . . should be greatly rejoiced at an assurance that the whimsical creature could attain no honorable place in this world, though I am perfectly resigned to his being transformed to a saint within twenty-four hours. . . . He went to Portsmouth, where he was be-dusted with all the honors of New Hampshire; but I found . . . that the sober part of the community were desirous that John Adams should be the Vice-President. . . . The other character acts with such increasing capriciousness that every man of reason and virtue is afraid of him. He is intending a journey in the ensuing week to Providence—probably from thence will go to Connecticut,—and I think . . . his flatterers have persuaded him of his election as President being more probable than Washington's. He declares publicly that he will not give Lincoln the command of the Castle—and by every means in his power attempts to mortify him." [30]

Behind Gore's reference to Lincoln lies a story of vindictiveness which illustrates how ruthless Hancock could be when a political antagonist stood in his way. Because the lieutenant governor was grossly underpaid it had been customary for the governor to hand him a sinecure in the form of the captaincy of the Castle, which carried an annual emolument of $1,000. Hancock may have picked the quarrel with Revere in 1779 to squeeze this plum out of his possession in anticipation of giving it to Cushing, who enjoyed it until his death. After the 1788 election Lincoln naturally had expected to get a taste of it, but Hancock had put it on ice with the explanation that he was thereby preserving for the commonwealth the money which it represented.

In this case, however, the man who usually was so scrupulous about staying within the limits of his authority had overstepped them, even in the opinion of an ordinarily rubber-stamp legislature. Although he did manage to quash a House resolution of the following February designed to unfreeze the Castle appointment, he eventually had to compromise by agreeing to fill the vacancy on the basis of a $533 fee. But by that time Lincoln was out of office; so Sam Adams, his successor, received the gift as one of the fruits of victory.

· 10 ·

Although negligible in itself, this controversy over the appointment revealed the almost autocratic nature of the Hancock regime. The outcome convinced the Federalists that they had lost their rear-guard action to retain a vestige of power through the lieutenant governorship: if Hancock could deprive their only remaining active standard bearer of a political perquisite established by long precedent, he could wipe out all opposition when the next test of strength should come in 1789, and he could rule Massachusetts for as many years as were left to him.

The governor had proved that he could overthrow any human adversary in a legislative chamber; but disease laid him low. He still was racked by gout, which was becoming constantly worse. But for its depredations and the resulting protracted confinement to his bedchamber, he might have beaten John Adams for the Vice Presidency. At least, he would have put up a stout fight for it.

As the 1788 campaign advanced into its critical stage Hancock must have sensed the hopelessness of his cause. But he tried to keep himself in the public eye through the social media which showed him off to best advantage. In September he was the cynosure of several elaborate affairs given by and for the officers of the French squadron then moored in Boston Harbor. Throughout the month he vied with Marquis de Sainneville, commandant of the fleet, for the distinction of being the perfect—and the more pretentious—host. On one occasion he competed for the accolade of America's Revolutionary ally with his arch rival in politics—John Adams—and such other uncongenial fellow guests as Bowdoin and Lincoln; but he managed to draw the major share of homage. In the government yacht on the way to and from the marquis' flagship he was saluted by the loudest bursts of cannon fire and the most vociferous cheers. A week later, after entertaining the Frenchmen at his mansion, he stole the show again by having himself driven, *in advance* of the departing visitors, to Long Wharf and leading the large crowd assembled there in three huzzas for the foreign notables as they passed between the ranks of the revived Independent Corps of Cadets to a waiting barge. This demonstration, of course, elicited one in return for the first citizen.[31]

But the publicity accruing to Hancock from these spectacles was too local to be of much assistance to his candidacy outside the state. That he was losing ground elsewhere—mainly because of his gout-enforced immobility—is indicated in Dr. Rush's letter of October 7 to Belknap: "Mr. John Adams will probably have all the votes of our State for the Vice-President's chair. Mr. Hancock['s] frequent indispositions *alone* will preclude him from that mark of respect from Pennsylvania." [32]

By the turn of the year even his once ardent adherents were giving up; and General Jackson confided on January 11 to General Knox: "People talk pretty loud and open that Mr. J. A. must and will be the man for V. Don't let this come from me—but you may be assured the other person will stand no chance. If it was merely his want of health it would be sufficient. He has not been out of his chamber more than once since you left here and is now confined to his bed with the gout."

On February 1, a few days before the election, Jackson sent to his business associate a medical communiqué which implied quite plainly that their favorite white hope was doomed to defeat: "Governor Hancock remains very sick and, I believe, will continue so until the General Government is set in motion." [33]

The returns of the balloting, counted on April 6, were not conducive to alleviation of Hancock's pain. Although the unanimous choice of Washington for President could not have surprised him greatly, his own failure to run better than fifth among eleven candidates for Vice President—with four votes * out of the sixty-nine cast—must have dismayed him. He probably was already reconciled to the election of Adams; but it must have galled him to receive not a single vote from the Massachusetts electors. He must have been particularly bitter against the Federalists, who were adequately represented in the Electoral College, for breaking their glib promises to support him in the Presidential race.

· 11 ·

The humiliated also-ran subordinated his feelings to the extent of writing Washington a note of congratulation, as is indicated by an acknowledgment from the new Chief of State nine days after his inauguration at New York, where the first Congress of the United States had gone

* Two from Pennsylvania, one each from South Carolina and Virginia.

into session on March 4.[34] But there is evidence—although questionable —that Hancock's wounded pride could not endure exposure to the patronizing pity of his enemies or participation in a public tribute to the head of the national government.

The occasion was the annual election of officers by the Ancient and Honorable Artillery Company—a ceremony which Thomas Hancock had built up into one of the most important on the Boston social calendar by entertaining the governor, Council, and other provincial dignitaries at the mansion after the military exercises on the Common. What occurred on June 1, 1789, is maliciously related by Belknap:

"Washington's picture was exhibited and his praises sung in Faneuil Hall with great ardor and sincerity. The most extravagant part of the story is that Governor H. had a *convenient* fit of the gout and could not appear on the common. . . . However, Lincoln proved himself an *older* general by insisting on a personal interview and actually entering the bedchamber, where the ceremonies were performed under the inspection of the physician and nurse. Much risibility was thereby occasioned among those who know the *real* character of the popular idol." [35]

These insinuations that the governor again was faking illness to avoid the necessity of lauding Washington and cooperating with Lincoln in the traditional ritual may have been unfair to the invalid of Beacon Hill. But it does seem as though he could have dragged himself out of bed as far as the parade ground across the street if he had been so minded. He at least is subject to suspicion, on the theory of the wolf-wolf cry, that his oft repeated plaint struck a false note in this instance.

Hancock had been well enough a few weeks previously to take part in the fanfare connected with the inauguration of his ninth term as governor. He had bowled over the impotent opposition of Bowdoin and had pulled Sam Adams, with whom he now was completely reconciled, along with him at the expense of Lincoln in the contest for the lieutenant governorship. The two old feudists had symbolized their rapprochement by taking their oaths of office clad in almost identical suits of American manufacture—broadcloth with silver buttons—for the purpose of encouraging home industry.

There was no fight left in the Federalists. Some of them not only had laid down their arms but were deriving masochistic pleasure from the utter collapse of their party in the place of its origin. Charles Gore wrote to King: "Our elections are settled and generally to my satisfaction. That Mr. Hancock is chief magistrate will at least tend to the peace of Massachusetts as much as though his rival has [sic] been successful." [36]

Hancock was truly master of all he surveyed from his elevated mansion—a view thus fulsomely described in the July issue of the *Massachusetts Magazine:*

"From the summer-house opens a capital prospect—West Boston and the northern part of the town—Charlestown—Cambridge—the Colleges —the bridges over Charles and Mystic rivers. . . . The south and west views are not less enchanting, as they take in Roxbury and the famous heights of Dorchester. . . . The cultivated highlands of Brooklyne and the rugged blue hills of Milton and Braintree . . . also are thrown upon the eye, together with innumerable farmhouses—cultivated villas—verdant fields—smiling hills, and laughing vales. . . . Upon the east those various islands which are interspersed in the harbor, from Castle William to the lighthouse, engage the sight by turns. . . . In a word, . . . this seat is scarcely surpassed by any in the Union." [37]

But, in spite of the resplendent sight that delighted his eyes, there was darkness in the governor's soul. He was virtually the undisputed ruler of a great state—but not of the greater United States. Yet he could console himself with the thought that it might be possible to fool the people into believing he was Washington's superior—in fact, though not in name—when the imminent showdown should come.

℘ XVI ℘

FIRST AND LAST BOWS

𝒜LTHOUGH ELECTED unanimously and regarded universally with affection as the father of his country, President Washington had reason to believe that not all his political children would submit readily to his authority. The young nation still suffered from severe growing pains. They were especially acute in New England, which had been the first section to give concrete expression to the movement for independence from Great Britain and was to be the last—because of the bitter-end stand of Rhode Island against ratification until the spring of 1790—to yield to genuine unification into the United States of America.

The new Chief Executive realized that the birthplace of the Whigs and the stronghold of their spiritual successors, the Antifederalists, would not willingly disavow the idea of state sovereignty and could not easily adapt itself to a strong central government. He was fully cognizant of the narrow margin by which the Constitution had escaped rejection in Massachusetts—and throughout the land. He was keenly aware of the jealous regard the Bay State felt for its rights and of the reluctance with which it had surrendered only enough of them to make the Union possible, under pressure of the master mediator, Hancock.

So when the Congress adjourned on September 29, 1789, to January 1, Washington decided to tour the least amenable part of the country in an effort to dispel doubt of his intentions, to gain support for his policies, and to win—compel, if need be—loyalty to his administration. To overcome fears that he had royal aspirations, persisting despite his stern rebuke of those who would have made him king, he set out from New York on October 15 with only two secretaries. His ultimate destination was Portsmouth; but the focal point of his journey, of course, was Boston. And the man who ruled regally in the capital of Massachusetts was determined that the head of the nation should not carry his democratic no-tions to extremes in the great commonwealth, lest they should reflect upon his own knowledge of punctilio. Along the line through New Haven and Hartford the President acquired six servants assigned by the governor. At Springfield he was met by military and civilian welcoming parties also furnished by Hancock.

Meanwhile the town of Boston had appointed a committee of selectmen and other prominent citizens to formulate plans for the reception of Washington—without consulting the chief executive of the state. Both the municipality and the governor had sent envoys to greet the President at the state line and announce the ceremonies arranged for his entrance into the capital. The civic deputation arrived first and apprised him of the lodgings provided for him at a public house. But the emissary from the Statehouse delivered a letter outlining a different program and inviting him to put up at the Beacon Hill mansion:

"I have . . . issued orders for proper escorts to attend you, and Colonel Hall, deputy adjutant-general, will wait upon you at Worcester and will inform you of the disposition I have made of the troops at Cambridge; . . . and request that you . . . would pass that way to the town, where you will receive such other tokens of respect from the people as will serve further to evince how gratefully they recollect your exertions for their liberties and their confidence in you as President of the United States of America."

Washington's reply, covering a presumable conviction that political capital was being made out of his visit, doubtless contributed to the chilly relations between the two proud patriots during his stay in Boston:

"I am highly sensible of the honor intended me. But, could my wish prevail, I should desire to visit your metropolis without any parade or extraordinary ceremony. From a wish to avoid giving trouble to private families I determined . . . to . . . decline . . . any invitation to quarters which I might receive while on my journey." [1]

Awaiting a better opportunity to repay what he apparently regarded as a snub, the governor wrote on Friday the 23rd:

"It would have given me pleasure had a residence at my house met with your approbation. I observe you had proposed taking an early dinner at Watertown and proceeding to Cambridge and from thence to Boston on Saturday afternoon. I . . . request that you would so far vary your former intention as to arrive in Boston by 1 o'clock. . . . I beg . . . that you, with the gentlemen of your suite, would honor me with your company at dinner on Saturday *en famille*." [2]

Back came another abrupt note of the same day making painfully clear that the Chief Magistrate of the United States did not intend to change his itinerary to suit the convenience of a mere state executive: "It is my determination to be at Cambridge tomorrow at 10 o'clock and from thence to proceed to Boston as soon as circumstances will permit, where it is probable I may arrive by 12 o'clock." But he would "accept Your Excellency's polite invitation to take an informal dinner with you." [3]

· 2 ·

Washington evidently was given to understand that Hancock would meet him at Cambridge; but only Lieutenant Governor Adams and the Council appeared. According to Benjamin Russell, a member of the town committee, the municipal authorities thought that the governor should have received the President in person as he crossed the state boundary near Springfield; but they claimed the privilege of doing the honors when he should reach the Neck at the entrance to the metropolitan area, and had a delegation waiting there for that purpose. Russell thus describes what occurred:

"The controversy was without result. Both authorities [the Adams party and the civic group] remained in their carriages while the aides and marshals were rapidly posting between them. . . . The day was unusually cold and murky. The President . . . had been mounted for a considerable time on the *Neck*, waiting to enter the town. He made inquiry of the cause of the delay and, on receiving information of the *important* difficulty, is said to have expressed impatience. Turning to Major Jackson, his secretary, he asked, 'Is there no other avenue to the town?' And he was in the act of turning his charger when he was informed . . . that he would be received by the municipal authorities. The arrangements . . . were then promptly executed, and the President was conducted [by both deputations], amidst the acclamations of his fellow-citizens, to the quarters in Court Street * provided for him by the town." [4]

Washington recorded in his diary that before going to his lodgings he had been escorted "through the citizens, classed in their different professions and under their own banners, till we came to the State House. . . . After . . . entering . . . and ascending to . . . a balcony . . . three cheers was given by a vast concourse of people. . . . The streets,

* A public house conducted by the widow of Colonel Joseph Ingersoll in what then was Queen Street.

the doors, windows and tops of the houses were crowded with well dressed ladies and gentlemen." He also was greeted there by Vice President Adams, who was taking advantage of the Congressional recess to renew friendships in Boston.

Finally installed at Widow Ingersoll's, he decided to show Hancock that the governor must be the first to pay personal respects, and sent regrets concerning his promise to dine at the mansion. His private journal reveals the reason:

"Having engaged . . . to take an informal dinner with the Governor . . . but under a full persuasion that he would have waited upon me so soon as I should have arrived, I excused myself upon his not doing it and informing me through his secretary that he was too much indisposed to do it, being resolved to receive the visit. Dined at my lodgings, where the Vice-President favored me with his company." [5]

By this time Washington had come to the conclusion that Hancock was resorting to his ever reliable gout as a pretext for remaining in the background in order to display his power to ignore such a preeminent personage; and he felt that matters had passed from the field of etiquette into that of politics, involving the relationship between supreme and subordinate authority. To General Heath and Thomas Russell, councilors who called on Saturday night at his boarding house to explain the governor's absence at the Neck, he expressed himself in these forthright and angry words:

"Gentlemen, I am a frank man and will be frank on this occasion. For myself, . . . I do not regard ceremony; but there is an etiquette due my office which I am not at liberty to waive. My claim to the attention that has been omitted rests upon the question whether the whole is greater than a part. I am told that the course taken has been designed and that the subject was considered in Council. . . . This circumstance has been so disagreeable and mortifying that I must say, notwithstanding all the marks of respect and affection received from the inhabitants of Boston, had I anticipated it, I would have avoided the place." [6]

When this statement, amounting to an ultimatum, was relayed to Governor Hancock there must have been great consternation in the official family. The candles of the mansion probably burned through the small hours of Sunday morning as Hancock conferred with his henchmen about what was to be done. It is not likely that he gave up his delusions of grandeur without heated argument. But he did finally bow to the inevitable by noon and asked Washington, by special messenger, for permission to call—ostensibly at the virtual risk of his life. His capitulation was couched in language suggestive of negotiations between hostile princes:

"The Governor's best respects to the President. If at home and at leisure, the Governor will do himself the honor to pay his respects in half an hour. This would have been done much sooner had his health, in any degree, permitted. He now hazards everything, as it respects his health, for the desirable purpose."

Not to be outdone in diplomatic formality—and not to be taken in, either, by the governor's pretense that he courted death in offering to pay the controversial call—the head of the nation accepted the proffer of submission from the chief magistrate of Massachusetts, seemingly with tongue-in-cheek solicitude for his physical well-being. Stressing his own superiority by the use of his full title, aping Hancock's salutatory sentence, and even putting an almost immediate time limit on acquiescence, Washington replied:

"The President of the United States presents his best respects to the Governor and has the honor to inform him that he shall be at home till 2 o'clock. The President needs not express the pleasure it will give him to see the Governor; but, at the same time, he most earnestly begs that the Governor will not hazard his health on the occasion." [7]

Hancock, according to his widow, was driven tenderly to the Widow Ingersoll's with a flock of retainers fluttering over him. Washington's diary makes no mention of this but notes that his visitor admitted it would have been wrong for the highest officer in the land to seek him out: he "assured me that indisposition alone prevented his doing it yesterday and that he was still indisposed; but, as it had been suggested that he expected to *receive* the visit from the President, which he knew was improper, he was resolved . . . to pay his compliments today." [8]

· 3 ·

In later years Dolly corroborated her husband's contentions as to his part in this incident, attributed other versions to his foes, and added a few harrowing details. Sumner paraphrases her as asserting:

"Mr. H. had enemies as well as other folks; and . . . yet, as Mr. H. had the gout in his foot and hands and could not move, they persuaded the General that he was disinclined to make the first call. . . . It is well known that Mr. H. was a great advocate of the sovereignty of the States, and it was represented to the General that Mr. H., being chagrined at not being chosen the first President of the United States, was determined

to insist on the first call. . . . Mr. Patrick Jeffery and other friends of
Mr. H. informed him that it was necessary for him to remove the impression which this opinion, now become general, had made; and the
Governor, the next day, was carried down to the General's quarters and
taken from his carriage in the arms of his servants. When the General
saw them bringing up a helpless man . . . she says, he found he had
been deceived and burst into tears. On Monday he sent word by the
marshal of the district, Jonathan Jackson, Esq., that he should call on the
Governor and hoped that he should have the pleasure of spending an
hour or two with him and Mrs. Hancock alone; which he did and . . .
was very sociable and pleasant during his whole visit."

For once Sumner took the trouble to check on the loyal lady's vivid,
but often fictionized, memory. John Brooks, governor of Massachusetts
from 1816 to 1823, told him:

"That he himself dined with General Washington that day at his quarters and that Mr. Jackson was there, also; and that Mr. Jackson frequently spoke of the Governor's conduct and that he had no doubt his
omission to call was intended; but when he [Hancock] found that he
was not supported by the gentlemen of the town, who thought he had
degraded himself and committed the dignity of the State . . . he got
over it as well as he could and feigned himself . . . sick." [9]

It is hard to conceive of the stoical, dignified Washington breaking
down and weeping over the obviously dramatized suffering of a man
whose reputation for faking illness must have been known to him. In
his daily memoranda he alludes to having had tea with Hancock while
making the rounds of the first families on Monday evening but says
nothing about the heart-rending invalid scene depicted by Dolly as having occurred on Sunday. Perhaps he was too disgusted to consider it
worthy of comment.

Although the ice was broken—or melted by the warm flood streaming
from the President's eyes—the two sticklers for political etiquette did not
meet again informally, probably because the Boston dogmatist froze up
once more. On Tuesday, in the course of other tributes, the Chief of
State "received the addresses of the Governor and Council" and was the
honor guest of Governor Hancock by proxy (because of a sudden relapse) at a dinner in Faneuil Hall. Former Governor Bowdoin and the
current representatives of the ever present French navy were his hosts
on Wednesday while Hancock continued in gouty—perhaps grumpy—
seclusion, although he sent his lady as deputy to a dance given for the
man of the hour. He remained conspicuously aloof when Washington,

attended as far as Cambridge by Vice President Adams, Bowdoin, and numerous other notables, departed for Portsmouth on Thursday.[10]

The governor's behavior had repercussions throughout the political circles of the Massachusetts metropolis long after the President returned to New York on November 13. King heard an echo from Charles Gore in December:

"His Excellency has attained to such a measure of health (blessed be God) as again to pay and receive visits. . . . Be assured that, whatever was his disorder or the cause of it, those who are considered as his enemies have treated him with an unexpected degree of delicacy. They have been silent—and his advocates dare not say his conduct was becoming." [11]

However delicate his adversaries may have been, Hancock apparently still had a sore conscience in January, 1790, for he sought exoneration from the General Court at the opening of its next session on the 19th, in an official report on the Presidential sojourn:

"Since the adjournment of the legislature the President of the United States has been pleased to honor the Commonwealth with a visit. Upon so pleasing an occasion I thought it to be my indispensable duty . . . to receive him with all the attention due to his personal merit and illustrious character, . . . and I feel myself assured that we shall meet your entire approbation in our proceedings." [12]

The governor's sense of guilt may have been made articulate by a journalistic uproar at the turn of the year when the town committee for the entertainment of Washington presented its case to the public. Belknap wrote to Hazard:

"Our selectmen and the governor and sheriff are quarreling in the newspapers about what happened on the day of the arrival of the President. . . . The selectmen . . . have said something . . . which must affect His Excellency very sensibly. They have . . . told the true reason of his not going out of town to meet the President. His indisposition was mental, not bodily. I suspect he will have but few votes in this town at the next election." [13]

On the surface this whole controversy seems to have revolved around a small point of etiquette—whether a governor was supreme in his own state and entitled to the deference even of the President within its bounds. But the issue went far deeper and had major significance for a young nation struggling to achieve unity, strength, and stability under constitutional government.

The President put his finger on the crux of the matter when he informed Heath and Russell that his claim to priority of respect was based upon the relationship of the whole to a part. His contention—an irrefutable one—was that if the Presidency of the United States was to mean anything it must command the fealty of *all* the citizens, irrespective of local eminence, popularity, or power. Social precedence, although inconsequential in itself, was as important as political primacy; for the one symbolized the other. And the father of his country was undoubtedly sincere in saying that he had no regard for ceremony in its personal manifestations. His well known modesty and selflessness prove that. His only concern was for the dignity and authority of the office he occupied. If those rights were to be flouted, in the slightest degree, the whole governmental structure might collapse. Even the great Commonwealth of Massachusetts and the most powerful governor on the continent must acknowledge the supremacy of the President.

This issue was particularly pertinent at a time when the states had just yielded the essence of their precious sovereignty with the utmost reluctance. If Hancock had made Washington defer to him, even in the insignificant conflict over punctilio, other governors would have been encouraged to whittle away the President's prerogatives until nothing was left of the power vested in him, and the Union disintegrated into its originally independent parts.

Hancock, of course, did not think things through to this inevitable conclusion. He would not deliberately have jeopardized the future of the nation to whose creation he had contributed so much. He could have had no more far-reaching motive than to hoodwink the people into believing that he was bigger than the Constitution and that he was a law unto himself.

· 4 ·

Although the foremost egotist of eighteenth century America had been compelled to eat crow, his voracious vanity must have been fed to satiety by an ode in the leading local newspaper toward the close of the year— a year during which he evidently was incapacitated, for the most part, by a bona-fide siege of the gout. The extent to which he was crippled is indicated not only by the dearth of data concerning his activities but also by Edmund Quincy in a biography of his father, Josiah Quincy, who attended a banquet in July at the mansion during which the governor "did not sit at meat with his guests but dined at a small table by himself in a wheel-chair, his legs swathed in flannel. He was a martyr to the gout." [14]

The ode, ranking John Hancock among the saints, appeared in the

Boston *Gazette* of November 29 and was inspired by the unveiling of a brick column on the top of Beacon Hill to commemorate the principal events and immortalize the outstanding personages of the Revolution:

> Great Hancock's worth thro' every distant clime
> Shall be resounded to the latest time;
> Millions shall bless the day that they were born,
> When God-like Hancock did these States adorn;
> On Fame's bright wings his glorious name shall soar
> Till stars shall fall and systems be no more;
> Immortal statesman! 'Round fair Freedom's shrine
> Heroes and sages hail him all divine;
> To Heaven's expanse may late his spirit rise
> And guardian angels waft it to the skies;
> Celestial choirs shall sound his lasting fame;
> Expiring time shall not erase his name;
> Seraphs his brows around with laurels grace;
> At God's Right Hand he'll take the sacred place;
> For deeds so generous and deserved renown
> Thy worth, Oh, Hancock, claims a Heavenly crown.[15]

The future saint must have derived considerable consolation from the thought that he would be at least on an equal footing with Washington in the world to come. It is a wonder that he bothered with mortal affairs at all after this preposterous panegyric; but he condescended to discuss mundane states' rights in his first message to the new General Court when it convened in January, 1791. His reelection to the governorship during the preceding April had been virtually automatic as Bowdoin, no longer a declared candidate, polled a courtesy vote of only 1,884 ballots.

Despite his compromise with the advocates of a strong federal government on the question of constitutional ratification, Hancock still was basically true to his principles. He believed that the best way to build up a firm central government was to strengthen the state framework, and his address is one of the clearest and most concise expositions of what came to be the traditional Antifederalist position. He declared:

"It remains for us, Gentlemen, to give our support to this system by maintaining in full energy the constitution of our own state, upon which, with those of the other states in the Union, the federal government is founded; for it must eventually stand or fall with those particular governments. The least alteration in the constitutional principles of one of them must essentially affect that. The federal government might, indeed,

by absorbing the powers of the state governments, change its own nature
and become a very different system from what it originally was. But to
maintain it as it now is will be best effected by maintaining them in as
much respectability as their several constitutions will admit of." [16]

He proved his sincerity by taking—for once—an unpopular but admirable step in the interest of a sounder financial policy for the commonwealth, two days after his regime was extended for another year on May
25, 1791, with the same virtually unanimous consent: he announced to
the Assembly that he would veto a bill for the raising of revenue by a
lottery. This pernicious practice had been resorted to frequently ever
since colonial times as a painless way to extract from the public the
money that should have been produced by taxation. It was a subterfuge
that impugned the integrity of the legislature and weakened the moral
fiber of the people.

· 5 ·

While reinforcing the economic foundations of the state Hancock did
not neglect to brace himself as a pillar of high society. With one of his
periodic displays of generosity he defrayed the cost of the election day
dinner at Faneuil Hall out of his own purse. The bill for food amounted
to £90; that for 163 bottles of wine and incidentals, to £65.6s.6d.

Two weeks after this affair he was host at another banquet which had
tragi-comic consequences. It was held at his mansion on June 6 as part of
the annual Ancient and Honorable Artillery Company ceremonies.
James S. Loring, a historian who may have been one of the guests, pictures the feast as follows:

"Among the company present were Col. 'Azor Orne and Solomon
Davis, Esq., a merchant who resided in Tremont Street. . . . He was
very facetious. A superb plum cake graced the center of the table. It was
noticed by the guests that Mr. Davis partook very freely of this cake and,
moreover, that the silver tankard of punch was greatly lightened of its
liquid by liberal drafts through his lips. As was the natural habit of Mr.
Davis, he set the table in a roar; and, one of his puns being specially felic-
itous, Colonel Orne remarked, 'Go home, Davis, and die—you can never
beat that!' Mr. Davis, on his way home, fell dead in a fit of apoplexy
near King's Chapel, and his pockets were found filled with plum cake."[17]

The governor, too, may have overindulged in his own rich repast, for
a letter from Daniel Sewell implies that he took a trip soon afterward
for his health: "I should have been happy in seeing Your Excellency

when at [New] York, but I understand . . . that you did not choose to have any company there." [18]

Hancock did no public business in the last half of 1791 that received special mention in the records; and, except for his part in a spectacular controversy over public morals, he lived out the two concluding years of his short span in comparative quiet. Death must have been increasingly on his mind, for there were obvious signs that his frail physique, gout-ridden and racked by a complication of other ailments, could not long survive. He must have been made more conscious of this by Eunice Burr's gently reproachful letter of May 1, 1792, concerning his neglect to erect a headstone over Aunt Lydia's grave in Fairfield. She nudged his conscience by asking him to let her "know if you would have any objection to Mr. Burr putting up a stone just to let it be known where the remains of our dear, honored, and lovely departed friend lies." [19]

That this note sharpened his long dulled sense of obligation to his foster mother's memory is indicated in one from Thaddeus Burr during June:

"In consequence of the conversation I had with . . . Captain Scott, communicating your request respecting the removal of the remains of your dear aunt, . . . I agreed with a Captain Bass of this place to transport them to Boston if practicable. I then . . . found the case and inner coffin not in a condition to be moved. . . . We shall now await your further instructions."

If there was a reply to this communication it has not been preserved. But a second letter from Burr, written on October 26, reveals that the governor and his lady had visited their old Fairfield friends in the meantime.[20] Their mansion had been burned to the ground, and Eunice had been roughly handled by Hessians in July, 1779. Perhaps to convince them that his heart was not as hard as it seemed, Hancock provided, shortly before he died, the lumber and glass for a new home, with the understanding that it was to be a replica of his own Beacon Hill show place. The frame, constructed in Boston, was delivered intact to the Connecticut town.

· 6 ·

Meanwhile Hancock had received another almost 100 per cent mandate from the people as governor for the year starting in May, 1792. On his first appearance in the new term before the General Court he delivered a speech on the meaning of democracy which ranks among the finest of the many and various interpretations placed by statesmen upon that concept down to the present day. The gist of it is:

"That a free government founded in the natural, equal rights of all the people is within the reach of human ability and to be prized as a principal support of natural happiness is an idea which has been long established in the minds of the greatest and wisest men in the world. . . . That government may be considered as truly free where all the people are, by the constitution and laws, upon the same rank of privilege and have an equal security for their lives, liberties, and property—where the laws do not create, but are calculated to prevent, all exclusive rights to fame or wealth and leave each citizen upon his own merit for the honors of his country and upon his own honest exertions for the acquirement of property." [21]

As governor of Massachusetts, he naturally laid more emphasis than a politician of our day upon the accumulation of property as an opportunity and object of life under a democratic government. To stress this point was proper and expedient, for the right to vote in the Bay State and several others was predicated on the possession of land.

Although an exponent of the most advanced political theories of the age, Governor Hancock was behind the times in his views on social morality. The issue which embroiled him in a sensational conflict arose in 1791, when a movement to repeal the forty-year-old law against theatrical performances was launched. This statute had been reinforced by similar decrees in Massachusetts and other states during a Puritanical reaction against the loose living of early Revolutionary days. As far back as 1778 the Continental Congress had passed a resolution that government officials should not attend stage plays.

In consequence a British stock company headed by an actor-manager named John Henry, who had made a highly successful American debut at New York in 1767, had gone to Jamaica in the West Indies and had remained there until the war was almost over. In 1782, returning with his troupe, Henry had established a precarious foothold at Annapolis; and in 1785, by amalgamating with another group of strolling players in New York, he had tried to promote "chaste and moral" plays for "truly respectable audiences" in both places.[22] Finally, by the summer of 1792, he thought himself well enough intrenched to challenge the legal strictures of New England in the belief that the diversion-hungry masses would support him in defiance of narrow-minded officialdom. But he decided to make an oblique assault upon the citadel of Puritanism by circumventing the ban against his business. He opened a repertory engagement in an old Boston stable. Advertised as a series of "moral lectures" to be given at the "New England Exhibition Room, Board Alley" (now Hawley Street), the program included "Feats on the Tight Rope," *The True-Born Irishman,* Richard Brinsley Sheridan's *The School for Scandal,* and Shakespeare's *King Richard III.*[23]

By November 7 Hancock's sense of duty had been so thoroughly aroused and his moral sensibilities so deeply offended that he felt obliged —especially since the man responsible was one of those hated Britons, an Irishman—to bring the affair before the Assembly. His message pointed out: "A number of aliens . . . have lately entered the state . . . under advertisements insulting to the habits and education of the citizens; have been pleased to invite them to . . . stage plays, interludes, and theatrical entertainments under the title . . . of *Moral Lectures.* . . . No means have been taken to punish a most open breach of the laws and a most contemptuous insult upon the powers of government."[24]

During a performance of *King Richard III* soon afterward Sheriff Jeremiah Allen, under orders of the governor and Council, arrested one Harper, who was playing the lead as the hunchbacked tyrant, in the midst of the scene on Bosworth Field. The audience became so incensed at being cheated out of their thrills at such a tense moment that they tore down and trampled a portrait of Hancock which Henry, probably to get on the right side of him, had hung on the front of a stage box.

The governor may have taken matters into his own hands without obtaining authority from the legislature to seize the star of the company; for the warrant had been issued without a sworn complaint and the prisoner was released, after a public trial, on the strength of that plea. If the hearsay accusations of John Quincy Adams, in a letter of December 16 to John Adams, are true he definitely overstepped the bounds of legality:

"At night . . . a mob of about 200 people . . . went up to the governor's house to ask his leave to pull down the playhouse. . . . He . . . as it is said, authorized them to proceed upon their riotous design. They accordingly . . . began to destroy the fences round the house but were soon dispersed by a justice of the peace of the other party. . . . There has been since then no further attempt to act more plays, and all the actors are now gone."[25]

But they came flocking back when, on the last day of 1792, the General Court bowed to the overwhelming popular will, rescinded the statute against Thespianism, and substituted one permitting plays to be performed in the capital of the commonwealth but continuing to exclude them from the other, less sophisticated towns. Boston's first regular theater was built during 1793 in Long Lane and was opened in February of the following year.

Never before had the people as a whole stood out against Hancock on a major issue affecting them directly. Their decisive rejection of his policy—an incongruous reversion, in a man of such generally liberal leanings, to the prudish precepts of his youth—indicated that he was losing his grip on his idolaters at last. Even an idol must keep up with the march of time.

· 7 ·

Governor Hancock was trying to brake the wheels of political progress, too, at this period. In an address to the General Court in November— amazing for its downright denial of the United States Government's right to command obedience from a state executive in a federal matter —he quibbled over the use of the word "shall" in a routine Congressional measure instructing every governor to have three lists of Presidential electors within his jurisdiction prepared and delivered to them prior to the assembling of the electoral college in December. With more heat than common sense he declared:

"When an act of Congress uses compulsory words with regard to any act done by the supreme executive of this commonwealth I shall not feel myself obliged to obey them because I am not, in my official capacity, amenable to that government. . . . Gentlemen, I do not address you . . . from a disposition to regard the proceedings of the general government with a jealous eye, nor do I suppose that Congress could intend that clause . . . as a compulsory provision. But I wish to prevent any measure to proceed through inattention, which may be drawn into precedent hereafter to the injury of the people or to give a constructive power where the federal Constitution has not expressly given it." [26]

Here was the old states' rights Hancock speaking again in a final show of opposition to centralized government. That the great Commonwealth of Massachusetts and its great governor should be dictated to by any outside agency, even in such a petty instance as this, still was inconceivable to him who had been so largely instrumental in having the authority delegated to the Congress four years before. His declaration to the legislature was a bald statement of the principle for which he had fought surreptitiously during his altercation with Washington over etiquette. Although pretending—and probably believing, in part—that he was defending his beloved people against Congressional encroachment upon their particular domain, he undoubtedly looked upon the federal prerogative "with a jealous eye." He had wielded virtually absolute power in his own bailiwick—relatively small geographically but disproportionately big politically—too long to surrender it without a struggle. But this fight was another losing one for the man whom the parade of historical evolution was passing by.

A secondary cause of Hancock's petulant objection to being ordered about by the Congress may have been that he did not want to have anything to do with the electors, who again, as he must have known, were to help elect Washington President unanimously and John Adams Vice President without giving their own governor a single vote. John Quincy Adams attributed his cantankerousness to this neglect, which was so general that his name was not even included in the group of five candidates put up for the new four-year term starting on March 4. Adams asserted:

"The unanimity of the electors in this state was, by all accounts, a sore mortification to His State Majesty. It angered him to the heart, and he vented his peevishness upon the first objects that presented themselves to him. . . . He made several difficulties about signing the warrant upon the treasury for the pay of the electors." [27]

The governor's irritability may have been increased, too, by recurring trouble with Harvard over the funds in his keeping. In September, Treasurer Storer had once more threatened him with legal action. The final farcical phase of these negotiations extended into 1793, when a committee appointed by the college offered to buy back the securities at par, even though the market price was only eighteen shillings. But the die-hard debtor was too smart to compromise himself by entering into such a shady deal.

The first eight months of his last year on earth were almost barren of his participation in public affairs—aside from perennial reelection to the governorship for an eleventh term—probably because of constantly deteriorating health. Except for a plea to the General Court on January 31 in behalf of legislation that would do away with capital punishment for burglary, outlaw cropping, branding, and the public whipping post, reduce the state debt, and commit the commonwealth to the support of a national bank, he confined himself to the workaday duties of his office until within three weeks of his death. [28]

But this did not mean that he was yet resigned to the inexorable fate of all mortals. On August 3 he penned to Sam Adams from Concord (where the Assembly was sitting because of a smallpox epidemic in Boston) a whither-are-we-drifting letter which reveals that he still was determined to do battle for the threatened political principles now espoused by both patriots. He and Adams, who had been lieutenant governor ever since 1789, were back on the old basis of intimacy that had bound them together in the early days of the Revolutionary movement. With an outburst of Latinity—possibly inspired by the honorary degree of Doctor of Laws conferred upon him by Rhode Island College (the present Brown University) and Harvard in 1788 and 1792, respectively—the governor wrote:

"I never more devoutly wished for *mens sana in corpore sano.* . . . I am alarmed. Watchman, what of the night? . . . My friend, what are we coming to? It is time to step forth and oppose the current of opinions and pursuits that are endeavoring to establish a system foreign to your ideas and mine. . . . I love my country but will not give up its liberties to the last drop of my blood. As for me, I am infirm; but . . . you will always find me prompt to plan and ready to execute when necessity requires. *Obsta Principies* is my motto and *Festina Lente* my maxim." [29]

· 8 ·

Six weeks later Hancock fulfilled this pledge by taking up the cudgels for the last time in defense of states' rights and giving the original impetus to a principle which, like those he had advocated in 1788, eventually was embodied in the Federal Constitution. Conducted on September 18 by Secretary Avery and Sheriff Allen, the governor made his final appearance before the General Court. He and James Sullivan, now state attorney general, had been summoned by Marshal Jackson to answer a suit brought in a United States court against the commonwealth by a nonresident. But Hancock had refused to obey and called a special session of the Assembly to outlaw the pending action. Unable to deliver the historic speech that he had prepared for the occasion, he had Avery do so. Its most pregnant passage reads:

"I cannot conceive that the people of this commonwealth, who by their representatives in convention adopted the federal compact, expected a state would be held liable to answer a compulsory civil process to an individual of another state or a foreign kingdom."

As a result of this oblique but effective enunciation of a tenet which is now recognized as one of the strongest bulwarks of state sovereignty, the Assembly resolved on the 27th that the privilege claimed by the litigant was "dangerous to the power, safety, and independence of the several states and repugnant to the first principles of a federal government." [30] In implementation of this resolution the legislature thereupon proposed what became, despite a prior Supreme Court decision upholding an alien's right to sue, the Eleventh Amendment of the Constitution.

After the reading of his message at the earlier meeting of the Court, Governor Hancock had struggled to his tottering legs and had spoken briefly but prophetically. Evidently realizing that his fighting days were nearly over, in spite of the gallant front presented to Adams in August, he had echoed the import of the words uttered by his grandfather more than half a century before:

"I feel the seeds of mortality growing fast within me. But I think I have, in this case, done no more than my duty as the servant of the people. I never did, and I never will, deceive them while I have life and strength to act in their service."

It is probable that Hancock never again stirred from his mansion—or even from his bed—after returning to Boston at the conclusion of this pledge to the common folk whom he loved sincerely, regardless of his many demagogic statements concerning them. The "seeds of mortality" continued to mature rapidly and finally choked off his breath on Tuesday morning October 8, 1793, in his fifty-seventh year. Death compensated somewhat for the long suffering that life had inflicted upon him. The agony lasted less than an hour.

On the 10th the *Independent Chronicle* thus reviewed the circumstances:

"The day previous to his death he appeared more alert than for many days before, which gave his friends some flattering hopes of his recovery. On the morning of his death he expressed no unusual complaints till about 7 o'clock, when he suddenly felt a difficulty in breathing. His physicians were immediately sent for, who gave him some temporary relief; but the dissolution of nature made such rapid progress that before 8 o'clock he resigned his soul into the hands of Him who gave it." [31]

· 9 ·

No son of Massachusetts had ever received the homage paid to John Hancock during a lifetime, and none had ever been so honored at the close. Indeed, it is safe to say that not another man in all America had been given, up to that time, a funeral such as was accorded him on Monday the 14th; and that no American—with the exception of Abraham

Lincoln—has since been escorted to his grave with comparable ceremony. Even the pomp-loving and affection-craving Hancock could not have wished for a more flamboyant tribute on the part of the classes or a more genuine expression of sorrow on the part of the masses.

The body had lain in state at the mansion throughout the week and had been viewed by thousands of mourners from every section of the commonwealth. According to the *Chronicle*, at sunrise on the day of the obsequies, which was unseasonably warm and pleasant, "the bells in all the public edifices in his town opened the scene by tolling without cessation an hour; and the flags in town, at the Castle, and on the masts of the shipping in the harbor were half-hoisted. At 1 o'clock all the stores and shops were shut, and numerous citizens . . . paid various marks of unfeigned respect to the deceased." [32]

An hour earlier virtually every military unit in Boston and several from adjacent towns had assembled on the Common under the command of General William Hull, who had done valiant service during the Revolution. Lined up behind the soldiery were all the state functionaries of any consequence and many of national repute. In the center of the official procession walked Acting Governor Adams, just ahead of the six eldest councilors, who served as pallbearers. An artillery guard of honor followed the corpse and surrounded the "Hancock," one of the brass fieldpieces spirited away from the Loyalist arsenal at Hancock's instigation on the eve of the War for Independence and now draped in black velvet.

Next in order rode Dolly and the rest of the family in one or more of the twenty-one carriages. Following the relatives were Vice President Adams; justices of the federal courts in the vicinity, wearing the traditional full dress of the eighteenth century judiciary—black gowns and club wigs—for the last time; ministers of foreign governments; leading authorities of Harvard College (forgiving, ostensibly at least, the unfair financial treatment they had received at the hands of the departed); municipal officers, church dignitaries, numerous other notables, and the ubiquitous "respectable gentlemen." Marching four abreast and stretching a mile and a half behind the officialdom, were the idolaters of him who—even Mercy Warren must have admitted—had attained in death a dignity belying her conception of him as a "silly image." An eyewitness named Henry Williams recorded in his journal: "Upon the most modest calculation, . . . there were upwards of 20,000 people in the procession. And the spectators—every house and street was thronged." [33] Contrary to what might be pictured as a spectacle of the utmost confusion, the

Chronicle reported that "the greatest order and regularity was observed—the most solemn silence and attention pervaded every rank of the multitude. . . . A general gloom was visible in every countenance." [34]

The cortège got under way at two o'clock, crossed the Common in a southwesterly direction to Frog Lane (now Boylston Street), then proceeded eastward by way of the present Washington Street, circled the Statehouse, where Sam Adams had to drop out because of fatigue; turned north to "Treamount" Street, and finally headed west to the Old Granary Burying Ground. The dirge beat on the muffled military drums was punctuated at intervals of a minute during the hour-long cavalcade by the doleful booming of cannon on the surrounding hills and at the Castle.

Although Hancock, according to Martha Quincy, had asked that he be buried without public display and without the firing of the customary salute to the chief magistrate at the grave, the second request was heeded no more than the first.[35] As his remains were deposited in the ancestral tomb beside those of his uncle at three o'clock a volley of rifle fire proclaimed that he had reached the end of his earthly road.

It had often been a rocky road, but always royal and ascendant, for the patriot in purple.

Epilogue

IN 1824, after being widowed for the second time, Dorothy Quincy Hancock Scott was the recipient of a *beau geste* without parallel in American history. She was paid royal homage by the Marquis de Lafayette during his last visit to the United States. Edmund Quincy thus describes the occasion:

"As he was passing through the streets that morning, in the midst of all the tumult of welcome, he . . . said to my father, 'Pray tell me, is the widow of John Hancock yet alive?'

"'O yes,' was the answer, 'and I have no doubt that we shall see her at one of the windows as we pass by.' . . .

"As they were passing along what is now Tremont Street, fronting the Common, my father espied the venerable dame seated in an honorable post of observation on a balcony overlooking the scene. . . .

"'Tell the coachman,' said the General, 'to draw up opposite the place.'

"This being done, Lafayette rose and saluted her with a profound bow, which she returned by as profound a courtesy, the crowd cheering the pair with great enthusiasm. And hers was the first private house which he entered in Boston." [1]

In jarring contrast to Lafayette's courtly gesture the Commonwealth of Massachusetts, despite its outward show of appreciation for Hancock's services at the time of his death, was disgracefully ungrateful and continued so for a century afterward. Soon after he was buried the state perpetrated a cruel injustice upon his widow, according to Martha Quincy.

Mrs. Hancock wished to pay for the funeral with money drawn from the estate but yielded to the General Court's insistence that the expenses be taken out of public funds, as was customary in the case of

361

governors who expired in office. Before the bill of $1,800 was presented, however, the legislature enacted a statute providing that the cost of a chief magistrate's obsequies should not be defrayed by the treasury. The Court injected the final fillip of heartless irony into the situation by revoking this measure after Dolly had settled the account and before another governor succumbed.[2]

Hancock could have saved his relict all this embarrassment by specifying—as he probably had intended—that the account be settled by resort to his ample fortune. But, in keeping with his laxity in most financial matters, he had put nothing in writing relative to the disposition of his affairs. Two weeks after he died intestate Mrs. Hancock was appointed administratrix. A year and a half later she received as her dower the mansion and grounds, appraised at £5,000; Hancock's Wharf and the buildings on or adjoining it, which were valued at £7,500.[3] To her subsequent regret she consented to accept this legacy, comprising only about one-sixth of the total valuation of her deceased husband's far-flung holdings, by agreement with the nearest of kin—Mother Mary Perkins and Brother Ebenezer Hancock—and Richard Perkins as legal representative of Sister Mary, who had passed on. Dolly raised £4,000 by selling the pasture behind the Beacon Hill homestead, shortly after acquiring possession, to the town of Boston for the erection of a new Statehouse, which was to become the west wing of the present huge and imposing seat of government.[4] But she was destined to spend her declining years in straitened, though genteel, circumstances, and her means amounted to less than $6,000 at the time of her demise. The remainder of Hancock's real property, and presumably his liquid assets, were divided among the other heirs in 1797.

The former First Lady of the nation, however, provided for her immediate future by marrying Captain Scott, now a widower. But she did so only after keeping him in suspense so long that he was driven to prayer in despair while some of her snobbish friends were attempting to break up the match because they considered the shipmaster beneath her station.[5] She finally gave in on July 28, 1796—the anniversary of her first marriage, two decades earlier—at the age of forty-nine. The Reverend Peter Thacher performed the ceremony in his Brattle Street Church.

Dolly lived with her second spouse in Portsmouth until his death on June 19, 1809. Then the hardy old dame went back to her Beacon Hill home and remained there until about 1816, when she sold it and after

a short stay in Central Court moved to a house in Federal Street, to
spend the rest of her eighty-three years.[6]

They were trying years for Mrs. Scott. Although the captain bequeathed her a wine cellar containing "300 gallons . . . of London
particular Madeira," he apparently left her little else.[7] In 1814 she
petitioned the court for an allowance from the Hancock estate on the
ground that she had lost her only productive piece of property—the
wharf—through a foreclosure proceeding. There is no record as to
whether this request was granted; but three months later she obtained
permission to sell the mansion tract, which could not otherwise have
been used for the discharge of debts.[8]

The erstwhile belle of Boston, however, continued to turn a cheerful
and pretty face to the world. That she was fashionably dressed, too,
at eighty is indicated by a Copley portrait painted in 1827. It shows her
wearing her white hair in stiff French puffs ranged across her forehead,
a muslin cap frilled with ribbons, and a plain black gown with an ex-
pansive Elizabethan ruff covering her throat.

But Dolly lived, for the most part, in the past. During the illness
which ended her days on February 3, 1830, she is supposed to have
amused herself by placing phantom guests around her dining table to
conjure up in imagination the festive old times. Although recollections
of those yesterdays were aroused most thrillingly by Lafayette's tribute,
she had the more solid satisfaction of knowing that many of her first
husband's enemies had changed their estimate of him.

As often happens in the case of a man whose personality is so positive
as to evoke whole-souled affection or implacable hatred from those with
whom he comes in contact, death jolted Hancock's foes into a realization that they had been blinded by prejudice while he was alive. It
made them aware of the important place he had filled in one of the
most significant eras of political advancement known to mankind. It
opened their passion veiled eyes to the fact that his passing had left a
vast void in the public life of his state and nation.

Thacher, his estranged pastor, preached the funeral sermon on October 20 in the Brattle Street Church at the Sunday service following
the interment. This homily, although moderately eulogistic, carries more
weight as a critique of Hancock's worth than the usual extravagant
praise which a majority of eighteenth century divines felt obliged to
bestow upon the departed spirit of a prominent and powerful parish-
ioner. With rare frankness the minister implied that the subject of
his discourse was somewhat less than a paragon. But he seconded the

opinion of all other commentators, friendly or hostile, concerning Hancock's popularity. He also expressed agreement with the consensus respecting his patriotism, his sacrificial nature, his charitableness, his skill as a mediator, and his value to the Revolutionary cause.[9]

This clergyman, who spoke so magnanimously of a disaffected communicant after his death, probably had felt far from Christian toward him beforehand; for their differences must have run deep to induce Hancock to withdraw—or contemplate withdrawing—from the church of his childhood. But Thacher could not have experienced a more radical change of heart than John Adams.

In 1791 Adams had been reminded that on one occasion he had pointed through the doorway of his North Braintree home to the near-by parsonage and declared: "Yes, there is the place where the great John Hancock was born. . . . John Hancock! A man without head and without heart—the mere shadow of a man!—and yet a Governor of old Massachusetts!" [10]

But in 1812 the ex-President of the United States—somewhat mellowed, yet still bearing many an ancient grudge—wrote to Richard Rush: "I could melt into tears when I hear his name. . . . If benevolence, charity, generosity were ever personified in North America, they were in John Hancock. What shall I say of his education? His literary acquisitions . . . his military, civil, and political services? His sufferings and sacrifices? I dare not say . . . at this time, what I think and what I know." [11]

In two letters addressed to William Tudor five years later Adams confessed a kind of retroactive fondness for his former enemy. His accompanying admissions of misjudgment, guilt, and remorse ring true. The first reads:

"I can say with truth that I profoundly admired him and more profoundly loved him. If he had vanity and caprice, so had I. And if his vanity and caprice made me sometimes sputter . . . mine . . . had often a similar effect upon him. But these little flickerings of little passions determine nothing concerning essential characters. . . . Though I never injured or justly offended him . . . I cannot but reflect upon myself for not paying him more respect than I did in his lifetime. . . . Nor were his talents or attainments inconsiderable. They were far superior to many who have been much more celebrated. He had a great deal of political sagacity and penetration into men. He was by no means a contemptible scholar or orator. Compared with Washington, Lincoln, or Knox, he was learned."

In the second letter to Tudor the penitent Adams bracketed Hancock with Otis and Sam Adams at the top of the list of Revolutionary leaders. He characterized them as "the first movers; the most constant, steady, persevering springs, agents, and most distinguished sufferers and firmest pillars of the whole Revolution." [12]

The purpose of this book has been to round out the portrait sketched by Thacher, Adams, and other contemporaries—to bring into relief the lights and shadows so that the reader may form his own impressions at the points where the shades merge into gray, as they must in a picture of such a contradictory character. Perhaps it would be helpful to focus attention at the last upon the quintessence of the pigments that have gone into the work. This is the fact that its protagonist was one of the closest approximations in American annals to that apocryphal creature—the "indispensable man." He was the man on horseback—with trappings—who is essential to the success of every revolution.

George Washington rode the symbolic steed but was too cold to fire the imagination of the masses. Sam Adams was the necessary intellectual radical but was too austere to win the people's affection. John Adams had the required combination of brains and political acumen but lacked the common touch. And so it goes as one thumbs through the catalogue of founding fathers. Each made a priceless contribution to the birth of a great nation, but none except Hancock could so arouse the enthusiasm of the multitude and sustain their loyalty to the cause in a region where it was strained to the utmost during the agonizing years of war and immediately subsequent peace.

What achievements of this many-faceted figure accounted principally for his virtual indispensability to the establishment of his country?

In the first place, Hancock did more than any other person to surround the Revolutionary movement with an aura of respectability. During the eighteenth century, when social standing had so much more influence upon world opinion concerning political rebellion than it does today, the value of an aristocrat—especially a fabulously rich one—to such a cause was inestimable. This was particularly true in the case of the Beacon Hill plutocrat, for he had the most far-reaching reputation of all Americans by virtue of his almost universal business connections. Furthermore, his decision to go counter to his own best interests—as it seemed at the time—in casting his lot with the revolutionists had an incalculably inspirational effect upon gentry and commonalty alike in the colonies. It may be argued plausibly that the surge toward freedom might have faltered and might even have lost its impetus entirely but for the timely renewed impulse imparted by his renegade patriotism.

Having helped so materially in bringing about the upheaval which pulled down the old order, Hancock took a prominent part in laying the cornerstone of the new. As President of the Second Continental Congress he eliminated the friction among the masons of the foundation with the unction of his personality and induced them to work together as well as could be expected.

After the blueprint of the national structure, in the form of the Declaration of Independence, had been drawn this contractor of nation building inscribed the first bold strokes which committed the artificers to carry out the plans of the brilliant architects of liberty. But for this intrepid act, undertaken alone at the risk of hanging for treason, the rest of the workers might have lost heart and abandoned the project. And if he had not driven them unremittingly to apply themselves to the forge of war in which the United States was hammered out, the whole enterprise might have collapsed.

Once the most majestic edifice of democracy ever reared had been created and began to stand free from all external support—even if shakily —Hancock played a major role by persuading Massachusetts, one of the key states, to ratify the Federal Constitution with amendments which rendered it thoroughly workable. All the arduous labor of years would have gone for naught if this governmental fulcrum had not been placed under the still loosely jointed and faulty construction.

Finally, as the initial constitutional governor of the tremendously influential Bay State, this man of many parts added important finishing touches to the house erected by and for freemen. He won—in one notable instance, at least—not merely for his own commonwealth but for every other state as well, certain rights which protected them from the encroachments of centralized authority and thereby insured the stability of the country as a unit.

In spite of what John Adams called "little flickerings of little passions," Hancock had an essentially strong and admirable character. If not absolutely indispensable to the evolution of America, he could have been dispensed with only at grave danger to the outcome of the grand process.

And so it was with symbolic propriety that Lafayette, the preeminent aristocratic democrat of the Old World, made the *beau geste* to the widow of his counterpart in the New World.

Notes and Citations

PROLOGUE (*Pages* 1-5)

1. Entry of Oct. 10, 1635, in Cambridge *Records* (Cambridge, 1901), 30.
2. Quoted in W. B. Sprague, *Annals of the American Pulpit*, I, 239.
3. *Ibid.*, 240.
4. *Ibid.*
5. J. Hancock, *Sermon Preached at the Ordination of Mr. John Hancock*, 23, 25.
6. George Washington to John Hancock, Nov. 2, 1777, in *Writings*, ed. W. C. Ford, VI, 133 n.
7. From 1717 to 1773 the General Court, or Assembly, of Massachusetts consisted of the royal Governor, the Council, and the House of Representatives. The Governor was appointed by the Crown; but the Council of twenty-eight members, unlike the corresponding body in most of the colonies, was elected annually by the outgoing Council and the incoming House. Sometimes also referred to as the Assembly, this House comprised two delegates from every town in the province except Boston, which had four. They, too, were elected every year. The Council originally exercised excutive, legislative, and judicial functions in conjunction with the governor; but by 1768 it had little more than legislative power, and the lower house wielded most of that.
8. J. Hancock, *The Prophet Jeremiah's Resolution*, 7, 9, 11.

CHAPTER 1 (*Pages* 7-23)

1. Thomas Dudley to Countess of Lincoln, Mar. 12-28, 1630 (see calendar note following), in Mass. Hist. Soc. *Collections*, 1st Ser., VIII, 36. Dudley had put his employer's estate, which had been encumbered with a debt of £20,000, on a sound financial footing during nine years' service. He had then retired to Boston in Lincolnshire (the American city of that name probably was so christened at his suggestion) but had soon returned to the service of Lincoln at the earl's urging. He had continued in that

capacity until he sailed for New England in 1630. Four years later he became governor of the Massachusetts Bay Colony.

2. *Ibid.*

3. *Ibid.,* 39.

4. *Ibid.,* and 41. The Court of Assistants of the Massachusetts Bay Colony was what would now be called a board of directors. Together with the governor and the deputy governor, it managed the colony. The charter provided for eighteen assistants, but no more than ten out of the two thousand persons in the province were considered politically wise enough to serve in 1630. According to another stipulation, the General Court (not to be confused with the later body of the same name), consisting of all "freemen," or original settlers, was to meet four times a year. The freemen were empowered to admit new members and make laws at these meetings, in which the governor and six assistants likewise took part. On Oct. 19, 1630, however, the leaders of the province induced the General Court to surrender its legislative rights to the Court of Assistants, thus blithely ignoring the charter; and up to 1634 the latter organization exercised all the functions of government.

5. L. R. Paige, *History of Cambridge, 1630–1877* (Boston, 1877), 9.

6. Entry of Aug. 14, 1632, in John Winthrop, *History of New England,* ed. James Savage, I, 104–105.

7. Entry of Dec. 24, 1632, in Cambridge *Records,* 4.

8. William Wood, *New England's Prospect,* 43. According to Lucius R. Paige, leading authority on the early history of Cambridge, it was not the model town thus pictured—or, at least, it did not live up to its auspicious beginnings: "For nearly 200 years after its foundation, Cambridge increased very slowly in population and wealth. . . . The schoolhouses and other public buildings were few and inexpensive; the streets and sidewalks were neglected and unlighted; thorough sewerage was unknown." (*History of Cambridge, 1630–1877,* 451–452.)

9. The name Hancock is spelled in five additional ways—Hancocke, Hancok, Hancoke, Hancoks, and Handcoke—in the Cambridge town records. This is due partly to the highly elastic spelling rules of the period and partly to the custom of having the town clerk take down names by ear as they were read out in meeting.

10. Entry of Jan. 5, 1634, in Cambridge *Records,* 10. The pioneering spirit that had driven Hancock and his neighbors to this untamed country still was egging them on toward wider horizons. Although only about 100 families in all, they were complaining of lack of elbowroom and were threatening to seek their fortunes anew in the wilderness from which they had so recently carved a niche of semicivilization by heart-wrenching toil. In the spring of 1634 the General Court, always loath to lose hard-working settlers, gave them permission to make whatever deal they could for expansion. Fortunately, Boston and Watertown had more land than they could handle and obligingly ceded to the ambitious Newtownites the territory embraced today by Brookline, Brighton, and Newton. But a string was attached to Brookline, then known as Muddy River. This was a proviso that the grant should be forfeited if Mr. Hooker and his Braintree company

should move away. They did pick up and go to Connecticut in 1636—partly because of the travel itch, partly because Massachusetts Bay was too small to contain a pair of such self-consciously eminent divines as Hooker and John Cotton. The loss of Brookline was more than offset almost immediately by a Court order extending the northern boundary of Newtown, now called Cambridge, a distance of eight miles into an unassigned area which took in the present sites of Arlington and most of Lexington. In consequence of later grants the town reached its maximum dimensions and acquired the shape of an hourglass—thirty-five miles long and a mile wide at the waist—in 1651. By 1688 it had finally assumed its modern size and contours after what eventually became Billerica and Newton had been incorporated as separate villages.

11. Entry of Feb. 8, 1635, in Cambridge *Records*, 18–19.

12. Despite all this beautiful civic planning, it appears that the Newtown authorities as often as not allotted a piece of land in a Charlestown or Watertown backyard to one of their own citizens during the years when Hancock was sinking his roots into the soil. Up to March 6, 1633, nobody really knew where Newtown ended and Charlestown began; and even the agreement entered into on that date by representatives of the two settlements appointed by the General Court reads like the prospectus of an old-time real estate speculator. It specifies "that all the land impaled by the New Town men, with the neck whereon Mr. Graves his house standeth, shall belong to New Town and that the bounds of Charlestown shall end at a tree marked by the pale, and to pass along from thence by a straight line unto the midway betwixt the westermost part of the governor's great lot and the nearest part thereto of the bounds of Watertown."—Entry of Mar. 6, 1633, in Massachusetts Colony *Records*, I, 102, quoted in Paige, *History of Cambridge*, 2.

13. Quoted in John Dickinson, "The Massachusetts Charter and the Bay Colony," in *Commonwealth History of Massachusetts*, ed. A. B. Hart, I, 106.

14. Entry of Mar. 12, 1637/8 (see calendar note following), in Mass. Colony *Records*, I, 221, quoted in Paige, *History of Cambridge*, 223.

15. Entry of May 13, 1640, in Mass. Colony *Records*, I, 180, quoted in *ibid.*

16. Members of the governing body in Newtown and Cambridge were called townsmen up to 1656; selectmen thereafter.

17. Entry of Oct. 28, 1636, in Mass. Colony *Records*, I, 183, quoted in Paige, *History of Cambridge*, 42.

18. *New England's First Fruits*, 12.

19. *Ibid.*, 13.

20. "Although Daye [Day] was recognized by the General Court December 10, 1641, as 'the first that set upon printing,' he was a locksmith . . . by trade. Perhaps his son Matthew had already received some instruction as a printer. . . . I think that Marmaduke Johnson, who came to assist in printing the Indian Bible, was the first thoroughly instructed printer in New England." (Paige, *History of Cambridge*, 44 n.) Day's printing plant did not get all the New England, or even Massachusetts Bay, business during

the thirty years when it had a virtual monopoly. Manuscripts of sermons written by the more eminent ministers, the better historical works, and other writings that merited finer typography than the Cambridge printer was equipped to furnish were sent to London as heretofore. But Nathaniel could obtain from him such light reading as the original New England almanac, compiled by William Pierce, mariner, and the Psalms in meter hot off the press.

21. Entry of Mar. 13, 1639, in Mass. Colony Records, I, 254, quoted in Paige, History of Cambridge, 383.

22. Entry of May 20, 1640, in Mass. Colony Records, I, 292, quoted in ibid., 384.

23. Entry of Jan. 14, 1666, in Cambridge Records, 165.

24. Entry of Mar. 27, 1765, in ibid., 145–146.

25. Entry of May 9, 1670, in ibid., 185.

26. Entry of Nov. 11, 1673, in ibid., 213.

27. Entry of Feb. 14, 1676, in ibid., 226.

28. Entry of Mar. 15, 1677, in ibid., 233.

29. Quoted in Paige, History of Cambridge, 572.

30. It was a common practice in early colonial days to name a child after an older one who had died. The resulting confusion in pedigrees must make many a genealogist feel like hanging himself on the nearest family tree. And—as if this were not enough to drive the lineage experts crazy—the Hancocks followed the practice on three subsequent occasions. There were also two Marys, two Abigails, and two Elizabeths. This circumstance makes the high rate of mortality in Nathaniel's household painfully apparent; but it was no higher than in most other families of like size at the time.

31. Entry of Mar. 30, 1694, in Cambridge Records, 305.

32. Entry of 1691, in ibid., 293.

33. Entry of May 12, 1693, in ibid., 302. The proprietors were the settlers of the town in whom title to its property was vested. They had power to make general divisions of land among the inhabitants and to grant particular tracts to individuals.

34. Ministers were expected to supplement their pay by cultivating their acres and selling the produce. They also received monetary gifts from well-to-do parishioners. Even on a strictly salaried basis they were much better paid than other professional men. Their income was greater than that of prosperous farmers and merchants, too. Besides, it went much further then than it would today.

35. Quoted in C. A. Staples, Address in Commemoration of the Ordination of the Reverend John Hancock, 11, 12.

36. C. Hudson, History of the Town of Lexington (rev. ed., 1913), I, 39, 50–51. Inflation had been on the increase in Massachusetts Bay since the turn of the century. In 1704, for instance, an ounce of sterling silver was valued at seven shillings in the currency of the colony, and by 1725 it represented twenty-seven shillings. Thomas Hutchinson writes, "The depreciation was grievous to all creditors but particularly distressing to the clergy and other salary men" (History of Massachusetts Bay, II, 174).

37. Ecclesiastical ordinations were gala social events at this period, when

life was still hard and almost entirely devoid of diversion. Although there is no account of the ceremonies held to consecrate John Hancock to the work of God except that they were attended by seven ministers from out of town, a description of those staged two years later at Woburn shows what they were like. They lasted four days, and sixty guests of the parish sat down every evening to dinner, consuming six and a half barrels of cider, twenty-eight gallons of wine, four of rum, and two of brandy; thirty-two horses belonging to the visitors were stabled at the expense of the hosts. The total cost was more than $400, according to modern monetary values—a lavish outlay for those times.

38. J. Hancock, Sermon Preached at the Ordination of Mr. John Hancock, 31, 35.

39. Ebenezer Hancock was called to assist his father in the dual capacity of minister and teacher under a complicated set of terms. He was to share with the Reverend John an annual salary of £400 and was to receive a settlement gift of £300 on the Bishop's decease. His scholastic duties were a continuation of those begun on his graduation from Harvard in 1728. The school in which he taught was known as a "running school" and now provided free tuition. Situated in the center of the town, it was not easily accessible to children living on the outskirts. To accommodate them the educational facilities were moved from one quarter to another every month. Lexington's younger generation had to do without reading, writing, and arithmetic for about two-thirds of each year.

40. J. Hancock, The Lord's Ministers, 1, 2, 3, 19. In complimenting his parishioners on their industry Hancock was not exaggerating, for they were prosperous enough to own twenty slaves in all. These Negroes were employed only as house servants and were treated well.

41. N. Appleton, The Servant's Actual Readiness, note on fly-leaf.

42. C. Hudson, History of the Town of Lexington (1st ed., 1868), 72. The wearing of mourning rings and the drinking of alcoholic beverages at funerals had been prohibited by the General Court in 1741 on pain of a £25 fine. This measure and similar ones had been taken because many families were impoverishing themselves in the attempt to keep up with wealthy neighbors in elaborate obsequies. Fifty suits of clothes and ninety dozen pairs of gloves were ordered for the services of Andrew Belcher, brother of the governor. Dr. Andrew Eliot was given 2,941 pairs of gloves by mourners at ceremonies where he officiated and realized £1,441 on them for his New North Meetinghouse in Boston.

43. N. Appleton, The Servant's Actual Readiness, 31–34.

44. Entry of June 29, 1726, in Records of First Church, North Braintree, quoted in H. A. Phillips's MS. Notes and Sources, in American Antiquarian Society, Worcester.

45. Quoted in C. F. Adams, Jr., Three Episodes of Massachusetts History, II, 618–619.

46. Entries of Jan. 21, 1728, and Aug. 12, 1728, to Sept. 28, 1735, in Records of First Church, North Braintree, requoted from Mass. Hist. Soc. Proceedings, 2nd Ser., VI, 487–488.

47. C. F. Adams, Jr., "Some Phases of Sexual Morality," in Mass. Hist. Soc. *Proceedings,* 2nd Ser., VI, 497.

48. John Hancock's birthday is recorded by some historians as January 12, 1736/7. The variation in dates is due to the official use of the old Julian calendar throughout the British Empire at the time Hancock was born. Under this system March 25 was the first day of the year. In the Roman Catholic Church and in all Roman Catholic countries it had been supplanted in 1582 by the Gregorian, or New Style, calendar introduced by Pope Gregory XIII and designating January 1 as the beginning of the year. But not until September 2, 1752, did England adopt the Gregorian calendar. This was widely employed even in Great Britain and her colonies long before 1752, but March 25 continued to be regarded as the first day of the year in English-speaking legal and ecclesiastical circles. Hence the alternative years, such as 1736/7, were recorded for the period between January 1 and March 25 before 1752. In that year eleven days were stricken from the Old Style calendar as representing the difference then existing between it and the new one. This accounts for the discrepancy between January 12 and January 23 cited indiscriminately by historians as Hancock's birthday. All dates in this book are New Style.

49. Records of First Church, North Braintree, quoted in W. S. Pattee, *History of Old Braintree,* 218.

50. John Adams to William Tudor, June 1, 1817, in *Works,* ed. C. F. Adams, X, 260–261.

51. E. Gay, *Sermon Preached at the Funeral of Mr. John Hancock,* 18, 23–24, 25.

CHAPTER II (Pages 24–41)

1. This designation appears on the title page of *New English Canaan,* the book that Thomas Morton wrote after he had returned to England, about his experiences in America. Clifford's Inn was, and still is, a London law society.

2. *Bradford's History of Plymouth Plantation,* ed. W. T. Davis, Original Narratives Ser. (New York, 1908), 237, 238.

3. T. Morton, "The New English Canaan," in P. Force, ed., *Tracts,* II, xv, 93.

4. Entry of Jan. 15, 1716, "Sewell Diary," in Mass. Hist. Soc. *Collections,* 5th Ser., VII, 71.

5. John Hancock was the third of fourteen men to hold the highest political office in the United Colonies, as President of the Continental Congress, before the official establishment of the United States under the Constitution with Washington as the first Chief Executive.

6. The facts on which this description of eighteenth century Braintree is based were taken from Charles Francis Adams, *History of Braintree,* 88–95.

7. J. Adams to Tudor, June 1, 1817, in *Works,* ed. C. F. Adams, X, 259.

8. A. T. Perkins, *Life of Copley*, 46–47.

9. Thomas Hancock eventually acquired for a pittance virtually the whole of Beacon Hill by shrewd, if not sharp, dealing. He bought two acres adjoining his original property for £220 from Shute Yeamans in 1752 and later satisfied the court that he was entitled to four or five more, by means of a defective deed drawn on the assumption that this tract was common land owned by the town of Boston. Actually the municipality had title only to six square rods and a right of way. Thomas and his nephew retained possession by pasturing cows in the area. In 1819 it was distributed among the numerous heirs in such small pieces that one legatee obtained a strip eighty feet deep but with a frontage of less than eighteen inches on Beacon Street. As late as 1902 one tiny parcel still belonged to a person who could trace his ancestry back to old Thomas.—W. W. Wheildon, *Sentry*, 91–95.

10. Thomas Hancock to James Glin, Dec. 20, 1736, and June 24, 1737, in Letterbooks, Baker Library, Harvard University.

11. Tyler & Hancock to Captain Partington, Aug. 1, 1737, in *ibid*. From about 1731 to 1741 Hancock had William Tyler as a partner in several ventures.

12. T. Hancock to Francis Wilks, June 24, 1737, in *ibid*.

13. T. Hancock to John Rowe, Jan., 1738, in *ibid*.

14. T. Hancock to Wilks, Dec. 20, 1738, and July 10, 1739, in *ibid*.

15. T. Hancock to Jarvis Maplesden, Nov. 28, 1739, in *ibid*.

16. "Many references are found to premature old age among the men of this period. A short life was encouraged by severe exposures, lack of mental exhilaration by means of literature or plays, and by the procedure common throughout most of the colonies of treating boys as adults at about the age when we are thinking of putting them into high school. An example is the father who wrote his son a stern letter when the boy had reached the age of nine; assuring him that hereafter, in all their dealings together, the lad was to be treated as a man. This over-stimulation of the mind and early assumption of the burdens of adulthood exerted a decided influence on the span of life of Massachusetts manhood. According to the scanty vital statistics available, few men lived beyond the age of fifty years and scarcely any over seventy years."—A. R. Curnick, "Social Life in the Revolutionary Period," in A. B. Hart, ed., *Commonwealth History of Mass.*, III, 281–282.

17. Quoted in L. Sears, *John Hancock* (Boston, 1912), 22. Most of the factual material on Hancock's school days is from this book.

18. Quoted in S. E. Morison, *Three Centuries of Harvard*, 103.

19. T. Hancock to Christopher Kilby, Sept. 10, 1748, in H. A. Phillips, MS. Notes and Sources, American Antiquarian Society.

20. T. Hancock to Kilby & Barnard, Feb. 15 and Nov. 11, 1749, in *ibid*.

21. T. Hancock to Kilby, Dec. 9, 1749, and May 6, 1750, in *ibid*.

22. Harvard Archives, quoted in J. Quincy, *History of Harvard University*, II, 95.

23. "From that time [1720] to 1763, when Hollis was built, the group of 'colleges' (except for the addition of Holden Chapel in 1744) was . . . Old Harvard, Massachusetts, and Stoughton College. . . . [They] formed an open triangle. . . . North of Old Harvard the Spencer Orchard . . . had been

set aside in 1712 as a . . . recreation ground. . . . South of Massachuetts was the college brew-house, and east of Stoughton the 'fellows' barn,' where presumably the hay cut in the Yard was stored."—S. E. Morison, *Three Centuries of Harvard,* 59.

24. Harvard Archives, quoted in L. Sears, *Hancock,* 31.

25. Most of the data on the life and curriculum at Harvard are taken from L. Sears, *John Hancock,* 26–39.

26. Quoted in S. E. Morison, *Three Centuries of Harvard,* 105.

27. Quoted in M. M. Carlton, *John Hancock,* 2.

28. Quoted in S. E. Morison, *Three Centuries of Harvard,* 115.

29. John Hancock to Mary Perkins, May 1, 1754, in L. Sears, *John Hancock,* 42–43.

CHAPTER III (Pages 42–60)

1. Bostonian Society *Publications,* XII, 99–100.

2. The analysis and interpretation of the Hancocks' business methods in this chapter and succeeding ones are based on Prof. W. T. Baxter's *The House of Hancock* (Cambridge, 1945).

3. T. Hancock to John Checkering, Oct. 22, 1736, in Letterbooks.

4. T. Hutchinson, *History of Massachusetts Bay,* III, 297.

5. J. Allen Narrative, in Mass. Hist. Soc. *Proceedings,* 1st Ser., XVI (1879), 69.

6. T. Hutchinson, *Massachusetts Bay,* III, 297–298.

7. T. Hancock to Mrs. Jarvis Maplesden, June 20, 1739, in Letterbooks.

8. T. Hancock to Wilks, Oct. 26, 1739, in *ibid.*

9. T. Hancock to Kilby, Aug. 2, 1740, in *ibid.*

10. T. Hancock to John Barnard, July 29, 1745, in *ibid.*

11. T. Hancock to George Brice, Mar. 13, 1736, in *ibid.*

12. T. Hancock to Kilby, Sept. 10, 1763, in *ibid.*

13. T. Hancock to Kilby, Nov. 12, 1748, and June 29, 1752, in *ibid.*

14. T. Hancock to John Tomlinson, Aug. 31, 1749, in H. A. Phillips, MS. Notes and Sources.

15. Edward Cornwallis to Lords of Trade, Nov. 27, 1750, in J. Winsor, ed., *Narrative and Critical History of America,* V, Pt. 1, 149 n. The Lords of Trade, or Board of Trade, were the British overseers of colonial affairs but had no power to make decisions as to policy. They could only advise the King and Privy Council.

16. Esther Forbes, *Paul Revere and the World He Lived In,* 48–51, is the source of most of the background material in this section.

17. J. Bennett, History of New England, in Mass. Hist. Soc. *Proceedings,* 1st Ser., V. 113.

18. *Ibid,* 124–126. "In 1725 Deacon Jonathan Williams of Brattle Street Church, a hard-headed grain dealer . . . having his mind always concerned with the Common because his duty was to collect for the town the fees derived from the pasturing of the cows there, conceived the idea of starting a

mall like Pall Mall in London. He sent to London and got a large number of small trees, which he planted along the future Tremont Street edge of the Common. . . . For many years Thomas Hancock, and later John Hancock, were especially commissioned by the town to care for . . . those trees, and the love with which they regarded them was shown by both having attempted, though not with permanent success, to start a similar mall along Beacon Street."—Bostonian Soc. *Publications*, XI, 21–22.

19. Boston *Evening Post*, Sept. 7, 1747, quoted in O. E. Winslow, ed., *Harper's Literary Museum*, 387.

20. Entry of Oct. 1, 1750, Goelet Journal, in *New England Hist. and Geneal. Register*, XXIV, 53.

21. J. Bennett, *op. cit.*, 125.

22. T. Hancock to Kilby & Barnard, Feb. 13, 1756, in Letterbooks.

23. T. Hancock, Domestic Memoranda, in Baker Library.

24. J. Adams to Tudor, June 5, 1817, in *Works*, ed. C. F. Adams, X, 259.

CHAPTER IV (Pages 61–79)

1. T. Hancock to Kilby, Aug. 4, 1755, in Letterbooks.

2. W. T. Baxter, *The House of Hancock*, 134.

3. Massachusetts *Archives*, V, 457, quoted in *ibid*.

4. T. Hancock to Lord Halifax, Sept. 15, 1755, in Letterbooks.

5. T. Hancock to Kilby, Apr. 19, 1756, in *ibid*.

6. T. Hancock to Kilby & Barnard, Nov. 21, 1755, in *ibid*.

7. Entry of Nov. 18, 1755, in John Tudor, *Deacon Tudor's Diary*, ed. W. Tudor, 9.

8. J. Hancock to Lydia Hancock, undated, in A. E. Brown, *John Hancock: His Book*, 7.

9. J. Hancock to Jonas Clark, undated. Original MS. in possession of California Fruit Growers Exchange, Los Angeles.

10. Mary Perkins to Ebenezer Hancock, May 10, 1760, in Hancock Papers, XXX.

11. T. Hancock to Kilby, Barnard & Parker (a third partner had been added to the firm), May 21 and May 23, 1760, in Letterbooks.

12. T. Hancock to John Pownall, June 7, 1760, in *ibid*. An enclosed receipt for the governor's passage shows that the fare was £150.

13. T. Hancock to J. Hancock, July 5, 1760, in *ibid*.

14. T. Hancock to Thomas Pownall, Sept. 24, 1760, in *ibid*.

15. J. Hancock to Daniel Perkins, Oct. 29, 1760, in Mass. Hist. Soc. *Proceedings*, XLIII (1910), 193–194. Hancock may have spent some of this "dull" period learning to swim in the Thames—an accomplishment he acquired while in England.

16. J. Hancock to E. Hancock, Dec. 27, 1760, in *ibid.*, 194–195. Molly was a maid, probably white. "Agniss," Prince, and Hannibal were Negro slaves.

17. "Memoirs of John Hancock, Esq.," in *New Lottery Magazine*, Aug., 1776.

18. J. E. Alden, "John Mein: Scourge of Patriots," in Colonial Soc. of Mass. *Publications*, XXXIV (1943), 596.

19. J. Hancock to T. Hancock, Jan. 14, 1761, in Mass. Hist. Soc. *Proceedings*, XLIII, 196, 197.

20. J. Hancock to D. Perkins, Mar. 2, 1761. Original MS. in possession of Bostonian Society, Boston.

21. T. Hancock to J. Hancock, Mar. 23, 1761, in Letterbooks.

22. J. Hancock to T. Hancock, July 11, 1761, in Mass. Hist. Soc. *Proceedings*, XLIII, 200.

23. T. Hancock to Kilby, Barnard & Parker, Oct. 22, 1761, in Letterbooks.

24. Jonathan Barnard to T. Hancock, July 14, 1761, in Amer. Antiq. Soc. *Proceedings*, N. S. XII (1899), 53.

25. T. Hancock to J. Hancock, Oct. 7, 1760, in Letterbooks.

26. J. Hancock to T. Hancock, Jan. 14, 1761, in Mass. Hist. Soc. *Proceedings*, XLIII, 195.

27. T. Hancock to J. Hancock, July 5, 1760, in Letterbooks.

28. T. Hancock to Tomlinson, Trecothick & Co., Nov. 6, 1761, in *ibid.*

29. T. Hancock to John Bastide, Jan. 29, 1762, in *ibid.*

30. In 1810 Isaiah Thomas, foremost colonial printer and publisher, wrote: "Kneeland and Green printed, principally for Daniel Henchman, an edition of the Bible in small quarto. This was the first Bible printed in America in the English language. It was carried through the press as privately as possible and had the London imprint of the copy from which it was reprinted, viz., 'London: Printed by Mark Baskett, Printer to the King's Most Excellent Majesty,' in order to prevent a prosecution from those in England and Scotland who published the Bible by a patent from the Crown; or, *cum privilegio*, as did the English universities of Oxford and Cambridge. When I was an apprentice I often heard those who had assisted at the case and press in printing this Bible make mention of the fact. The late Governor Hancock was related to Henchman and knew the particulars of the transaction. He possessed a copy of this impression."—"History of Printing in America," in Amer. Antiq. Soc. *Transactions*, V (1874), 107–108.

31. T. Hancock to Matthew Woodford, July 8, 1762, in Letterbooks.

32. T. Hancock to Woodford, Aug. 2, 1763, in *ibid.*

33. T. Hancock to Jonathan Barnard & Co., Jan. 1, 1763, in *ibid.*

34. T. Hancock to William Beth, Mar. 18, 1763, in *ibid.*

35. T. Hancock to Barnard & Co., June 7, 1763, in *ibid.*

36. T. Hancock to Barnard & Co., undated, in W. T. Baxter, *The House of Hancock*, 171.

37. T. Hancock to Barnard & Co., Nov. 14, 1763, in Letterbooks. Harrison had become a member of the firm on Kilby's retirement.

38. *General Court of Massachusetts*, 24. Thomas Hancock had capitalized on the intense interest in this subject by publishing, jointly with Daniel Henchman, a volume entitled *A Dissertation Concerning Inoculation of the Small Pox*. "The inoculation . . . was dangerous not only to the individual but to the community. 'Venom' was taken from 'the best sort of smallpox,'

as much as would lie on the point of a needle, and put directly into an open wound. In this way a light case usually developed, which was, however, real smallpox and exactly as contagious. The patient was soon up and about with as complete immunity as though he had taken it 'in the natural way.' "—E. Forbes, *Paul Revere* (Houghton Mifflin Company, Boston, 1942), 78. Reprinted by permission of the publishers.

39. Margaret H. Mascarene to John Mascarene, Jan. 30, 1764, quoted in S. A. Eliot, *History of Cambridge*, 63–64.

40. T. Hancock & Co. to Barnard & Harrison, July, 1764, in Letterbooks.

41. Mar. 13, 1736, in *ibid.*

CHAPTER V (Pages 80–101)

1. Suffolk County Probate Court *Records*, File No. 13484, Boston. Even unto death Thomas Hancock was secretive about his financial affairs. The paragraph in his will naming John residuary legatee concludes: "And I order that no inventory of my estate be given into the Probate Office but such security as the law requires when none is given." The purpose of this stipulation may have been to guard his nephew against parasites, schemers, and poor relations who might try to borrow from him or defraud him of his patrimony. In the absence of any contemporary record of his cash legacy, the estimate of £80,000 made by most historians who have touched on the subject would seem to be based on guesswork. But it probably is fairly accurate.

2. Mrs. Hancock was one of only twenty-two Bostonians who possessed carriages, according to a census taken in 1768.

3. J. Adams to Tudor, June 1, 1817, in *Works*, ed. C. F. Adams, X, 259–260.

4. J. Hancock to Barnard & Harrison, Aug. 17, 1764, in A. E. Brown, *John Hancock: His Book*, 46.

5. J. Hancock to Barnard & Harrison, Dec. 6, 1764, in Letterbooks.

6. J. Hancock to Devonshire & Reeve, Dec. 7, 1764, in *ibid.*

7. Boston *Evening Post*, Dec. 25, 1764, quoted in J. S. Loring, *Hundred Boston Orators*, 73. This store was situated near the head of the present South Market Street.

8. J. Hancock to Barnard & Harrison, Jan. 21, 1765, in Letterbooks.

9. J. Hancock to Barnard & Harrison, Apr. 18, 1765, in *ibid.*

10. J. Hancock to Barnard & Harrison, Apr. 5 and May 13, 1765, in *ibid.*

11. J. Hancock to Barnard & Harrison, July 6, 1765, in *ibid.*

12. J. Hancock to Lamar, Hill & Bissett, July 23, 1765, in *ibid.*

13. The first volume of Hutchinson's highly important *History of Massachusetts Bay* had been published early in 1765; but the second, which was still in manuscript, narrowly escaped destruction at this time, along with valuable records of the province. The Reverend Andrew Eliot rescued most of the mud-spattered sheets from the gutter, and they were published later in England.

14. J. Hancock to Barnard & Harrison, Jan. 25, 1766, in Letterbooks.
15. J. Hancock to Barnard & Harrison, Sept. 30 and Oct. 14, 1765, in *ibid.*
16. J. Hancock to Barnard & Harrison, Oct. 21, 1765, in *ibid.*
17. Most of the facts in the description of the Pope's Day celebrations are taken from E. Forbes, *Revere*, 93–98.
18. "Reminiscences," in *New England Hist. and Geneal. Register*, VIII, 191.
19. Quoted in E. Forbes, *Revere*, 126.
20. "Portrait of an Empty Barrel," in *Harper's Magazine*, CLXI (1930), 431.
21. J. Hancock to Thomas Longman, Oct. 28, 1765, in Letterbooks.
22. J. Hancock to Barnard & Harrison, Dec. 21, 1765, in *ibid.*
23. J. Hancock to Barnard & Harrison, Jan. 18, 1766, in *ibid.*
24. Diary entry of Feb., 1763, in *Works*, ed. C. F. Adams, II (Boston, 1850), 144.
25. J. Adams to Tudor, June 1, 1817, in *Works*, ed. C. F. Adams, X, 260.
26. Entry of May 19, 1766, in John Rowe, *Letters and Diary*, ed. A. R. Cunningham, 95.
27. J. Hancock to Harrison & Barnard, May 27, 1766, in Letterbooks. Harrison had become senior partner when the elder Barnard retired in favor of his son.
28. J. Hancock to Harrison & Barnard, Nov. 10, 1766, in A. E. Brown, *John Hancock: His Book*, 135.
29. E. E. Pierce, in Introduction to Rowe, *Letters and Diary*, 25–26.
30. Entry of Dec. 2, 1766, in *ibid.*, 116–117.
31. J. Hancock to Harrison & Barnard, Dec. 3, 1766, in A. E. Brown, *John Hancock: His Book*, 135.
32. J. Hancock to Harrison & Barnard, Apr. 22, 1767, in Letterbooks.
33. J. Hancock to Harrison & Barnard, Sept. 2, 1767, in *ibid.*
34. J. Hancock to Harrison & Barnard, Oct. 16, 1767, in *ibid.*
35. J. Hancock to George Haley, Oct. 16, 1767, in *ibid.*
36. J. Hancock to Harrison, Barnard & Sprag, Nov. 2, 1767, in *ibid.*

CHAPTER VI (Pages 102–127)

1. Customs Commissioners to Lords of Treasury, Mar. 28, 1768, in Public Record Office, London, quoted in W. T. Baxter, *The House of Hancock*, 260.
2. Hutchinson to R. Jackson, Apr. 17, 1768, in Massachusetts Archives, XXVI, 299, Statehouse, Boston.
3. W. T. Baxter, *The House of Hancock*, 261.
4. The Writs of Assistance empowered customs officers to search any house or ship for smuggled goods.
5. Quoted in W. T. Baxter, *The House of Hancock*, 262.
6. *Ibid.*, 263.
7. Quoted in W. V. Wells, *Life of Samuel Adams*, I, 186.

8. S. Adams to Dennys de Berdt, Sept. 27, 1768, in *Writings*, ed. H. A. Cushing, I (New York, 1904), 245–246.

9. Quoted in W. T. Baxter, *House of Hancock*, 268. Litigation over minor phases of the *Liberty* case dragged on until the Revolution, according to John Adams: "A painful drudgery I had of his cause. There were few days through the whole winter when I was not summoned to attend the Court of Admiralty. It seemed as if the officers of the Crown were determined to examine the whole town as witnesses. . . . They interrogated many of his near relations and most intimate friends and threatened to summon his amiable and venerable aunt. . . . I was thoroughly weary and disgusted with the court, the officers of the Crown, the cause, and even with the tyrannical bell that dangled me out of my house every morning; and this odious cause was suspended at last only by the battle of Lexington." (*Works*, ed. C. F. Adams, II, 215–216.)

10. Entry of June 14, 1768, in Boston Town *Records*, XVI (1886), 254.

11. Bernard Papers (Letterbooks), VI, 321, quoted in Mass. Hist. Soc. *Proceedings*, LV (1923), 257.

12. J. Hancock to George Haley, June, 1768, in A. E. Brown, *John Hancock: His Book*, 158.

13. W. V. Wells, *op. cit.*, 207.

14. Hutchinson to Thomas Whately, Aug., 1768, in Thomas Hutchinson, *Diary and Letters* (Boston, 1773), 6.

15. W. V. Wells, *op. cit.*, 213.

16. Hutchinson to Whately, Oct. 4, 1768, in Thomas Hutchinson, *op. cit.*, 9.

17. L. W. Labaree, *Royal Government in America* (New Haven, 1930), 198–199.

18. J. Hancock to Haley & Hopkins, Nov. 4, 1769, in A. E. Brown, *John Hancock: His Book*, 166–167.

19. Speeches quoted in E. Forbes, *Paul Revere*, 155.

20. *Works*, ed. C. F. Adams, II, 229–230.

21. This account of the Boston Massacre is based on the version in E. Forbes, *Revere*, 151–168—a distillation of the legal evidence contained in P. W. Chandler, *American Criminal Trials*, I, 303–418, and the personal observations in B. B. Thatcher, ed., *Traits of the Tea Party*, 96–122.

22. J. Belknap, Memoranda, in Mass. Hist. Soc. *Proceedings*, 1st Ser., III (1859), 308–309.

23. Entry of Mar. 5, 1770, in J. Tudor, *Deacon Tudor's Diary*, ed. W. Tudor, 33.

24. S. Adams to J. Hancock, May 11, 1770, in *Writings*, ed. H. A. Cushing, II, 9.

25. William Palfrey to Haley & Hopkins, June 13, 1770, in Letterbooks.

26. J. Hancock to Haley, Dec. 27, 1770, in *ibid.*

27. J. Hancock to E. Hancock, Jan. 11, 1771. Original MS. in possession of John Hancock Mutual Life Insurance Co., Boston.

28. J. Hancock to Haley & Hopkins, 1771, in A. E. Brown, *John Hancock: His Book*, 171.

29. Hutchinson to person unknown, Apr. 5, 1771, in Hutchinson Correspondence (Bancroft Transcripts), II, New York Public Library.

30. Hutchinson to J. Pownall, May 30, 1771, in Massachusetts Archives, XXVII, 174.

31. Hutchinson to person unknown, June 5, 1771, in Hutchinson Correspondence, II, New York Public Library.

32. Quoted in W. V. Wells, *Life of Samuel Adams*, I, 398.

33. T. Hutchinson, *History of Massachusetts Bay*, III, 346–347.

34. J. Hancock to Haley & Hopkins, Oct. 11, 1771, in Letterbooks.

35. J. Hancock to Haley & Hopkins, Nov. 14, 1771, in A. E. Brown, *John Hancock: His Book*, 172.

36. Hutchinson to Thomas Gage, Dec. 1, 1771, in Massachusetts Archives, XXVII, 258.

37. Hutchinson to Francis Bernard, Jan. 29, 1772, in *ibid.*, 286.

38. Quoted in A. E. Brown, *John Hancock: His Book*, 176.

39. S. Adams to Arthur Lee, Apr. 22, 1773, in R. H. Lee, *Life of Arthur Lee*, II (Boston, 1829), 203.

40. Quoted in A. E. Brown, *John Hancock: His Book*, 176.

41. S. Adams to Lee, Apr. 12, 1773, in W. V. Wells, *Life of Samuel Adams*, I, 470.

42. Hutchinson to Lord Hillsborough, June 15, 1772, in Hutchinson Correspondence, III.

CHAPTER VII (Pages 128–152)

1. Quoted from S. K. Lothrop, *History of the Church in Brattle Street*, 101.

2. Entry of Mar. 10, 1772, in Boston Town *Records*, XVIII (1887), 72.

3. Entry of Mar. 3, 1774, *Letters and Diary*, ed. A. R. Cunningham, 264.

4. Boston *Gazette*, Oct. 2, 1772.

5. Quoted in L. Sears *John Hancock*, 128–129.

6. Quoted in J. C. Miller, *Sam Adams*, 280.

7. Entry of June 4, 1773, *Letters and Diary*, ed. A. R. Cunningham, 246.

8. Benjamin Hallowell to J. Pownall, Sept. 29, 1773, in B. F. Stevens, ed. *Facsimiles of Manuscripts in European Archives*, XXIV, Doc. No. 2029, p. 5.

9. Entry of Nov. 3, 1773, in John Rowe, Extracts from the Unpublished Diary of . . . , *Proceedings in Masonry*, Mass. Grand Lodge, 426.

10. Quoted (entry of Nov. 29, 1773) in *ibid.*, 427.

11. T. Hutchinson, *History of Massachusetts Bay*, III, 310–311.

12. Lieutenant Colonel Leslie to Lord Dartmouth, Dec. 6, 1773, in *Home Office Papers*, ed. R. A. Roberts, IV, 175–176.

13. Entry of Dec. 8, 1773, in John Rowe, *op. cit.*, 428.

14. Quoted in W. V. Wells, *Life of Samuel Adams*, II, 114.

15. Entry of Nov. 30, 1773, in Rowe, *loc. cit.* "The people assembled in Boston took the name of 'the Body,' instead of a 'legal town meeting,' and began with that spirit with which all established powers ought to act in the

exercise of their legal constitutional authority."—T. Hutchinson, *History of Massachusetts Bay*, III, 309.

16. John Andrews to William Barrell, Dec. 1, 1773, in Mass. Hist. Soc. *Proceedings*, 1st Ser., VIII (1866), 325.

17. Hutchinson to person unknown, Dec. 3, 1773, quoted in W. V. Wells, *Life of Samuel Adams*, II, 116.

18. Hutchinson to Lord Dartmouth, Dec. 17, 1773, in Hutchinson Correspondence, III.

19. Quoted in E. Forbes, *Revere*, 197.

20. B. B. Thatcher, ed., *Traits of the Tea Party*, 177–178.

21. Andrews to Barrell, Dec. 18, 1773, in Mass. Hist. Soc. *Proceedings*, 1st Ser., VIII (1866), 325–326.

22. Entry of Dec. 16, 1773, Rowe, *loc. cit.*

23. B. B. Thatcher, ed., *op. cit.*, 193.

24. J. Hancock to Haley & Hopkins, Dec. 21, 1773, in Letterbooks.

25. T. Maxwell, "The Command at the Battle of Bunker Hill, as Shown in the Statement of Major Thompson Maxwell," *New England Hist. and Geneal. Register*, XXII (1868), 57–58.

26. T. Hutchinson, *History of Massachusetts Bay*, III, 315, 313–314.

27. James Scott to J. Hancock, London, Feb. 21, 1774, in *Old-Time New England*, XXV (1934), 35–36.

28. J. Hancock, *Oration Delivered March 5, 1774*, 8–10, 12–13, 18, 19.

29. Diary entry of Mar. 5, 1774, in *Works*, ed. C. F. Adams, II, 332.

30. Noah Webster to Ebenezer S. Thomas, July 29, 1840, in Mass. Hist. Soc. *Proceedings*, 3rd Ser., XLIII (1910), 155.

31. E. S. Thomas, *Reminiscences of the Last Sixty-five Years*, II, 169.

32. Entry of Mar. 8, 1774, in John Rowe, *Letters and Diary*, ed. A. R. Cunningham, 265.

33. Entry of July 1, 1774, in *Diary and Letters*, ed. P. O. Hutchinson, I (1884), 166–167.

34. Haley to J. Hancock, July 20, 1774, in Hancock MSS., Baker Library.

35. Henry Pelham to John S. Copley, July 17 and Nov. 2, 1774, in Mass. Hist. Soc. *Collections*, 7th Ser., LXXI (1914), 232, 267–268.

36. Quoted in A. E. Brown, *John Hancock: His Book*, 185.

37. Andrews to Barrell, Aug. 16, 1774, in Mass. Hist. Soc. *Proceedings*, 1st Ser., VIII (1802), 342.

CHAPTER VIII (Pages 153–174)

1. Earl Percy to Duke of Northumberland, Aug. 15, 1774, in Hugh, Earl Percy, *Letters from Boston and New York, 1774–1776*, ed. C. K. Bolton, 34.

2. The ten children of Edmund Quincy IV and Elizabeth Wendell Quincy, in order of birth, were: Edmund V, Henry, Abraham, Elizabeth, Katherine, Jacob, Dorothy I (who died in infancy), Sarah, Esther, and Dorothy II.

3. Edmund Quincy to Henry Frankland, Nov. 30, 1756, in S. H Swan,

"Story of an Old House," *New England Magazine,* N. S. XVII (1897), 178–179.

4. E. Quincy to Elizabeth Wendell Quincy, July 26, 1756, in E. C. D. Woodbury, *Dorothy Quincy,* 17.

5. Diary entry of Jan. 3, 1759, in John Adams, *Works,* ed. C. F. Adams, II, 60.

6. Diary entry of late Feb. or early Mar. 1759, in *op. cit.,* 62. Samuel and Ned (Edmund) were sons of Col. Josiah Quincy.

7. Entries of Oct. 2, 9, 12, 13, and Nov. 5, 1750, in Goelet Journal, *New England Hist. and Geneal. Register,* XXIV (1870), 53–55, 61.

8. " 'Dorothy Q.,' Who Became Dorothy H.," *Americana,* XIV (1920), 412.

9. Entry of Feb. 22, 1770, in John Boyle "Journal of Occurrences in Boston," *New England Hist. and Geneal. Register,* LXXXIV (1930), 262.

10. Samuel Salisbury to Stephen Salisbury, Mar. 19, 1771, in C. L. Nichols, "Samuel Salisbury," Amer. Antiq. Soc. *Proceedings,* N. S. XXXV (1926), 51.

11. R. Perkins to E. Hancock, Aug. 31, 1771, in Hancock Papers, XXX.

12. J. Adams to Tudor, June 1, 1817, in *Works,* ed. C. F. Adams, X, 260.

13. E. Quincy to Dorothy Quincy, June 18, 1773, in Colonial Soc. of Mass. *Publications,* VI (1904), 320–321. The abbreviations refer to Governor Hutchinson and Lieutenant Governor Oliver.

14. Quoted in F. W. C. Hersey, "The Misfortunes of Dorcas Griffiths," Colonial Soc. of Mass. *Publications,* XXXIV (1943), 22.

15. Boston *Evening Post,* Sept. 19, 1774.

16. Andrews to Barrell, Sept. 26 and 27, 1774, in Mass. Hist. Soc. *Proceedings,* 1st Ser., VIII (1866), 368, 369.

17. *Pennsylvania Gazette,* May 3, 1775.

18. "Extract of a Letter from London to a Gentleman in Massachusetts," Apr. 25, 1775, in P. Force, ed., *American Archives,* 4th Ser., II (Washington, 1839), 386.

19. Quoted in E. C. D. Woodbury, *Dorothy Quincy,* 69.

20. Entry of Sept. 6, 1775, in *Diary and Letters,* ed. P. O. Hutchinson, I, 528–529.

21. *Virginia Gazette,* Dec. 2, 1775.

22. Entry of Mar. 6, 1775, in John Barker, *The British in Boston,* ed. E. E. Dana, 25–26.

23. Quoted in Mass. Hist. Soc. *Proceedings,* 1st Ser., V (1862), 211.

24. "Letter to a Gentleman in New York," Mar. 22, 1775, in P. Force, ed., *American Archives,* 4th Ser., II (1839), 211.

25. Andrews to Barrell, Mar. 20, 1775, in Mass. Hist. Soc. *Proceedings,* 1st Ser., VIII (1866), 401.

26. "Letter to a Gentleman, etc.," *loc. cit.*

27. Andrews to Barrell, Mar. 20, 1775, *loc. cit.*

28. J. Hancock to D. Quincy, Mar. 25, 1775. Original MS. in Boston Public Library, Mellen Chamberlain Collection.

29. James Warren to Mercy Warren, Apr. 6, 1775, in *Warren-Adams Letters,* I—Mass. Hist. Soc. *Collections,* LXXII (1917),—45.

30. Helena Bayard to D. Quincy, Apr. 14, 1775, in E. C. D. Woodbury, *Dorothy Quincy*, 60.

31. Diary entry of May 20, 1775, in Dorothy Dudley, *Theatrum Majorum: The Cambridge of 1776*, ed. A. Gilman, 22.

32. J. Hancock to Christopher Leffingwell and William Hubbard, Apr. 15, 1775. Facsimile in possession of John Hancock Mutual Life Insurance Co., Boston.

33. Paul Revere to corresponding secretary of Massachusetts Historical Society, Jan. 1, 1798, in Mass. Hist. Soc. *Collections*, 1st Ser., V (1798), 106–107.

34. J. Hancock to Elbridge Gerry, Apr. 18, 1775, in New York Public Library, Manuscript Division, Hancock Miscellaneous Papers.

CHAPTER IX (Pages 175–198)

1. Revere to corresponding secretary of Massachusetts Historical Society, Jan. 1, 1798, in Mass. Hist. Soc. *Collections*, 1st Ser., V (1798), 107.

2. Facsimile of Revere deposition in Bostonian Society, Boston.

3. Deposition of William Munroe, Mar. 7, 1825, in E. Phinney, *History of the Battle of Lexington*, 33–34.

4. W. H. Sumner, "Reminiscences," *New England Hist. and Geneal. Register*, VIII (1854), 187.

5. Caesar Rodney to Thomas Rodney, May 11, 1775, in G. H. Ryden, ed., *Letters to and from Caesar Rodney*, 58.

6. Elizabeth Clark to Lucy W. Allen, Apr. 19, 1841, in Lexington Hist. Soc. *Proceedings*, IV (1912), 91–92.

7. W. H. Sumner, "Reminiscences," in *New England Hist. and Geneal. Register*, VIII (1854), 187–188.

8. Jonathan Sewell to John Lowell, Sr., Apr. 24, 1777, in E. E. Salisbury, *Family Memorials*, 345.

9. J. Hancock to Massachusetts Committee of Safety, Apr. 24, 1775, in P. Force, ed., *American Archives*, 4th Ser., II (1839), 384–385.

10. J. Hancock to D. Quincy, May 7, 1775, in E. E. Salisbury, *Family Memorials*, 378–330.

11. Silas Deane to Elizabeth Deane, May 7 and 12, 1775, in Conn. Hist. Soc. *Collections*, II (1870), 222–223, 227–228.

12. Entry of May 10, 1775, in Samuel Curwen, *Journal and Letters*, ed. G. A. Ward, 29.

13. S. Deane to E. Deane, May 12, 1775, *op. cit.*, 229.

14. Most of the material for this description of Philadelphia was drawn from C. and J. Bridenbaugh, *Rebels and Gentlemen*, 3–22, and Howard Fast, *Citizen Tom Paine*, 94–113.

15. Quoted in L. Sears, *John Hancock*, 179.

16. Entry of May 24, 1775, in W. C. Ford, *Continental Congress, Journals*, ed. II. (1905), 59.

17. Thaddeus Burr to Tapping Reeve, May 15, 1775. Original MS. owned by Fairfield Historical Society, now on deposit in Yale University Library, Annie Burr Jennings Memorial Collection.

18. W. H. Sumner, "Reminiscences," *New England Hist. and Geneal. Register,* VIII (1854), 188.

19. Dorothy Dudley to Esther Livingstone, Aug. 30, 1775, in Dorothy Dudley, *Theatrum Majorum,* ed. A. Gilman, 33.

20. John Lowell, Jr., to Lydia Hancock, June 5 and 17, 1775, in H. A. Phillips MS. Notes and Sources, Amer. Antiq. Soc., Worcester.

21. Proscription of Thomas Gage, June 12, 1775, in P. Force, ed., *American Archives,* 4th Ser., II (1839), 969.

22. J. Hancock to D. Quincy, June 10, 1775, in H. C. Walsh, "Three Letters from Hancock to 'Dorothy Q.,'" *New England Magazine,* N. S. VI (1892), 532, 533.

23. John Adams, *Works,* ed. C. F. Adams, II, 417.

24. *Ibid.,* 416.

25. J. Hancock to Joseph Warren, June 18, 1775, in E. C. Burnett, ed., *Letters of Members of the Continental Congress,* I, 134.

26. J. Hancock to Gerry, June 18, 1775, in P. Force, ed., *American Archives,* 4th Ser., II (1839), 1019.

27. J. Hancock to Washington, July 10, 1775, in L. Sears, *John Hancock,* 119.

28. Washington to J. Hancock, July 21, 1775, in P. Force, ed., *op. cit.* 1710.

29. J. Hancock to D. Quincy, June 21, 1775. Facsimile in New York Public Library. Copyright, 1938; quoted by permission of the American Autograph Shop, Merion Station, Pa.

CHAPTER X (Pages 199–220)

1. J. Adams to James Warren, July 24, 1775, in *Warren-Adams Letters,* I, 88–89.

2. J. Adams to Abigail Adams, July 24, 1775, in John and Abigail Adams, *Familiar Letters,* ed. C. F. Adams, 85.

3. John Adams, *Works,* ed. C. F. Adams, III, 32.

4. Benjamin Harrison to Washington, July 21, 1775, in E. C. Burnett, ed., *Letters of Members of the Continental Congress,* I, 170.

5. J. Adams to James Warren, June 27, 1775, in *Warren-Adams Letters,* I, 145.

6. E. Quincy to D. Quincy, July 22, 1775, in *New England Hist. and Geneal. Register,* XI (1857), 165–167.

7. Mass. Hist. Soc. *Proceedings,* 2nd Ser., VI (1891), 396.

8. New York *Gazette,* Aug. 28, 1775.

9. E. Quincy to H. Quincy, Sept. 9, 1775, in S. H. Swan, "Story of an Old House," *New England Magazine,* N. S. XVII (1897), 180.

10. J. Adams to James Warren, Sept. 19, 1775, in *Warren-Adams Letters*, I, 112.

11. William Gordon, *History of the United States*, II (New York, 1801), 283.

12. Entry of Sept. 27, 1775, in Continental Congress, *Journals*, ed. W. C. Ford, III (1905), 476.

13. Quoted in E. Forbes, *Paul Revere*, 296.

14. Revere to corresponding secretary of Mass. Hist. Soc., Jan. 1, 1798, in Mass. Hist. Soc. *Collections*, 1st Ser., V (1798), 106–111.

15. Quoted in E. Forbes, *Paul Revere*, 297.

16. J. Adams to B. Rush, Feb. 21, 1813. Original MS. in Boston Public Library, Alexander Biddle Papers.

17. J. Adams to James Warren, Oct. 21, 1775, in *Warren-Adams Letters*, I, 157.

18. Entry of Oct. 28, 1775, in Christopher Marshall, *Passages from the Remembrancer*, 55.

19. J. Adams to A. Adams, Nov. 4 and Dec. 3, 1775, in John and Abigail Adams, *Familiar Letters*, ed. C. F. Adams, 121–122, 127–128.

20. Entry of Nov. 24, 1775, in Christopher Marshall, *op. cit.*, 58–59.

21. M. A. Quincy, "Reminiscences," in *Our Country*, ed. A. L. Phelps, 304.

22. Diary entry of Dec. 22, 1775, in *American Historical Review*, I (1896), 298.

23. J. Hancock to Washington, Dec. 22, 1775, in P. Force, ed., *American Archives*, 4th Ser., IV (1843), 379.

24. Lord Stirling to J. Hancock, Dec. 17, 1775, and Jan. 10, 1776. Original MSS. in New York Historical Society, William Alexander Papers.

25. J. Hancock to Philip Schuyler, Jan. 10, 1776, in E. C. Burnett, ed., *Letters of Members of the Continental Congress*, I, 306.

26. J. Hancock to Thomas Cushing, Jan. 17, 1776, in Mass. Hist. Soc. *Proceedings*, 3rd Ser., LX (1927), 99–100.

27. Cushing to J. Hancock, Jan. 30, 1776. Original MS. in Historical Society of Pennsylvania, Simon Gratz Collection.

28. J. Hancock to Massachusetts Assembly, Jan. 31, 1776, in E. C. Burnett, ed., *op. cit.*, 333.

29. J. Hancock to Cushing, Feb. 1, 1776, in Mass. Hist. Soc. *Proceedings*, 3rd Ser., LX (1927), 101–102.

30. W. H. Sumner, "Reminiscences," *New England Hist. and Geneal. Register*, VIII (1854), 189.

31. J. Hancock to Cushing, Feb. 13 and 16, 1776, in Mass. Hist. Soc. *Proceedings*, 3rd Ser., LX (1927), 102–103, 105.

32. Articles of agreement, Mar. 1, 1776. Original MS. in U.S. Naval Academy Museum, Annapolis, Md.

33. J. Hancock to Cushing, Mar. 6–7 and Apr. 27, 1776, in Mass. Hist. Soc. *Proceedings*, 3rd Ser., LX (1927), 105, 106–108.

34. John Adams, *Works*, ed. C. F. Adams, III, 34–35.

35. J. Hancock to Lord Stirling, Mar. 15, 1776. Printed copy in New York Public Library, MS. Division, Hancock Miscellaneous Papers.

36. Washington to J. Hancock, Mar. 19, 1776, in P. Force, ed., *American Archives*, 4th Ser., V (1844), 420.

37. Isaac Cazneau to J. Hancock, Apr. 4, 1776, in W. K. Watkins, "How the British Left the Hancock House," *Old-Time New England*, XIII (1923), 194–195. The damages resulting from the British occupation of Hancock's mansion amounted to about £4,737, according to a survey made by Bant.

38. The description of Boston after the evacuation is based on E. Forbes, *Paul Revere*, 306–307.

CHAPTER XI (Pages 221–249)

1. J. Hancock to Washington, May 16, 1776, in P. Force, ed., *American Archives*, 4th Ser., VI (1846), 473.

2. J. Hancock to Washington, May 21, 1776, in J. Sparks, ed., *Correspondence of the American Revolution*, I, 205.

3. J. Hancock to Washington, June 3, 1776, in E. C. Burnett, ed., *Letters of Members of the Continental Congress*, I, 471, 472.

4. J. Hancock to New Hampshire Convention, June 4, 1776, in *ibid.*, 473–474.

5. Boston *Gazette*, May 20, 1776.

6. Entry of July 2, 1776, in Continental Congress, *Journals*, ed. W. C. Ford, V, 507.

7. J. Hancock to New Jersey Convention, June 11, 1776, in T. B. Myers, ed., *Letters and Manuscripts of the Signers*, 217.

8. J. Hancock to Washington, June 11, 1776, in P. Force, ed., *op. cit.*, 812.

9. J. Hancock to Cushing, June 12, 1776, in Mass. Hist. Soc. *Proceedings*, LX (1927), 110–111.

10. Quoted in H. Friedenwald, *The Declaration of Independence*, 136–137.

11. S. Higginson, *Ten Chapters in the Life of John Hancock*, 11–12.

12. M. Chamberlain, "The Authentication of the Declaration of Independence," in Mass. Hist. Soc. *Proceedings*, 2nd Ser., I (1885), 293.

13. J. Hancock to Maryland Convention, July 4, 1776, in E. C. Burnett, ed., *op. cit.*, 526–527.

14. J. Hancock to Washington, July 6, 1776, in *ibid.*, II, 2.

15. J. Hancock to William Cooper, July 6, 1776, in Mass. Hist. Soc. *Proceedings*, LX (1927), 113.

16. J. Adams to Samuel Chase, July 9, 1776. Original MS. in Boston Public Library, Alexander Biddle Papers.

17. Washington to President of Congress, July, 1776, in E. C. Burnett, *The Continental Congress*, 189.

18. Quoted in Mass. Hist. Soc. *Proceedings*, 3rd Ser., LX (1927), 113n.

19. Quoted in J. H. Hazelton, *The Declaration of Independence*, 209.

20. Benjamin Franklin, *Works*, ed. J. Sparks, I, 408.

21. J. Hancock to Maryland Assembly, Jan. 31, 1777, in E. C. Burnett, ed., *Letters of Members of the Continental Congress*, II, 228.
22. J. Hancock to Cushing, June 16, 1776, in Mass. Hist. Soc. *Proceedings*, 3rd Ser., LX (1927), 112.
23. J. Hancock to Massachusetts Assembly, July 16, 1776, in E. C. Burnett, ed., *op. cit.*, 13–14.
24. J. Hancock to Cushing, July 30, 1776, in Mass. Hist. Soc. *Proceedings*, LX (1927), 114.
25. Josiah Bartlett to John Langdon, Oct. 7, 1776, in E. C. Burnett, ed., *op. cit.*, 117.
26. J. Hancock to Cushing, July 30, 1776, in Mass. Hist. Soc. *Proceedings*, LX (1927), 114.
27. Entry of Oct. 16, 1776, in Continental Congress, *Journals*, ed. W. C. Ford, VI, 882.
28. Congress Papers, No. 58, Aug. 6, 1776, quoted in L. Lorenz, *John Paul Jones*, 75.
29. Writing to James Fenimore Cooper in the 1840's, Janet Taylor, Jones' niece, said she had the commission in her possession. The existence of her letter, which did not come to light until 1943, was pointed out to the author of this book by Capt. H. A. Baldridge, Curator of the Naval Academy Museum, where the MS. is now.
30. Washington to J. Hancock, Aug. 18, 1776, in P. Force, ed., *American Archives*, 5th Ser., I, 1026.
31. J. Hancock to Washington, Aug. 24, 1776, in E. C. Burnett, ed., *op. cit.*, 60.
32. Nephew or niece of D. Hancock to person unknown, Nov., 1793. Original MS. in Boston Public Library, Chamberlain Collection. The writer may have been Martha A. Quincy, who spent the last ten years of her grandaunt's life with her and was the principal beneficiary under her will.
33. William Bant to J. Hancock, Oct. 19, 21, Dec. 2, 16, 1776. Original MSS. in Boston Public Library, Chamberlain Collection.
34. S. Adams to E. Adams, Dec. 19, 1776, in Samuel Adams, *Writings*, ed. H. A. Cushing, III, 329.
35. J. Hancock to Robert Morris, Jan. 14, 1777, in New-York Hist. Soc. *Collections*, Publication Fund Ser., XI (1878), 412–414.
36. J. Hancock to R. Morris, Jan. 17, 1777, in S. V. Henkels, *Confidential Correspondence of Robert Morris* (Catalogue No. 1183, Item 8).
37. E. Hancock to Washington, Jan. 30, 1777, in George Washington, *Writings*, ed. J. C. Fitzpatrick, VI, 486n.
38. Diary entry of Feb. 17, 1777, in John Adams, *Works*, ed. C. F. Adams, II, 435.
39. J. Hancock to R. Morris, Feb. 18, 1777, in E. C. Burnett, ed., *op. cit.*, 260.
40. J. Hancock to R. Morris, Feb. 18, 1777, in New-York Hist. Soc. *op. cit.*, 419–420.
41. J. Adams to A. Adams, Feb. 21, 1777, in John and Abigail Adams, *Familiar Letters*, ed. C. F. Adams, 248.

42. Diary entry of Feb. 21, 1777, in John Adams, *Works*, ed. C. F. Adams, II, 435.

43. J. Hancock to R. Morris, Feb. 26, 1777, in New-York Hist. Soc. *op. cit.*, 421–422.

44. J. Hancock to R. Morris, Feb. 27, 1777, in E. C. Burnett, ed., *op. cit.*, 286.

45. J. Hancock to Dorothy Hancock, Mar. 3, 1777, in Autographs of the Signers of the Declaration of Independence, Pierpont Morgan Library, New York.

46. J. Hancock to D. Hancock, Mar. 4, 1777. Original MS. in possession of John Hancock Mutual Life Insurance Co., Boston.

47. J. Adams to A. Adams, Mar. 7, 1777, in John and Abigail Adams, *op. cit.*, 249–250.

CHAPTER XII (Pages 250–272)

1. J. Hancock to Archibald Bullock, Jan. 8, 1777, and to Maryland Assembly, Feb. 20, 1777, in E. C. Burnett, ed., *Letters of Members of the Continental Congress*, II, 208–209, 233–234, 266–267.

2. J. Hancock to D. Hancock, Mar. 10–11, 1777, in A. E. Brown, *John Hancock: His Book*, 216–218.

3. J. Hancock to D. Hancock, Mar. 11, 1777, in H. C. Walsh, "Three Letters from Hancock to 'Dorothy Q.,'" *New England Magazine*, n.s. VI (1892), 535–536. On one occasion, when parsnips were not available in Philadelphia, Hancock had some shipped from Boston.

4. L. Lorenz, *John Paul Jones* (U.S. Naval Institute publication), 110–112.

5. W. Gordon, *History of the United States*, II, 284.

6. "The second *Hancock* was taken over by the Navy from the War Department Nov. 8, 1902. Her service in the U.S. Navy included duty in South American waters, 1902–1903. She was receiving ship at New York, 1904–1913. Later she had transport duty in the West Indies and Mexican waters, 1914–1917. The *Hancock* was at St. Thomas, Virgin Islands, in connection with the transfer of the islands when the commanding officer of the *Hancock* (Capt. Edwin T. Pollock, U.S.N.) took formal possession of them from Denmark in the name of the United States in March, 1917.

"The *Hancock*, one of the vessels transporting the first American Expeditionary Forces to France, sailed June 14, 1917, and made two trips to France and two to the Azores, in addition to transport duty in the Caribbean, during the World War. Capt. William Lord Littlefield, U.S.N. (deceased), one of the commanding officers of the U.S.S. *Hancock* during World War I, received the Navy Cross with the following citation:

" 'For distinguished service in the line of his profession as commanding officer of the U.S.S. *Hancock* and the U.S.S. *Charleston*, engaged in the important, exacting, and hazardous duty of transporting and escorting troops and supplies to European ports through waters infested with enemy submarines and mines.'

"The second *Hancock* also made a trip to England with personnel and equipment for the ex-German vessels allocated to the United States in 1920. She was receiving ship at Pearl Harbor, T.H., 1921–1925, and placed out of commission and stricken from the Navy list Sept. 10, 1925, at Mare Island, Calif. *Hancock* No. 2 was sold May 21, 1926."—Headquarters First Naval District, Boston.

The aircraft carrier *Hancock* was launched on Jan. 24, 1944, at the Bethlehem Fore River Shipyards, Quincy, Mass., under the auspices of the John Hancock Mutual Life Insurance Co. The company raised $60,000,000 to defray the cost of construction by a special sale of War Bonds.

A packet named the *Hancock* plied between New York and Newport, R. I., during 1790, and a merchant vessel called the *John Hancock* was added to the Liberty fleet in 1942.

7. Entry of Sept. 9, 1777, in Continental Congress, *Journals*, ed. W. C. Ford, VIII, 726–727.

8. J. Hancock to Washington, Sept. 12, 1777, in E. C. Burnett, ed., *op. cit.*, 492.

9. Entry of Sept. 23, 1777, in "Extracts from the Diaries in the Moravian Archives at Bethlehem, Pa.," *Pennsylvania Magazine*, XIII (1889), 72.

10. Entry of Sept. 25, 1777, in Christopher Marshall, *Extracts from the Diary*, ed. W. Duane, 130.

11. J. Hancock to R. Morris, Oct. 5, 1777, in New York Hist. Soc. *Collections*, Publication Fund Ser., XI (1878), 431.

12. Henry Laurens to John L. Gervais, Oct. 16, 1777, in E. C. Burnett, ed., *op. cit.*, 522.

13. J. Hancock to Washington, Oct. 17, 1777, in J. Sparks, ed., *Correspondence of the American Revolution*, II, 8–9.

14. J. Hancock to Pennsylvania Assembly, Oct. 17, 1777, in New York Public Library, MS. Division, Hancock Miscellaneous Papers.

15. J. Hancock to D. Hancock, Oct. 18, 1777, in *New England Hist. and Geneal. Register*, XII (1858), 106.

16. Washington to J. Hancock, Oct. 22, 1777, in George Washington, *Writings*, ed. W. C. Ford, VI, 132–134.

17. J. Hancock to Washington, Oct. 25, 1777, in E. C. Burnett, ed., *op. cit.*, 534.

18. Entries of Oct. 25, 31, 1777, in Continental Congress, *op. cit.*, IX, 839, 852–853.

19. S. Adams to James Warren, Oct. 30, 1777, in E. C. Burnett, ed., *op. cit.*, 537.

20. Entry of Oct. 31, 1777, in Continental Congress, *op. cit.*, 853.

21. Diary entry of Nov. 7, 1777, in J. Sparks, ed., *Library of American Biography*, 1st Ser., VI, 121–122.

22. Diary entry of Nov. 17, 1777, in John Adams, *Works*, ed. C. F. Adams, II, 441.

23. J. Hancock to D. Hancock, Nov. 8, 1777, in A. E. Brown, *John Hancock: His Book*, 222.

24. Entry of Nov. 19, 1777, in William Heath, *Memoirs of the American War*, 148. *Independent Chronicle*, Nov. 27 and Dec. 4, 1777.

25. James Lovell to S. Adams, Jan. 1, 1778, in E. C. Burnett, ed., *op. cit.*, III, 2n.

26. German officer to persons unknown, Dec. 10, 1777, in *Massachusetts Magazine*, I (1908), 52.

27. J. Hancock to Samuel Langdon, Apr. 11, 1775, and Langdon to Hancock, Mar. 18, 1776, in MS. Archives, Widener Library, Harvard University.

28. When Hancock returned the papers he kept three Harvard account books dating from 1669 to 1752. They were found in a stable behind his mansion about 1861 and restored to the institution before the Beacon Hill show place was razed in 1863.

29. Gordon to J. Adams, Mar. 27, 1777, in Massachusetts Hist. Soc. *Proceedings*, 3rd Ser., LXIII (1931), 338.

30. J. Quincy, *History of Harvard University*, II, 197.

31. Harvard corporation resolution of Jan. 22, 1778, in MS. Archives, Widener Library.

32. J. Quincy, *op. cit.*, 204.

33. "On December 3 [1792] Hancock sent a verbal message to Treasurer Storer that he would pay the debt on January 1, if apprised of the amount. Storer sent him a bill for £1,495, 14s. 2d. . . . But Hancock died on October 8, 1793, before paying a penny."—S. E. Morison, *Three Centuries of Harvard* (Harvard University Press, Cambridge, 1936), 156. Reprinted by permission of the publishers.

34. J. T. Adams, "Portrait of an Empty Barrel," *Harper's Magazine*, CLXI (1930), 432.

35. Inventory and appraisal of Hancock estate, in Suffolk County (Mass.) Probate Court Records, File No. 20215.

36. J. Quincy, *op. cit.*, 206.

37. J. Quincy, *op. cit.*, 514.

38. All letters in the section on the Hancock-Harvard controversy mentioned without citation may be found in the Manuscript Archives at the Harvard College Library.

CHAPTER XIII (Pages 273–295)

1. J. Hancock to R. Morris, Jan. 12, 1778, in S. V. Henkels, *Confidential Correspondence of Robert Morris* (Catalogue No. 1183, Item 16).

2. Entry of June 25, 1778, in William Pynchon, *Diary*, ed. F. E. Oliver, 54–55.

3. New York *Gazette*, Feb. 2, and *Pennsylvania Ledger*, Mar. 11, 1778.

4. *Acts and Resolves of the Province of Massachusetts Bay*, Feb. 13, 1778, XX, 291.

5. Gordon to Washington, Jan. 12, Mar. 2, 1778, in Massachusetts Hist. Soc. *Proceedings*, LXIII (1931), 371–372, 382.

6. S. Adams to James Warren, May 25, 1778, in *Warren-Adams Letters*, II, 11–13.

7. S. Adams to E. Adams, Feb. 1, 1781, in Samuel Adams, *Writings*, ed. H. A. Cushing, IV, 246.

8. James Warren to S. Adams, May 10 and 31, 1778, in *Warren-Adams Letters*, II, 9–10, 13–14.

9. Entries of June 3, 6, 12, 1778, in Samuel Holten Journal, Essex Institute *Historical Collections*, LV (1919), 163–164.

10. J. Hancock to D. Hancock, June 20, 1778, in Massachusetts Hist. Soc. *Proceedings*, XLVIII (1915), 506.

11. J. Hancock to D. Hancock, June 23, 1778, in H. C. Walsh, "Three Letters from Hancock to 'Dorothy Q.,'" *New England Magazine*, n.s. VI (1892), 537.

12. S. Adams to E. Adams, July 9, 1778, in Samuel Adams, *op. cit.*, 41.

13. J. Adams to S. Adams, July 9, 1778, in W. V. Wells, *Life of Samuel Adams*, III, 29. The paragraph referring to Hancock in this letter, which was signed by a British Tory with the pseudonym Charles de Weissenstein and was sent supposedly from Brussels on June 16, reads: "As the conspicuous public part which some American gentlemen have taken may expose them to the personal enmity of some [of] the chief persons in Great Britain, and it is unreasonable that their services to their country should deprive them of those advantages which their talents would otherwise have gained them; the following persons shall have offices or pensions for life, at their option. . . : Messieurs [Sam] Adams, Hancock, Washington, Franklin."— "Project for Allaying the Present Ferments in North America," in B. F. Stevens, ed., *Facsimiles of Manuscripts in European Archives Relating to America*, VIII, Doc. No. 836, p. 2.

14. Entry of Aug. 8, 1778, in Price Diary, *New England Hist. and Geneal. Register*, XIX (1865), 334.

15. J. Hancock to Washington, Aug. 12, 1778, in Massachusetts Archives, CXCIX, 413.

16. J. Hancock to D. Hancock, Aug. 18, 1778. Original MS. in Boston Public Library, Chamberlain Collection.

17. James Warren to S. Adams, Aug. 18, 1778, in *Warren-Adams Letters*, II, 42–43.

18. J. Hancock to D. Hancock, Aug. 19, 1778. Original MS. in Massachusetts Hist. Soc., Bowdoin and Temple Papers.

19. J. Hancock to Jeremiah Powell, Aug. 22 and 25, 1778. Transcript in New York Public Library, MS. Division, Hancock Miscellaneous Papers.

20. Entry of Aug. 26, 1778, in Price Diary, *New England Hist. and Geneal. Register*, XIX (1865), 336.

21. James Warren to S. Adams, Aug. 27, 1778, in *Warren-Adams Letters*, II, 44.

22. S. Higginson, *Ten Chapters in the Life of John Hancock*, 16–21.

23. *Acts and Resolves of the Province of Massachusetts Bay,* May 1, 1779, XXI, 470.

24. Marquis de Lafayette to Washington, Sept. 1, 1778, in J. Sparks, ed., *Correspondence of the American Revolution,* II, 198–199.

25. S. Adams to James Warren, Sept. 12, 1778, in Samuel Adams, *Writings,* ed. H. A. Cushing, IV, 60–61.

26. Nathanael Greene to Washington, Sept. 16, 1778, in J. Sparks, ed., *Correspondence of the American Revolution,* II, 207.

27. W. H. Sumner, "Reminiscences," in *New England Hist. and Geneal. Register,* VIII (1854), 189–190. Hancock owned only one cow in 1774 and probably had not acquired any more during the busy intervening years.

28. James Warren to S. Adams, Sept. 30, 1778, in *Warren-Adams Letters,* II, 48.

29. A. Adams to J. Adams, Sept. or Oct., 1778, in John and Abigail Adams, *Familiar Letters,* ed. C. F. Adams, 342.

30. Samuel Phillips Savage to S. Adams, Oct., 1778, in W. V. Wells, *Life of Samuel Adams,* III, 55–56. S. Adams to Savage, Nov. 1, 1778, in Samuel Adams, *op. cit.,* 87–88.

31. James Warren to J. Adams, Oct. 7, 1778, in *Warren-Adams Letters,* II, 52–53.

32. Entry of Dec. 17, 1778, in Thomas Hutchinson, *Diary and Letters,* ed. P. O. Hutchinson, II, 230.

33. James Warren to S. Adams, Feb. 12, 1779, in *Warren-Adams Letters,* II, 87.

34. Gordon to J. Adams, May 8, to Horatio Gates, June 8, 1779, in Massachusetts Hist. Soc. *Proceedings,* LXIII (1931), 411, 413.

35. Revere to William Heath, Oct. 24, 1779, in Massachusetts Hist. Soc. *Collections,* 7th Ser., IV (1904), 325.

36. G. O. Trevelyan, *George the Third and Charles Fox,* I, 279. Charleston was captured by General Clinton on May 12, 1780.

37. J. Hancock to D. Hancock, 1780. Original MS. in possession of Mrs. Edward P. Wight of Portsmouth, N.H.

38. James Warren to J. Adams, July 11, 1780, in *Warren-Adams Letters,* II, 135.

39. Gordon to J. Adams, July 22, 1780, in Massachusetts Hist. Soc. *Proceedings,* LXIII (1931), 436–437.

CHAPTER XIV (296–318)

1. James Warren to S. Adams, Sept. 17, 1780, in *Warren-Adams Letters,* II, 138.

2. S. Adams to E. Adams, Oct. 10 and 17, 1780, in Samuel Adams, *Writings,* ed. H. A. Cushing, IV, 209–212.

3. Gordon to J. Adams, Oct. 19, 1780, in Massachusetts Hist. Soc. *Proceedings,* LXIII (1931), 445.

4. Entry of Oct. 25, 1780, in William Pynchon, *Diary,* ed. F. E. Oliver, 77.

5. W. Gordon, *History of the United States*, III, 498.
6. Entry of Oct. 26, 1780, in William Pynchon, *op. cit.*, 77.
7. Quoted in A. E. Brown, *John Hancock: His Book*, 266.
8. W. Gordon, *loc. cit.*
9. Quoted in A. E. Brown, *op. cit.*, 267–270.
10. J. Quincy, *History of Harvard University*, II, 200.
11. James Warren to S. Adams, Nov. 2, Mercy Warren to J. Adams, Nov. 15, 1780, in *Warren-Adams Letters*, II, 144–145, 147.
12. S. Adams to John Scollay, Dec. 30, 1780, in Samuel Adams, *op. cit.*, 236–238.
13. *Laws and Resolves of Massachusetts, 1780–1781*, Feb. 8, 1781, 11.
14. Entries of Mar. 14, 16, 21, 1781, in William Pynchon, *op. cit.*, 89, 90.
15. Washington to J. Hancock, July 8, to President of Congress, Aug. 2, to George Clinton, Aug. 5, to Benjamin Lincoln, Aug. 6, 1781, in George Washington, *Writings*, ed. J. C. Fitzpatrick, XXII, 340, 447, 468, 470–471.
16. J. Hancock to John Wendell, May 22, 1782, in B. Wendell, "A Gentlewoman of Boston," *Amer. Antiq. Soc. Proceedings*, n.s. XXIX (1919), 266, 267.
17. W. Sullivan, *Familiar Letters on Public Characters*, 12–13.
18. Entry of July 17, 1782, in William Pynchon, *op. cit.*, 129.
19. Entry of Nov. 13, 1782, in *Journal of Massachusetts House of Representatives*, III, 377–378, Statehouse, Boston.
20. Catherine Wendell Davis to J. Wendell, Nov. 1782, in B. Wendell, *op. cit.*, 267.
21. W. C. Todd, "Lord Timothy Dexter," in *New England Hist. and Geneal. Register*, XL (1886), 381.
22. M. A. Quincy, "Reminiscences of the Hancocks," in A. Phelps, ed., *Our Country*, 299, 300.
23. J. Hancock to Washington, Oct. 15, 1783, in J. Sparks, ed., *Correspondence of the American Revolution*, IV, 50.
24. Heath to J. Hancock, Apr. 18, 1783, in Mass. Hist. Soc. *Collections*, 7th Ser., V (1905), 388–389.
25. J. Hancock to Scott, Nov. 14, William Hoskins to Winckworth Tonge, Aug. 14, 1783, in Letterbooks.
26. J. Hancock to Scott, Nov. 14, 1783.
27. W. H. Sumner, "Reminiscences," *New England Hist. and Geneal. Register*, VIII (1854), 189.
28. Gordon to Gerry, Dec. 24, 1783, in Massachusetts Hist. Soc. *Proceedings*, LXIII (1931), 500–501.
29. James Warren to J. Adams, Feb. 26, 1784, in *Warren-Adams Letters*, II, 236.
30. *Continental Journal*, Mar. 4, 1784, quoted in M. F. Ayer, *Early Days on Boston Common*, 38.
31. J. Hancock to General Court, Jan. 29, 1785, quoted in Boston *Herald*, June 11, 1890.
32. Charles Gore to Rufus King, Mar. 20, Gerry to King, Mar. 28, 1785, in C. R. King, *Life and Correspondence of Rufus King*, I, 81, 75–76.
33. Gerry to King, May 27, 1785, in *ibid.*, 100.

CHAPTER XV (Pages 319–341)

1. John Quincy Adams to Abigail Adams, July 17, 1785, in J. Q. Adams, *Writings*, ed. W. C. Ford, I (1913), 19n.

2. Gordon to J. Adams, Aug. 13, Oct. 4, 1785, in Mass. Hist. Soc. *Proceedings*, LXIII (1931), 515, 522. James Warren to Gerry, Oct. 4, 1785, in *Warren-Adams Letters*, II, 265.

3. James Sullivan to King, Oct. 25, 1785, in C. R. King, *Life and Correspondence of Rufus King*, I, 111–112.

4. J. Hancock to King, Nov. 30, 1785, in *ibid.*, 114.

5. King to J. Hancock, Dec. 4, 1785. Original MS. in Historical Society of Pennsylvania, Charles F. Jenkins Collection.

6. Henry Jackson to Henry Knox, Dec. 12, 1785. Original MS. in Massachusetts Historical Society, Henry Knox Papers.

7. Nathan Dane to James Bowdoin, Jan. 10, 1786, in E. C. Burnett, ed., *Letters of Members of the Continental Congress*, VIII, 283.

8. *Independent Chronicle*, Feb. 1, 1787.

9. J. Hancock to Knox, Mar. 14, 1787. Original MS. in Mass. Hist. Soc., Knox Papers.

10. King to Gerry, Mar. 25, 1787, in E. C. Burnett, ed., *op. cit.*, 564.

11. James Warren to J. Adams, May 18, 1787, in *Warren-Adams Letters*, II, 292–293.

12. J. Q. Adams to J. Adams, June 30, 1787, in J. Q. Adams, *Writings*, ed. W. C. Ford, I, 31–32.

13. S. B. Harding, *The Contest over the Ratification of the Federal Constitution . . . Massachusetts*, 45.

14. T. C. Amory, *Life of James Sullivan*, I, 222–223.

15. King to George Thatcher, Jan. 20, 1788, in *Historical Magazine*, 2nd Ser., VI (1869), 266.

16. J. T. Austin, *Life of Elbridge Gerry*, II, 75–76. King to Knox, Feb. 3, 1788, in F. S. Drake, *Life of Henry Knox*, 98.

17. W. V. Wells, *Life of Samuel Adams*, III, 258–259.

18. Convention of the Commonwealth of Massachusetts *Debates and Proceedings*, 225.

19. Belknap to Ebenezer Hazard, Feb. 10, 1788, in Mass. Hist. Soc. *Collections*, 5th Ser., III (1877), 17.

20. G. H. Haynes, "The Conciliatory Proposition in the Massachusetts Convention of 1788," in Amer. Antiq. Soc. *Proceedings*, n.s. XXIX (1919), 309–310.

21. G. Bancroft, *History of the United States*, VI, 395n.

22. S. B. Harding, *op. cit.*, 85n.

23. *New Hampshire Gazette*, Feb. 20, 1788.

24. Philadelphian to person unknown, July 2, 1788, in E. C. D. Woodbury, *Dorothy Quincy, Wife of John Hancock*, 200, 201.

25. J. Adams to M. Warren, July 20, 1807, in Mass. Hist. Soc. *Collections*, 5th Ser., IV (1878), 334–335.

26. Quoted in E. C. D. Woodbury, *op. cit.*, 200.

27. S. Higginson, *Ten Chapters in the Life of John Hancock*, 62

28. *Independent Chronicle* and *New Hampshire Gazette*, Aug. 21, 1788.

29. Entry of Aug. 18, 1788, in J. Q. Adams, Diary, in Mass. Hist. Soc. *Proceedings*, 2nd Ser., XVI (1903), 449.

30. Christopher Gore to Theodore Sedgwick, Aug. 31, 1788. Original MS. in Mass. Hist. Soc., Knox Papers.

31. *Independent Chronicle*, Sept. 18 and 25, 1788.

32. B. Rush to Belknap, Oct. 7, 1788, in Mass. Hist. Soc. *Collections*, 6th Ser., IV (1891), 149.

33. Jackson to Knox, Jan. 11, Feb. 1, 1789. Original MSS. in Mass. Hist. Soc., Knox Papers.

34. Washington to J. Hancock, May 9, 1789, in E. C. D. Woodbury, *op. cit.*, 206.

35. Belknap to Hazard, June 2, 1789, in Mass. Hist. Soc. *Collections*, 5th Ser., III (1877), 134.

36. Charles Gore to King, June 7, 1789, in C. R. King, *op. cit.*, I, 361.

37. "Description of the Seat of His Excellency John Hancock, Esq., Boston," in *Massachusetts Magazine*, I (1789), 395–396.

CHAPTER XVI (Pages 342–360)

1. J. Hancock to Washington, Oct. 21, Washington to J. Hancock, Oct. 22, 1789, in George Washington, *Writings*, ed. J. Sparks, X, 490, 17.

2. J. Hancock to Washington, Oct. 23, 1789, in J. Sparks, ed., *Correspondence of the American Revolution*, IV, 290–291.

3. Washington to J. Hancock, Oct. 23, 1789, in George Washington, *op. cit.*, 48.

4. Benjamin Russell to Jared Sparks, May 22, 1835, in *ibid.*, 492.

5. Entry of Oct. 24, 1789, in George Washington, *Diaries*, ed. J. C. Fitzpatrick, IV, 34–35.

6. Quoted in L. Sears, *John Hancock, the Picturesque Patriot*, 297–298.

7. J. Hancock to Washington, and Washington to J. Hancock, Oct. 26, 1789, in George Washington, *Writings*, ed. J. Sparks, X, 493.

8. Entry of Oct. 25, 1789, in George Washington, *Diaries*, ed. J. C. Fitzpatrick, IV, 36.

9. W. H. Sumner, "Reminiscences," *New England Hist. and Geneal. Register*, VIII (1854), 190, 191.

10. Entries of Oct. 26–29, 1789, in George Washington, *Diaries*, ed. J. C. Fitzpatrick, IV, 36–39.

11. Charles Gore to King, Dec. 3, 1789, in C. R. King, *Life and Correspondence of Rufus King*, I, 369.

12. Massachusetts State Papers, Ch. 3352, Jan. 19, 1790.

13. Belknap to Hazard, Jan. 30, 1790, in Mass. Hist. Soc. *Collections*, 5th Ser., III (1877), 212.

14. E. Quincy, *Life of Josiah Quincy*, 38.

15. Boston *Gazette*, Nov. 29, 1790.

16. Massachusetts State Papers, Ch. 3491, Jan. 26, 1791.

17. J. S. Loring, *Hundred Boston Orators*, 109.

18. Daniel Sewell to J. Hancock, Aug. 11, 1791. Transcript in New York Public Library, MS. Division, Hancock Miscellaneous Papers.

19. Eunice Burr to J. Hancock, May 1, 1792, in Baker Library, Hancock Papers.

20. T. Burr to J. Hancock, June 3 and Oct. 26, 1792, in Baker Library, Hancock Personal Letters.

21. *Laws and Resolves of Massachusetts*, 1792–1793, June 6, 1792, 682.

22. Quoted in Mass. Hist. Soc. *Proceedings*, 3rd Ser., LXII (1930), 57.

23. Quoted in L. Sears, *John Hancock, the Picturesque Patriot*, 318.

24. Massachusetts State Papers, Ch. 3705, Nov. 7, 1792.

25. J. Q. Adams to J. Adams, Dec. 16, 1792, in J. Q. Adams, *Writings*, ed. W. C. Ford, I, 123.

26. Massachusetts State Papers, Ch. 3707, Nov. 12, 1792.

27. J. Q. Adams to J. Adams, Dec. 16, 1792, in *op. cit.*, 124.

28. Massachusetts State Papers, Ch. 3916, Jan. 31, 1793.

29. J. Hancock to S. Adams, Aug. 3, 1793, in Baker Library, Hancock Domestic Letters. His father had quoted *"Principies (Principiis) Obsta"* to express his opposition to the Great Awakening and had translated it freely as "to crush the cockatrice in the egg."

30. Massachusetts State Papers, Ch. 45, Sept. 18 and 27, 1793.

31. *Independent Chronicle*, Oct. 10, 1793.

32. *Ibid.*, Oct. 17, 1793.

33. Entry of Oct. 14, 1793, in H. H. Williams' Family Journal, quoted in W. H. Sumner, *History of East Boston*, 332.

34. *Independent Chronicle*, Oct. 17, 1793.

35. M. A. Quincy, "Reminiscences of the Hancocks," in A. L. Phelps, ed., *Our Country*, 314.

EPILOGUE (Pages 361–366)

1. E. Quincy, *Life of Josiah Quincy*, 404–405.

2. M. A. Quincy, "Reminiscences of the Hancocks," in A. L. Phelps, ed., *Our Country*, 314–315.

3. Suffolk County Probate Court Records, File No. 20215.

4. Entry of May 13, 1795, in Boston Town *Records*, XXXI (1903), 396–397.

5. Esther Quincy Sewell to Scott, Aug. 11, 1796, in E. C. D. Woodbury, *Dorothy Quincy, Wife of John Hancock*, 231–232.

6. The mansion tract was sold piecemeal in later years. In 1855 the forty buildings on part of the property were valued at $1,500,000 (Boston *Herald*, June 30, 1918). In 1859 a committee appointed by the Massachusetts Senate to negotiate for the purchase of the Beacon Hill homestead with a view to

preserving it as a memorial recommended that the Hancock heirs be offered $100,000. Although the price was satisfactory to all parties, the deal never went through. The historic house and grounds finally were bought by Gardner Brewer and J. M. Beebe, Boston merchants, in 1863, and the show place was torn down. It has been reproduced at Ticonderoga, N. Y. Horace A. Moses, the paper manufacturer of Springfield, Mass., gave most of the money for the replica, and presented it to the New York State Historical Association as a museum and library.

7. Quoted in Colonial Soc. of Mass. *Publications*, VI (1904), 318.

8. Original decree granting permission, dated Jan. 30, 1815, in Mass. Hist. Soc.

9. P. Thacher, *Sermon Preached to the Society in Brattle Street, Boston, Oct. 20, 1793*, 16, 18–19.

10. Quoted in L. Sears, *John Hancock, the Picturesque Patriot*, 230.

11. J. Adams to Richard Rush, July 31, 1812. Original MS. in Historical Society of Pennsylvania, Gratz Collection.

12. J. Adams to Tudor, June 1 and 5, 1817, in John Adams, *Works*, ed. C. F. Adams, X, 259–261, 263.

Bibliography

MANUSCRIPTS

Alexander (William) Papers, New York Historical Society.
Articles of Agreement, U.S. Naval Academy Museum, Annapolis, Md.
Biddle (Alexander) Papers, Boston Public Library.
Bowdoin and Temple Papers, Massachusetts Historical Society, Boston.
Chamberlain (Mellen) Collection, Boston Public Library.
Decree granting permission to sell real estate, Massachusetts Historical Society, Boston.
Gratz (Simon) Collection, Historical Society of Pennsylvania, Philadelphia.
Hancock Domestic Letters, Letterbooks, Manuscripts, Papers, Personal Letters, New England Historic Genealogical Society (on deposit in Baker Library, Harvard University, Cambridge, Mass.).
Hancock Miscellaneous Papers, New York Public Library.
Hancock (John) Letters, Bostonian Society; California Fruit Growers Exchange, Los Angeles; Mrs. Edward P. Wight, Portsmouth, N.H.; John Hancock Mutual Life Insurance Company, Boston; Pierpont Morgan Library, New York.
Hancock (Thomas) Domestic Memoranda, New England Historic Genealogical Society (on deposit in Baker Library, Harvard University, Cambridge, Mass.).
Hutchinson (Thomas) Correspondence (Bancroft Transcripts), New York Public Library.
Jenkins (Charles F.) Collection, Historical Society of Pennsylvania.
Jennings (Annie Burr) Memorial Collection, Fairfield Historical Society, Fairfield, Conn.
Knox (Henry) Papers, Massachusetts Historical Society.
Manuscript Archives, Harvard College Library.
Phillips (Henry A.) Notes and Sources, American Antiquarian Society.
Revere (Paul) Deposition, facsimile in Bostonian Society Library.
"The Historical Love Letter," facsimile in New York Public Library.

399

NEWSPAPERS

Boston *Evening Post.*	*New England Chronicle.*
Boston *Gazette.*	*New Hampshire Gazette.*
Boston *Herald.*	New York *Gazette.*
Connecticut Courant.	*Pennsylvania Gazette.*
Independent Chronicle.	*Pennsylvania Ledger.*
Massachusetts Spy.	*Virginia Gazette.*

OTHER SOURCES

Primary

Acts and Resolves of the Province of Massachusetts Bay, Vols. XX, XXI, in Statehouse, Boston.

Adams, John, *Works,* ed. Charles Francis Adams, Vols. II, X, Boston, 1850, 1856.

—— and Abigail Adams, *Familiar Letters During the Revolution,* ed. Charles Francis Adams. New York, 1876.

Adams, John Quincy, Diary, Mass. Hist. Soc. *Proceedings,* 2nd Ser., XVI (1903), 295–464.

—— *Writings,* ed. Worthington C. Ford, Vol. I. New York, 1913.

Adams, Samuel, *Writings,* ed. Harry A. Cushing, Vols. I–IV. New York, 1904–1908.

Allen, J., Narrative, Mass. Hist. Soc. *Proceedings,* 1st Ser., XVI (1879), 69.

American Antiquarian Society *Proceedings,* n.s. Vol. XII (1899).

Appleton, Nathanael, *The Servant's Actual Readiness for the Coming of His Lord.* Boston, 1752.

Barker, Lieut. John, *The British in Boston: Being the Diary of . . . ,* ed. Elizabeth E. Dana. Cambridge, Mass., 1924.

Belknap, Jeremy, Memoranda, Mass. Hist. Soc. *Proceedings,* 1st Ser., Vol. III (1859), 308–309.

—— Minutes of the Massachusetts Convention to Ratify the Federal Constitution, *Ibid.,* 296–297.

Bennett, Joseph, History of New England, Mass. Hist. Soc. *Proceedings,* 1st Ser., V (1862), 113, 125.

Bernard Papers, Mass. Hist. Soc. *Proceedings,* 3rd Ser., LV (1923), 257.

Boston Town *Records,* Vols. XVI, XVIII, XXXI. Boston, 1886, 1887, 1903.

Bostonian Society *Publications,* Vols. XI, XII. Boston, 1914, 1915.

Boyle, John, "Journal of Occurrences in Boston, 1759–1778," *New England Hist. and Geneal. Register,* LXXXIV (1930), 262.

Bradford, William, *History of Plymouth Plantation, 1606–1646,* ed. William T. Davis (Original Narratives of Early American History). New York, 1908.

Brown, Abram E., *John Hancock: His Book.* Boston, 1898.

Burnett, Edmund C., ed., *Letters of Members of the Continental Congress,* Vols. I–VIII: Washington, 1921–1936.

Colonial Society of Massachusetts *Publications*, Vol. VI. Boston, 1904.

Connecticut Historical Society *Collections*, Vol. II. Hartford, 1870.

Continental Congress, *Journals*, ed. Worthington C. Ford, Vols. II, III, V, VI, VIII, IX. Washington, 1905–1907.

Convention of the Commonwealth of Massachusetts, *Debates and Proceedings*. Boston, 1856.

Curwen, Samuel, *Journal and Letters*, ed. George A. Ward. Boston, 1864.

"Description of the Seat of His Excellency John Hancock, Esq.," *Massachusetts Magazine*, 1 (1789), 395–396.

Dudley, Dorothy, *Theatrum Majorum: The Cambridge of 1776* (diary and letters), ed. Arthur Gilman. Cambridge, Mass., 1876.

Ellery, William, Diary, in *Library of American Biography*, ed. Jared Sparks, 1st Ser., VI, 121–122. New York, 1854.

"Extracts from the Diaries in the Moravian Archives at Bethlehem, Pa.," *Pennsylvania Magazine*, XIII (1889), 72.

Force, Peter, ed., *American Archives*, 4th Ser., II, IV, V, VI; 5th Ser., I. Washington, 1839–1848.

Franklin, Benjamin, *Works*, ed. Jared Sparks, Vol. I. Boston, 1856.

Gay, Ebenezer, *Sermon Preached at the Funeral of Mr. John Hancock*. Boston, 1744.

General Court of Massachusetts. Boston, 1930.

Goelet, Francis, Journal, *New Eng. Hist. and Geneal. Register*, XXIV (1870), 53–55, 61.

Gordon, William, *History of the United States*, Vol. II, New York, 1801; Vol. III, London, 1788.

Hancock, John, (I), *Sermon Preached at the Ordination of Mr. John Hancock*. Boston, 1726.

—— *The Lord's Ministers Are the People's Helpers*. Boston, 1735.

—— *The Prophet Jeremiah's Resolution to Get Him unto Great Men*. Boston, 1734.

Hancock, John (II), *An Expostulatory Letter Addressed to the Reverend Mr. Nathanael Eells*. Boston, 1743.

Hancock, John (III), *Oration Delivered Mar. 5, 1774*. Boston, 1774.

Heath, William, *Memoirs of the American War*, ed. R. R. Wilson. New York, 1904.

Henkels, Stanislaus V., *Confidential Correspondence of Robert Morris* (Catalogue No. 1183). Philadelphia, 1917.

Historical Magazine, 2nd Ser., Vol. VI (Morrisania, N.Y., 1869).

Holten, Samuel, Journal, in Essex Institute *Historical Collections*, LV (1919), 163–164.

Home Office, *Papers*, ed. R. A. Roberts, Vol. IV. London, 1899.

Hutchinson, Thomas, *Diary and Letters*, ed. Peter O. Hutchinson, Vols. I, II. Boston, 1884, 1886.

—— *History of Massachusetts Bay*, Vol. II, Cambridge, Mass., 1936; Vol. III, London, 1828.

—— and others, *Copy of Letters Sent to Great Britain*. Boston, 1773.

Laws and Resolves of Massachusetts, 1780–1781, 1792–1793. Statehouse, Boston.

Lexington (Mass.) Historical Society *Proceedings*, Vol. IV (1912).
Magazine of American History, Vol. XXIV (1890).
Marshall, Christopher, *Extracts from the Diary of* . . . , ed. William Duane. Albany, 1877.
—— *Passages from the Remembrancer* of . . . , ed. William Duane. Philadelphia, 1839.
Massachusetts Archives, XXIV, XXVII, CXCIX. Statehouse, Boston.
Massachusetts Historical Society *Collections*, 1st Ser., V (1798), VIII (1802); 5th Ser., III (1877), IV (1878), 6th Ser., IV (1891); 7th Ser., IV (1904), LXXI (1914).
—— *Proceedings*, 1st Ser., VIII (1866); 3rd Ser., XLIII (1910), XLVIII (1915), LX (1927), LXII (1930), LXIII (1931).
Massachusetts Magazine (new), Vol. I (1908).
Massachusetts State Papers, Ch. 45, 3352, 3491, 3705, 3707, 3916. Statehouse, Boston.
Maxwell, Thompson, "The Command at the Battle of Bunker Hill, as Shown in the Statement of Major Thompson Maxwell," *New Eng. Hist. and Geneal. Register*, XXII (1868), 57–59.
May, Joseph, Journal, in William V. Wells, *Life and Public Services of Samuel Adams*, III, 258–259. Boston, 1866.
"Memoirs of John Hancock, Esq.," *New Lottery Magazine, or Fortunate Repository*, London, Aug., 1776. (Available in Boston Public Library.)
Morton, Thomas, "The New English Canaan," in P. Force, ed., *Tracts and Other Papers*, Vol. II. Washington, 1838.
Munroe, William, Deposition, in Elias Phinney, *History of the Battle of Lexington*. Boston, 1825.
Myers, Theodorus B., ed., *Letters and Manuscripts of the Signers*. New York, 1871.
New England Historical and Genealogical Register, Vols. XI, XII (1857, 1858).
New England's First Fruits. London, 1643.
New York Historical Society *Collections*, Publication Fund Ser., Vol. XI. New York, 1878.
Old-Time New England, Vol. XXV (1934).
Percy, Hugh, Earl, *Letters from Boston and New York, 1774–1776*, ed. Charles K. Bolton. Boston, 1902.
Price, Ezekiel, Diary, *New Eng. Hist. and Geneal. Register*, XIX (1865), 334, 336.
Pynchon, William, *Diary*, ed. Fitch E. Oliver. Boston, 1890.
Quincy, Martha A., "Reminiscences of the Hancocks," in *Our Country*, ed. Almira L. Phelps. Baltimore, 1864.
Records of First Church, North Braintree, Mass., in Mass. Hist. Soc. *Proceedings*, 2nd Ser., VI (1891), 487–488.
Records of the Town of Cambridge, 1630–1703. Cambridge, Mass., 1901.
Report from Headquarters First Naval District, Boston.
Rowe, John, Extracts from the Unpublished Diary of . . . , in *Proceedings in Masonry, Mass. Grand Lodge, 1769–1792*. Boston, 1895.
—— *Letters and Diary*, ed. Anne R. Cunningham. Boston, 1903.

Ryden, George H., ed., *Letters to and from Caesar Rodney*. Philadelphia. 1933.

Salisbury, Edward E., *Family Memorials*. New Haven, Conn., 1885.

Sewell, Samuel, Diary, Mass. Hist. Soc. *Collections*, 5th Ser., VII (1882), 71.

Smith, Richard, Diary, *American Historical Review*, I (1896), 298.

Sparks, Jared, ed., *Correspondence of the American Revolution*, Vols. I, II. Boston, 1853.

Stevens, B. F., ed., *Facsimiles of Manuscripts in European Archives Relating to America*, Vols. VIII, XXIV. London, 1891, 1895.

Suffolk County Probate Court Records. Boston.

Sullivan, William, *Familiar Letters on Public Characters, and Public Events; from the Peace of 1783 to the Peace of 1815*. Boston, 1834.

Sumner, William H., "Reminiscences," *New Eng. Hist. and Geneal. Register*, VIII (1854), 187–191.

Thacher, Peter, *Sermon Preached to the Society in Brattle Street, Boston, Oct. 20, 1793*. Boston, 1793.

Thatcher, Benjamin B., ed., *Traits of the Tea Party; Being a Memoir of George R. T. Hewes*. New York, 1835.

Thomas, Ebenezer S., *Reminiscences of the Last Sixty-five Years*, Vol. II. Boston, 1840.

Thomas, Isaiah, "The History of Printing in America," *Amer. Antiq. Soc. Transactions*, V (1874), 107–108.

Tudor, John, *Deacon Tudor's Diary*, ed. William Tudor. Boston, 1896.

Warren-Adams Letters, Vol. I—Mass. Hist. Soc. *Collections*, Vol. LXXII (1917).

Washington, George, *Diaries*, ed. John C. Fitzpatrick, Vol. IV. Boston, 1925.

—— *Writings*, ed. John C. Fitzpatrick, Vols. VI, XXII. Washington, 1932, 1937.

—— *Writings*, ed. Worthington C. Ford, Vol. VI. New York, 1890.

—— *Writings*, ed. Jared Sparks, Vol. X. New York, 1847.

Winslow, Ola E., ed., *Harper's Literary Museum*. New York, 1927.

Winthrop, John, *History of New England, 1630–1649*, ed. James Savage, Vol. I. Boston, 1853.

Wood, William, *New England's Prospect*. Boston, 1865.

Secondary

Adams, Charles Francis, Jr., *History of Braintree, Mass*. Boston, 1891.

—— "Some Phases of Sexual Morality and Church Discipline in Colonial New England," *Mass. Hist. Soc. Proceedings*, 2nd Ser., VI (1891), 497.

—— *Three Episodes of Massachusetts History*. Boston, 1892.

Adams, James T., "Portrait of an Empty Barrel," *Harper's Magazine*, CLXI (1930), 431–432.

Alden, John E., "John Mein: Scourge of Patriots," *Colonial Soc. of Mass. Publications*, XXXIV (1943), 596.

Amory, Thomas C., *Life of James Sullivan*, Vol. I. Boston, 1859.

Austin, James T., *Life of Elbridge Gerry*, Vol. II. Boston, 1828.

Ayer, Mary F., *Early Days on Boston Common*. Boston, 1910.

Bancroft, George, *History of the United States*, Vol. VI. New York, 1885.

Baxter, W. T., *The House of Hancock*. Cambridge, Mass., 1945.

Bridenbaugh, Carl and Jessica, *Rebels and Gentlemen*. New York, 1942.

Brooks, Van Wyck, *The World of Washington Irving*. New York, 1944.

Burnett, E. C., *The Continental Congress*. New York, 1941.

Carlton, Mabel M., *John Hancock: Great American Patriot*. Boston, 1922.

Chamberlain, Mellen, "The Authentication of the Declaration of Independence," Mass. Hist. Soc. *Proceedings*, 2nd Ser., I (1885), 293.

Chandler, Peleg W., *American Criminal Trials*, Vol. I. Boston, 1841.

Curnick, Arthur R., "Social Life in the Revolutionary Period," in *Commonwealth History of Massachusetts*, ed. A. B. Hart, III, 281–282. New York, 1929.

Dickinson, John, "The Massachusetts Charter and the Bay Colony," in *Commonwealth History of Mass.*, ed. A. B. Hart, I, 106. New York, 1927.

Drake, Francis S., *Life of Henry Knox*. Boston, 1873.

Drake, Samuel G., *History and Antiquities of the City of Boston*. Boston, 1854.

Eliot, Samuel A., *History of Cambridge*. Cambridge, Mass., 1913.

Fast, Howard, *Citizen Tom Paine*. New York, 1943.

Forbes, Esther, *Paul Revere and the World He Lived in*. Boston, 1942.

Friedenwald, Herbert, *The Declaration of Independence*. New York, 1904.

Harding, Samuel B., *The Contest over the Ratification of the Federal Constitution in . . . Massachusetts*. New York, 1896.

Haynes, George H., "The Conciliatory Proposition in the Massachusetts Convention of 1788," Amer. Antiq. Soc. *Proceedings*, n.s. XXIX (1919), 309–310.

Hazelton, John H., *The Declaration of Independence*. New York, 1906.

Hersey, Frank W. C., "The Misfortunes of Dorcas Griffiths," Colonial Soc. of Mass. *Publications*, XXXIV (1943), 22.

Higgins, Lucy P., " 'Dorothy Q.,' Who Became Dorothy H.," *Americana*, XIV (1920), 408–419.

Higginson, Stephen, *Ten Chapters in the Life of John Hancock*. New York, 1857.

Hudson, Charles, *History of the Town of Lexington*. Boston, 1868, 1913.

Hunt, Freeman, *American Anecdotes*, Vol. I. Boston, 1830.

King, Charles R., *Life and Correspondence of Rufus King*, Vol. I. New York, 1894.

Labaree, Leonard W., *Royal Government in America*. New Haven, Conn., 1930.

Lee, R. H., *Life of Arthur Lee*, Vol. II. Boston, 1829.

Lorenz, Lincoln, *John Paul Jones*. U.S. Naval Institute, Annapolis, Md., 1943.

Loring, James S., *Hundred Boston Orators*. Boston, 1852.

Lothrop, Samuel K., *History of the Church in Brattle Street, Boston*. Boston, 1851.

Miller, John C., *Sam Adams, Pioneer in Propaganda*. Boston, 1936.

Morison, Samuel E., *Three Centuries of Harvard*. Cambridge, Mass., 1936.

Musick, John R., *John Hancock: A Character Sketch*. Dansville, N.Y., 1898.

Nichols, Charles L., "Samuel Salisbury—a Boston Merchant in the Revolution," in Amer. Antiq. Soc. *Proceedings*, n.s. XXXV (1926), 51.

Paige, Lucius R., *History of Cambridge*. Boston, 1877.

Perkins, Augustus T., *Sketch of the Life of John Singleton Copley*. Boston, 1873.

Pattee, William S., *History of Old Braintree and Quincy*. Quincy, Mass., 1878.

Quincy, Edmund, *Life of Josiah Quincy*. Boston, 1867.

Quincy, Josiah, *History of Harvard University*, Vol. II. Cambridge, 1840.

Sears, Lorenzo, *John Hancock, the Picturesque Patriot*. Boston, 1912.

Shipton, Clifford K., *Andrew Oliver*. Boston, 1943 (reprinted from *Sibley's Harvard Graduates*, Vol. VII).

Sprague, William B., *Annals of the American Pulpit*. New York, 1857.

Staples, Carlton A., *Address in Commemoration of the Ordination and Settlement of the Reverend John Hancock*. Arlington, Mass., 1900.

Swan, Sarah H., "The Story of an Old House," *New England Magazine*, n.s. XVII (1897), 178–180.

Todd, William C., "Lord Timothy Dexter," *New Eng. Hist. and Geneal. Register*, XL (1886), 381.

Trevelyan, George Otto, *George the Third and Charles Fox*, Vol. I. London, 1912.

Umbreit, Kenneth B., *The Founding Fathers*. New York, 1941.

Walsh, Henry C., "Three Letters from Hancock to 'Dorothy Q.,'" *New England Magazine*, n.s. VI (1892), 532–533, 537.

Watkins, Walter K., "How the British Left the Hancock House," *Old-Time New England*, XIII (1923), 194–195.

Wells, W. V., *Life of Samuel Adams*, Vols. I–III. Boston, 1865–1866.

Wendell, Barrett, "A Gentlewoman of Boston," Amer. Antiq. Soc. *Proceedings*, n.s. XXIX (1919), 267.

Wheildon, William W., *Sentry, or Beacon Hill*. Concord, Mass., 1877.

Williams, Henry H., *Family Journal*, in W. H. Sumner, *History of East Boston*. Boston, 1869.

Winsor, Justin, ed., *A Narrative and Critical History of America*, Vol. V, Pt. 1. Boston, 1887.

Woodbury, Ellen C. D., *Dorothy Quincy, Wife of John Hancock*. Washington, 1905.

Index

Adams, Abigail, 200, 207, 208, 249, 289

Adams, James Truslow, 271

Adams, John, 59-60, 81, 95-96, 116, 119, 160, 185, 199, 204, 205, 206-207, 213, 217, 228, 249, 269, 274, 298, 314, 325, 326, 332-333; baptized by J. Hancock II, 22; drinking habits, 27; playmate of JH, 27; counsel for JH, 109; defends British troops, 120; and Whig machine, 129; moved by oration of JH, 146; credits JH with authorship, 147; in First Continental Congress, 149; social life in North Braintree, 156-157; entry into Philadelphia, 188; recommends Washington for commander in chief, 195-196; favors iron glove, 200; suspects friendship of JH for B. Harrison, 200-201; supplies army, 201-202; calls on JH, 207-208; early in fight for independence, 224, 225; on Declaration committee, 226; suspects JH of seeking plum, 245-246; at dinner for JH, 246-247; advocate for officers, 255; returns to North Braintree unheralded, 264-266; offered peerage, 281, 391; minister to Court of St. James's, 319; designs of JH against, 320; touted for Chief Justice of U.S., 335; break with J. Warren, 335-336; welcomed by JH, 336; boomed for Vice Presidency, 337, 339; competes for French accolade, 338; dines with Washington, escorts him to Cambridge, 345, 347-348; reelected Vice President, 356; in funeral procession of JH, 359; change of heart toward JH, 364-365

Adams, John Quincy, 208; birthplace, 27; expressions on JH, 319, 326, 337, 354, 356

Adams, Samuel, 56, 104, 208, 243, 274, 281, 283, 286, 290, 291, 325; party of, thwarted by JH, 3; raises banner of rebellion, 80; petitions against taxation, 85; in political clubs, 85, 95; rabble rouser, 87, 90-92; organizes correspondence committees, 87, 131-132; influence on JH, 90; forces Oliver to resign, 93; elected to General Court, 95, 99, 115, 123, 126, 132, 148; discusses JH, 95-96; disgusted with JH, 97; reprieved through JH, 100-101; defends JH, 108-109; rants about liberty, 110; finds revolution necessary, 112; helps organize independent Assembly, 113; denies instruction right of George III, 115-116; urges demonstration, 117; in Boston Massacre, 119-120; on troops committee, 120; dissuades JH from resigning, 121; calls nonimportation failure, 122, keeps Revolutionary movement alive, 125; reconciled with JH, 126; early life, appearance and character, 128-130; uses Loyalist letters for propaganda, 132-134; petitions recall of Hutchinson and Oliver, 134; in tea agitation and Boston Tea Party, 135-141; and JH's Boston Massacre oration, 146; arrest recommended, 147; in choice of Congressional delegates, 149; locks General Court, 149; goes to First Continental Congress, 162; life threatened, 163-

407